BEHAVIORAL MATHEMATICS
FOR GAME AI

DAVE MARK

Charles River Media
A part of Course Technology, Cengage Learning

COURSE TECHNOLOGY
CENGAGE Learning

Australia, Brazil, Japan, Korea, Mexico, Singapore, Spain, United Kingdom, United States

Behavioral Mathematics for Game AI
Dave Mark

**Publisher and General Manager,
Course Technology PTR:** Stacy L. Hiquet

Associate Director of Marketing: Sarah Panella

Content Project Manager: Jessica McNavich

Marketing Manager: Jordan Casey

Acquisitions Editor: Heather Hurley

Project Editor: Karen A. Gill

Technical Reviewer: Kevin Dill

Editorial Services Coordinator: Jen Blaney

Copy Editor: Ruth Saavedra

Interior Layout: Shawn Morningstar

Cover Creator: Dave Mark

Cover Designer: Mike Tanamachi

Indexer: Broccoli Information Management

Proofreader: Mike Beady

© 2009 Course Technology, a part of Cengage Learning.

ALL RIGHTS RESERVED. No part of this work covered by the copyright herein may be reproduced, transmitted, stored, or used in any form or by any means graphic, electronic, or mechanical, including but not limited to photocopying, recording, scanning, digitizing, taping, Web distribution, information networks, or information storage and retrieval systems, except as permitted under Section 107 or 108 of the 1976 United States Copyright Act, without the prior written permission of the publisher.

For product information and technology
assistance, contact us at
**Cengage Learning Customer and Sales Support,
1-800-354-9706.**

For permission to use material from this text
or product, submit all requests online at
cengage.com/permissions.

Further permissions questions can be e-mailed to
permissionrequest@cengage.com.

All trademarks are the property of their respective owners.

Library of Congress Control Number: 2008940614
ISBN-13: 978-1-58450-684-3
ISBN-10: 1-58450-684-9

Course Technology, a part of Cengage Learning
20 Channel Center Street
Boston, MA 02210
USA

Cengage Learning is a leading provider of customized learning solutions with office locations around the globe, including Singapore, the United Kingdom, Australia, Mexico, Brazil, and Japan. Locate your local office at: **international.cengage.com/region.**

Cengage Learning products are represented in Canada by Nelson Education, Ltd.

For your lifelong learning solutions, visit **courseptr.com.**
Visit our corporate Web site at **cengage.com.**

Printed in the United States of America
1 2 3 4 5 6 7 11 10 09

A Little History and a Lot of Dedication

I first got into computers in the early 1980s. By the late 1980s, my very *non*technical grandfather, Gilbert Todd, advised me to "grab onto them computers and stick with 'em… that's where the future is." I did just that, but more out of my own inexorable need to be involved in technology than from his encouragement. After a brief spin in the music business, I got back into computers in the mid-1990s by doing all manner of IT consulting.

In 2002, my wife Laurie and I had just started dipping into the game business by forming Intrinsic Algorithm. On May 20 of that year, my dad drove me to the airport to head off to what was my first Electronics Entertainment Expo (E3) conference. My 88-year-old grandfather wanted to come along for the ride. As an ex-pilot, he enjoyed watching the planes. He knew that I was going out to Los Angeles to some sort of computer game–related conference, although he probably believed that it was a little more of a heady event than what the then-ubiquitous loud music, spectacular lights, and "booth babes" would have suggested to him.

As I got out of the car in front of the terminal and retrieved my luggage from the trunk, my grandfather gave me the best handshake his aging body could generate and told me, "You head out there and tell 'em how it's done."

I didn't have the heart to argue with my grandfather and say that I wasn't going to E3 to *tell* anyone anything, but rather to soak up as much of the state of the industry as I could. I simply thanked him for the encouragement and told him that I would do my best to "set 'em straight."

Those words were the last thing my grandfather said to me. On May 25, 2002, the Saturday after the show and the night before I was due to fly back, he had a heart attack and died.

My grandfather's final words to me—which none of us knew at the time would be so—have rattled around in my brain for the past six years. Just like the trip that I left for on that day, I have spent more time listening and learning than telling anyone how anything is done. However, as I started writing this book, my grandfather's words came back to me once again. I couldn't help but think that, perhaps, his advice was more timeless than the handful of days that I spent wandering through the expansive LA Convention Center. Maybe his encouragement was issued without an expiration date. Or maybe I should just assume that it is still in effect.

Regardless, here I am six years later writing a book on game AI. So, PawPa, I may be a bit late, but I'm ready to head out there and tell 'em how it's done. Thank you.

In the meantime, there are others who have been helping me along the way who deserve some thanks:

To my parents, who bought me my first Apple IIc back in 1984—although they were a bit less enthusiastic when I used it to play games. See? I told you I could make something out of that!

To my best friend in my teen years, Gregg Bieser, who did more than simply play games with me on our respective Apples. It was with Gregg that I made my first awkward—even *abortive*—efforts to make my own games.

To my AP Computer sidekicks and friends, Phil, Bob, Scott, and Rick, whose love of strategy board games and RPGs (fueled by the strangely never-diminishing supply of caffeine at Phil's house) helped crystallize in me what I wanted my own games to look and play like some day.

To my younger brothers, Jared and Kevin, who, at elementary school ages in the 1980s, were my guinea pigs as AD&D players. In retrospect, being a Dungeon Master at 15 years old was the first time I turned mathematics into behaviors.

To the late Eric Dybsand, who, at the 2003 GDC, told me I knew what I was talking about—even when I didn't think I did. Respawn soon, my friend! In the meantime, I hope you can get this book delivered to wherever you are. It seems like you were right. Oh, do me a favor and loan a copy to PawPa while you are at it. He won't understand a word of it, but it will make him proud.

To Steve Woodcock, not only for being there from the beginning, but for sticking around during the hard part, and then telling me it was time to get back on the horse after I had fallen off.

To Alex Champandard for both giving me plenty of good advice and handing me the "megaphone and soapbox" that a weekly column can turn into.

To Steve Rabin for his supply of wisdom regarding "AI Wisdom" and trusting me to help hold the reins to something bigger than both of us.

To Heather Hurley and Karen Gill at Charles River Media for helping me make the jump from 13 pages to 500.

To my tech editor, Kevin Dill, for reading every word and number—and reminding me about the geometry of triangles.

To my in-laws, Larry and Lenora Reynolds, who loaned Laurie and me some bootstraps they had lying around—and were patient with us when we wore them out.

To my son Steven, who constantly reminds me that games can bridge generations—and teaches me that my thumbs are too slow.

To my daughter, Kathy, who constantly reminds me that games can be about more than shooting stuff—and teaches me how to observe people in ways that continue to amaze me.

To my son Aaron, who constantly reminds me of what I was like when I was his age—which kinda scares both of us.

To my stepdaughter Beth, who constantly reminds me that it *can* be fun to completely beat the snot out of an opponent.

And, finally, thanks must go out to my wife and business partner, Laurie. Starting Intrinsic Algorithm was *my* dream. *Her* dream was helping me achieve *mine*. During the conversation at a restaurant in late 2001 that launched us into the game business, she gave me the best bit of advice I've ever had. When I asked her, "But what if I can't do it? What if I fail?" she simply shrugged and said, "Well, then we'll know."

Thanks, dear. You don't know what that meant to me, then and now. This book is dedicated to *your* dedication.

Thank you all,
Dave Mark

About the Author

Dave Mark is the president and lead designer of Intrinsic Algorithm, LLC, an independent game development studio and AI consulting company in Omaha, Nebraska. He has been programming since 1984 when he was in high school where, much to the dismay of his teacher, he wrote his first text adventure on the school's DEC PDP-1144.

After a brief detour in the music business as a composer/arranger, keyboard player, and recording engineer during the early 1990s, Dave re-entered the technology arena in 1995. In 2002, he came to the startling realization that the corporate IT consulting and development world is a little short on creativity and fun. As a result, Dave left to start Intrinsic Algorithm LLC with his wife, Laurie.

He is a contributor to the *AI Game Programming Wisdom* series of books, a regular columnist at AIGameDev.com, and a founding member of the AI Game Programmers Guild.

Dave continues to attend the University of Life. He does not plan to graduate anytime soon.

Author's Preface

As I have read different books on a variety of subjects over the years, I have found a variety of styles to be effective for communicating ideas. In addition to simply reading the text of a book on a technical subject, I have often appreciated the extra effort that went into creating examples of the concept. I enjoy diagrams and graphs so that I can simply have a place to anchor my thoughts as I ponder the issue. Where appropriate, I like seeing the formulas used, already normalized into a form that can be dropped into code. And, of course, I find actual code snippets very helpful when the problem is one of programming.

Some of these elements have been more helpful than others. Some of them have been used to the point of overkill such that it was next to impossible to extract meaningful content from the clutter. On the other hand, I have often felt that I have been left wanting a diagram, a table, or a bit of code so that I could put things into perspective.

To that end, as I set out to write this book, I made myself a promise to attempt to find the balance that would be the most helpful to you, the reader. Throughout this work, I attempt to cover four different approaches: theory, math, examples, and code.

Much of the discussion in this book will be about the theory behind the concepts. This will be where I lay out the concept of a point as groundwork. While this might seem to be the part of the book that is the least directly relevant to game programming, it is also where much of the important material is. Everything spills out of these ideas. Rather than bland recitation, I try to make the theory accessible through example and anecdote.

If necessary, the theory sections will show the relevant mathematics of the concepts. Please note that, unlike some other books, my goal is not to overwhelm you with esoteric proofs of *how* I got to where I did, but to give you as a developer an end product that you can find useful in production.

IN THE GAME

Very often throughout the book, I will lay out hypothetical game-like situations that show how to use a theoretical concept. While these examples may be game genre–specific, the concepts themselves can usually be applied universally. You will be able to quickly identify these sections by the icon at the left that will appear at the beginning of each in-game example. Note that there's a listing of all the In the Games following the table of contents.

PUTTING IT IN CODE

Where appropriate, I will offer up examples of how tools are used in programming situations. Sometimes these functions will be ones that you can use in your own projects. In these cases, you can find the code on the book's Web site at http://www.courseptr.com/downloads.

For clarity's sake, I list some of the naming conventions that I use in my projects and, therefore, in this book.

- Type and `struct` names are in all caps: `MY_TYPE`.
- `Struct` names are preceded by a lowercase "s": `sMY_STRUCT`.
- Variables and functions are in initial caps: `MyFunction( MyVariable )`.
- Member variables of a class are generally preceded with a lowercase "m": `mMyMemberVariable`.
- List and vector names are preceded by a lowercase "l" and "v," respectively. I combine these when necessary, such as in a member of a class that is also a vector. In this case, the name is preceded by "mv," such as in `mvMyMemberVector`.

Given that discussions of differences in programming style are often likened to religious wars, I hope my naming conventions do not cause you to view me as a heretic or to lob this book onto a blazing pyre of sacrilegious tomes with evil code-naming conventions.

Oh yeah, open and close braces for functions belong in the same column, but open braces for `if` and `while` statements belong at the *end* of the `if` or `while` line. I want to follow the column from the end brace to the command that started it all. If you think differently, then you… you… you're just *wrong!* So there!

OK… sorry. That was uncalled for. I truly hope that my quirks don't annoy you or make this book harder to understand. I'm just old. I learned some of these habits in 1984. Blame my high school computer teacher.

sigh

Throughout all of the sections, we will encounter terms that are worth noting. To help you locate and remember these items, they will be bolded and marked with the **important lingo** arrow in the margin.

Sometimes, I will add a cautionary note or an aside of some sort. This will be set apart with the stylized, yet familiar comment brackets you see here.

In addition to seeing in-game examples, you will encounter numerous examples from "life"—mine as well as those around me. Since, as AI programmers, we are often in the business of re-creating lifelike situations and behaviors, I find this approach fitting. Also, I hope that you forgive me for a sense of humor. It is my attempt to keep you from falling into the mind-numbing stupor that technical books have been known to induce. In a manner of speaking, I'm doing it for your own good. Don't just learn—enjoy!

Contents

Part I   **Introduction**   1

1   **Why Behavioral Mathematics?**   3
- Games and Choices   4
- Going Beyond Looks   10

2   **Observing the World**   15
- Identifying Factors   16
- Finding Hidden Factors   22
- Quantifying Observations   24
- Needing More Than Observations   28

3   **Converting Behaviors to Algorithms**   29
- Using Numbers to Select   30
- Using Numbers to Define   33
- Using Algorithms to Construct Numbers   37

Part II   **Decision Theory**   43

4   **Defining Decision Theory**   45
- Normative Decision Theory   45
- Descriptive Decision Theory   48
- The Best of Both Worlds   51

5   **Game Theory**   55
- Starting Simple   56
  - Matching Pennies   57
  - Prisoner's Dilemma   61

    Asymmetric Games   69
- Cutting the Cake   70
- Ultimatum Game   72
- Dictator Game   75
- Trust Game   76

6   Rational vs. Irrational Behavior   79

Perfect Rationality   80
- The Pirate Game   80
- Superrationality   85
- Guess Two-Thirds of the Average Game   87

Bounded Rationality   96
- Misusing Irrelevant Information   97
- Ignoring Relevant Information   100

Rational Ignorance   105
- The Cost of Information   105
- The Cost of Calculation   107

Combining It All   109

7   The Concept of Utility   111

Decisions under Risk   112
- Pascal's Wager   113
- No Pain, No Gain   115

Utility of Money   121
- Value vs. Utility   121
- Utility vs. Risk   123

Utility of Time   140
- Production over Time   141
- Distance over Time   145
- Changes in Utility over Time   150

Our Utility of Utility   165

8 Marginal Utility 167
    Value vs. Utility vs. Marginal Utility 168
    Changes in Marginal Utility 169
        Decreasing Marginal Utility 170
        Increasing Marginal Utility 177
    Marginal Risk vs. Marginal Reward 181
    Defining Thresholds 187
    Multiple Utility Thresholds 188
    The Utility of Marginal Utility 194

9 Relative Utility 195
    Hedonic Calculus 196
    Multi-Attribute Utility Theory 198
    Inconsistencies 205
        Problems with Perception 206
        Problems with Categorization 207
        Problems with Understanding 207
    Apparent Contradictions 210
        Giffen Goods 210
        Moral Dilemmas 219
    The Relative Benefit of Relative Utilities 225

Part III Mathematical Modeling 227

10 Mathematical Functions 229
    Simple Linear Functions 229
    Quadratic Functions 231
        Shifting the Quadratic 231
        Tilting the Parabola 233
        Reshaping the Parabola 234
    Sigmoid Functions 236
        The Logistic Function 236
        The Logit Function 239
    Ad Hoc Functions 240

11 Probability Distributions — 241
- Identifying Population Features — 242
  - Segmenting the Population — 244
  - Analyzing a Single Segment — 247
- Uniform Distributions — 248
- Normal (Gaussian) Distributions — 250
  - Properties of Normal Distributions — 250
  - Generating Normal Distributions — 254
- Triangular Distributions — 269
  - Simplified Normal Distributions — 269
  - Parametric Building — 270
- Uneven Distributions — 272
- Parabolic Distributions — 274
- Poisson Distributions — 276
- Distributing the Distributions — 279

12 Response Curves — 285
- Constructing Response Curves — 286
  - Building Buckets — 289
  - Retrieving a Result — 294
- Converting Functions to Response Curves — 296
  - Simple 1-to-1 Mappings — 296
  - Advanced 1-to-1 Mappings — 297
- Converting Distributions to Response Curves — 303
  - Data Structure — 304
  - Entering Data — 304
  - Selecting a Result — 308
  - Adjusting Data — 311
- Search Optimization — 314
- Hand-Crafted Response Curves — 316
- Dynamic Response Curves — 317

13 Factor Weighting — 319

- Scaling Considerations — 319
  - Imposing Artificial Limits — 319
  - Absolute vs. Relative Weights — 322
  - Granularity — 325
- Weighting a Single Criterion — 329
  - Concrete Numbers — 329
  - Abstract Ratings — 329
- Combining Multiple Criteria — 331
  - Normalizing — 331
  - Weighted Sums — 339
- Layered Weighting Models — 341
  - Constructing a Layer — 342
  - Propagation of Change — 345
  - Compartmentalized Confidence — 346
- Everything Is Relative — 348

Part IV Behavioral Algorithms — 349

14 Modeling Individual Decisions — 351

- Defining Decision — 351
- Deciding What to Decide — 353
- Analyzing a Single Option — 355
  - Identifying Factors — 356
  - Identifying Relationships — 375
  - Building Connections — 379
  - Scoring the Option — 382
- Comparing Options — 385
- Selecting an Option — 386
- Testing the Algorithm — 387
- Summarizing the Decision Process — 392

15	**Changing a Decision**	**395**
	Monitoring a Decision	396
	Time Frames	396
	A Hybrid Approach	401
	Perseverance and Decision Momentum	405
	Ignoring Futility	408
	Building Decision Momentum	409
	Our Final Decision on Changing Decisions	415
16	**Variation in Choice**	**417**
	Reasons for Variation	418
	Variation between Actors	419
	Variation by a Single Actor	420
	Embracing Randomness	422
	Selecting from Multiple Choices	424
	Random from Top n Choices	425
	Weighted Random from Top n Choices	430
	Weighted Random from All Choices	441
	Scores and Weights	444
	Epilogue	**447**
	Index	**451**

In the Game Listings

Know When to Walk Away, Know When to Run	33
Expanding the Engagement Decision	39
Matching Punches	59
Dueling Rocket Launchers	65
Scouting the Enemy	107
Counting the Enemy	108
The Tortoise and the Harried	119
Protecting the Barracks	130
Settlers and Warriors	143
Taking Fire	156
Building Soldiers	171
Declining Health	177
How Many Troops?	191
The Engagement Decision Revisited	200
Wizardry and Wands	216
Hippocratic Morals	224
How Much Weight?	332
Are We There Yet?	334
Who's Next?	336
Which Dude to Kill?	355
Dudes Revisited	403
Flotilla of Futility	406

Part I: Introduction

Part I sets the table for the rest of this book in that it introduces us to the mindset that we will want to carry into our quest for improving our artificial intelligence (AI) agents through behavioral mathematics.

Chapter 1, "Why Behavioral Mathematics?" asks us to ponder what it is we are trying to accomplish when we create opponents in games.

Chapter 2, "Observing the World," offers up the suggestion that many of the clues to creating intricate, deep, and meaningful behaviors are all around us.

Chapter 3, "Converting Behaviors to Algorithms," gives us a general overview of the approach that we will use when trying to place our observations into something that we can place into our game engine.

1 Why Behavioral Mathematics?

Game artificial intelligence (AI) has been an expanding and changing term in the past five to ten years. Even today, if you ask people what "game AI" entails, you will get significantly different answers. For a long time, however, most of those answers could be tied to specific and simple functions.

- "It's what makes the character walk toward me."
- "It's what makes the enemy shoot at me."
- "It's what makes the animation change from 'idle' to 'attack.'"

Those are all well and good—although taken at face value, not very encompassing. In a general sense, you would be hard-pressed to really justify calling those things "artificial intelligence." They are too simple. In some ways, they could be accomplished by a flip of a coin, a roll of the dice, or simply by a single "If…then" statement such as the player entering a room.

Lately, there has been a massive expansion of the ideas that fall into the purview of game AI. In the name of "realism" in games, many of these expansions and explorations have been flowing in the direction of trying to mimic behaviors—either by individuals, teams, or complex systems. Given the inherent complexity of individual psychology and group dynamics, sometimes this task seems to be more Sisyphean than Herculean. We can never *quite* be finished. Just when we think we have emulated behaviors, another caveat appears, and our algorithmic rock rolls back to the bottom of the hill. We will never solve the challenge of replicating human, animal, or alien behavior on the technological side because we will likely never be able to solve those behaviors on the *psychological* side. The only thing we can do is continue to examine and study and break things down as far as we can. Maybe the next time we push the rock up hill, it will feel a lot easier.

GAMES AND CHOICES

There is a saying in the game industry that originated from industry pioneer Sid Meier. He suggested, "A game is a series of interesting choices." That statement is, in my opinion, reasonable in a vague sense. However, with a little exploration, you can bracket things a little better. For example, if you were to pursue that concept by negation to the extreme, you would be left with the statement, "If there are no choices for the player, it is not a game." That is certainly true. What would be left is the monodirectional narrative that games have been replacing for decades now. Aside from the initial choice of what to watch, television and movies do not provide choices for the viewer. They are not interactive. They are not games.

Books have historically fallen into the same category. The exception to this is the "choose your own adventure" books. Unlike typical narratives, they allow the reader to make choices that, while very simple, do affect the outcome of the story. It is the addition of that simple mechanism that lifts the book from narrative entertainment into the realm of interactive entertainment. And, if the alternate paths and endings were divergent enough to be construed as "positive" or "negative," one could make the case that there is now a goal—and a corresponding concept of "winning" and "losing." In a sense, the book has now become a game.

Rock-Paper-Scissors, the staple mechanism of alleviating sheer boredom and selecting hapless people for distasteful tasks, has but one choice event with three possible selections in any given round (Figure 1.1). Flick the fingers, and you are done. All that is left is to count the score. That hardly makes for long-term entertainment. (In fact, it may be disqualified from consideration in Sid's definition in that there isn't even really a *series* of choices.)

		Player A		
		Rock	Paper	Scissors
Player B	Rock	---	Paper covers Rock	Rock breaks Scissors
	Paper	Paper covers Rock	---	Scissors cut Paper
	Scissors	Rock breaks Scissors	Scissors cut Paper	---

FIGURE 1.1 The decision matrix for the game Rock-Paper-Scissors.

In Tic-Tac-Toe, the number of possible choices starts at nine initially and gets worse from there. (Actually, it only *looks* like nine. Given that the board is symmetrical on two axes, the true number of starting moves is three: corner, side, and middle. Interestingly, the second player either has five or two responding moves depending on the initial selection by the first player.) Still, there are more choices per game than are available in Rock-Paper-Scissors. Anyone over the age of eight, however, realizes after about 10 times through the game that all the choices lead to the rather bleak outcome of a draw. (Startlingly, the WOPR supercomputer in the movie *WarGames* needed significantly more time than that to reach this conclusion.) So, while there are certainly *more* choices in play, the game isn't necessarily better.

Blackjack has only a few choices of what to do at any given point: hit, stand, double, and split. There are plenty of scenarios that the player can find himself in, however. A glance at one of the cute little Blackjack cheat cards (Figure 1.2) will show that there are 280 different meaningful combinations of what's on the table at any given time. While that is a significantly larger possibility space than Tic-Tac-Toe and certainly Rock-Paper-Scissors, a second glance at the cheat card will show that there is a statistically "right" way to play each of those combinations. So, while there are plenty of choices, they aren't necessarily "interesting." In fact, seasoned Blackjack players have that cheat sheet memorized—removing it, for all intents and purposes, from the realm of choice entirely. They simply play the way that millions of models have shown to be statistically advantageous.

Wandering down the casino aisle, you may encounter the Poker room. Again, there aren't many choices in the standard poker game. Aside from folding a hand, the choices largely revolve around how much to bet. And yet, the choices that *are* in play are far more interesting than those of Blackjack. What makes them that way? After all, just like Blackjack, it really comes down to the probability statistics. "What is the *likelihood* that my hand is better than yours?"

To understand the difference between the two games that makes Poker's choices more interesting than those in Blackjack, we must realize that there is another concept in play. There's someone else in the room that is *also* making a "series of interesting choices." Theoretically, just like Blackjack, the number of possible Poker hand combinations could be calculated. Just like Blackjack, there are a finite number of scenarios—although I would hate to see the size of the little cheat card. Given that information—and even being forced to use some inference about the other hands—you could make a reasonable assertion about the relative strength of your hand. Your interesting choice would be reduced to what you were willing to risk given the potential of winning and losing. The game would still take on the form of Blackjack—albeit a bit more complicated. Except for the one knotty factor that no amount of statistical modeling can entirely take into consideration—the guy on the other side of the table with the dark glasses and stupid hat that keeps rattling his chips is making an "interesting choice" as well.

BLACKJACK BASIC STRATEGY

		Dealer Showing								
		A	10	9	8	7	6	5	4	3	2
Pairs	A A	SP	SP	SP	SP	SP	SP	SP	SP	SP	SP
	10 10	S	S	S	S	S	S	S	S	S	S
	9 9	S	S	SP	SP	S	SP	SP	SP	SP	SP
	8 8	SP	SP	SP	SP	SP	SP	SP	SP	SP	SP
	7 7	H	H	H	H	SP	SP	SP	SP	SP	SP
	6 6	H	H	H	H	H	H	H	H	H	H
	5 5	H	H	D	D	D	D	D	D	D	D
	4 4	H	H	H	H	H	SP	SP	H	H	H
	3 3	H	H	H	H	SP	SP	SP	SP	SP	SP
	2 2	H	H	H	H	SP	SP	SP	SP	SP	SP
Hard Hands	17+	S	S	S	S	S	S	S	S	S	S
	16	H*	H*	H*	H	H	S	S	S	S	S
	15	H	H*	H	H	H	S	S	S	S	S
	14	H	H	H	H	H	S	S	S	S	S
	13	H	H	H	H	H	S	S	S	S	S
	12	H	H	H	H	H	S	S	S	H	H
	11	H	D	D	D	D	D	D	D	D	D
	10	H	H	D	D	D	D	D	D	D	D
	9	H	H	H	H	H	D	D	D	D	H
	8-	H	H	H	H	H	H	H	H	H	H
Soft Hands	A-9	S	S	S	S	S	D	D	D	D	D
	A-8	S	S	S	S	S	D	D	D	D	D
	A-7	H	H	H	S	S	D	D	D	D	D
	A-6	H	H	H	H	H	D	D	D	D	H
	A-5	H	H	H	H	H	D	D	D	H	H
	A-4	H	H	H	H	H	D	D	D	H	H
	A-3	H	H	H	H	H	D	D	H	H	H
	A-2	H	H	H	H	H	D	D	H	H	H

H HIT   S STAND   D DOUBLE   SP SPLIT

PLAYER'S HAND

* SURRENDER IF ALLOWED

NEVER TAKE INSURANCE

FIGURE 1.2 The Blackjack "basic strategy" card shows the mathematically optimum play for every combination of what the player has and what the dealer is showing.

My Choices...Your Choices...

The astute reader might notice that, in a game of Rock-Paper-Scissors or Tic-Tac-Toe, the other player *is* making a choice. Upon further examination, however, what can we really say about those choices? In Rock-Paper-Scissors, for example, there are only three options. As a player, you have no information about what your opponent is going to do (unless we dig into some major data analysis on long-term play patterns of our opponent—or just happen to know that he has a particular affinity for geology). Therefore, there is no real guide for the strategy that we should adopt throughout the course of our 3-second game. At that point, we are left with the somewhat-tepid realization that all three of our options are, for purposes of selection, the same. All the results are tied up in the scoring matrix alone. Whether we admit it or not, our selection is basically random. Or, in theory, it would be no better than a random selection. So, while we can operate under the pretense that we are making a choice of which option to play, truly our act of volition doesn't matter.

If you put that mentality on the other side of the table from you in the form of a human player (assume for the sake of example continuity that it is the same guy with the dark glasses and stupid hat), it fails to provide any sort of challenge over and above playing against the roll of an Official Rock-Paper-Scissors Decision Die (ORPSDD). You are playing against a random selection machine. The only difference is that the human player may be more likely to react to your victory dance than would the ORPSDD. In fact, as long as the taunting was not included in the test, I would suggest that an ORPSDD would admirably pass the **Turing Test** (see sidebar).

TURING TEST

The oft-cited Turing Test was conceived by famed AI researcher Alan Turing. He suggested that a machine entity could not be deemed "intelligent" unless it performed the action being tested in a manner indistinguishable from a human.

Currently, the test is used in a far more loose sense than what Alan Turing originally proposed. That leads to its being used in situations for which it was not intended—much as the term "litmus test" is used in far more situations than the chemical test that it truly is.

In a broad sense, the term "Turing Test" has become the equivalent to saying "believable." If one says that an AI entity "passes the Turing Test," it generally means that it looks as good as a human player. This believability is always going to be limited in scope, however. Usually, only a specific behavior or set of behaviors is being judged. This scope is, by necessity, also limited to game-relevant situations. For example, an agent may run, hide, and shoot in a manner that looks like a real player. However, if you try to engage this same agent in a conversation about the weather, the agent is going to be exposed for the narrowly designed entity that it is.

That being said, the phrase "it passes Turing" is a colloquially understood badge of honor that means "it looks and acts pretty darn well." As such, it is a goal to strive for as an AI designer and programmer.

Tic-Tac-Toe has a few more options, as I mentioned earlier. However, the state space of the game is so small that at any given moment the choices we have before us can be reduced to "correct," "incorrect," or "delaying the inevitable." If the point is to win the game, there really is no choice involved. At least not much more than answering the question, "Do you want to win the game?" So, while there are more choices in play for both you and your opponent, victory comes down to a failure on either your part or that of Mr. Glasses & Hat to correctly answer the question, "Do you want to win the game?" (Figure 1.3). Assuming a static level of continual lucidity for both of you, the only way someone is going to lose is if he *allows* the other person the advantage by intentionally letting him win through an incorrect play. Put another way, until someone *chooses* to lose, the actual choices made in the game are irrelevant. You are playing against a rigid, predictable, rule-based machine. In a way, it is almost an *inverse* Turing Test. To win (or draw), you simply play the same way a computer would.

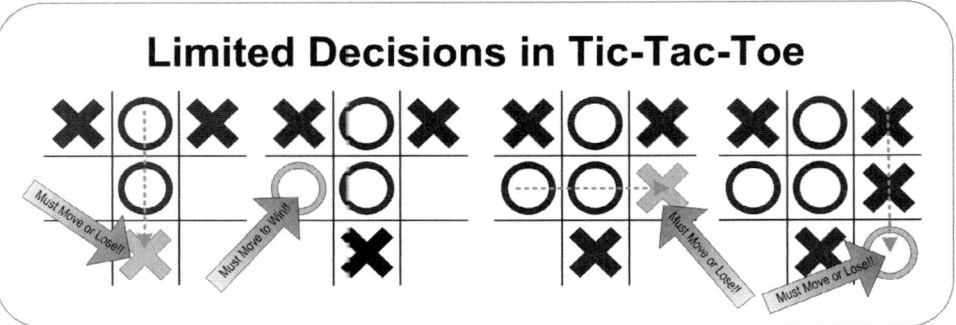

FIGURE 1.3 The decisions in Tic-Tac-Toe are usually limited based on whether you want to win or lose. In the game above, the player (X or O) had to play the locations dictated by the arrows or else lose the game in the next move.

Blackjack gives the appearance of playing against another entity. In the typical casino setting, the House as represented by the Dealer. (For the sake of saking, let's put the Dealer in dark glasses and a stupid hat.) According to the actual rules of the game, your opponent has *no* choices whatsoever. There is no random chance in the selections he is making like there is in Rock-Paper-Scissors. The random chance comes from the nature of the game itself—specifically, the order of the cards in the deck.

While there *is* a strict rule-based system in Blackjack (hit on less than 17, stand on 17 or more), it differs from the one in Tic-Tac-Toe. (That is, "I choose to win; therefore, I should move here.") In this case, the rules aren't in the decision model of the Dealer specifically; they are in the rules of the *game* as a whole. Unlike Tic-Tac-Toe, no matter how badly the Dealer *wants* to win (or lose, for that matter), his choices are entirely cast in stone. The Dealer isn't "selecting" anything; he is playing the game. He's reading a script, as it were. You are playing against a rigid, predictable opponent in the realm of a completely random environment. It is really no different from the Craps table nearby. You aren't playing against the man with the curvy stick and the loud banter. You are playing against precalculated payoff odds in a completely random environment (represented, in this case, by dice instead of cards).

That being said, Blackjack is yet another "made-for-Turing" game. From the player or dealer's standpoint, everything is calculatable and, therefore, predictable. If you win, it has nothing to do with your besting the abilities and decisions of your opponent. Your "opponent," in a sense, is the random ordering of the cards, not the Glasses & Hat stoic on the other side of the table. (And most Dealers, regardless of the regalia, won't respond whatsoever to your victory dance anyway. But security may.)

In Poker, however, your opponent is a vital part of the game. While you are both dealing in the realm of randomness, you are both allowed to *react* to that randomness—each to his own advantage. This differs from Rock-Paper-Scissors, where the randomness *is* the game. While you are dealing in the realm of choices, you are both allowed to pursue choices that *may* or *may not* lead to victory. This differs from Tic-Tac-Toe, where each choice is specifically, and almost obviously, tied to the condition of victory. While you are both dealing in the realm of rules, neither of you is rigidly limited in your core gameplay decisions so as to completely disconnect the decision from the desire to win. This differs from the Dealer in Blackjack, where the available decisions are so narrowly prescribed that the Dealer becomes a nonentity in the game.

In the game of Poker, the constraints of your opponent's gameplay are not so narrow as to be either entirely random or entirely predictable. As a player, you are aware that not only do *you* have many interesting choices to select from, but so does your opponent. What's more, because there is a cyclical interaction between you and your opponent, your selection process must necessarily involve all the potential selections your opponent may make. Taken an iteration forward, you must be aware that your opponent is likely to base his reaction on the selection you *do* make. For that matter, taken an iteration backward, perhaps your opponent's previous choice was made based on *his* assumption that *you* would take his decision into account. In comedy, this effect is referenced by some variant of "I know *you* know that *I* know what you *think* I know." In mathematics, it is known as a combinatorial explosion. In games, it sure does make for Sid's "interesting choices."

And therein lies the quest as AI designers and programmers. Given that our game studios often lack both the ability and the budget to hire live orcs, dragons, aliens, Nazi soldiers, or even bunnies to hop around nearby, our games face a paucity of opponents that are able to don the dark glasses and stupid hats that symbolize our nemeses. And, it has been shown that, if we choose to march out denizens to face them that are entirely random, entirely predictable, or mercilessly constrained in their behavior and try to pass them off as intelligent, thoughtful, and responsive entities, our gaming clientele is unforgiving. Frankly, those do not lead to necessarily "interesting choices" for the player. Therefore, our goal as AI designers and programmers must be to give the player those "interesting choices" by imbuing our AI progeny with the ability to make "interesting choices" of their own. We can leave the dark glasses and stupid hat to the art department.

GOING BEYOND LOOKS

For purposes of full disclosure, I have to admit that I have little artistic talent. I understand some of the concepts; I can draw perspective of blocky objects using a vanishing point, for example. I can even copy an existing drawing to some extent. To this day, I have a fantastic painting of a pig that I made in seventh grade that was copied from a picture in a magazine (Figure 1.4). However, that about exhausts my talent for the medium.

FIGURE 1.4   An original Dave Mark, circa 1981.

Looking Like a Pig

Despite my dearth of ability to perform in that particular discipline, I would still feel secure in making the claim that artists in the game industry have life a bit easier than do AI programmers. After all, they can *see* what it is that they are supposed to be accomplishing. Before they begin to draw a pig, they can look at a pig. They can make changes to parts of their pig that are less than accurate—in effect, fine-tuning their pig-replication abilities. They can show their picture of a pig to anyone else who wanders by and ask, "What does this look like?" Unless the artist subscribes to a more Picasso-esque approach, the reaction should be, "Hey! It's a pig!" (Unfortunately, my art teacher didn't buy my claim of being a disciple of Picasso.) People know what a pig looks like. It can be rigidly defined as a collection of expected parts. For example, everyone knows that a pig has four feet. If your pig has five feet, one of which is located in front of an inexplicably present dorsal fin, viewers will be mildly disturbed.

Artists also are comfortable with re-creating the environment. A light on one side of an object makes a corresponding shadow on the other. We've all seen it; we all know that it would be incorrect otherwise. The ability to perform observation and criticism doesn't simply lead to the *realization* that an error needs to be addressed; it often leads to the solution itself. For example, "Make the floor darker on the side of the object opposite the light." Even though I lack the ability to necessarily fix it properly, even I as a nonartist can often suggest the solution.

From a technical standpoint, the solutions are often fairly intuitive as well. For example, to make the color of the blue floor darker in the shadows, use a darker color of blue. To make the buildings in the distance look smaller, draw them smaller. Truly, the models of how to accomplish many of the core features of art have been somewhat solved for hundreds of years.

Acting Like a Pig

In contrast, game AI provides some challenges in a number of respects. For instance, we can't just show our AI-enabled pig to someone and ask, "Does this *act* like a pig?" The answer can't be rattled off as easily as one regarding the *look* of a pig. Certainly, there are some obvious failure scenarios such as said pig flying about the room in proverbially unlikely fashion. That should tip some of us off that something is amiss. However, it is far more difficult to state for certain while watching Mr. Swine's behavior unfold onscreen that it is, indeed, acting the way a proper pig should. There is a layer of abstraction involved that is not easy to translate through.

With the artwork, we *see* real life and then we *see* the representation of it. There is an implicit equality there. If what we see in real life doesn't match what we see in the representation, we can determine that it is wrong. Even if equality is not reached, we are cognizant of a point of diminishing returns. We are accepting of a representation that is pretty darn close to what we see in reality.

When watching behavior, however, we have to pass our understanding of that behavior through a filter of judgment. "Is that the *correct* thing for the pig to do?" To answer this question of equality, we would have to have an established belief about what the real-life pig would have been doing in the first place. While we can give generalized answers to that question, none of us can state for certain that *every* pig will act in a certain way *every* time that a situation occurs.

Moving beyond pigs to behaviorally more complicated life-forms (such as humans—although there may be some exceptions), the solution set gets significantly larger. As that happens, our confidence in what we believe the entity in question "should be" doing slips dramatically. While we may be more comfortable in thinking of *possibilities* of human behavior than those of a pig (seeing that we are, indeed, human), the fact that there are so many subtle shades of those behaviors makes it statistically less likely that any one of them is the "right thing" to be doing.

Just as our ability to define what it is these life-forms should be doing wanes, we are ever more hard-pressed to judge an artificial representation of an entity's behavior. In Tic-Tac-Toe, it was obvious when the opponent was playing right or wrong—the ramifications were immediately apparent. In Poker, even looking over a player's shoulder at his cards, it is often difficult to judge what his behavior "should be." The combination of the possibility space of the game with the range of thought processes of different players makes for a staggering array of choices. The best we can come up with is, "That may be a decent choice, but this is what *I* would do if I were him." And that statement itself needs to be taken with a grain of salt since we may not be taking the correct—or *more* correct—approach ourselves.

Making Pigs Act Like Pigs

What this means is that AI programmers have it tough. Unlike the artist who can see his subject and gauge the relative accuracy of his work to it, AI programmers don't necessarily know where they are headed. Certainly, we can have ideas and wishes and goals—especially in the short run. ("I want my pig to eat at *this* trough.") We are also well aware that those can tend to backfire on us. ("Why is my stupid pig eating at *that* trough when it is on *fire*?") However, as the complexity of our world grows, we have to realize that there may not *be* a goal of perfection such as the goal of photo-realism in art. Behavior is too vague and ephemeral to explain, thereby making it impossible to accurately mimic. Additionally, the goal in many games is to support the overarching narrative or role of a character. Achieving *perfect* behavior for a background character in a crowded city scene is different from attempting to construct realistically responsive behavior for that same character. Often, the best we can do is to embrace methods that give us a good shot at coming close to something that looks reasonable.

But how do we do that without going the route of complete randomness of the Rock-Paper-Scissors player, the monotonous predictability of the Tic-Tac-Toe opponent, or the rigid mindlessness of the rule-bound Blackjack dealer? Somehow we have to be able to create the mind of the Poker player. We have to approach the game from the inside of that Poker player's psyche.

We have to embody that soul with the ability to perceive the world in terms of relevant, not relevant, interesting, dangerous. We have to give him a way to conceptualize more than just "right or wrong," but rather shades of differentiation: better, worse, not quite as bad as. We have to create for him a translation mechanism to our own thought processes. And it is this last part that is the most difficult. To do that, we have to do so in a language that both of us can understand, yet one that is robust enough to convey all that we perceive and ponder. And that language is thankfully one that computers know best; in fact, it's the only one they know—that of mathematics.

The trick is, how do we convert behavior into mathematics? It isn't quite as simple as the what-you-see-is-what-you-get (WYSIWYG) model of the artists. ("Make the blue floor in the shadow darker by making the blue darker.") There is no simple translation from behaviors into numbers and formulas. (For what it's worth, I already checked AltaVista's translation tool, Babel Fish. No help there!) Certainly, researchers have been taking notes, conducting surveys, and accumulating data for ages. That doesn't help us to model some of the behaviors that as game developers we find necessary but are so second-nature to us that no researcher has bothered to measure them.

So we are on our own—left to our own devices, as it were. The best we can do is to observe the world around us, take our own notes, and conduct our own surveys. Then, using tools to make expression, calculation, and selection simpler, we can attempt to create our own interface into our hat-wearing Poker player so that he can proceed to make "interesting choices" as our proxy.

It is my hope that, through this book, I will be able to suggest to you how to observe the world and construct those mathematical models and interfaces for decision making. Will your AI pigs become model swine in all areas of their lives? I don't know. That's not entirely up to me. However, that result is hopefully going to be far better than if I were to attempt to paint one for you.

2 Observing the World

The most important skill to develop that will help you in constructing reasonable behaviors is something you will not learn how to do in this book. You must, of course, know what it is you are trying to re-create. If you are attempting to create a behavior for an entity that is *not* familiar (space aliens come to mind, although there *are* people who claim to be subject matter experts), you are at least going to want to find something that is similar to base your models on. Once you know what it is you are trying to re-create, you need to be able to *observe* what that entity generally does.

If you have taken a biology class in school, for example, you may have created what is often referred to as an "observation log." This is really not much more complicated than it sounds. At my high school, our biology teacher had a pet owl in the classroom. When it came time to do the observation log, the students would grab pencil and paper and, for 45 minutes, watch the owl and make a note of everything it did. These observations were generally very simplistic (apparently owls don't do much when sitting on a perch in a school classroom). They made notes such as:

- Turns head left
- Blink
- Turns head center
- Blink
- Blink
- Ruffles feathers
- Blink
- Repositions right foot

Certainly, there doesn't seem to be a lot we can glean about the behaviors of owls from observations such as these. Yes, we have compiled a list of possible things that an owl *could* do at any one point in time, but it doesn't give us a lot of information about *when* and *why*.

Often, the secret to the conceptual side of behavioral mathematics is to sit back and try to see what is *really* going on. Things are not often as clear-cut as they seem on the surface. Because of that, there is a layer of abstraction that is less visible but far more powerful. What sounds cause him to turn his head? Perhaps the owl ruffles his feathers only when the fan turns on? Is there a pattern to the blinking? What is he thinking when he moves that foot? Is he even thinking about it at all? Does he say to himself, "Now I'm going to move my foot"? Probably not. But there is *something* going on inside that owl's head on either a conscious or unconscious level, and the outward signs of that thought process are what makes our owl look and act like an owl.

What's more important is comparing the actions of one owl to those of another, or comparing the actions of the owl in one situation to his actions in another.

The complexity that differentiates one Poker player from another is not in the absolute linearity of processing mundane probability statistics, but in the subtle nuances of human behavior. Many of the things we do that set us apart from one another are unconscious—or at least born from beliefs that are, themselves, complicated in their origins.

IDENTIFYING FACTORS

It isn't enough to simply *observe* actions and reactions. We must *identify* those actions for what they are. We must have an explainable correlation between cause and effect. The difference is similar to the difference between hearing and listening. We hear things all around us at all times, but often we don't actually listen to what we hear. When we actually listen to things, we separate out distinguishable sounds from the aggregate sonic disturbance in the background. The same can be said about hearing a person speak but not necessarily listening to what he is saying—a staple of marital discord. (So I've been told. I *always* listen *very* attentively to what my wife says!)

The point is, it is only when we separate different observations from the background that we can put them into their proper local context. At that point, by identifying them, we have taken a necessary step toward isolating them for further analysis. Because there is no shortage of things to observe and identify, the trick is to determine which of those items are important enough to proceed with.

Surprisingly, this process is a little dichotomous for us as humans. Some things jump right out at us as important. On the other hand, most creatures (humans included) have a little evolutionary quirk called **latent inhibition** built into us as well. Latent inhibition is a filter system. On an instinctual level, it allows animals to observe the world and classify things as either important or unimportant to survival. If something is deemed to be unimportant, the mind no longer pays attention to it. That way, we don't waste precious clock cycles in our brains reprocessing something that has already been classified as irrelevant.

> **LATENT INHIBITION AND CREATIVITY**
>
> It has been observed that people with lower levels of latent inhibition—that is, those who do *not* shut out their environment as much as others do—tend to be more creative than those with normal levels of latent inhibition. The theory is that these people do not dismiss things as irrelevant as quickly as do their peers. Instead, they keep coming back to them and, in doing so, may be better able to understand not just *what* the subject of the observation is but how that subject fits into the world in a relative sense.
>
> While this seems like a desirable trait to have in a creative endeavor such as game design and development—and, admittedly, it does come in handy—lower levels of latent inhibition are also strongly correlated with psychosis or even diagnoses of mental illnesses such as schizophrenia, attention deficit disorder, and bipolar disorder.
>
> Be careful what you wish for.

However, in some pursuits, this time-saving device gets in the way of doing important work. Sometimes, in our process of observation and investigation, we need to consciously *suppress* our latent inhibition (which makes for an interesting double negative, doesn't it?). By doing that, we can reexamine things that are in our environment. Often, the most interesting and relevant ways our world works are things that we take for granted—right under our proverbial noses. It is through suppressing our latent inhibition that we can see enough detail to begin to sketch out the structures of the decision-making process.

Running the Fifth Grade

A number of years ago, when my daughter Kathy was 10, I was treated to a 20-minute dissertation in which she explained her entire reasoning for running for *vice* president of the fifth grade at her elementary school. First, she explained to me why she was running for the number-two spot. Her reasoning was that, since everyone wanted to be president, there was significant competition for that spot. There were only a few candidates for VP, however (Figure 2.1). I probed her somewhat on this decision, asking her why *she* didn't want to be president instead of only vice president. After all, the president would have more power (for what that's worth in the fifth-grade student council). She firmly explained that she would have *no* power if she didn't get elected at all. She also noted that the difference between the two positions was rather negligible. By being elected VP, she would be able to help advise and guide this august governing body. What we will explore later in this book is the problem that my 10-year-old not only ascertained intuitively but was able to explain in age-appropriate, nonmathematical terms—that a good chance of getting less is better than a poor chance of getting more.

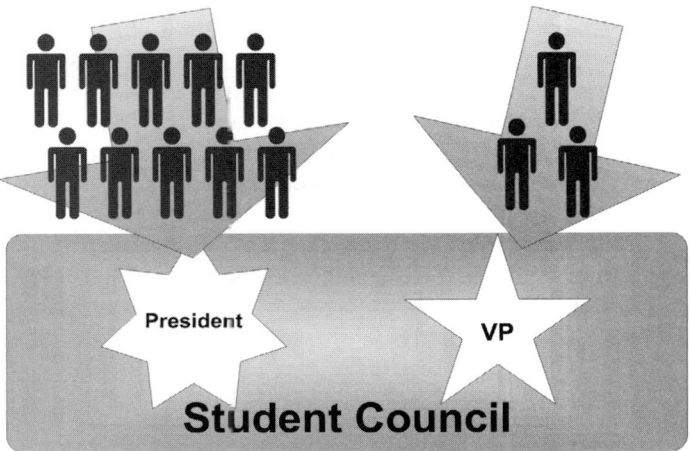

FIGURE 2.1 All other factors being equal, there is a 10% chance of becoming president and a 33% chance of becoming vice president. Running for VP offers a better possibility of being elected to the student council.

Another observation that she made was her perceptions about *why* people were supporting the candidates that they were—even prior to the speeches. She told of two phenomena that she had witnessed and identified. First, she talked about how the people who bothered to put up posters and hand-make stickers got a lot of the buzz. She thought it was silly that people would support someone simply because they had more posters (or cooler posters, I suppose). However, she was aware of how the process was happening. If people didn't *know* about a candidate, there was no one to support that candidate. What's more, the more posters and stickers that a kid had up, it would broadcast—in a simplistic sort of way—that the kid was actually serious about running for office. Again, this had nothing to do with issues... just a matter of exposure.

The second phenomenon that she noted was the "power of the group." Kids who were on the fence about a candidate could easily be swayed simply by the fact that someone they knew was supporting a particular person. The more people a kid encountered (especially in their own social circle) who supported a particular candidate, the more legitimacy was lent to that candidate (Figure 2.2). Kathy explained that it was just like the exposure via posters and stickers, but was more influential. While you may see and remember a poster, you *trust* your friends.

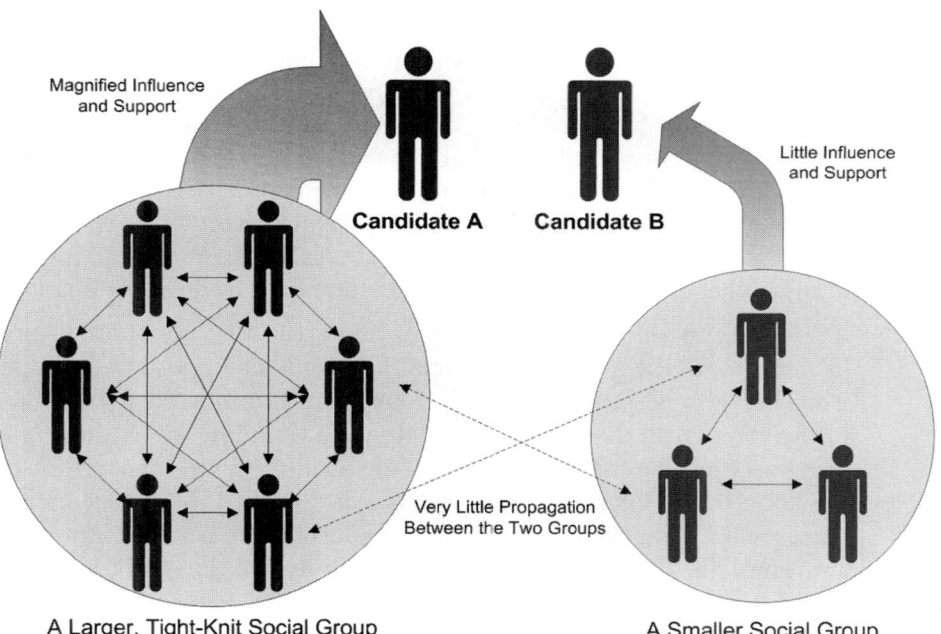

FIGURE 2.2 The larger the network of kids exchanging their opinions on a candidate, the more "information momentum" is created and reinforced in that group. This leads to more people supporting that candidate.

Even more powerful, she continued, was the fact that you didn't want to seem like you were going *against* your friends. Fear of social reprisal was a far more important (if insidious) reason to support a candidate. You might not support a candidate about which you had no opinion specifically because someone you *didn't* like was doing so. Despite the fact that she was appalled at this mindless peer pressure, she expressed with no small amount of mirth that often this propagation was bidirectional. Other than a subtle flow downstream from the "cool kids," you couldn't really tell which kid was the original one to support a candidate. Each one was doing it because they thought the other wanted them to. It just sort of happened as a group. Again, my daughter, in all her wisdom, had grasped an important concept. She had observed and attempted to codify the complex rules of information and influence propagation across the social network of a diverse group of 10-year-olds.

One last weighty issue (which was actually the reason for her phone call that day) was the consternation she felt about her campaign speech. Kathy was torn between whether to deliver meaningful, adult-sounding content or make more exciting, kid-friendly promises. She felt that she needed to include the relevant, responsible ideas she would bring to the student council. On the other hand, she feared that this sort of material would come across as boring and uninspiring to her peers. She knew she needed to mix in some kid stuff such as promising to push for ice cream on Fridays and what-not. (She was honest enough not to promise to actually *deliver* on these issues, but only to do her best to get them enacted.) With that approach, she knew she could inspire her juvenile electorate. Of course, going solely with that approach had its own caveats in that she feared that she would sound just like the other candidates or not be taken as someone who was serious about the job.

In the end, she decided on a compromise, selecting from both the more adult-like topics and the more kid-like ones that would be important to the people who would possibly be voting for her. She took a similar mindset that, if she didn't appeal to the voters with the happy-happy stuff, she would never get the opportunity to bring up what she felt needed to be addressed. (As a note, I'm writing this part of the book in the thick of the campaign season for a U.S. presidential election. It makes reminiscing about my daughter's "substance vs. fluff" dilemma all that more amusing.) She had analyzed the possible mindsets of her audience and selected a mixed strategy that balanced the needs of the fifth grade, the necessity of getting elected to satisfy those needs, and her own desire to be intellectually honest. She knew that to craft her speech appropriately, she would need to get into their heads and predict their reactions.

Observations without Order

All of these issues were rattling around in my daughter's brain that week. She had observed and analyzed the relative odds of the positions of president and vice president. She had observed the results that an increase in the numbers of posters and stickers could achieve. She had observed how opinions could be swayed by secondary factors such as the opinions of others in proximity and the social pressures that are endemic to a school environment. And my poor, conflicted offspring observed that, in some contexts, an idea without substance could actually have *more* influence than something concrete.

What she lacked was a way of putting this all into the proper framework and perspective with the appropriate weights and measures. To select the proper approaches to these problems, she would have had to accurately weigh how each factor affected the other children. For example, while she knew that posters and stickers were valuable for name recognition, she did not know whether those methods were more or less important than having an "in" to the right social networks. She didn't even have a way of quantifying the relative merits of posters vs. stickers. Was one poster worth ten stickers? Twenty? Only five?

She also had no way of assigning values to the general *categories* of serious and childish issues, much less the value of each individual topic. Simply put, she needed to crawl inside the brains of typical fifth graders and not just determine what was important to them on both conscious and subconscious levels, but express *how* important each factor was relative to the other. If she had been able to do this bit of mental wizardry, she would have been able to then construct a mathematical model that informed her about what decisions she should make.

Of course, she didn't do this detailed analysis in such an open, scientific way. Much of it was based on things she would intuit simply from observing the goings on around her. After all, she's only a 10-year-old girl (although a remarkably insightful one). Whether the reasons for behavior are conscious or unconscious, however, there are often ways of probing that layer of abstraction to see what is there. Most of it is based on the idea of determinism—or cause and effect. Taken as a whole, the hundreds of causes producing hundreds of effects can be a bit daunting—even to the point where the fact that there *is* a direct link between things is completely obscured. Observed and described individually, though, we can start to see how they all work individually yet combine to work together.

Evidence of these sorts of effects is all around us. The challenge is to take these observations and convert them into numbers and formulas that we can use. This is at the heart of the process we must use in crafting behavioral game artificial intelligence (AI). To create an agent that would make the decisions (such as my daughter), we must also be able to model other aspects of the world (such as her peers). Each of the components above shows an individual system that could be modeled. When you put them together, you get bigger and more complex decisions.

In the end, Kathy plotted her course with noble intent and shrewd political savvy yet came up short of the coveted office of fifth-grade vice president. After all, she was working uphill… she wasn't one of the "popular kids" and she refused to promise "ice cream Fridays."

FINDING HIDDEN FACTORS

Large decisions such as the ones that Kathy faced in her quest for fifth-grade totalitarianism can be daunting. What's more, the relationship between the various pieces and parts can be obscure and intertwined. How, then, do we approach unwinding this mass of threaded relationships until we have broken them down to their component parts? Once we have reached a reasonably atomic level, we can begin to make judgments about *just that one item*. The smaller the decision, the fewer factors are involved in analyzing it. The fewer the factors, the easier it is to see how they interrelate. Therefore, the trick is to start small… and then simply ask, "What is important?"

The Layer between Supply and Demand

If I may play the role of the proud father once again, I will relate what my youngest son, Aaron, surprised me with the same time as Kathy's socio-political epiphany. Aaron is a little more than a year younger than his sister and was, therefore, nine years old when this lightning bolt struck.

We were playing *Zoo Tycoon* together (which I whole-heartedly recommend as a teaching tool for elementary school children). We had been working on a new zoo for a while and had a handful of exhibits up and running. Aaron, pausing in thoughtful analysis commented, "Dad, we've got some interesting stuff for people to see now… and there are more people coming into our park. We should think about raising the park admission price. That way we would have more money to build with."

Eager to turn this into one of those vaunted "teaching moments," I asked him how much he thought we should raise the admission. He sat back slightly and narrowed his eyes in thought and then gave a response that seemed very odd coming out of a fourth-grader. The following is probably an over-dramatized recollection of the exchange due to my unconscious desire to make my kid look brilliant. However, to the best of my knowledge, it is pretty darn close to what he really said that day.

Aaron: "Well… I'm not sure. But we can't raise it too much."

Curious Dad: "Why not?"

Aaron: "Because if we raise it too much, we could actually lose money."

Astounded Dad: "Really? Aren't we raising it so we can make more money?"

Aaron: "Yeah… but if the price is too high, then less people will come. We will make lots of money off the ones that do come in, but we won't get the money of the people who decide not to come in."

Amazed Dad: "So how do we know what price is right?"

Aaron: "Well... we should raise it a little at a time and keep watching to see how many people are coming in. If less people come in, then we know that it was too much."

Proud Dad: "Son, you just expressed a concept that many 40-year-olds don't understand."

Aaron had made the observation that he wasn't operating in a static environment. His prospective customers may react to his decisions. Therefore, to make the correct decision, he needed to be able to somewhat predict what their behavior would be. What Aaron needed to determine was what the interface was between *his* decision and the reaction of the guests. There must be a relationship that can be figured out that would predict, within reason, their behavior. Of course, we all know that what he was expressing was the connection between price and demand. If something costs little, it is more attractive; as the price increases, it is less attractive.

If that is put into a consumer model (and additionally considering that difference in consumers' ideas as to what the "right price" is), you will find that a rising price will satisfy fewer and fewer people. Once the number of willing buyers falls to a certain point, it doesn't matter what we charge them; we won't be making as much money as before. Taken to the extreme, you could charge one million dollars for a zoo pass, but you probably won't get many takers. Alternatively, if we try to get more customers by cutting the price, we could reach a point where we are getting lots of business but not making any money. Again, the extreme end would be massive numbers of guests for free. There is a businessman's joke that says, "We'll make it up in volume." Uh... no you won't.

Turning Human Decisions about AI into AI Decisions

Interestingly, as this was a computer game, and the park guests in *Zoo Tycoon* did react appropriately to changes in price, we know that some clever designer had actually created a formula for that behavior. As humans playing the game, our job was to determine what this formula was. We know that attitudes would move in a certain direction, but we didn't know how much. As I mentioned, my son's approach was to move the price a little at a time and observe the changes in behavior. Eventually, we would be able to determine the right price for our zoo admission. (Of course, since our zoo was constantly changing in what it offered, the right price was a moving target—a sign of a good algorithm design. More on that later.)

However, in game AI, the roles are slightly different. The decision that we humans were making is one that could be applied to an AI agent such as a shopkeeper in a role-playing game (RPG). What is the right price to charge for a particular item? If all else was equal, the role of zookeeper would have to do just as we did—take into account the unknown formula that went into crafting the decision model of the guests. Rather than simply guessing (which is not a very suitable task for computers), we would be tasked with determining what formula(s) *we* would use to take into account what the *other* agents would be doing.

It is in that neutral territory that behavioral mathematics comes into play, and likewise, where we need to use observation and a little inference to construct those behavioral algorithms properly to adequately fill that gap.

QUANTIFYING OBSERVATIONS

Converting ideas into numbers alone might not be as hard as it seems, however. Quantifying things not just in *ordinal* terms (e.g., A is greater than B) but in precisely relative terms (e.g., A is *twice as big* as B) nudges us closer to the realm that computers can use to calculate and therefore closer to what we can use in game AI. In this case, we must ask another question. Just as the prior query was "What is important?" this one could be phrased, "How much more important is it?"

Counting on the Edge of a Razor

I will illustrate with an example from my own life that came as something of an epiphany to me—and, given the circumstances, was a sure sign that I needed to step away from AI development for a day or two. It came while I was shaving.

If you happen to use refillable razor cartridges as I do, they may come in a plastic container of five cartridges (Figure 2.3). If I were to ask you the odds of any of those particular cartridges being in use, you would likely give the mathematically simple and straightforward answer of one in five—or 20%. That would certainly be reasonable to assume. However, there is a subtle difference to be illustrated here. If you were to randomly select from my five cartridges, each of the five would have a 20% chance of being selected by you. Likewise, if you knew nothing else of the situation, a random selection that you made would have a 20% chance of being the correct cartridge. However, that *doesn't* mean that each cartridge has a 20% chance of being in use at any given moment.

What if I told you that I always use the cartridges in order, from the top one in the container down to the bottom one? Would that change your decision? Why? After all, you were not asked the order in which I use them. You were not asked to guess which one I would use next based on which one I was currently on. You don't know how long ago I purchased the refill pack. You don't know for how long I typically use one blade.

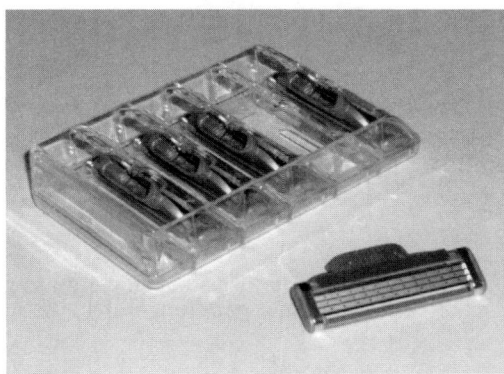

FIGURE 2.3 All blades may be created equal, but that doesn't mean they get used equally.

But wait… that last item *is* relevant, isn't it? If you use those refill packs, or anything similar for that matter, you may immediately recognize the point. For many of us, a distinct pattern of behavior surrounds those blades. When I first open a new pack and click the first blade into place, there is a quiet, almost subconscious oath to myself. "This is a *new* pack. I'm going to make it *last*." That mindset lasts for a while until finally, in an act of self-preservation, I have to switch to the second blade. Once I begin using that second blade, the mystique of the "first blade" is gone. I may as well change as needed. My diminished regard for conservation continues through the second, third, and fourth blades. The other end of the tray leads to a similar thought process as the first, however. This one is a bit more conscious on my part—and therefore has a bit more weight. That mentality is "This is the *last one* in the pack. I should make it last before busting open a new one."

If this subtle, but noticeable, shift in my allegiance to certain blades is taken into account, there is no longer a blanket assumption of equal usage that underlies the earlier premise. If we know the order of the blades, we can suggest that there is a slight bias toward the first and last blades in the pack—more so toward the last one. Therefore, rather than a straight 20% across the board, the distribution of usage may look more like Figure 2.4.

Notice that there is a slight bias toward blade 1 and a slightly larger bias toward 5. Obviously, the other three come in slightly under their starting point of 20%. The numbers I selected are by no means scientific. In fact, I have no idea if they are accurate about my blade usage or not. (In my less-funded college days, blade 5's usage would have been significantly higher due to "make it last because I can't *afford* to buy a new one.") If I were to use this hypothesis as a model for simulating my true blade usage, however, I believe it would be more accurate than a simple 20% across the board. In any event, it would certainly be more interesting.

Blade	Percent of Time	
1	22	"I'm going to make it last!"
2	17	I have my reasons for using blades 1 and 5 longer than the others.
3	17	
4	17	
5	27	"I can't afford a new one."

FIGURE 2.4 There is a bias toward using the first and last blades in a pack longer than the other three.

Just as my relatively lean college days led to a more significant reliance on the final blade, other people could have other patterns. Someone who is better off may not be concerned about moving on to the next refill tray, thereby not sticking with that fifth one long enough to risk a medical emergency. Someone who has a specific weekly pattern of usage may find he is *always* on the third blade before his "big date night" and will switch to the fourth to get that "clean, close shave" the commercials try to tell us is a strict requirement for actually being male. (I admit that I'm reaching a little bit on examples now.)

Now, razor blade usage patterns may not seem terribly relevant to games, but the illustration is more of the thought process involved than it is of the specific example. There are differences in how a given individual approaches each blade, and there are differences in how multiple individuals approach the whole blade-usage predicament. The point is that many typical behaviors can be quantified this way. What's more, the quantification can be done in such a way as to emulate the depth and personality of the subject.

Turning Observations into Numbers

Observing the distribution of possible choices is only the first step, of course. AI agents are there to act, not analyze. However, from a conceptual basis, the transition is not difficult. Using the razor blade example, if we proceed with the premise that the figures in Figure 2.4 are accurate usage percentages, it would be reasonable to assume that those same percentages would apply to the likelihood of me using any one of those five blades at a particular time.

So, if I were faced with an entire tray of five blades that I had used before, and the order has been preserved, you could make an educated guess as to which blades I would be likely to select.

In this case, we know that blade 5 is likely to be used the most, followed by blade 4. Blades 2 through 4 are the least used of the batch and would therefore be the most attractive to me. You could make an assumption based on these facts that might look like Figure 2.5. At first glance, the distribution of the percentages looks fairly inverse of the spread in Figure 2.4 (the probability of any particular one being in use). However, is that really what we are trying to accomplish?

Blade	Percent of Time
1	18 — "I probably used this longer."
2	23
3	23
4	23
5	13 — "I probably wore this one out!"

At any given time, what is the attractiveness of using each blade?

FIGURE 2.5 The relative attractiveness of each blade is based on how long I likely used it.

Making a Decision Based on the Numbers

Since I am aware of my proclivity toward over-using blades 1 and 5, if for some reason I have to go back and select a blade to reuse, I will make a conscious *choice* of selecting from blades 2, 3, and 4 (Figure 2.6). It is statistically more likely that those are less-worn, therefore making them more attractive to use. On the other hand, knowing that I probably used blade five to the breaking point, I'm not going to be terribly likely to even consider it. That much is obvious. However, despite the fact that blade 1 is probably in far better shape, I'm still going to be quite certain that it is worse than any of blades 2, 3, or 4. Why would I even consider blade 1, even though it may be in reasonably serviceable condition? It is far more likely that I would choose from that middle trio. The result of this is that the odds of selecting blades 1 or 5 are pretty much nonexistent. The probabilities of blades 2–4 climb accordingly.

Notice the subtle difference between the underlying logic of the numbers in Figure 2.5 and Figure 2.6. The former was simply a relative inverse of the usage statistics. The latter took into account an *intelligent decision* that I, as the shaver, would have made because I knew about the scenario that created the data in Figures 2.4 and 2.5. Despite the relatively small amount of difference between the conditions of the blades, I knew that if I had to choose one that was in better shape, it would have to be drawn from the three in the middle.

Figure 2.4 is based on observation. Figure 2.5 is based on inferences from the data in Figure 2.4. Figure 2.6 is designed to model an *intelligent decision* that could be made from the inferences in Figure 2.5. I will cover ways of modeling these types of decisions throughout this book.

Blade	Percent of Time	
1	6	"This is likely worse than 2 - 4"
2	31	After the blades have been used, which blade might I *select* to use again?
3	31	
4	31	
5	1	"This is likely the worst one."

FIGURE 2.6 Based on the what I expect the conditions of the blades to be after using them before, which blade might I select to use again?

NEEDING MORE THAN OBSERVATIONS

As we have laid out, to be able to craft our *pretend* worlds, we need to be able to observe and understand what is going on in our *real* worlds. Much can be discovered simply by observing what happens around us. We can identify the relevant factors and relationships—sometimes intuiting and inferring things that are not readily apparent. Most importantly, we must think about this information in a manner that allows for quantification. In some cases, this is simple. For example, my daughter could certainly make the claim that making three election posters was better than making only one. At other times, however, making direct comparisons is not possible. Could my daughter Kathy make the same claim that making three posters is the same as making three stickers? What *is* the difference between three posters and three stickers?

Even more difficult to ascertain is the relationships between items that cannot be counted. How much is it worth to have one popular kid evangelizing about your campaign for president of the fifth grade? How do we put a number on that? How do you put a value on promising ice cream Fridays?

And yet, if we are to construct an algorithm to make decisions about such things, we need to condense all this information into a form that can be digested by those algorithms. We need to be able to put these very issues into the language of mathematics and numbers. After all, when it comes to computers and the algorithms they so happily process, the power is in the numbers. Without the algorithms, we cannot make our decisions. Therefore, we need to somehow take these observations and comparisons about the behaviors we witness and turn them into numbers and algorithms.

Conveniently, that's our next stop…

3 Converting Behaviors to Algorithms

Different fields of work have their tools. Some are the typical physical tools such as the hammers and nails that carpenters use. Some are more conceptual such as a standard business process in the business world. In the game industry, artists have their standard tools as well. Some are physical such as modeling and animation software packages, and some are conceptual such as the idea of using the texture-mapped triangle. In my view, however, there is an intermediary between a pure tool and the end product.

A writer, for example, uses tools ranging from the word processor to pen and paper to the venerable quill pen and stone tablet. There are more abstract tools as well. The formalized rules of sentence structure and verb conjugation provide guidelines for what the reader expects from the writer's method of delivery. The words he uses, however—the fine points of the *language* he chooses to express his thoughts—are the intermediary. It is through the selection of words that the idea is articulated.

A classical artist uses brushes as his tools of choice. At first glance, one would label the paints as tools, too. I would contend that the paints are more of a *language* of expression—the liaison between the pure tool and the end product. There are suggestions as to what paints to blend to achieve certain colors and the proper way to mix them for various effects. However, it is up to the artist to decide how to achieve what he is attempting to portray. The paints are what allow the expression of creativity. They are what give variety and depth of character to the work.

Game artificial intelligence (AI) has its standard toolbox. Many algorithms and data structures are repeated over and over throughout all the games on the shelf. In fact, given the wide range of in-game behaviors that are exhibited, there are actually startlingly few methods on the list. In this case, a technique such as A*, a behavior tree, a state machine, or even a planning algorithm is a raw tool. Left to their own devices, however, those algorithms don't create behavior any more than words alone create a soliloquy or paints alone create an image of a supine swine. The nuance isn't in the method itself; the depth of behavior comes from the data that is inserted into the algorithm.

Using Numbers to Select

The finite state machine (FSM) depicted in Figure 3.1 is an example of something that is often seen in games. This sort of linearity of action is evident—and even common—in the most rudimentary game AI. For instance, an enemy in a first-person shooter (FPS) or a role-playing game (RPG) may start out in an idle state. Once a criteria is established, such as the player entering a certain radius, the enemy changes to an approach state. This is similar to the transition from state A to state B in Figure 3.1. There is no other option. If the player doesn't approach, state B is never entered. Continuing on, once the player is within range, the enemy may switch to state C, attack. If it never reaches the player, there is no other option; it stays in state B. Likewise, state D could represent "die," the transition triggered by its health reaching zero. If the health never reaches zero, it doesn't die (and keeps attacking). There's not a lot of AI going on here.

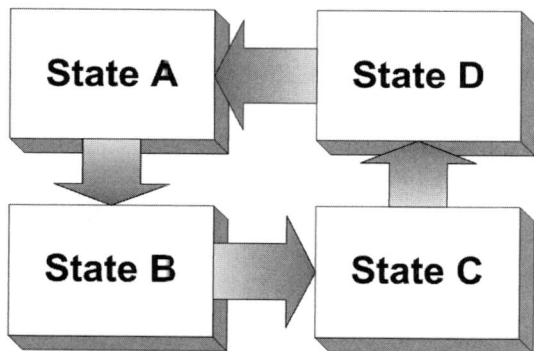

FIGURE 3.1 A very simple FSM with one static transition to and from each state.

The fault is not in the FSM, itself, however. After all, a state machine is a tool. As simply a tool, there is very little depth to it. In fact, with the assumption that simple logical triggers are behind the transitions (the arrows in Figure 3.1) from one state to the next, there is an implication of rigid predictability. If you know those transition cases, you know the next state. In the case of the FPS enemy, eventually a player will figure out that entering a certain radius triggers the transition from idle to approach. There is no variation whatsoever, and, accordingly, there is not a lot of drama. It is reminiscent of the predictability of Tic-Tac-Toe. "If the player can win next turn, block his movement."

By comparison, the state machine in Figure 3.2 provides something subtly different. While there are four states, just as in the one in Figure 3.1, state A can transition to states B, C, and D. Even given that expansion of potential "next moves" gives a small increase in the depth of the behavior.

For example, let's say state A is still the idle state of our FPS enemy. However, states B, C, and D are three different methods of attack. Perhaps B is still approach with the hopes of engaging in melee once the enemy arrives within range. State C, on the other hand, could be a ranged attack of some sort, and state D could represent casting a powerful spell. Now, as the enemy changes from idle, we may not necessarily know what is going to happen next.

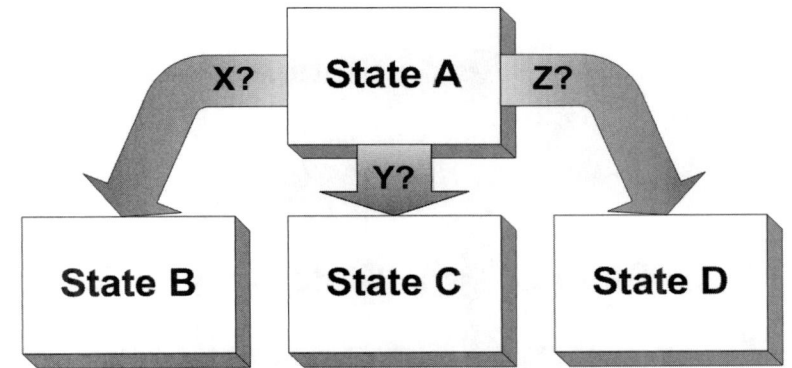

FIGURE 3.2 State (A) in this FSM could transition to any of three other states (B, C, or D) giving more than one possibility of what could happen next. The reasons those transitions occur are not defined but could simply be concrete rules or random chance.

However, if the transitions themselves were rigidly defined, there would still be predictability that would not take long to discern. For example, in the diagram, condition X leads to state B, condition Y leads to state C, and condition Z leads to state D. If the player can determine what conditions X, Y, and Z are, then the predictability of the agent has returned. Maybe conditions X and Y are triggered based on whether the player has a melee or ranged weapon out at the time—with the enemy responding in kind. If the enemy selects "approach" (state B) every time the player has a melee weapon out (condition X) and "ranged attack" (state C) every time the player brandishes his own ranged weapon (condition Y), then things are going to get mundane quickly. In this case, the transitions are reminiscent of the earlier explanation of the rules the dealer has to follow in Blackjack: If my cards are less than 17, hit; if they are 17 or greater, stand.

There is one more addition that would add some depth of character to this state machine. This addition would provide for the unpredictability that is reminiscent of the Poker player. One way of creating this sort of variety is to make the conditions themselves somewhat fuzzy. Using Figure 3.3 as an example, if there were percentage chances of transitioning to each of states B, C, and D, then a specific "next move" could be nailed down.

Using our FPS enemy example, perhaps the only trigger for a transition is still a radius, but the next state (i.e., approach, ranged attack, or spell) is based on the percentages established by X, Y, and Z. That way, while the player would know that the enemy will no longer be idle, there is no way to predict what is going to happen next. The player has to be prepared to react to each eventuality.

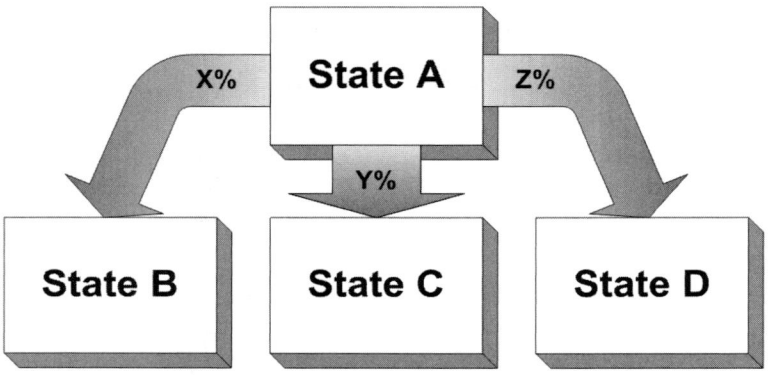

FIGURE 3.3 The transitions from state A to states B, C, and D are controlled by the percentages expressed by X, Y, and Z, respectively.

What's more, those percentages' chances can be dynamic as well. Rather than the X% chance of transition to state B always being the same value, we could allow it to change based on other factors. The result is that we may have a vague idea of *tendencies*, but there is always the potential for surprise. It is that unknown that lends *character* to our characters. Without that, our characters are automatons with the predictability of mechanical clocks.

The challenge—or to continue my metaphor, the *artistry*—comes through the process of *building* those fuzzy conditions. Just as the mixes of colors on an artist's palette are infinite, there are truly infinite possibilities on how to construct mathematical models. The models can be realistic, caricatures, or completely abstract. (My pig was an attempt at realism but ended up more as a caricature.) Even in the realm of realism, there are plenty of possibilities of how such realism can be represented.

In this case, the brush is an FSM, and, just like a paint brush, left to itself, it is largely incapable of providing the expression that we desire. By adding the mathematical models to the relatively expressionless FSM, we can paint a picture for our player—one that has the nuance that presents our vision in a robust, detailed, immersive way.

Just like the Poker player, our agent is now making "a series of *interesting* choices." And as the player experiences and interacts with our agent, he will likewise be able to make "a series of *interesting* choices." According to Sid's premise, at that point we have a game.

> **FSMs**
>
> FSMs have long been a staple of game AI. However, as behaviors grew more complex, the numbers of states grew as well. Accordingly, the number of potential transitions between the states grew at an exponential rate. The complexity of managing these states and their transitions began to work against the simple efficiency that was originally the attraction of the FSM.
>
> One of the criticisms of FSMs was that they were rigid and predictable. I don't completely subscribe to that theory. FSMs still have their place in game AI. Dismissing them outright is to say that the hammer is not a useful tool because it can't perform *all* possible construction tasks. However, often they are matched with other, more expressive structures where they can play a supporting role. In fact, by utilizing some of the techniques in this book, you can expand and extend FSMs to a great degree while managing some of the increased complexity.

USING NUMBERS TO DEFINE

For the numbers that we use to make decisions to be meaningful, they must represent something. If the transition percentages in Figure 3.3 were simply random, they wouldn't represent anything more than their own randomness. They wouldn't "stand for" anything. At that point, the effect of using them to guide the agent from state A to states B, C, or D would be lost in a chaotic shuffle.

IN THE GAME Know When to Walk Away, Know When to Run

To make those transitions mean something in a behavioral context, the numbers themselves need to be constructed so that they represent something meaningful in that same context. For example, if states B, C, and D were replaced by the three actions attack, hide, and flee, respectively (Figure 3.4), we would need to find a meaningful parameter (or collection of parameters) that would be relevant to the decision. Depending on the type of game and the data available, we may choose something as simple as the agent's health.

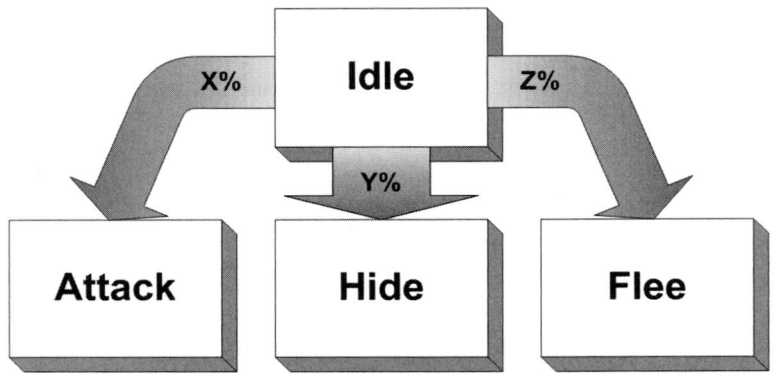

FIGURE 3.4 The transitions from the idle state to the attack, hide, and flee states are controlled by the percentages expressed by X, Y, and Z, respectively.

The example in Figure 3.5, shows three different definitions of the state that our agent's health could be (good, damaged, and critical). For each of those, there are three percentage values for each of the three actions (attack, hide, and flee). Part of defining those behaviors would be assigning those values. When our agent is in good health, how often do we want him to attack? To flee? What about when the agent is damaged? Should he *ever* attack when he is in a critical state of health? At that point, we are defining when those actions should be taken.

		Health		
		Good	Damaged	Critical
Action	Attack	85	40	10
	Hide	10	40	30
	Flee	5	20	60

FIGURE 3.5 Definitions of the transition percentages (X, Y, and Z) to the attack, hide, and flee states based on whether the agent's health is good, damaged, or critical. Note the arrow showing the approximate trend from attack to flee.

Of course, we would have to define what good, damaged, and critical health means. Does "good" mean 100%? Anything above 80%? 75%? That is yet another definition that must be made. The algorithm that processes the decision itself does not change. What is adjusted is the way the numbers are arranged. And *this* is where most of the subtlety comes into decision making.

To make even more robust algorithms, we may not use any categories at all. Instead, we could build a formula that takes into account the health value and converts it somehow into various percentages that we will then use to make our decision. For example, we may elect to use the following formulas to create our transition percentages:

$$Attack = (Health \times .7) + 10$$

$$Hide = (100 - Attack) \times .3$$

$$Flee = (100 - Attack) \times .7$$

At any given moment, we could use the agent's current health value to calculate the three percentages that we need to decide what the agent is going to do next. (Actually, we only need two, as the third option would be in effect if the first two are not selected.) Graphing those three formulas, we would get the results in Figure 3.6.

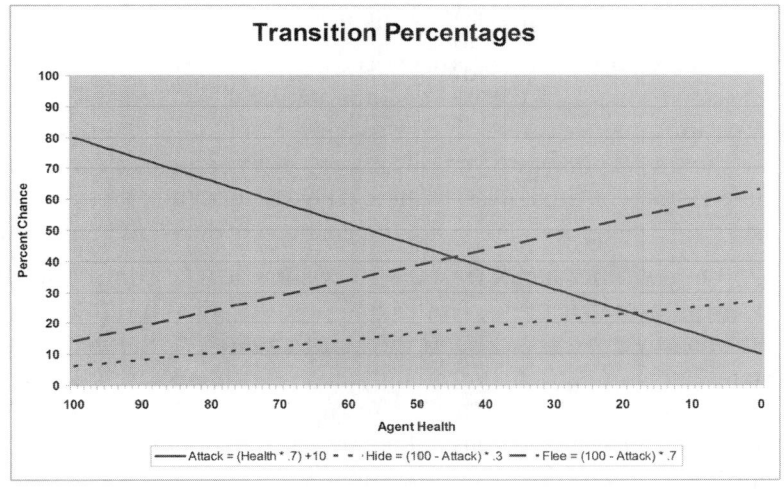

FIGURE 3.6 Based on the formulas shown, the percentages for the state transitions (y-axis) to attack, hide, and flee change automatically as the agent's health (x-axis) changes.

As you can see, the numbers follow a pattern similar to the static figures we created in Figure 3.5. We start with about an 80% chance of attacking and small chances of hiding of fleeing. As health reaches zero, the chance of attacking approaches 10%, and that of fleeing arrives at 63%, with hiding coming in at 27%.

Somewhere in the middle, we pass through values similar to what we had initially defined for the damaged value.

By changing the formulas we can tweak the behaviors to tailor them to what we are trying to accomplish. For example, I decided that, even if the agent is about to die, there should still be a 10% chance that it would attack. Depending on the behavior I was trying to emulate, this might be unreasonable. A different formula would yield something entirely different. Let's change the attack formula to the following:

$$Attack = (Health - 15) \times 0.95$$

We now have a result in which the initial attack percentage is about the same (80.75) but falls to zero as the agent's health gets to 15%. Below that, the only options are to hide or flee with the appropriate percentages. (Note that we would have to be careful to not use the negative numbers generated by this formula in the calculations of our hide and flee values.) This change leads to a completely different behavior for the agent—and a very different experience for the player. As before, the player will see severely wounded agents using the various retreat behaviors more and more often, but they will *never* see a critically wounded agent attacking.

Using a formulaic approach leads to smoother changes in values and, if constructed properly, is often very computationally efficient. There are also plenty of variations that we can apply to this approach. Rather than simply linear formulas, we can use exponential, logarithmic, or even complex polynomial expressions to define our behaviors. Each of these types of lines and curves has its own characteristics and, therefore, can be used to create very different behavioral responses.

On the other hand, we experience some loss of control by putting things entirely in formulaic terms. Notice that in the original three-column version (Figure 3.5) there was a subtle rise in the hide value when the agent was in the damaged state. Using our strictly linear approach (Figure 3.6), we lost that subtlety. In fact, it may have been difficult to find an appropriate combination of formulas that satisfied *exactly* what we wanted. If a formula makes things too sterile, a hand-crafted approach may be more appropriate.

There is generally no "right answer" to which approach to use. The number of possibilities is, for all intents and purposes, infinite. The trick is to select one that best approximates whatever it is that we are trying to emulate. We will investigate more of theses strategies in Part III, "Mathematical Modeling."

Using Algorithms to Construct Numbers

Individual numbers alone aren't always enough to do the trick. There usually isn't a clean one-to-one ratio between something we would like to consider (an input) and the decision we need to make (an output). It is often important for us to consider a variety of inputs. Additionally, these inputs may be of significantly different types. This complicates things further.

For instance, if we are simply looking at our health compared to our opponent's health, we are comparing two values that mean the same thing and may very well have the same scale. On the other hand, if we were to consider our health and the number of bullets left in our gun, we would have to determine which of these is more important and by how much. Do we put the bullets in terms of health? Health in terms of bullets? Or do we abstract things out to a level that takes both types of information into account? At this point, we have stepped out of simply using numbers and formulas… we are now creating more complex chains of logic and calculation to make our decision.

Making the Grade

If I can tap into my parenting again, my kids' school district has this fancy Web-based portal so that I can see every bit and piece of their grades. More than simply getting a letter grade or even the current grade percentage, I get to see the grades for every single assignment, project, quiz, and test. It goes even deeper than that… I get to see how many points each of the above was worth to begin with. So a 20-point quiz is worth more than a 15-point quiz. A 50-point homework assignment is worth a *lot* more than a 10-point one. Heck, even getting 40% on the 50-point homework (i.e., 20 out of 50 points) is worth *twice as much* as getting 100% of the 10-point one. Of course, the grade on the 50-point assignment is also worth five times as much as the grade on the 10-point one.

What makes things more interesting is that a 30-point test or quiz is not necessarily equal to a 30-point homework assignment. The reason? The grading system allows for layers of combination weighting that is similar to our example above. The work is grouped into categories such as homework, projects, labs, quizzes, and tests depending on the way the teacher has arranged the class. Each category (similar to our mid-level groupings) is then given a weight. The weights are combined with the respective scores in each category, and a final grade is determined.

Stepping through an example makes things a bit clearer. Here are some sample grades that I just made up. (My own kids' grades at the moment aren't all that interesting or conducive to an example.) In this example (Figure 3.7), there have been two tests, two quizzes, and four homework assignments. Each of those (white boxes) shows the number of points scored out of the maximum possible. For example, the first test grade was 35 out of a possible 50.

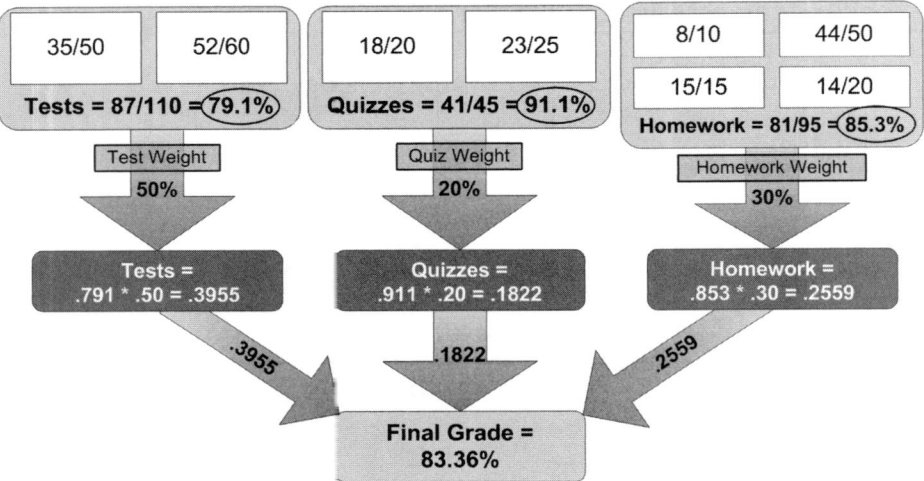

FIGURE 3.7 A hierarchy of individual grades grouped into three categories: tests, quizzes, and homework. Each item has its own weight, as does each of the three categories. By combining them accordingly, we can arrive at a final grade.

In each category, the total points scored and the total points possible are added up, for tests in this instance, leading to 87 out of 110, or 79.1%. When a grade has been found for each of the three categories (e.g., quizzes = 91.1 and homework = 85.3), they will then be combined.

Compartmentalization

Note the top row of arrows in Figure 3.7. Tests are worth 50% of the total grade, quizzes 20%, and homework 30%. This has nothing to do with the total number of points accumulated in each category. For example, despite the fact that there are 95 total homework points, that doesn't mean that it is nearly as important as the 110 test points. The points in each category only have meaning *inside* their respective categories. The only number that comes out of that category is the final percent scored, which, as mentioned, is applied to the weighting for that category. Proceeding through the simple math, we arrive at weighted values for each of the three categories that, when added together, give us a final grade value—in this case, 83.36%.

There are extraordinary benefits to this model. By setting up these categories and layers, we compartmentalize things to the extent that there is essentially a firewall between the different areas. We are free to set the number of points for any given homework assignment relative *only* to other homework assignments. If we feel that there is a proper balance between the relative importance of the four assignments, we can feel confident with the value coming out of the *entire* homework category.

What's more, if we added a fifth homework assignment, we would not have to consider the *weight* of that assignment beyond the homework category. We don't have to consider if the points for the new assignment are in balance with the quiz tomorrow or the test this Friday. As long as it blends in well with the existing four assignments, we are finished. The *result* would cascade out and down toward the final grade just like any other changes, but only based on the already established relationship that *all* homework be taken together and (in this case) figure in as 30% of the final grade.

Noting a couple of more items of interest in the example in Figure 3.7, the 91% grade on quizzes seems good until you realize that, at 20%, the quiz weighting isn't enough to bring the grade up that much. Even if the teacher gave 20 more quizzes and nothing else, if you maintain that 91% grade on them, the final grade would not change. Even if the quizzes were worth 100 points each and you received a grade of 91% on them, the final grade would not change. That is another one of the features of building decision algorithms in a modular fashion such as this.

That simple act of grouping like factors together to determine an aggregate also cuts much of the complexity down. If all items, whether test, quiz, or homework, were to be tallied up without weighting, every time we added a new one of *any* of those, we would have to compare its weight to *all* of the others that have come before. In actuality, in the school environment, if you wanted to maintain a certain spread of the weights, you would even have to plan into the future and preweight everything you would do for the whole term. So by simply constructing a logical, mathematical algorithm, we not only make things simpler to use, but maintain more control over what we want to see as an end result.

IN THE GAME   Expanding the Engagement Decision

In the "engagement decision" example in the previous section, we used only one criterion, "agent's health," to decide whether we should attack, hide, or flee. Unfortunately, the data that we use to construct our decisions is rarely as simple as that. Something as simple as "agent's health" is usually not the *only* consideration in making a decision. Often, we need to account for other factors. For example, in the engagement decision above, we may want to take into account such things as:

- Agent's health
- Enemy's health
- Agent's weapon
- Enemy's weapon
- Number of enemies

- Proximity to a leader
- Proximity to an important location
- Agent's "anger" level

If we were so inclined, we could measure each of the above criteria and build a formula that takes it all in and spits out one single number. Needless to say, a formula that took all of that into account in the appropriate manner would get fairly unwieldy.

Alternatively, we could combine some of the above factors into intermediate values that would then be utilized in constructing the final decision (Figure 3.8). For instance, we could combine the agent's health and the enemy's weapon into a value representing the risk that is presented to the agent. On the flip side of that, the agent's weapon combined with the enemy's remaining health could be combined into a measure of the threat to the enemy. These two values could then be combined into an indication of the total threat balance between what the agent could receive and dole out.

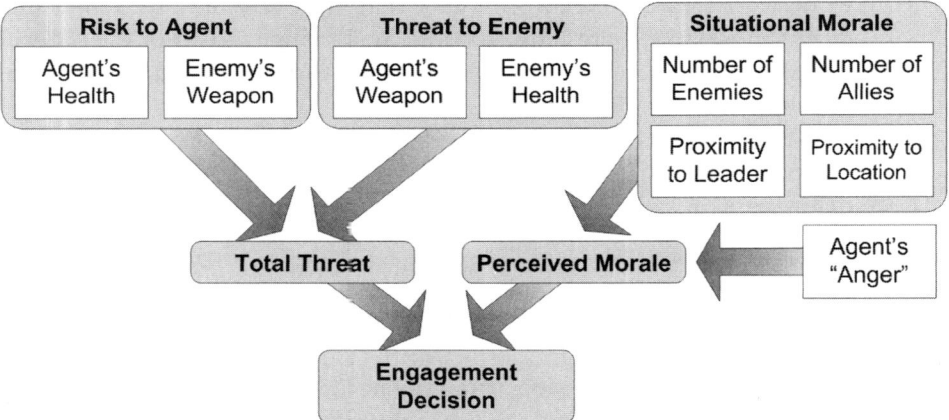

FIGURE 3.8 A hierarchy of factors can be combined in layers to eventually arrive at a single decision. In this case, nine factors are combined and recombined until the final "engagement decision" is calculated.

By analyzing the number of friends and foes, where the agent's leader is, and the proximity to an important location (like a base), we could determine the morale that the agent may have at the time. However, if we were to combine these factors with the agent's anger level, we could arrive at a "perceived morale" that might represent how flying into a rage might color the agent's decision making. In the end, we can funnel all of the above into one final "engagement decision."

Now we have taken the nine criteria that we started with and combined them into more of a modular format. We are still using them all, but the relationships between them have become more meaningful. Each time we combine factors, however, we will have to determine how to weight them and massage them to get the effect we want.

Going back to our engagement decision example, even starting small, in constructing the risk to agent value, we need to determine how important the two factors—agent's health and enemy's weapon—are, respectively, to that value. Are they equal? Is the agent's health more important than the weapon? Do we calculate it in terms of how long the agent can expect to live at a particular *rate* of damage? Combining intermediate values can be a little more obscure. How do we process total threat and perceived morale so that we are sure we are going to generate an appropriate balance?

In large part, when dealing with complex, multilayered processes, the key is to be confident with each step along the way. If you feel good about what went into two smaller decisions, you can more accurately combine those two results into a larger one. Likewise, when debugging or even tweaking a full decision, it is important to work backward appropriately. If you are not satisfied with one layer, it may not be the direct inputs to that layer that are the problem. You must question everything that leads to that point. Referring again to Figure 3.8, if you are not happy with the result you are getting from the total threat value, you have to question not just how you are *combining* risk to agent and threat to enemy together, but the factors that you used in arriving at those figures to begin with.

All of these approaches are the steps to a very complicated process of crafting decisions. Once done, however, the resulting behaviors can be deep and powerful… and yet easily changed and maintained.

That being said, don't expect "solutions" in this book. Unlike an area such as pathfinding, there isn't one *problem* here, much less a single *answer* to that problem. Using the metaphor from the beginning of this chapter, as you proceed through the book you can expect to find plenty of brushes, paints, palettes, and other tools of the trade. You will learn some of the researched and studied history of the art and how what those masters discovered can be applied in your own work. You may find suggestions for what colors mix well to accomplish certain effects. I will even invite you to look over my shoulder to see how I paint some sample works. However, there is no way I can tell you how to do your own painting. There are simply too many ways to do it.

All the artistry must be your own.

Part II: Decision Theory

In Part II, we will explore the roots of what goes into making decisions.

Chapter 4, "Defining Decision Theory," looks at the two major types of decision theory, their uses, their weaknesses, and how they can be blended together.

Chapter 5, "Game Theory," walks through some of the classic decision scenarios and investigates what we can glean from them to use in our own games.

In **Chapter 6, "Rational vs. Irrational Behavior,"** we discuss the differences between purely rational behaviors, purely *irrational* behaviors, and seemingly irrational behaviors that actually make sense.

Chapter 7, "The Concept of Utility," explains how objective measurements in the world can be converted to a perspective that an artificial intelligence (AI) agent can understand.

Chapter 8, "Marginal Utility," explores how the utility of an object or action is sometimes a moving target that changes based on the perspective of the observer.

Chapter 9, "Relative Utility," discusses how the utility of one object or action can be compared, contrasted, and even combined with the utility of another object or action, and how this can either assist in a higher goal or lead to conflicting information.

4 | Defining Decision Theory

Decision theory seems, by its name, to be a fairly straightforward concept. At first blush, it would seem to be the theory of making decisions. While that is technically correct, these waters are deceptively deep and even a bit turbid. The notion of what actually constitutes a decision is sometimes called into question—which doesn't make it any simpler to advance a theory about it.

Regardless of what we settle on as a definition of *decision*, there are plenty of theories about not only the "right" way to come to one, but also theories on why humans and other such decision-making entities often fail miserably to make that right decision.

NORMATIVE DECISION THEORY

There are a couple of different subdivisions of the larger umbrella of decision theory. The primary one is the area of **normative** or **prescriptive** decisions. Think of this as relating to what is normal or should be prescribed in the situation—that is, what *should* be done given the facts. Facts are (in fact) a *requirement* of normative decision theory. The only way a decision that should be made can be determined with such certainty is with certain assumptions in place (Figure 4.1). The decision maker:

- Has *all* of the relevant information available
- Is able to *perceive* the information with the accuracy needed
- Is able to perfectly *perform* all the calculations necessary to apply those facts
- Is perfectly *rational*

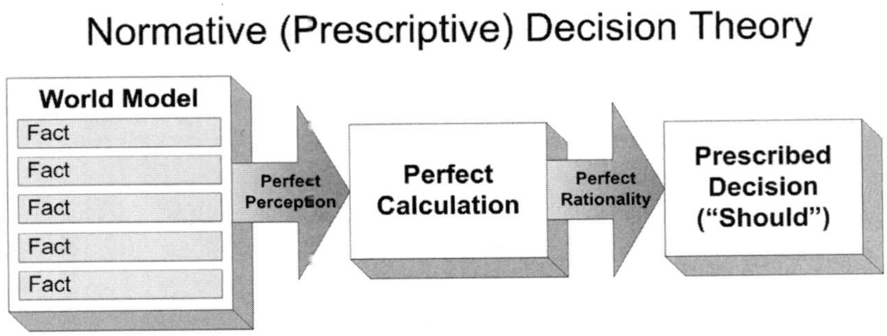

Normative (Prescriptive) Decision Theory

FIGURE 4.1 Normative decision theory takes a perfectly perceived model of the world, accurately performs all the necessary calculations, and rationally selects the most appropriate decision.

Most other game AI agents use normative (prescriptive) decision theory. In fact, this is the area that encompasses much of game AI today. A pathfinding algorithm uses all four of the above criteria and returns the path that an agent *should* take. Likewise, a planner that utilizes A* to find a way to solve a goal theoretically returns the "best" steps to take to accomplish its intended goal. A stereotypical bot in a first-person shooter (FPS), as an entity tied to the game world, has all the information about its environment available to it, can perceive it all—through cheats if necessary—and is able to perform any and all necessary calculations to make a perfect head shot on anyone it pleases, and they are rational to a fault.

It would seem that normative decision theory is perfectly suited for computers and, by association, game AI. If, as a designer or programmer, we are specifically concerned with looking at our game world and solving a problem to tell our agents what they should do, normative decision theory seems to be the channel through which we must pass. While this is the case to some extent, there are caveats.

Predictable "Shoulds"

In Chapter 1, we examined how some games have a very defined pattern of what *should* be done on any given move. In Tac-Tac-Toe, given any board arrangement, there is one play that you *should* do if you want to win (or not lose). Not only does that instruct us about what to do on our turn, but we can be reasonably certain that our opponent will respond with the corresponding move that he *should* make to counter it. Accordingly, in our opponent's eyes, our move is just as predictable.

In Blackjack, the moves on any given arrangement of cards are a bit more obscure due to the mathematical complexity involved. However, the best mathematical solution is printed in vivid colors on the cheat cards. Those moves represent a statistical aggregation representing what we *should* do. Does it always work? No…

The effectively random nature of dealing cards makes it possible that we will lose the hand despite making the suggested play. However, if one were to do the math, the result still shows us that our best chances lie in a certain direction. Therefore, we *should* follow it. Any kind dealer (and even the often overly helpful people at the table) will tell you what your play *should* be—making it fairly apparent that the proper Blackjack play is predictable.

Therein lies the problem. Using normative decision theory exclusively as a source of game AI makes those decisions and actions very predictable. If, as a player, you can track the same criteria the agent is using to make those decisions, you can then match them with the decision the agent makes when those criteria are in place. As these patterns repeat, you will be able to determine what those "shoulds" are. Thus, you can predict with complete accuracy what the AI agent is going to do at any given time. All you are doing is connecting the cause and effect model that the agent is depending on completely for its thought process. You have exposed what seems to be a complicated process for the Rube Goldberg machine that it is: Everything happens for a reason—everything happens in order… because it *should*.

The other problem with using normative decision theory is that it is entirely mechanical. I don't necessarily mean mechanical in the sense of completely deterministic as explained above. I mean it in the *perceived* sense that it doesn't seem human. Certainly, much of that effect is due to the rigid cause and effect chain. However, there is another factor in play: Not *all* people act the same way *all the time*. If you were to face 10 enemies that are using the same model, and they *all* act the same way *every time* they are faced with a constellation of criteria, the notion of humanity (or any other *–ity* you want to apply here) is lost. We are exposing our agents for the completely mathematical and logical bots that they are. Not only does that not look "real," but how long do you think it generally takes for the cause and effect rules to make it onto the Web or into strategy guides? "If you want to beat [this game], do [this]—the AI will do [that]… every single time."

Using normative decision theory for game agents causes people playing against them to subscribe to using it as well. We have reduced the exchange to the deterministic equivalent of Tic-Tac-Toe. There is an answer for everything on both sides. If you want to win, you must follow it. To harken back to Chapter 1 and Mr. Sid's idea of interesting choices, it would seem that we have unwittingly removed both the "interesting" *and* the "choice" from the experience. There must be a better way.

DESCRIPTIVE DECISION THEORY

The other side of the decision theory coin is the realm of **positive** or **descriptive** decision theory. In this case, *positive* is not the antonym of *negative*, but rather spun off the word *posit*, that is, to lay down an assumption or theory. In fact, despite the affirmative nature of the word, positive decision theory deals in such a manner as to *not* make a judgment about what *should* be done.

The other choice of words, *descriptive*, is somewhat clearer in this respect. Descriptive decision theory simply *describes* a correlation, for example, between cause and effect or other such relationships. This is the realm of study of what people *tend to do*, rather than what they *should do* (Figure 4.2).

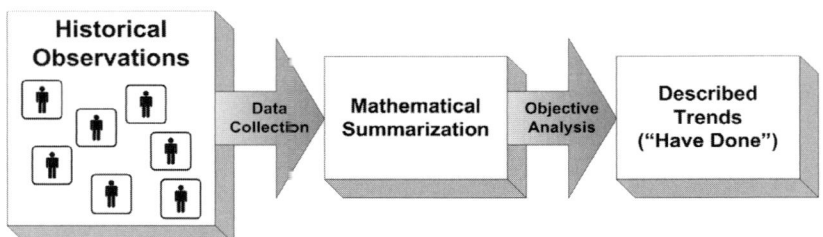

FIGURE 4.2 Positive decision theory uses historical observations of behavior, and summarizes and analyzes that data to express what has been done in the past.

Part of the problem is that of converting scale. In Isaac Asimov's *Foundation* trilogy, the character Hari Seldon was a proponent of what he called "psychohistory." He believed that by studying the past actions of large groups of people, you could predict the future actions of large groups of people. Notice that the first part of that sentence looks much like our descriptive decision theory, that is, studying the past actions of large groups of people. However, Seldon was very aware that the data from psychohistory could not predict the actions of a single person. Asimov's example (which actually is borrowed from real-world physicist Daniel Bernoulli) was that of the action of molecules of a gas. While science has a pretty good handle on how large quantities of gaseous molecules act in concert, they can't predict the action of any single one of those molecules. Therefore, while psychohistory is valuable for predicting the path of masses, it doesn't help us determine what may happen on a more granular scale—such as that of the individual.

For example, I've heard it said that "four out of five dentists surveyed recommend sugarless gum to their patients who chew gum." That is a description of the aggregate of the dentists surveyed. Literally, when the data was summarized, 80% of them recommended sugarless gum. The other 20% just wanted more repeat business.

There are a few things that we *can't* assume based on this data. First, we cannot make the case that dentists *should* recommend sugarless gum four-fifths of the time and recommend the dental time bomb the rest of the time. It also *doesn't* mean that any one dentist recommends sugarless gum 80% of the time and regular gum to the rest of his patients. Descriptive decision theory doesn't deal with the specifics of individual behaviors like that. However, from the description provided by this data, we can pull a random dentist off the street, ask his opinion, and feel reasonably certain (80% so) that he is going to recommend sugarless gum to us. (Come to think of it, is there *any* gum that has sugar in it anymore?)

Past Performance May Not Be an Indication

So, the problem with theory is that it's… well… *theoretical*. It is not really what "is" in a concrete sense but what "seems to be" if you back up far enough to blur out all the detail. If I can draw from a prior life of mine, when I was a musician studying theory and composition, my mother bestowed upon me her copy of the book *Harmony* by Walter Piston. While reading about music theory is almost as dry as reading about game AI, there was a line in the preface that caught my eye. Walter said, "Theory must *follow* practice… theory is not a set of *directions* for composing music. It tells us not how music will be written *in the future*, but how music has been written *in the past*" (emphasis mine). What Mr. Piston was pointing out is that music theory is *descriptive* in nature rather than *prescriptive*. It gives us a window into what has become accepted practice over time rather than what should be done by anyone writing music today. (One could make the point that today's musicians seem to take Piston's edict the wrong way around… and, accordingly, that the creative variety of today's music suffers in merciless homogeneity.)

The only way we can make a connection between what *has been done* (descriptive decision theory) and what *should be done* (normative decision theory) is to assume that what has come before had a valid, reasonable rationale. That is, the decisions that the collection of dentists made were for a reason. We may not know what that reason is, but, if we trust the dentists, we can decide that their collective opinion is reasonably correct.

One problem with using these assumptions is that we may be misled by what has been collected. In investment program commercials, we hear this as "past performance may not be an indication of future results." The same could be said for sports teams over the course of many years. Just because a team has a history of success over the years, that doesn't mean they are going to do that well during the upcoming season. (Or, in the case of my Cubbies... uh... never mind.)

Another problem that can occur is when we end up in a cyclical arrangement. That is, when the availability of data on what has been done by others in the past is used to drive the decisions of others in the future. At times, this seems like it would be a good idea. If I were a dentist trying to decide on what sort of gum I would recommend to my patients, I may look at what *other* dentists before me have recommended. In our clichéd "four out of five" scenario I may decide that sugarless gum must have merit enough that my colleagues are suggesting it to their patients. Therefore, I should do so as well. There are problems with this approach, however.

What if They Are Wrong?

As we covered above, we have to assume that the data is relevant and well informed. Sometimes it is not. There is a well-known (and oft-repeated) phenomenon in politics, wherein polling data is used as news. If we were to see a poll on an issue or a person who told me that a majority of people felt a certain way, I might be inclined (like the dentist above) to assume that there is something to the position. As time passes and more people believe the data and shift their opinions accordingly, the poll itself shifts more. This may not be due to any sort of legitimacy of the topic in question. It may be entirely due to the fact that people trust each other's opinions and think that the next person (as reported by the poll) must know more about the issue than they do.

The more people that are reported as supporting the position, the more strongly my conviction that there must be some relevance or benefit to it, despite the fact that I may know nothing about the issue. If we were to make a decision based on that information, we would have committed a grievous error. We have taken descriptive decision theory (the polling data) and used it as a replacement for the prescriptive decision theory (what we *should* do with the information).

As I related in Chapter 3, my daughter Kathy noticed the effect that the descriptive data had in the fifth-grade election. People were willing to base their support for a candidate on the knowledge that a group of friends supported that candidate as well (i.e., the survey). For what it's worth, in the milieu of a fifth-grade student council election, there *is no* prescriptive decision theory that can be presented. There is no reason that you *should* vote for any one kid over another. In that case, the perceived opinion of the group is good enough. In Kathy's observation, each kid believed that the other had a perfectly valid reason for supporting that candidate... and they never bothered to compare notes. It was an exhibition of the social momentum of peer pressure at its finest. You wouldn't need Hari Seldon's psychohistory to predict the voting habits of 10-year-olds.

In a similar vein, the practical joke of stopping in a crowded place to stare and point up at something that isn't there is a great example of how you can influence the public in this way. The more people start mimicking you, the easier it is to get other people to look as well. Their thought process is just the same as the polling data. They don't have the facts that would be required for a *prescriptive* motive telling them they *should* look up. Instead, they have placed all their trust in the *descriptive* sense of "Everyone else is doing it… I'm sure *they* wouldn't be doing it without reason."

THE BEST OF BOTH WORLDS

Certainly, there are merits in both of these areas, but while normative decision theory (the bot) has obvious examples of how it should be used to make decisions in games, how does descriptive decision theory come in? After all, we don't tap into a database of survey information à la *Family Feud* to help our bots make decisions. About the closest thing we have to that is capturing player data ahead of time and attempting to make our decision models from that. If game AI were that simple, these sorts of books wouldn't be necessary. However, there *is* something to be gleaned from the use of descriptive decision theory.

In game AI, we are tasked with something of a hybrid. On the one hand, we are trying to determine, on any given game frame, what our agents *should* do. We are trying to create a decision for the moment—the arena of normative decision theory. That may or may not be a simple undertaking, depending on the decision or situation.

On the other hand, whether or not we can come to a decision about what *should* be done, we are trying to emulate and/or re-create behaviors that look like what people (or animals, or space aliens…) *tend to do*. Of course, these decisions may or may not be what they *should do*. Hopefully, those tendencies that we analyze with descriptive game theory (and attempt to re-create) will also be near enough to the "most logical choice" as per normative game theory so that they don't look ridiculous—slightly misguided or a bit erroneous perhaps, but not outright silly.

The result of all of this is that, to construct decisions that are meaningful and realistic, we can't tie ourselves to the omniscient and purely rational tenets of normative decision theory. Looking again at the list of requirements for that to be in place:

- Has *all* of the relevant information available
- Is able to *perceive* the information with the accuracy needed
- Is able to *perfectly perform* all the calculations necessary to apply those facts
- Is perfectly *rational*

… none of those are at all human, and therefore any decision based on that model is bound to be flawed in its efforts to *look* human (or animal, etc.).

If we swap a few things into those four items, however, we can start to sense a model that is a bit more like what we encounter in reality.

- Has *some of* the relevant information available
- Is able to perceive the information—albeit with *some inaccuracies*
- Is able to perform the calculations necessary *within a margin of error*
- Makes decisions that involve factors *other than* perfect rationality

In each of the italicized areas above, we have washed out some of the perfect computational ability that computers just happen to be good at. In its place, we now have some more fuzzy ideas and nebulous concepts. How do we know *how much* information to make available? How do we construct *some inaccuracies* in the perception? How do we insert a *degree of error* into calculations? How much error? And what sorts of factors do we include other than perfect rationality? For that matter, what other factors *are there*?

This is where we can put *positive* or *descriptive* decision theory to work. By starting with the raw logic of what they *should* do, applying an analysis of what people, animals, or even orcs *tend to* do, we can build models that guide what they *will* do in our games (Figure 4.3).

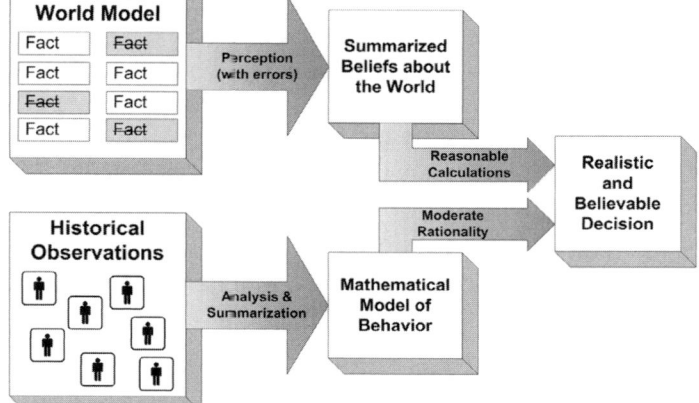

FIGURE 4.3 Combining normative and positive decision theory takes the limited world model perceived by an agent, adds the potential for errors, and creates a belief about the world. When combined in a moderately rational fashion with a behavior model constructed from observations of what people tend to do, it yields varied, yet believable realistic behaviors.

Assembling all of this together is a balancing act. Whereas each of the areas is relatively self-contained and self-reliant on its own, once the walls are down, we encounter inconsistencies and even outright contradictions. In that case, which is more important? Do you start with one and modify it with the other? Is there an underlying law that points us in the right direction regardless of the rigors of logic or the vagaries of observed behavior? Is there a theory that encompasses all of the above? Interestingly, there is, or, at least, there has been a reasonable attempt to explore and codify these issues.

To paraphrase Fraulein Maria, let's start at the very beginning… a very good place to start. We must decide on a manner for determining what our agents *should* do. And for that, we tap into the wonderful world of John von Neumann.

5 Game Theory

While plenty of study from a variety of disciplines has tackled the behemoth of decision theory, perhaps one of the most successful (and conveniently relevant to us) forays into this realm is the collection of efforts made in the area of **game theory**.

Game theory has never been a mainstream subject. Initial references to it date back as far as the early 1700s. However, the spectacular mathematical genius John von Neumann is generally credited as being the "father of game theory." In 1928, he published a series of papers on the subject. A more visible launching point of the concept occurred in 1944 with the publishing of the book *Theory of Games and Economic Behavior* that von Neumann co-authored with economist Oskar Morgenstern. Not long afterward, in 1951, John Nash took game theory to another level with his analysis of equilibria. More on that later.

On the whole, however, game theory went through ebbs and flows of interest. Limited mostly to esoteric, military, or scientific arenas, it has also seen use in the areas of political science, sociology, biology, computer science, logic, and even philosophy. In the 1980s, it finally caught on in the world of economics—over 50 years after von Neumann's original papers and more than 35 years after Neumann and Morgenstern published their massive dissertation on the subject.

Despite its name, game theory is only loosely connected to the concept of games. In fact, the name "game theory" is something of an unfortunate misnomer (which may have led to the delay in it being considered seriously by the scientific community). The core concepts tend more toward a generic analysis of decision making—some of which can be applied to games. One of the most important tasks that the field of artificial intelligence is charged with is imbuing agents with the ability to make decisions—some of which can be applied to games. It would seem, then, that the ideas that are endemic to game theory would be a natural starting place for a study on how to create decisions in artificial agents in games.

GAME THEORY DEFINITIONS

When reading about game theory, you will occasionally see references to the following terms.

- Two-person: A game played by two people. Alternatively, this can apply to two teams of people working together toward the same goals (e.g., Bridge).
- Zero-sum: A game that has a balancing end condition such as one winner and one loser (e.g., Chess, Checkers, Tic-Tac-Toe), or whatever is gained by one player is lost by the other player (e.g., Poker with a fixed amount of money at the table).
- Non-zero-sum: A game where there are degrees of winning and losing (e.g., Poker, a lottery, a contest where you get to keep your score such as Bridge).
- Perfect knowledge: A game where each player sees everything that is going on (e.g., Chess, Checkers, Tic-Tac-Toe).
- Imperfect knowledge: A game where some information is hidden from the player (e.g., Battleship, Poker, anything with a "fog of war").
- Cooperative: A game where the players can form binding commitments.
- Symmetric: A game where both sides have the same information and play by the same rules.
- Asymmetric: A game where one side has different rules and/or different information than the other.

Starting Simple

Fourteenth-century English logician and Franciscan friar William of Occam is credited with one of the most useful notions in all of science. **Occam's razor** states, "Entia non sunt multiplicanda praeter necessitatem." For those of you who don't speak Latin (I admit that I must include myself here), this roughly translates as "entities must not be multiplied beyond necessity." There have been plenty of restatements of this edict that are a bit clearer. Two of the more oft-quoted are "all other things being equal, the simplest solution is the best" and "the simplest explanation that covers all the facts is usually the best."

Brother Occam would have been pleased with John von Neumann. Despite the fact that he was a brilliantly talented mathematician (he was famously known for declining to use the supercomputer he actually helped invent because he could do the calculations faster in his head), Mr. von Neumann knew when flash and style were inappropriate. One of the useful aspects of his presentation of game theory is that it boiled down decision making into small enough parts that it is easy to discern the concepts in play. Examples in game theory are often characterized by simple rules and equally transparent decision possibilities. (The actual proofs of von Neumann and Morgenstern's assertions of game theory are not even remotely as compact—to the point that *Theory of Games and Economic Behavior* is largely unreadable.) John von Neumann starts small—with the concept of the two-player, zero-sum, perfect knowledge game and works up from there.

Through this reverence to Occam's razor, we are given the smallest possible building blocks from which we can learn and with which we can build later. Using these examples, we can establish a foundation of understand about what goes into decisions, not only from a logical standpoint, but from a mathematical one as well. It is this application of mathematics to decision theory that allows us to model the subtlety to which I referred in Chapter 1.

Matching Pennies

In Chapter 4 of *Theory of Games and Economic Behavior,* von Neumann and Morgenstern begin with a section entitled "Some Elementary Games," which has a subsection, "The Simplest Games." They weren't kidding. The first one they introduce is one not so obscurely called Matching Pennies. It is similar to Rock-Paper-Scissors but with two choices instead of three. (I told you they weren't kidding!) It is a zero-sum game in that one player's loss is another's gain.

The game involves two players and two pennies. (I grudgingly use the term *game* despite the lack of interesting choices... but that's just my two cents.) Each player hides his penny and turns it to either heads or tails. They then simultaneously show each other their pennies, and the enormously complex ordeal of scoring the round ensues. As you can see in Figure 5.1, if the pennies match—either both heads or both tails—then player A is the winner. Conversely, if the coins do not match, then player B is the winner. (I'm not sure how it is determined who will be player A, but I would suggest that they could flip a coin.)

The lesson to be learned here is strictly one of terminology. Matching Pennies is a game in which there is no "pure strategy." That is, there is no "best response." A **pure strategy** is a complete definition of what a player *should* do at any given time. That is, *if* you play this way, you will win (or at least will maximize your chances of doing so). For example, as we discussed before, Tic-Tac-Toe has a pure strategy. If you want to win, you have to make certain moves. If you make those moves, you maximize your chances—which, in the case of Tic-Tac-Toe, generally leads to a draw. At worst, it doesn't lead to a loss. At best, if your opponent makes a mistake (by not playing the pure strategy), you will win.

	Player A	
	Heads	Tails
Player B — Heads	A: +1 (win) B: -1 (lose)	A: -1 (lose) B: +1 (win)
Player B — Tails	A: -1 (lose) B: +1 (win)	A: +1 (win) B: -1 (lose)

FIGURE 5.1 The decision matrix for Matching Pennies. If both players select the same face, player A wins. If the players select opposite faces, player B wins.

Pure strategies are a gold mine when playing games, but they are a death knell for game developers. If players discover a pure strategy for playing against your artificial intelligence (AI), they will be able to win all the time with very little thought or effort. On the other hand, if AI agents can determine a pure strategy that causes them to play the same way every time, they become very predictable and, thus, very boring.

In Matching Pennies, since there is no knowledge of the game environment, nothing to perceive, and no calculations to make, even normative decision theory can't come to the rescue and tell us what we *should* do on any given play. Therefore, there is no pure strategy to play. There is no "best" thing to do at any one time.

Interestingly, despite there being no "best" strategy, over time there *is* a *worst* strategy… always selecting the same face for your coin. If you were to do that, it wouldn't take long for the other person to determine your pattern and respond accordingly. Likewise, a parallel worst strategy is to always alternate between heads and tails. Your opponent should be able to pick up on your method and play in such a way that your predictable repetition words to his advantage. Notice that at that point, we have not introduced some knowledge to be aware of… the pattern of play. If an agent were able to discern that and calculate accordingly (i.e., extending the pattern), then it could make a pretty good stab at what it *should* play as per normative decision theory.

Barring that, about the only hope we have is to apply some sort of psychology and hope to ascertain what your partner's pattern is—and, therefore, his next move. If your opponent is even reasonably adept at obfuscation, though, nothing short of the Jedi Mind Trick is going to yield any better results than chance.

Mixing It Up

This opposite approach from pure strategy is called a **mixed strategy**. In this approach, you select between a variety of strategies that are available to you. Often, you can assign probabilities to these decisions to select which one you can do. This is something that we address in depth later on. Suffice to say that in Matching Pennies, there are only two choices at any one time.

That being said, the best approach is to vary your plays in a somewhat random fashion. Of course, if you do that, you are no better off than if you had flipped your coin. Taken one step further, why flip two coins and see if they match when you and your opponent could simply flip a single coin and be done with it? But now I'm arguing with the entire premise of this delightfully simple game. Occam would not approve.

As I mentioned, the game is roughly analogous to Rock-Paper-Scissors. The difference is that there are three possible plays in Rock-Paper-Scissors rather than simply two. That makes the scoring grid 3×3 as well. Regardless, as with Matching Pennies, there is no "pure strategy" to Rock-Paper-Scissors that you can follow to achieve any more success.

IN THE GAME	**Matching Punches**

At first, it would seem that something as simple as Matching Pennies would have no real comparison to the world of computer and video games. However, over the years plenty of games have used this mechanism in some form or another. In fact, one could claim that some games still do.

If we were to imagine a fighting game of the simplest sort, we could start to draw a parallel. Let's say that player A has two attacks—high and low punches. Player B, on the other hand, has two defenses—high and low blocks. The goal of the game is for player A to get past player B's block and score a hit. If B's block is in the same area as A's attack (i.e., high vs. high), then A fails to score a point. If B's block is in the wrong area (i.e., high vs. low), then A scores a hit.

Given the parameters of this game, we can analyze it in exactly the same way as Matching Pennies. There is no "best" strategy to play—other than not repeating the *same* sequence over and over. The only thing you can do is observe the other player for potential clues that he is playing dumb and repeating patterns. If both players are mixing their choices appropriately, the best you can attempt to accomplish here is a random button-masher.

Putting It in Code

Although this may seem obvious, I may as well drop it in. If you were to put the *entire* AI for Matching Pennies or the above hypothetical fighting game into code, this is what it might look like.

```
typedef enum { MV_HEADS = 0,
               MV_TAILS = 1} PENNIES_MOVE;


PENNIES_MOVE MyGame::SelectPenniesMove()
{
    PENNIES_MOVE ThisMove = PENNIES_MOVE(rand() % 2);
    return ThisMove;
}
```

It seems kind of pointless, doesn't it? We have one single function that returns 0 or 1, in this case, representing heads or tails. Incidentally, if you make the function return three choices instead of two, you have the AI for Rock-Paper-Scissors.

```
typedef enum { MV_ROCK = 0,
               MV_PAPER = 1,
               MV_SCISSORS = 2} RPS_MOVE;


RPS_MOVE MyGame::SelectRPSMove()
{
    RPS_MOVE ThisMove = RPS_MOVE(rand() % 3);
    return ThisMove;
}
```

As I suggested in Chapter 1, games such as these only have the *appearance* of playing against another person. If your best bet is to play randomly, the only choice is whether to do so or not. If you choose to play randomly, and your opponent does so as well, then we do not have a game that meets the condition of "interesting choices." It also becomes tiring rather quickly. (I do not believe this is a coincidence.)

Prisoner's Dilemma

One of the more oft-cited examples of game theory is the Prisoner's Dilemma. It was originally framed by Merrill Flood and Melvin Dresher working at the famed RAND Institute think tank in 1950. Albert W. Tucker formalized the game with prison sentence payoffs and gave it the name Prisoner's Dilemma. In the spirit of von Neumann, it is a two-person, perfect knowledge game. However, unlike Matching Pennies, it is *not* a zero-sum game… both people can "win" to varying degrees. Likewise, both players can "lose" as well. And that, we will see, is what becomes an important, yet deceiving factor in this contest.

In its most often cited form, the Prisoner's Dilemma uses a hypothetical situation of two suspects being arrested by the police. The police have insufficient evidence for a conviction on a major crime that carries a 10-year sentence. The police separate both prisoners and visit each of them to offer the same deal. If one testifies (i.e., "defects") for the prosecution against the other and the other remains silent, the betrayer goes free and the silent accomplice receives the full 10-year sentence. If both remain silent, both prisoners are sentenced to only six months in jail for a minor charge. If each betrays the other, each receives a five-year sentence. Each prisoner must choose to betray the other or to remain silent. Each one is assured that the other would not know about the betrayal before the end of the investigation. The question posed is, given these parameters—including the specifics of the lengths of the prospective sentences—how should the prisoners act?

From a mathematical standpoint, the issue is deceptively simple to solve. However, not everyone notices the solution right off. At first glance (Figure 5.2), the choices seem to be:

- If I stay silent I *could* go to jail for 10 years.
- If I tell on my partner, I could *go free*.

The above assertions, however, don't quite cover all the possibilities. Specifically, they leave out the fact that you truly don't know what the other person will do—and that *his* choices make a significant impact on the results. In fact, it is because the other person's psychology and resultant choices are in play (and yet unknown) that this is a particularly intriguing problem.

Strictly Dominant Strategies

Let's begin with the assertion that the potential actions of the other prisoner are unknown and, we will have to assume for now, unpredictable. Any solution we devise, therefore, has to give equal credence to both possibilities—that the person in the next room over could betray us or keep silent. Keeping that in mind, the choices we have before us can apply a 50% chance to each of the potential outcomes of that choice. Using that logic, our choices now carry the following potential penalties.

Stay silent:

- 50% chance that we serve 6 months (if he stays silent as well)
- 50% chance that we serve 10 years (if he rats us out)

Betray our partner:

- 50% chance that we go free (if he stays silent)
- 50% chance that we serve 5 years (if he tells on us as well)

We are tempted to do a purely mathematical solution for this. By applying the percentages to the time periods, we can reduce the unknown action of our cohort to a single figure. In this case, staying quiet would amount to

$$(50\% \times .5\,years) + (50\% \times 10\,years) = 5.25\,years$$

Likewise, if we were to betray our partner, we would be facing

$$(50\% \times 0\,years) + (50\% \times 5\,years) = 2.5\,years$$

	Prisoner A	
	Stay silent	Betray
Prisoner B — Stay silent	Each serves 6 months	A: Goes Free B: 10 years
Prisoner B — Betray	A: 10 years B: Goes Free	Each serves 5 years

FIGURE 5.2 The decision matrix for Prisoner's Dilemma. Depending on the actions of the two prisoners, a variety of results could occur.

So, in a situation where we treat each of our partner's choices as equally possible, it would seem that it is in our best interest to betray him. The two possible outcomes given our action are zero and five years… or an average of 2½ years. That is certainly better than the average of 5½ years that we face if we stay quiet.

Put logically, rather than mathematically, this seems to make sense as well. We are putting the possibility of 10 years of incarceration out of play. Instead, we are looking at a *maximum* of five years. We are also putting the six-month sentence out of play as well, but who cares? We are keeping the possibility of doing *no time whatsoever* alive and well! We have the best maximum, the best minimum, and the best average result all on our side of the ledger. There doesn't seem to be a weakness to this approach. In fact, if we accept all our premises as valid, our **solution concept** is what is referred to in game theory as a **strictly dominant strategy**. That is, our strategy of ratting out our partner makes us better off *no matter what he does*.

From a strictly game theory standpoint, we have achieved what we set out to find—an optimal solution given all the possibilities. We determined that cooperating is strictly dominated by defecting. That is, the "defect" strategy is inherently weaker. (Even defective, I suppose.)

Can We Improve on "The Best"?

A quandary arises when we analyze our premises, however. For the sake of argument, we replaced our inability to know what our partner's choice was going to be with equally probable outcomes—50% each. That gave us a mechanism for taking into account the unknown. Unfortunately, we also treated our partner as if he was no more intelligent than the randomly shuffled deck of cards that the Blackjack dealer in Chapter 1 was using. We ascribed no rationality to him whatsoever. By reducing him, in effect, to a flip of a coin, we are not even taking into account that he was *capable* of making a choice.

Again, this may not seem to matter on the surface. After all, we have already determined the strictly dominant strategy for ourselves (to defect). That strategy is in our best interests of self-preservation in that it guarantees us the lowest sentence regardless of what the other person does. If it is in my best interest to utilize that strategy, would my partner not be of the same mind and defect as well?

The answer to this may lie in personalizing things in the other direction. If our partner chooses the strategy of defecting, he has looked at *us* as a 50/50 wildcard as well. He has determined that *we* are not capable of rational thought and, therefore, has taken matters entirely into his own hands… optimizing his own benefit by choosing to betray *us*. Of course, if he *does* betray us and *we* betray *him*, it looks like we are both going to do five years.

Even if we were to adjust our payoff formulas to account for an imaginary "likelihood" that he will choose to defect, say making it 80% instead of 50%, we would get the following:

$$(20\% \times 0\,years) + (80\% \times 5\,years) = 4\,years$$

Never mind the 2½ year *average* potential sentence that we were looking at. The premise on which it was based (a 50% probability for *each* of our partner's choices) was flawed the whole time. He wasn't a coin flip. He was a rational human (in dark glasses and a stupid hat) who was fully capable of making (interesting) choices that served *his* own best interest.

Pareto Optimality

Of course, if we now accept the notion that our partner is a rational human, out for his own benefit, we may have to include the idea that he would view *us* the same way. Perhaps all is not lost. If we *both* view each other as completely reasonable and wise, and, in doing so, assume the other would view *us* as just as enlightened, we may have to reanalyze our payoff matrix.

We have recently come to the conclusion that, despite our happy thoughts of a 2½-year average sentence, we are looking at five years if we both choose to defect. That 2½-year sentence doesn't really exist. It was a mathematical fiction based on our application of probability. Now that we are working under the assumption that it is no longer likely that we will get off entirely with no time at all, the six-month option that we allowed to be taken off the table looks a lot more attractive. What if he is thinking the same way?

To simulate what would happen if we could read each other's minds, we may as well pretend that we can speak with our partner in crime. To be honest, if we were to do so, this entire exercise would no longer be a dilemma. We could simply agree to keep our mouths shut, serve our six months, and go home. That would achieve what is called a **Pareto improvement**. A Pareto improvement occurs when the solution shifts so that at least one of the players has a better situation at no detriment to the other. In this case, the shift actually benefits *both* players. In fact, a quick glance at the Prisoner's Dilemma matrix shows that the scenario of both prisoners keeping quiet is actually the **Pareto *optimum*** because no further improvements can be made.

The irony of the situation is that, in acting in what is ostensibly our own best interests (betraying our partner), we actually avoid the *optimal* solution for both of us. It seems to be a contradiction that acting in our own self-interest does not include the actual best option for ourselves. The mistake that was made, however, was the original assumption we made about our partner… that we could have *no idea* what it was that he would do. That may or may not be the case—it depends on our knowledge of our partner. It could still very well be wise to betray him if we have reason to believe he is going to do the same to us. If we believe he is not only intelligent enough to recognize the hidden "out," but also thinks enough of *us* to assume that *we* would take it as well, then we can choose to keep quiet and meet him for a cheeseburger in six months. We will examine this more in Chapter 6.

| IN THE GAME | **Dueling Rocket Launchers** |

To see how this sort of game theory staple is important, let's put the Prisoner's Dilemma into a hypothetical game setting. To design a scenario that accurately reflects the quandary of the Prisoner's Dilemma, we need to look at the parameters that surround the choice. First, we must have two parties with two identical choices facing them. Second, we must have a conservative choice and an aggressive choice. Both of those choices must have a reasonably positive outcome and a somewhat negative outcome based on how they match up with the other player's choice. That is, we need to have a 2×2 scoring matrix where the positives and negatives roughly match those in the original Prisoner's Dilemma.

Imagine we are in a shooter type environment as shown in Figure 5.3. Both players start in a position of being mostly hidden from the other player. The cover we are behind protects us from anything *except* rockets. If a rocket were to strike our hiding place, we would be killed. We are fully healthy but lightly armed. We can fire on our opponent from our cover, but only do very light damage to him. Likewise, if he stays hidden, he can do light damage to us as well.

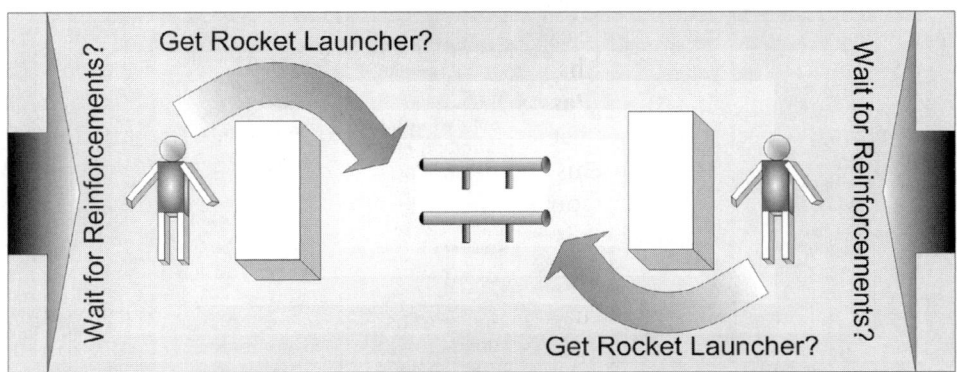

FIGURE 5.3 Either agent could elect to run into the open and grab a rocket launcher or to hide and wait for reinforcements.

Out in an open area between us and our enemy are two rocket launchers. If either player gets a rocket launcher, he will be able to fire it at the hiding place of the other player—killing him. Because the small arms fire is not accurate when firing at people on the move, running to retrieve a rocket launcher will not bring about any damage. However, if *both* players run to acquire rocket launchers, they will then be able to shoot rockets at each other as they run around. If this happens, it is assured that both of them will take heavy damage, although not as bad as what would have happened if they had simply stayed hidden as a vulnerable, unmoving target for the enemy's rocket launcher.

Both teams are waiting for reinforcements that will arrive soon and simultaneously. If we are heavily damaged when the others arrive, we could possibly die (50%). This chance of death is not as certain, however, as if an enemy's rocket were to strike us while we are hidden (100%). If we are only lightly damaged by the small arms fire we took while hidden, we will have only a 5% chance of dying when both sides' reinforcements show up. (In all cases, these risks are mirrored by our enemy, that is, he's facing the same possibilities for the same choices.)

Making the Choice

The choice before our agent is this: Do we chose to stay in hiding, perhaps taking occasional pot shots at our hidden enemy, and wait for the reinforcements to show up, or do we rush out to grab one of the two rocket launchers and either kill the enemy where he is hiding or run around trying to kill him while he does the same to us? It is a little easier to visualize the decisions and results by placing them in a grid just like the one we used for Matching Pennies and Prisoner's Dilemma (Figure 5.4).

		Enemy	
		Hide & Wait	Get R/L
Our Agent	Hide & Wait	Agent & Enemy both take minimal damage (5%) - survive until reinforcements show up	Enemy gets R/L, kills hidden Agent (100%) and remains unhurt (0%)
	Get R/L	Agent gets R/L, kills hidden Enemy (100%) and remains unhurt (0%)	Agent & Enemy both take heavy damage (50%) - might get killed when reinforcements show up

FIGURE 5.4 The 2×2 decision matrix for the rocket launcher example is surprisingly similar to that of the Prisoner's Dilemma.

The decision process is much the same as well. If we are trying to maximize the damage to save ourselves from harm, just as we did in the Prisoner's Dilemma, we may want to look at the possible outcomes of our choices from that standpoint. If we were to run out and grab the rocket launcher, there are two possibilities. First, if the enemy stays hidden, we acquire the big gun without opposition, aim, and blow him and his cover sky high with no damage to ourselves (Figure 5.5). That doesn't sound too bad.

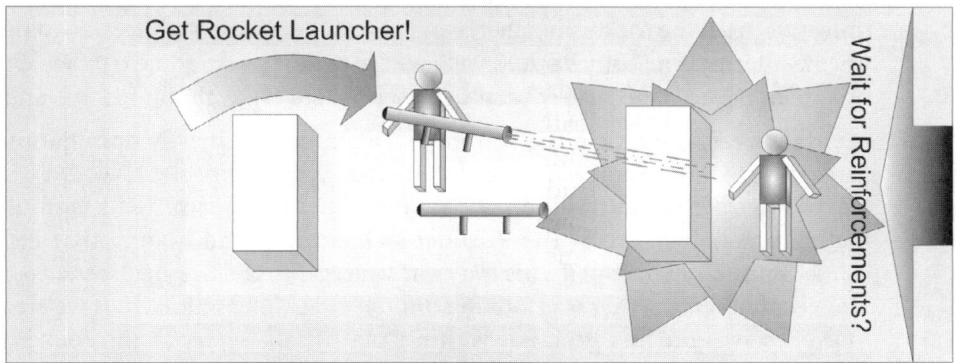

FIGURE 5.5 The scenario of one agent rushing to get the rocket launcher while the other one hides is analogous to the Prisoner's Dilemma scenario of one prisoner betraying while the other stays silent. In either case, the former wins and the latter loses entirely.

Second, if he *does* run out to grab a rocket launcher for himself, we begin the shoot-and-hop dance in the middle of the arena, take some damage, doing some damage, and hoping that when the reinforcements show up for both sides we aren't too messed up to get through it alive. However, we realized that being damaged at that point isn't terribly attractive. Still, it gives us a fighting chance. We are still alive. In fact, the two outcomes of this choice are both rather positive. We either blow our enemy to heck or we knock him down a few pegs. There isn't any *immediate* risk of death… only the heightened possibility of death later on once the rest of the troops arrive.

The same cannot be said for one of the possible outcomes were we to stay put. If we remain in hiding and our *enemy* runs out to get the rocket launcher, we aren't going to last long. At that point, we are good and dead—reinforcements or not. However, that outcome is not certain. He *may* choose to not run out there at all, instead using his own woefully inadequate peashooter to harass us the way we are doing him. Once the respective reinforcements show up, the battle will begin in earnest, with us having only sustained minor damage. However, it *is* pretty much an all or nothing prospect to remain where we are. We live or we die. And it's that last part that is a little disturbing. Aren't we trying to *avoid* death?

The Strictly Dominant versus Optimal Strategies

So, just like in the original Prisoner's Dilemma, we have found a strictly dominant strategy. Before, it was to betray our partner. By doing so, we were guaranteed no worse than five years of prison, no matter what our partner did. In this case, by running out to get the rocket launcher, we are guaranteeing that we are not going to die in the near term. If he comes out as well, we are going to take some damage, but at least we are not dead… no matter what our enemy does. That all sounds well and good.

However, just like in the Prisoner's Dilemma, the strictly dominating strategy isn't the *optimal* strategy. The optimal strategy, *in a joint sense*, would be for both parties to stay put and wait for the reinforcements to arrive. This is similar to not betraying our partner in the Prisoner's Dilemma—and hoping that he does the same. But, as I mentioned, this is a *joint* strategy. In the original scenario, we could believe that our partner was looking out for us as well as himself. If we are supporting ourselves on this premise, we find that it falls apart in the rocket launcher example. Why would our *enemy* be looking out for *our* best interests as well as his own? That line of thinking is based on the fallacy of our premise.

In both the Prisoner's Dilemma and rocket launcher problems, the other person isn't looking out for *our* interests at all. He is looking out for *his own interests* and, in looking at what *we* might do, believes (rightly) that we are looking out for *our own interests*. Confused yet? It is the classic "I believe that he believes that I believe…" cliché. Put another way, if I believe that my enemy is interested in "living to fight another day" and that he realizes that I might also subscribe to that notion, we are both going to wait it out and only fight when the reinforcements arrive.

What's to prevent him from charging out of cover, grabbing a rocket launcher, and blowing my hidey-hole sky high? Probably the fear that I might charge out and start blasting as well.

But can I make my decision based on that? What is preventing *me* from charging out and blasting *him* into proverbial smithereens? Only my own distaste at limping back with half health when the troops from both armies arrive—a situation that I may not survive. I would much rather play it safe for now, and I assume that he is thinking the same thing. That is the optimal solution: both of us playing it safe until the rest of the group shows up.

Certainly, there could be plenty of other issues that we would need to consider if this were a true game environment. What does death mean, for example? In an online game, is there a respawn rate? In a real-time strategy (RTS) game, how many units like me can my general build? And how fast? Are we close to a goal such as capturing a strategic point where we may want to throw everything we have at the attack? Are we defending a strategic point and need to do so for as long as possible —therefore causing us to be conservative and careful? All of these could possibly be valid points, but they also complicate things somewhat—and make Friar Occam shift a little uncomfortably in his chair. For purposes of making the point, we have to resort to our standard disclaimer of "all other things being equal." (Trust me, as we progress further through this book, we will dismiss the good friar from the room so we can start having some real fun.)

Sure, the puzzle isn't completely "solved." It remains a dilemma, but it's not as cryptic as it once was. (Unfortunately, it's also not as superficially clear-cut either.) What you realize through the process is that the correct decision depends on other information that wasn't given and that, in a hypothetical, depersonalized setting, you can't ferret out for yourself (e.g., the knowledge of whether or not your partner is a selfish moron or a suicidal, berserking maniac). That is the point I am trying to make.

Many problems have mathematical solutions that take a limited number of parameters into account. Often, those lead to strictly dominating strategies. At that point, the problem is solved and the hunt is over. However, by putting other factors into play, such as a rational, intelligent person with a possible twist of malice… or loyalty… on the other side of the table, we have created something that goes beyond a simple mathematical solution. We have created a dilemma that, in our established vernacular, is an "interesting decision."

ASYMMETRIC GAMES

Up to this point, the games we have touched on have been symmetrical. Both sides have had the same decisions, risks, and rewards available to them. Certainly, that is not always the case. In fact, even in a symmetrical game such as an FPS or RTS, plenty of situations will arise where an individual encounter is not symmetrical. Theoretically, those encounters are, in and of themselves, complete games with decisions to be made.

Our rocket launcher example above would be entirely different if the rules were changed so that the unarmed player A was deciding to grab the rocket launcher while player B was already armed with a sniper rifle. Staying put behind meager cover is now no longer a low-risk solution, which makes taking your chances running into the open a lot more attractive.

Sometimes the lack of symmetry is in the goals and sometimes it is in the available choices. In Chapter 1, we touched on the game of Blackjack. This popular casino game is deceptively asymmetric. When it comes to scoring the hands, both the players and the dealer are held to the same criteria.

- Have a higher valued hand than the opponent.
- Don't go over 21.

Given this information only, the game looks as if it is the same on both sides. In fact, you could play Blackjack head-to-head against a friend rather than in the traditional sense against a dealer and you *would* be playing symmetrically. Both players would be able to freely ask for hits, stands, splits, and doubles at will. However, the dealer doesn't have those options. The rules are very specific about what he can and cannot do.

- If he has less than 17, he must hit.
- If he has 17 or higher, he must stand.

This is why Blackjack is a winnable game. Very often it behooves the player to elect to stand with a hand of less than 17. The dealer doesn't have that option available… and the player knows it. So, while the scoring is identical, the gameplay differs significantly. Blackjack is an asymmetrical game.

Needless to say, there is an entirely different dynamic to games where there are different choices to be made on each side. However, there is still an important factor that needs to be taken into account just as much as in symmetrical games: What is the other player likely to do and how should I adjust my strategy to accommodate that? Sometimes this is easy to compute, and other times, you have to make a concerted effort to "get inside the mind" of the other party.

CUTTING THE CAKE

One situation that many people may be familiar with is that of cutting something in half to share. In this process, a cake or other such desirable item needs to be divided between two people. The first person makes the cut, and the second person selects which piece he wants.

Most of us wouldn't necessarily think of this process as a game. In fact, it really isn't a game at all. However, the point that it illustrates does speak quite a bit to game theory, and, like some of the examples that will follow, this act is definitely asymmetrical, as the very simple rules show. One person is the "Cutter," and the other is the "Decider." There is no overlap in their responsibilities. Neither has any say in the other's role, and yet each must rely on the other person.

The decision of the second person is the more obvious as long as we assume that the person is going to attempt to get as much cake as he can. (I don't think that's a far stretch, do you?) The key point—and therefore the more interesting decision—falls to the first person—the Cutter. Where does the Cutter divide the cake so that he can also maximize the amount of cake he would get?

I am going to put off the obvious solution for a moment so that we can formally approach the logic involved. The Cutter has the power to do one of three things (ignore the symmetry for the moment). He can make piece A bigger (and B smaller, of course), he can make piece B bigger (at the expense of A), or he can do his darndest to make them the same size. If he makes A bigger, the Decider is likely to select A. If he makes B bigger, the Decider is, once again, likely to select B. In both cases, the Cutter comes out on the short end of the spatula and gets a smaller piece. However, as the Cutter minimizes the difference between the two pieces—even to the point of theoretical equality—the Decider loses the ability to even *detect* which of the two pieces is bigger, much less to select it.

Even if the Decider could tell the difference down to miniscule amounts, as the size of the larger piece approaches the size of the Cutter's inevitably smaller piece, that smaller piece is increasing in size as well. If we assume that the meticulous measurements of the Decider will *always* allow him to pick the larger piece, the best the Cutter can hope for is half the cake minus some nanoscale amount. Obviously, it is in the Cutter's best interest to make that amount as small as possible since it is the only thing standing between him and a complete half of the cake.

From a game theory standpoint, the only way the Cutter can determine his strictly dominant strategy is to take into account what the Decider may do given each of the possible ways of cutting the cake (Figure 5.6). So, like the Prisoner's Dilemma, the strictly dominant strategy is to attempt to maximize your own position. Unlike the Prisoner's Dilemma, however, the optimum strategy is the same as the dominant one. You simply can't improve the dominant strategy any further.

The main similarity to the Prisoner's Dilemma, however, is that the key to finding that strategy is to think beyond your own position and put yourself into the mind of the opponent. That is, "How would the other person react to the choice I make?" If you didn't have to take this into consideration, the "game" would be as simple as taking as much cake as you like and leaving the rest for the other person. After all, they wouldn't have a choice but to accept what you offered them.

/*
In late 2007, a rumor began circulating claiming that "the cake is a lie." I can assure you that this is, in no way, a reference to the cake in this example. Any attempt by nefarious sorts to imply that the cake in this example is a falsehood or other such fabrication will be dealt with swiftly.
*/

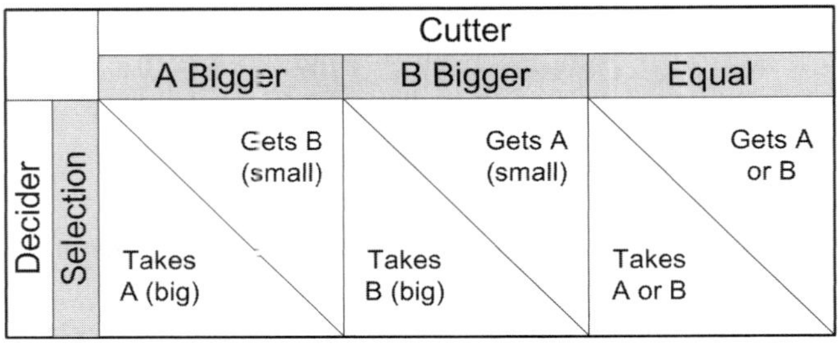

	Cutter		
Decider Selection	**A Bigger**	**B Bigger**	**Equal**
	Gets B (small) / Takes A (big)	Gets A (small) / Takes B (big)	Gets A or B / Takes A or B

FIGURE 5.6 When cutting the cake, if it is assumed that the Decider will always take a larger piece, the only way the Cutter does not get a smaller piece is if they are equal.

ULTIMATUM GAME

Admittedly, the cake example in the previous section would be much simpler if we didn't allow the other person to select which piece he wanted. However, there is another popular twist on asymmetrical decision theory that is in a similar vein. In this scenario, often referred to as the Ultimatum Game, there are still two differing roles—the Giver (similar to the Cutter) and the Decider. Once again, the Giver is in charge of dividing and distributing a finite amount between himself and another person. As much as I would like to continue using confection as our medium of exchange, I find that this example works better with money.

Let's assume that we, as the Giver, have been entrusted with $100 to distribute between ourselves and another person (the Decider). We are told that we propose to give a non-zero amount to the other person (the titular ultimatum). Whatever we don't give to that person, we will be allowed to keep for ourselves, with one major caveat: The Decider can select to accept or refuse our offering. If the Decider keeps his cut, we (as the Giver) get to keep ours as well. If the Decider turns down the offer for whatever reason, we do *not* get to keep our share of the money either. In effect, the Decider is electing that *neither* of us will get anything at all. The $100 is returned to the mysterious source from whence it came.

This game has been used often in psychological studies, with interesting results. People's actions differ significantly from those that would be dictated by using simple mathematics alone.

To determine where things go awry, we first need to analyze the decision facing the Giver. Theoretically, we must select a value that the Decider will accept. The reason for this is plainly obvious. If the Decider is displeased with our offering, he will reject us, and we will get nothing. (Does it sound like we need a volcano and a small farm animal in this example?) However, if we please the Decider, we will get to keep whatever is left. Mathematically, the problem is, how do we get the most that we can out of the $100 without risking getting nothing at all?

We have set up the classic struggle between greed and fear (which we will talk about more in a bit). It would seem that we need to decide on some threshold below which our gift would upset the Decider. Once we are confident of that threshold, we could increase our cut of the pot up to that point. For example, if we decide that the Decider would be happy with $20, we could offer him that and attempt to keep the $80 for ourselves. On the other hand, the Decider might not be pleased with anything less than a 50/50 split like we had in the cake example above. In that case, we would want to offer $50 and keep $50 for ourselves. Perhaps, if we don't offer an actual *majority* of the $100 to the Decider, he may turn us down out of spite—making sure *we* don't get anything either.

In a way, the Decider is holding us hostage. He could easily make sure we don't get anything no matter *what* we offer! So how do we determine what the Decider is likely to do? Again, our strategy requires us to flip the situation around and look at the problem from the point of view of the Decider.

Looking from the Other Side

If I am now the Decider, after the Giver proposes the amount that he is offering me (x), my choices are as follows:

- Accept amount x.
- Decline x and receive nothing.

Given that the rules of the game are that the Giver *must* offer a non-zero amount, $x > 0$ will *always* be true. Therefore, if I accept, I will *always* be better off than if I decline. Even if the Giver elects to offer me $1—or one *cent*—accepting that token amount would net me more than if I had declined.

Viewed in a decision matrix (Figure 5.7), this much is obvious. Incidentally, I could have left it at one box since x is a variable and the choices for the Decider are all the same. Additionally, I could have expressed this solution as a simple graph. I separated the Giver's choices into three columns, however, to illustrate a point.

Switching our mindset back to that of the Giver, we should realize that no matter what we offer the Decider, he is going to be better off accepting than declining. If we, therefore, assume that he will accept any legal (i.e., non-zero) offer, we should offer him the smallest possible amount (let's use $1 for now) and claim the rest ($99) for ourselves.

		Giver		
		X is small	X is medium	X is large
Decider	Accept	100 - x / x	100 - x / x	100 - x / x
	Decline	0 / 0	0 / 0	0 / 0

FIGURE 5.7 The decision matrix for the Ultimatum Game shows that the only possibility for either participant to get anything is for the Decider to accept the Giver's offer.

The Failure to Act Rationally

Yet, when this test is given by psychologists, that is *not* what happens. They have discovered that there *is* a threshold below which the Decider will *not* accept the gift. For whatever reason—likely the feeling of being "stiffed"—the Decider elects to take nothing and suffer as long as the Giver is suffering along with him. In nonclinical terms, it is the equivalent of "Oh yeah? Fine! Be that way! I'll show you!"

What we have seen is that the Decider is *not* acting in his best interests mathematically and logically. Theoretically, he is not acting "rationally." It would be rational to choose to receive something of value over receiving nothing at all. However, although it might be irrational, apparently it is also not unexpected.

It turns out that plenty of people playing the Giver side of the game actually *do* offer more than the bare minimum to the Decider. Just as it is irrational for the Decider to turn down a certain thing (via accepting whatever is offered), by the same rules, it would be irrational for the Giver to offer anything more than the minimum. And yet, more often than not, they do so.

There could be two reasons for this. First, it could be that the Giver doesn't have a good grasp on the theory that goes into making the decision from the point of the Decider (i.e., something is better than nothing). Second, it could be that the Giver is well aware that there could be something insulting about being completely rational. That is, despite realizing the complete rationality of trying to maximize his own position, he may realize that the Decider might *not* elect to do the completely rational thing by accepting.

Put more succinctly, the Giver may find it rational to assume that the Decider will *not* do the rational thing—and, therefore, the Giver should bypass what would *normally* be rational for him to do. Any clearer yet?

This illustrates a divide between the types of decision theory examined in Chapter 4. The mathematical approach of normative decision theory (the "shoulds") is not reflected in what people tend to do in practice (i.e., descriptive decision theory). As we move on, we will find plenty of these seeming contradictions, and they may make us begin to second guess the seemingly reliable normative approach to attempting to replicate behaviors.

DICTATOR GAME

A game (if it can be called that) similar to the Ultimatum Game is the Dictator Game. The setup is the same. A pot is available to the Giver. However, the other person is now no longer the Decider; he can't decide to do anything at all. He will accept whatever the Giver elects to offer him. In a way, the Giver is now the Decider as well. (We will now refer to the other person in this exchange simply as the Receiver—since that is his only role.)

Because the Receiver now has *no* control whatsoever in the arrangement, we (as the Giver) could simply elect to give him the minimum amount (e.g., $1) and be done with it. This would maximize the amount that we keep for ourselves: $99. In fact, if the rules allowed for it, we could elect to give the Receiver nothing at all, and there would be nothing he could do about it. From a decision theory standpoint, it is obvious that the most logical solution for the Giver is to minimize the gift (x) because it maximizes his own take ($100 - x$).

However, once again, psychological testing shows to us that people don't always act rationally. In numerous trials, it has been shown that the Givers usually give more than the minimum amount. *How much* they give is not important. The point is simply that they do so when they don't have to. After all, every dollar they give away is one they can't keep for themselves. What could cause them to do this?

One suggested solution is similar to the first one in the Ultimatum Game—the Giver simply fails to maximize his own position. This doesn't seem quite as likely in the Dictator Game, however. In the Ultimatum Game, the failure to understand how to maximize his own position would have likely been born out of a failure to put himself in the shoes of the Decider, whose predicament was simply the inevitable decision between something and nothing, and seeing how that affected his own choice. In this case, the Giver doesn't have to put himself in the shoes of the other person at all. This should make the decision *simpler* than the Ultimatum Game.

The other suggested solution is that there is a factor involved that is not being tracked and measured by the rules of the game—*altruism*. It could be that the people playing the role of Giver in the Dictator Game are gaining some sort of satisfaction out of sharing with others that outweighs whatever monetary losses they are taking.

Certainly, this could be related to the structure of the game and the testing environment. If some dude in a lab coat were to hand me $100 and say "Could you share some of this with a stranger, please?" I wouldn't have too much of a problem with it. I'm still walking out with more money than I came in with. However, if you were to approach me and say "Take some of your *own* assets and share them now," you would likely get a slightly more rude answer.

TRUST GAME

One final twist on these sorts of games is a spin on the Dictator Game. We need to reset the names again, as we are now getting a little circular. Once again, we have a Giver who will bestow an amount on the Receiver. However, in a sort of mirror twist, the amount the Giver has to split is based on an initial gift by the eventual Receiver (Figure 5.8).

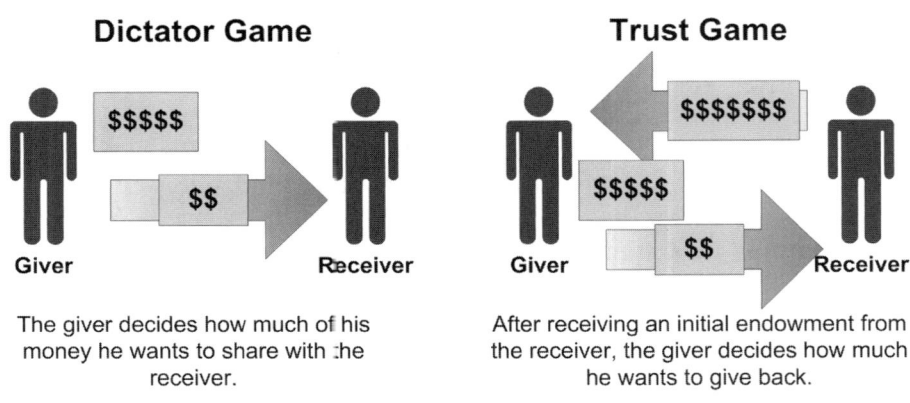

FIGURE 5.8 The difference between the Dictator Game and the Trust Game is that in the Trust Game, the Receiver gives a sum of money to the Giver in the hopes of getting some of it back.

At first glance, it would seem silly for the Receiver to give the Giver anything at all in the hope of getting it back. Therefore, to prime the pump, the pot is generally sweetened somewhat by the researchers through matching funds or some other enticement, so that the Receiver is encouraged to actually give *something* to the Giver. Yes, it's twisted.

The reason that this is interesting is that, once in possession of the funds, the Giver doesn't *have to* give anything (back) to the Receiver. Just like the Dictator Game, to maximize his own portion, it is in the Giver's best interest to *not* give anything to the Receiver, and yet the Givers still tend to do so. Perhaps it is altruism again. Yet, once again, altruism is not possible to track via strictly mathematical models.

However, there does seem to be another factor in play. If the Receiver doesn't give a lot of money to the Giver in the first place (and the Giver knows this), then the Giver is less likely to give more of it back to the Receiver. This introduces another dynamic—one that seems to affect the factor of altruism. Let's call this one "spite."

If the Receiver trusts the Giver with a large amount of money, for example, the Giver may feel the same altruism that he would feel in the Dictator game. However, as the amount of money the Receiver trusts the Giver with declines, so does the likelihood and size of the amount the Giver gives back. It is as if the Giver is saying "OK, fine… if you don't trust me, I'm not going to reward you."

Interestingly, when these experiments are repeated with the same partners, they very rarely end in what is actually the perfect single game equilibrium of "no trust." That is, the Receiver gives nothing at all to the Giver. One could account for this in that the researchers are kicking in a little to encourage it to begin with, but still, it also may have something to do with the fact that something else is going on in the Receiver's psyche. Does the Receiver have a "need" to feel trust*worthy*? Is that pride? Avoidance of shame? You can see how the more we delve into this, the further away from simple logical, mathematical explanations we drift.

We also can begin to see why there are often differences between the purely mathematical normative decision theory models and the more anecdotal descriptive decision theory ones. It is not only the inability of agents to calculate in a completely rational fashion but also the inclusion of messy emotions like fear, spite, pride, and shame that make decisions a bit more difficult to predict. Remember the difference between Tic-Tac-Toe and Poker? The calculations were simple to make in Tic-Tac-Toe. Your opponent's move was just as simple to predict. With Poker, we add a little more complication and a *lot* of psychology, and the choices get very interesting.

6 Rational vs. Irrational Behavior

One of the problems that von Neumann and others had with their application of game theory was the expectation that people behave rationally and, in doing so, will always attempt to select the best outcome. As we saw from some of the examples in Chapter 5, this is not always the case. Often, people either fail to select the best option or even elect *not* to for whatever reason. The result is the reason for such a difference between normative decision theory and descriptive decision theory. In that gap lies a whole lot of irrational behavior.

Of course, trying to figure out *what* those behaviors are is a bit of a knotty problem. Computers are good at figuring out the *rational* answers. Coming up with an *irrational* but reasonable-*looking* answer is another trick entirely. Most of us are accustomed to the notion that irrationality is something to be avoided or even shunned. And yet, as we have seen so far—and will continue to explore—irrationality is not only very real but it is what bestows depth of character on behaviors.

There is a significant problem in trying to work with irrational behavior, however. While generally there is only one *correct* (i.e., rational) answer to a problem, the solution set on irrational behavior tends to be a bit wider. That is not to say that everything that is not the "correct" answer is going to look reasonable. Some things *are* just plain wrong.

If you recall in Chapter 1, I wrote about my beloved pig painting. While my prone porcine portrayal was less than perfect, it was well within the bounds of "piggishness." It didn't have the fifth leg sticking out of the top of its back like a dorsal fin. While not perfect, it was reasonably pig-like. There are, in truth, an infinite number of ways that one could paint a pig, but only a select number of them would fall within an acceptable range that observers would accept as "looking like a pig." Sure, some of them might be categorized as "an odd-looking pig" but would still be thought of as reasonable enough to not be confused with, say, a horse, an iguana, or a platypus (although a platypus is confusing enough on its own).

In the end, while normative decision theory and the utility-maximizing algorithms that fall out of it provide us with the sterile "should do" answers, we need to look a little further into the basis of reason and rationality to begin to replicate it.

Perfect Rationality

Because irrationality is so difficult to define, it is actually easier to start this foray by starting from the summit of the mountain of rationality and working down. Agents are said to have **perfect rationality** if they *always* act in the best possible manner, even if they have to perform extensive and difficult calculations to do so.

If, for the sake of example, we were to reduce this to a simpler game space, we could use the game of Tic-Tac-Toe. As we noted in Chapter 1, the choices available at any point in the game can be narrowed down to a decision between whether or not we want to win. If we do want to win, there is an obvious selection. If we do not want to win, there is an equally obvious selection. Therefore, our success at Tic-Tac-Toe is based entirely on whether or not we want to win. A perfectly rational player will *always* play those correct moves. If we were to elect to play incorrectly on even one of those moves, we would no longer be considered perfectly rational.

Other examples of perfect rationality can be applied to the games from Chapter 5. The prisoner who, without any other information to go on, elects to betray his partner in the Prisoner's Dilemma is exhibiting perfect rationality. The person who gives the minimum in the Ultimatum and Dictator games is acting in a perfectly rational fashion. Cutting the cake exactly in half so as to minimize exposure to the expected (and perfectly rational) greed of another player is perfectly rational. Even the person who plays a mixed strategy in Matching Pennies to keep from tipping off his opponent to patterns is being perfectly rational.

If an optimal solution exists, the perfectly rational agent will take it every time. What could be so wrong about that? It turns out that perfect rationality has serious weaknesses that can only be exposed by running it through a test drive. For that, we need a test track so we can see perfect rationality in action.

The Pirate Game

The Ultimatum Game is an interesting conflict between two people with its "take it or leave it" game of chicken. As we noted above, it is also an excellent example of how perfect rationality can lead to an extreme solution—in this case offering the bare minimum payout to the other person. The possibilities get even more intriguing when it is extended to multiple people. The Pirate Game does just this.

In the Pirate Game, we have a number of *rational* pirates (for this example we will use five). Despite my desire to come up with really cool pirate names, we will refer to them as A, B, C, D, and E. The alphabetical monikers actually help us with the next issue, that the pirates have a strict order of seniority: A is superior to B, who is superior to C, who is superior to D, who is superior to E.

As a group, the five pirates find 100 gold coins and are trying to decide how to distribute them. In the pirate's world the rules of distribution are as follows.

- The most senior pirate should propose a distribution of coins.
- The pirates should then vote on whether to accept this distribution.
- The proposer is able to vote.
- The proposer has the *casting* vote in the event of a tie.
- If the proposed allocation is approved by vote, that proposal goes into effect.
- If the vote fails, the proposer is thrown overboard from the pirate ship and dies.
- The next most senior pirate makes a new proposal to begin the process again.

Pirates base their decisions on four factors. Each pirate:

1. Is entirely rational.
2. Wants to survive.
3. Wants to maximize the amount of gold coins he receives.
4. Would prefer to throw another overboard, if all other results would otherwise be equal.

At first glance, it would seem that pirate A, being outnumbered by his peers, might have to minimize his own allocation to avoid getting kicked off. After all, if the other four pirates think he is taking too much, they would stand to benefit by declining his proposal and sending him down the stereotypical plank. At that point, the total would only be divided among the four of them, rather than five. This, however, is not the solution—and is surprisingly divergent from his optimal approach.

Iterating Perfectly Rational Decisions

The pure strategy solution becomes more apparent if we work backward. To do so, let's assume that somehow we managed to get down to the final two pirates, D and E. Knowing that, as senior pirate, he has the deciding vote over E, D proposes 100 for himself and zero for the hapless E. E can't do anything about it, so this would be the final result when it is just the two of them.

Pirate	Gold	Vote
D	100	Yes*
E	0	No

If we were in a situation where three pirates are left, C, D, and E, then C would know that D will perform the strategy above and offer E nothing in the next round. Therefore, C will offer E one coin, and keep the rest for himself—D getting nothing. E, being perfectly rational, also realizes that if it comes down to D and himself, he is going to get nothing. Therefore, the one coin from C looks pretty good compared to nothing, and E elects to vote for C's proposal.

Pirate	Gold	Vote
C	99	Yes*
D	0	No
E	1	Yes

Of course, in order for the three-pirate scenario to come about, something must have gone amiss with the four-pirate scenario. If B, C, D, and E were remaining, B (again, being perfectly rational) would know that the three-pirate proposal by C would have gone as above. Therefore, he needs to placate D because D knows the next round will not go well for him. If B offers D one coin, D will take that offer; it beats getting nothing from C. Having bought D's vote with one coin, and knowing that he has the deciding vote in a tie, B is no longer concerned with C or E's opinions and offers them nothing. The vote will be two to two but with B's vote as the kicker.

Pirate	Gold	Vote
B	99	Yes*
C	0	No
D	1	Yes
E	0	No

Of course, B could have taken the same approach as C and offered E the one gold coin. After all, since E knows he won't get any *more* than one coin if B is tossed overboard, you would think that he would vote for that proposal. However, remember that according to rule 3 above, each pirate is eager to throw the others overboard. In that case, he would be interested in throwing B overboard since he can get that single gold coin from C in the next round *and* dispense with a rival. E would therefore *not* vote yes simply because he is offered one gold piece the same way that D would. Knowing this, B would go with the original plan of buying D's vote.

Of course, A is all-knowing and purely rational as well, and will therefore have a pretty good handle on all of the above scenarios. As we saw, if B were in charge of distribution, C and E would be left out in the cold with nothing at all. A knows this—and knows that those are the two votes he needs. What's more, he knows that the price of those votes is simply one gold piece. C and E, being rational, will realize that the one gold coin is better than either nothing at all or, in the case of C, eventually being thrown off. With all of this in mind, A's proposal is as follows.

Pirate	Gold	Vote
A	98	Yes*
B	0	No
C	1	Yes
D	0	No
E	1	Yes

One final note: like B's option above, A could possibly distribute those two coins another way, for example, giving one to D instead of C. However, just like E in the example above, D would rather chuck A overboard as pirates seem inclined to do and collect his one gold coin from B in the next round. Therefore, A will simply give the one gold coin to C rather than D.

/*

For those of you who are familiar with recursion, this is a perfect example of how a problem can be solved by starting with the smallest possible scenario (in this case, two pirates) and working backward… applying the same rules at each level, but with the knowledge gained from the prior ones. Given that, if you have enough gold to support the pirate population, you can solve the Pirate Game for any number of greedy mateys. (You can even do up to 200 pirates with 100 gold coins.)

For those of you who are not *familiar with the definition of* recursion, *this is the way it was presented to me in my AP computer class in high school.*

recursion n: 1. *(see* recursion*)*

*/

The lesson to be learned here is that, even when agents are purely rational and have perfect information on hand (or on hook), sometimes the rational thing to do needs a little digging to find. In this case, A had to take into account what D, C, and B would propose (in that order) and how each would vote for each of those proposals. All of those issues together get rolled up into what A needs to propose. This is the normative decision theory approach. We have been told, mathematically and algorithmically, what we *should* do.

Questioning Iterative Rationality

The solution we arrive at using iterated rationality differs from the first-glance approach. When we looked at the game initially, we figured that pirate A needed to propose at least a *marginally* fair settlement. In fact, if we were to run a live Pirate Game with real people, it is very likely that, like the Ultimatum, Dictator, and Trust games in the previous chapter, pirate A would propose something significantly different from the proven optimal solution. Modeling behaviors based on this is the descriptive behavior theory approach, that is, what people tend to do in that situation. In this case the people *tend* to do things they should *not* do.

What mechanism would cause him to do this? Certainly not the naked altruism as is seemingly the only explanation in the Dictator Game. Pirates aren't known for their philanthropic leanings. This would suggest something else as the cause of the illogical offers.

If it is not benevolent other-centric interest (even on a subconscious level), perhaps it is more *self*-interest? Basing the decision on self-interest, it would seem, would more likely have led us to the maximal (that is, *greedy*) solution we got. So how can self-interest lead us in the *wrong* direction? There is a different way that self-interest can be represented. Remember that money was not the only consideration in the game. Pirates were trying to avoid the very real threat of becoming fish food as well. Therefore, it is a legitimate expression of self-interest to say, "If I appear too greedy, they will kick me off." To that end, a pirate may tend to give *more* than is required mathematically to avoid a particular fate.

At this point, we have arrived at a similar mindset that plagued the Ultimatum Game. That is, "If I give too little, I will be rejected by the other person simply out of spite—and will receive nothing." In the case of the Ultimatum Game, the thinking error was that the other person (the Receiver) would reject an offer that was too small and instead take nothing. Of course, that is illogical for the Receiver to do. His decision matrix shows that getting anything at all—even one dollar—is better than nothing. Therefore, the Giver should only offer *one* dollar and expect it to be accepted. But that is not what *real* players of the Ultimatum Game do.

In the Pirate Game, the mindset is similar, but the consequences are slightly different. Instead of getting no money, there is the possibility of getting no money *and* getting death on top of it all. (And, as we all know, one of the classic blunders is "never go in against a pirate when *death* is on the line!") Any given senior pirate may believe he has to worry about *looking* altruistic to his subordinates not only so they will accept his proposal, but so he will survive the whole process. As we discovered, however, this first-blush approach is not even remotely correct. Aside from buying a vote or two at a very small price, the ranking pirate can simply keep the rest for himself—and no one can do anything about it. At least not without sacrificing themselves later on in the process.

So, if we were to put this into a game situation, which method do we use? The normative one provided us with the answer of what a pirate *should* do. The descriptive one provided us with the answer of what pirates (or at least pretend ones) *tend* to do. The former is the optimum solution; the later is the more "realistic."

SUPERRATIONALITY

In the Prisoner's Dilemma, we touched on the difference between the strictly dominant strategy of defecting and the Pareto optimal strategy of keeping quiet. In that case, the only way the optimal strategy could be accomplished was if our partner elected to stay quiet as well. The only way we could feel comfortable making that decision was if we knew that our partner would recognize the optimum strategy… and believed that *we* were going to follow it as well. Therefore, the important issue is not simply one of *us* behaving rationally but also acting under the assumption that all *other* players act rationally as well. This is known as **superrationality**, as coined by Douglas Hofstadter in one of the eclectic articles in his 1985 book, *Metamagical Themas* (ISBN 0-465-04566-9).

Admittedly, making a rational decision whose success must be based on the fact that everyone *else* in the room is also making a rational decision is sometimes a bit of a stretch. In fact, in some cases all it would take is *one* person to not act rationally to send the entire framework into a tumble. As we will explore later, this is one of the greatest handicaps in normative decision theory as discussed in Chapter 4. Remember that the requirements for normative decision theory are:

- Has *all* of the relevant information available
- Is able to *perceive* the information with the accuracy needed
- Is able to perfectly *perform* all the calculations necessary to apply those facts
- Is perfectly *rational*

This is all well and good if we are dealing with a puzzle that does not involve other thinking agents. However, merely by their inclusion, we are potentially disqualifying the first two items on the list. Short of some form of omniscience, we can't read the other players' minds—therefore putting all the relevant information behind a screen of doubt. Even information we can perceive will not necessarily be completely accurate. As we can see, while normative decision theory and the "shoulds" that it spits out for us can be rather helpful in solving some sorts of problems, it begins to show weaknesses when other people are involved.

Four Out of Five Pirates Surveyed...

In the Pirate Game, we questioned pirate A's decision because it doesn't fit with our gut feeling of what he ought to do. Part of the reason for this is that our view of the *other* pirates may be a little off. One of the initial guiding premises of the set up of the game was that "all the pirates are rational." Once again, it is that *unreasonable* assumption of superrationality that disqualifies a purely normative approach from believability. If the other pirates are *not* rational, then all of the calculations we did above are meaningless. If they are not purely rational, then those messy things like fear, spite, shame, and even simple calculation errors will creep into their decision making. If their decision making is compromised and unreliable, then we can't accurately put ourselves in their shoes, can we?

Therefore, whether or not we are purely rational is not the only question that needs to be addressed if we are to formulate our approach. If we are rational and so are the rest of them, all is well, but if even one of them is not rational, it can significantly skew any sort of predictive result.

Of course, in the Prisoner's Dilemma, it was in our best interests to work together. In the Pirate Game, the competitors all want to launch each other overboard and get more gold for themselves. Can we really assume they are both perfectly rational and have *our* best interests in mind as well?

So, perhaps our quandary lies in that we are trying to solve the wrong problem. Rather than trying to ascertain the "right answer" that optimizes our solution in the perfectly rational world, we need to try to model behavior that takes into account that people aren't purely rational with all of the information and calculation ability.

The answer to the question is more of a function of what *game problem* we are trying to solve. Also, the answer may be affected by what it is we are trying to accomplish in this particular calculation. If we need mathematical accuracy, then the normative approach is the best one to use. If we need psychological believability, the descriptive one is preferable. And someplace in the middle we can draw traits from both. In fact, only by juxtaposing the two approaches were we led to the fact that the descriptive approach (e.g., being altruistic) was downright incorrect from an efficiency standpoint. Only by analyzing the two of them simultaneously were we able to determine that the normative approach (e.g., mathematical exhaustion) didn't take into account potential psychological factors. That is, the "shoulds" seemed perfectly viable until we brought in the data that suggested that real people simply don't do what they "should do."

So, maybe our gut instinct wasn't too far off. All of this wonderful math and logic that computers speak so well and artificial intelligence (AI) programmers are so fond of goes right out the window. If our pirates are to look and act *realistically* they may not act completely rationally. If they don't act completely rationally, they won't use the algorithms that generate the optimum outcome. So, without the fancy mathematics to help us, what *would* be the right settlement for pirate A to offer so as to avoid an unfortunate diving expedition?

While there may be no immediate solution, there are certainly lessons to be learned here.

GUESS TWO-THIRDS OF THE AVERAGE GAME

Thankfully, in the Pirate Game, the rules stated that "all pirates are rational." While the assertion of superrationality (that is, every participant is perfectly rational) seems to be a bit of a stretch based on the stereotypical presentation of pirates, it certainly made arriving at a solution a lot simpler. As we iterated through each step of the process, we could solve each of those steps with the assertion "…and therefore, he will do *this*." That assumption of rationality left us a single outcome for each of the subsolutions, which, in the end, built up to one single outcome as the "best" arrangement for the lead pirate to propose.

At the time, we hinted at the fact that the mathematically optimum solution that we arrived at was different from what we would have guessed as mere *nonrational* pirates. Most of us would have offered our buccaneer colleagues more than was necessary to purchase their acquiescence. Thankfully, our fellow pirates would have been just as nonrational and probably would not have known the difference. As long as our offer made sense to them (whether they liked it or not), they would have likely gone along with it because it "felt right."

A popular example similar to the Pirate Game that exemplifies this lack of rationality is a game called Guess Two-Thirds of the Average. The title is not very cryptic. The game literally involves asking a group of people to guess a number between zero and 100. The goal is to guess closest to what two-thirds of the average of all the guesses would be. For example, if the average guess of all of the participants was 75, then the winning guess would be the one closest to 50. If the average of all the guesses was 33, the winner would be the one who guessed closest to 22.

Once again, just like the Pirate Game, many of us reading the rules of this game are already formulating little plans in our heads as to how we would approach this. I certainly did—and I was wrong. Kind of. Unlike the Pirate Game, there is no explicit edict of superrationality. That is, the participants *may* be perfectly rational, but it is likely that they are not. This injects a level of uncertainty into the decision. The quandary that this presents, ironically enough, is that one of the decisions that must be made is whether or not to act completely rationally (if you know how). This depends on whether or not—and even to what extent—one thinks the other players are going to be rational.

In the Prisoner's Dilemma, this manifested itself rather well. The strictly dominant strategy was to betray the other player because that promised the best results *no matter what the other person did.* However, as we explored, the *optimal* strategy was for both players to keep quiet. The only way a player would select this option, however, was if he *knew* that the other person was going to act in the completely rational fashion and keep quiet as well. If the other person's rationality is not known (or he is known to be a loose cannon anyway), then the fall back is the strictly dominant strategy.

In the Guess Two-Thirds Game, we are faced with a similar dilemma—but on a larger scale. We need to decide if the other players of the game are going to be acting rationally or not before we can decide if we should play the rational strategy or not. What's more, now that we have strayed away from the simplicity of von Neumann's game theory examples, we have to account for far more variables. With the Prisoner's Dilemma, we had to ascertain the rationality of *one* person to determine which of the two choices he would make. In this case, how *many* of the other players are going to be rational? And to what extent?

Iteratively Eliminating Irrational Answers

The problem here is that there is no strictly dominating strategy from which to start. That is, we can't say, "This is the best way to play *no matter what other people do.*" Unlike in the Prisoner's Dilemma, we can't say, "Betraying gives us the best chance." Interestingly, there is a unique *pure* strategy. In the Prisoner's Dilemma, this strategy was to keep silent with the knowledge that our partner was going to do so as well—because he was *rational*. Similarly, in the Guess Two-Thirds Game, this approach leads us to the best possible result if everyone in the game is acting purely rationally. However, we get a far different answer than we would expect.

To arrive at this answer, we need to walk through the exercise from the beginning, just like we did with our miserly brigands. In this case, we do this by iteratively eliminating strictly dominating strategies. To do that, we must *find* the strictly dominated strategies. By using that information to our advantage, we can narrow our solution set down significantly.

Just as a strictly dominating strategy was one that was the best for the situation *no matter what*, a strictly dominated strategy is one that is the worst for the situation *no matter what.* In the Guess Two-Thirds Game, there is no strictly dominating strategy, but there *are* strictly dominated strategies. That is, there are ways to play that will *always* lose—*no matter what.*

The reason for this is that there are mathematical impossibilities in the game. Because the rules of the game state that people select numbers between 0 and 100, we know that it is impossible for the *average* guess to be above 100. Certainly, it could *be* 100, but only if everyone in the game guessed 100. (Don't laugh; as we will see later, there *are* people who do this.) If the average *cannot* be above 100, then the two-thirds point *cannot* be above 66.67. It would therefore be irrational to guess anything above 66. So, cross off a big chunk of the possibilities.

Now, because we are working from the premise that everyone is rational, we must assume that they *know* that guessing above 66 is irrational. Therefore, we also know that *no one* is going to guess above 66. Well, if *no one* is going to guess above 66, then we can also assert that the two-thirds point will *not* be above 44 (two-thirds of 66). Because none of our rational co-players will guess above 44, we know the two-thirds point will not be above 29.48 (two-thirds of 44). Lather, rinse, repeat… (Figure 6.1).

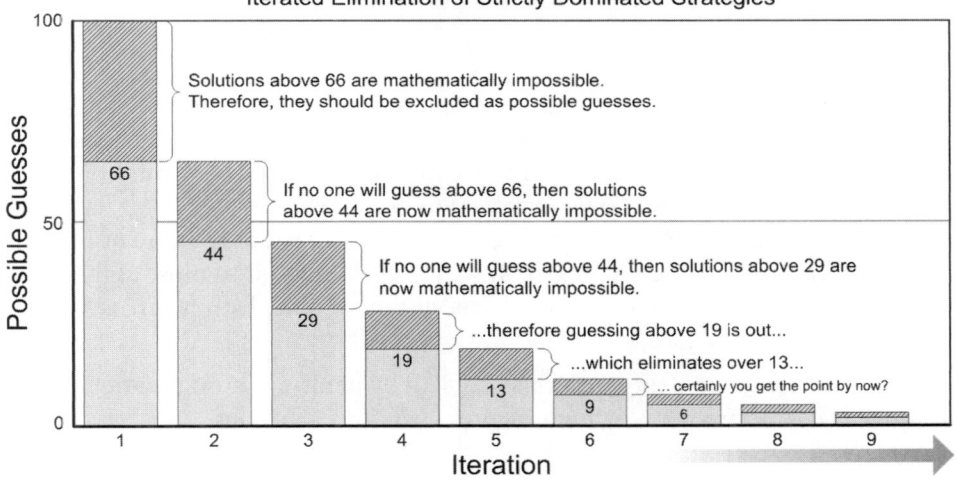

FIGURE 6.1 By iteratively eliminating the strictly dominated strategies (i.e., those that have no possibility of winning), we determine that the only pure strategy is that of guessing zero.

Eventually, by eliminating the possible guesses of rational players, we get to the point where any guess above 0 is irrational. That means, in the Guess Two-Thirds of the Average Game, the pure strategy guess is… zero. Of course, this answer only exists in the world of superrationality. Everyone has to be playing by the same purely rational strategy, and the odds of *that* happening are fairly slim.

Guessing the Guesser's Guesses

Much like the problem that existed in the Pirate Game, this *pure strategy* doesn't fit well with what we *feel* the solution should be. The difference is that in the Pirate Game, by proposing something less than the 98 coins for ourselves, we were not being rational. We were the ones being irrational by not realizing that *we* were in the driver's seat. The solution in the Pirate Game would have been to calculate the most rational proposal, tell it to the other players, and then get them to see that they have no choice. If we failed to propose the 98 coins for ourselves, it was because we were not being rational ourselves.

In this case, the solution is not entirely in our hands. It is a moving target based on the *other* players' degree of rationality and, subsequently, their guesses. Since we can't assume that the other players are entirely rational, and we aren't in the position to propose the solution and explain the way things are simply "going to be 'round here," we have to take into account the questionable rationality of the other players ahead of time. That's why the *pure strategy* of guessing zero is not necessarily the right one.

But what *is* the right guess? As we suggested earlier, there really isn't one. Any given run of the game could generate wildly different answers with wildly different averages. However, there may be an *optimal* guess. This would be one that takes into account what people may *tend* to do. Remember, we don't have to figure out what each individual person is going to do; we need only figure out what the group is going to do in an aggregate. If we are close enough to most of them, the average will fall in line with our general expectations. Someplace in here is a sweet spot... if only we could find it.

Rather than approach this problem by iterating through rational solutions, we need to approach it by iterating through *likely* solutions.

Because the goal of the game is to determine what two-thirds of the average would be, we need to first determine what we believe the average of all the other player's guesses will be. If people were either completely unaware of the rules or mathematics of the game (or completely random), we could assume that the guesses would be spread evenly across the range from zero to 100. The average of all these guesses would be near 50. In that case, our guess should be two-thirds of that, or 33.

But what if even *some* of the other players are thinking the same way we are? Would they guess 33 as well? If so, a disproportionate number of *educated* guesses at 33 would be mixed into the purely random background noise of irrational people. The average of all the guesses would now drop below 50 slightly—as would the two-thirds point. For example, if the average of the guesses is now 45, then two-thirds would be 30. Our guess of 33 would have been too high. Maybe a guess of 30 is more accurate. But what if other people are thinking the same thing we are and, instead of guessing 33, elect to guess 30 instead? That drags down the average even more, and likewise our two-thirds target.

Certainly you can see where this is headed. The more people who are acting rationally in the group, the more the average (and associated two-thirds target) is affected. What's more, some people may be acting rationally at the shallower level (for example, guessing 33), and some may be acting slightly *more* rationally by taking into account the first level of rational players. Even others may be assuming that *everyone* is acting rationally at a shallow level and that the average guess is going to be 33 instead of 50. That would make their two-thirds guess 22! Kinda makes your head spin, doesn't it?

In 2005, the Department of Economics at the University of Copenhagen in Denmark ran a well-publicized trial of the game in the Danish newspaper *Politiken*. They offered a cash prize of 5,000 Danish kroner (about $1,000) to whoever had the closest guess. They attracted over 19,000 submissions via an Internet site. Needless to say, that wasn't a bad sample size. (In fact, about 1 in 300 Danes participated!) The average of the guesses in their trial was 32.407, which led to a winning target of 21.605.

Upon examination of the histogram of the submissions (Figure 6.2), a couple of things stand out. First, there was a wide distribution of guesses—including some people who actually *did* guess 100. In fact, while it is definitely the sparsest area of the chart, a surprising number of people guessed above the "impossible point" of 66.7.

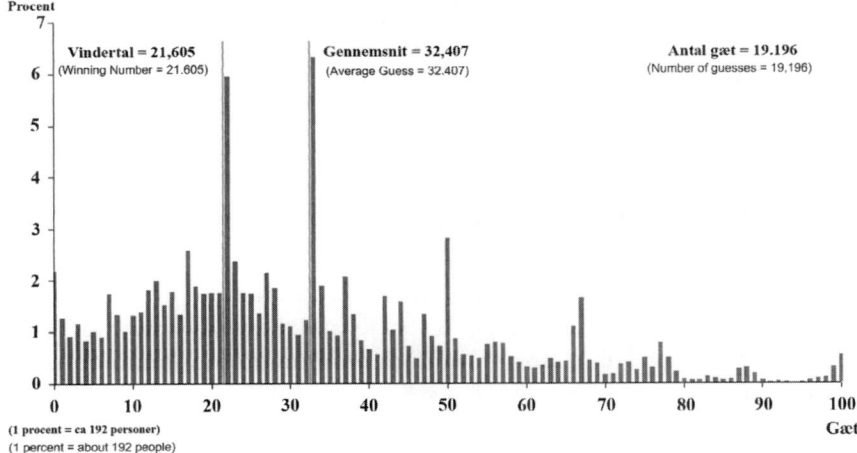

FIGURE 6.2 The results of the Danish experiment show that the two most popular guesses were 33 and 22. Indeed, the average guess was 32.4, making the winning target 21.6. Graphic from "Making an Educated Guess" Working Paper, Department of Economics, University of Copenhagen by Jean-Robert Tyran and Frederik Roose Øvlisen (2009) used with permission.

The guess receiving the largest number of votes (over 6%) was 33. Remember that we had touched on 33 being a potential solution—but only if all of the other votes were equally distributed between zero and 100, making the average guess 50. So, some people were obviously thinking along those lines. However, their fatal flaw was expecting that even distribution. Just as superrationality—the rationality of all participants—is an unreasonable expectation, expecting that *all* of the participants are completely *irrational* is just as flawed a premise.

The guess receiving the second-most number of votes—and, at 6%, only slightly behind the 33 guess—was 22. Once again, the mindset seemingly at work here is one that we touched on earlier. The people who guessed 22 were counting on the fact that a large majority of the *other* folks were going to be guessing 33. They were hoping some players would be at least thinking about their answer (unlike the players who guessed 100, for example), but not thinking *too* much. By taking those people into account, and then basing their actions on that information, people who guessed 22 were, in fact, very close to the solution.

Measuring the Depth of Rationality

So, it would seem that assuming that at least a *portion* of the population was *partially* rational is a valid strategy that leads to an optimal solution. The question is, how many of the participants are going to be rational and to what extent? We know the answer lies between two extremes. Also, as we have seen, the answer presents itself as a continuum that is represented by how many iterations people go through in attempting to outguess the other people.

For example, we have the random players whose guesses are spread all over the possible range from 0 to 100. Those players are not thinking at all about what anyone else could do. This is evidenced by the fact that people are willing to even select numbers of the impossible result threshold of 66.67. Let's give these people a rationality index of 0. In essence, they are simply randomly picking numbers. Statistically, the average of their guesses should be close to 50 (Figure 6.3).

The next group of people takes the "zero rationality" folks into account. They work from the assumption that people are going to be all over the map with their guesses, figure that the average will be 50, and then guess around 33. They have performed one level of iteration through the logic progression. Let's give them a rationality index of 1.

The people who are aware that the level-one people exist would also then take those votes into account. With the presumption of the 33 vote being a big draw, they would then guess 22. We will assign this group a rationality index of 2. They have performed two iterations of thought—they assumed there would be level ones who would count on the existence of level zeros.

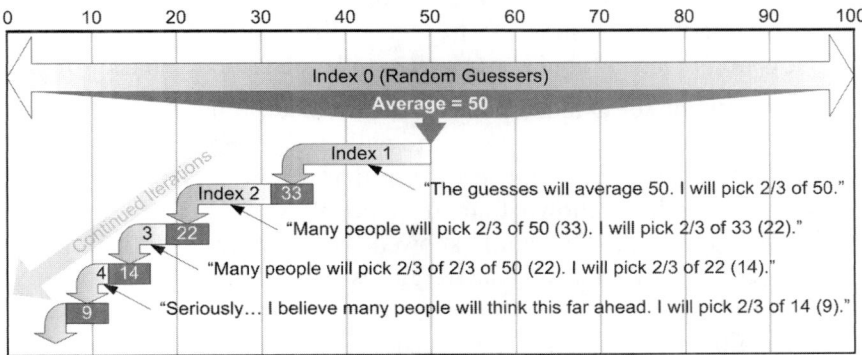

FIGURE 6.3 Each group of people will take into account the groups before them. For example, the index 1 group will assume the index 0 people are guessing randomly. The index 2 group will assume the index 1 people are basing their guess on index 0, and so on.

If some people take the level-two guessers into account and base their own guesses on that (i.e., 15), we would give them a rationality index of 3. Again, as before, they performed three layers of calculation, in that they are assuming that plenty of levels twos exist based on the level twos' belief about the level ones which are, in turn, based on the assumption of the level zeros.

If you were to proceed all the way down to the bottom, you would get to a guess of *one* at rationality index 10. That is, someone would have to assume that level nines exist who are basing their own guess on the assumption that level eights exist, and so on.

How Low Will You Go?

So, how many iterations are people either capable of doing, willing to do, or believe is appropriate to do? Separating out those three reasons for not proceeding further is a little difficult, but coming up with how many iterations of logic people do is easily measured. As we saw in the Danish example, if a significant number of people "get it," it tends to show up on the histogram of the results. In this case, there were plenty of index 0 people, about 6.5% were index 1 (guessing 33), and about 6% were index 2 (guessing 22). After that, things tend to blur out and are no longer apparent from the histogram. This is not a coincidence.

Many researchers have toyed with the game and found that those patterns repeat. By changing the game to "guess 70% of the average," for example, you would expect the most popular guesses to change accordingly. It turns out that this was, indeed, the case. Most people were random (index 0), many people guessed 70% of the expected average of 50, or 35 (index 1), and another large batch guessed 70% percent of 35, or 24 (index 2). Just like in the Danish example, index 3 either didn't show up or was diffused enough that it blended into the background.

Changing the game to other rules provided similar results. When various studies around the world have been run with multipliers such as 0.7, 0.9, 1.1, and 1.3, the pattern was repeated. It turns out that people very rarely get to level three. In fact, studies have shown that most people end up with a rationality index of between 0 and 3. (One study showed that computer science folks ended up the highest, with an average of 3.8 iterations. That isn't to say they won; they probably didn't because they were thinking *too* far beyond the other guessers.) So, we can determine that, for some reason, people don't bother going any further than a couple of iterations into the logic. This could be for a variety of reasons.

- They don't think of it.
- They can't do the calculations.
- They don't believe it is relevant because *other* people can't or won't.

An interesting twist to this is that the rationality index that people get to is based on who the other players are. For example, if you give the game twice to an economist who knows he is playing against the general public the first time and a bunch of other economists the second time, he will change his answer accordingly. He will assume that the other economists will iterate further than the general public and adjust his selection to a lower number (a higher rationality index) accordingly. This leads us to the assumption that some people aren't stopping their iterating process because they can't think that far, but rather that they are doing so because they realize it is pointless to continue.

If we think back to the *pure strategy* of this game, we were led to the logical conclusion that we should guess zero. We arrived at that conclusion under the assumption of the superrationality of the participants, which we know to be unreasonable. The above observation shows that—excluding the 2% of Danes who guessed *zero*—many people *are* aware of that unreasonable expectation of ubiquitous rationality.

Logical Irrationality

What we have found is that, when faced with the very likely absence of superrationality, it actually becomes less efficient to be purely rational. With our first approach to solving the Guess Two-Thirds Game, we were being purely rational at each step.

We were iteratively eliminating logically impossible answers and, in doing so, assumed that the entire population of guessers would do so as well. Eventually, this led us to the purely rational answer of guessing zero.

In our second attempt at solving the problem, we started with the premise that the population was *not* superrational; that is, some people may be rational, but it is not likely that *everyone* is. By taking away the aura of superrationality, it would seem that our problems have been solved. However, we still had to decide how to rationally proceed from that standpoint. As we showed, this can be done in stages—which we labeled as index 0, index 1, and so on. The same caveat is in play, however. If we proceeded on logically, we would eventually end up back in the territory of guessing zero once again.

Both of these approaches lead us to the wrong answer. While we may have wonderful proofs of the perfect *rationality* of guessing zero, it is simply not a *good* answer to this problem. In the first method, our premise of superrationality was flawed. Put another way, it is irrational for us to assume that everyone else is rational. In the second method, we started with the right idea. We gave up on the notion that *everyone* was rational (giving us the index 0 guessers) but still had to count on the fact that at least *some* of them were (the index 1 guessers). So, it is rational to assume that *some* other people are rational, but how far can we take that? At some point, the seemingly rational chain of iterated processes has to be abandoned. We can no longer assume that things will be the way they "should be" because, at some point, other people will no longer be acting the way they "should."

Therefore, it is in our best interests to, somewhere along the way, abandon the rational method of arriving at an answer and say, "Enough!" We are logically concluding that we are going to no longer be purely rational. It is *logical* to act *irrationally* simply because the environment that we are making the decisions in is irrational as well. If the other people involved aren't going to be completely rational, then it is not logical for us to be completely rational. (I don't recommend using that justification during an argument with your wife. And definitely don't do it where your kids can hear… you don't want it coming back at you later!)

The whole idea can be summed up in a single quote from Mr. Spock, *Star Trek's* renowned purveyor of logic and rationality. When Captain Kirk asked Mr. Spock if a particular action was "the logical thing to do," Spock replied, "No, but it is the *human* thing to do." And isn't this, after all, what we are trying to accomplish in crafting our AI?

BOUNDED RATIONALITY

So, through an analysis of the Guess Two-Thirds Game, we have discovered that it is sometimes illogical to be perfectly rational—even when we *can* be. The reason for this is that we can't count on superrationality. We know superrationality does not exist because, even despite our best intentions, humans are not always rational in their decision making. Of course, humans are not completely *random* either. If perfect rationality is the pinnacle of the mountain, random decisions are the boulders strewn around the base. Someplace along the slope between these two extremes is where the bulk of human decision making is positioned.

But what makes up these decisions? What keeps us from making perfectly rational choices, even when we may *want* to do so? Even when we realize that it *is* in our best interests to do so? What is the barrier that gets between the slope of the mountain where we are and the pinnacle of perfect rationality? It turns out that, while there are many different pitfalls along the way—too numerous to list, in fact—many of them can be generally categorized the same way. In a word, *error*.

The term **bounded rationality** has come to represent the notion that people often are not or cannot be completely rational. This is usually due to failings in the ability to perceive or calculate adequately. If we were, once again, to go back to our list of criteria for normative decision theory, we would find that many of the expectations therein are the impossibilities (or at least unlikelihoods) that get in the way of perfect rationality.

- Has *all* of the relevant information available
- Is able to *perceive* the information with the accuracy needed
- Is able to perfectly *perform* all the calculations necessary to apply those facts
- Is perfectly *rational*

Beginning at the top, we often do not have *all* the relevant information available. In the case of the Guess Two-Thirds Game, for example, we simply do not have the ability to know what everyone else is going to guess. That isn't to say that information isn't there; we simply can't access it. Even when the information is available to us, we may not realize it as being present or important.

The second item is only slightly different. Even if we know the information is there and that it is relevant, we may not be able perceive it with the accuracy needed to lead us in the right direction. That is a simple human failing of not only our physical senses, but of attention and comprehension.

Calculating Which Calculations to Use

One of the most important problems that humans have with mimicking perfect rationality—and therefore normative decision making—is the third point on the list. We simply are not wired to make many of the calculations that are necessary. This is not limited to performing math and whatnot. Surprisingly, we do more of that than we realize. Simply catching a fly ball requires us to instinctively perform a startling number of differential calculus equations, yet this is something that small children can do many years before they are comfortable with long division. The problem of flawed calculation is a little more subtle than that.

Often, the calculations that need to be made are not the ones we are handed and can write down on paper. Instead, the problem of calculation is determining what calculations need to be made in the first place. This is similar to the perception of information issue above. Faced with an endless array of potential factors and an exponentially larger number of combinations of those factors, simply deciding what to include and what to exclude is an enormous feat.

Both including *too much* information and not including *enough* information in our decision-making process can lead to failures to arrive at logical conclusions. These are two of the important "boundaries" that lead to bounded rationality.

MISUSING IRRELEVANT INFORMATION

Thankfully, as we mentioned in Chapter 2, most sentient life forms have a built-in filter known as latent inhibition. This helps us sort through things in our environment and dismiss those which are not relevant. If, as a kid, we were in left field dutifully doing our differential calculus to catch the incoming fly ball, we would probably concede that the length of Suzie Miller's straw relative to the depth of her cup and her volume of remaining Cherry Coke is not relevant to our task at hand (or at glove).

However, latent inhibition is not infallible. Sometimes things slip through that we may *think* are relevant but actually are not. In fact, even being aware of these points may detract from our calculation ability, such as our awareness that Suzie Miller is watching us run for the lazy fly ball and thinking that we need to look cool while making the catch. At that point, we might get a little too muddled to do all that heady differential calculus. (Please note: This is, by no means, autobiographical. When I was performing athletically as a kid, I *never* got muddled by girls watching me. No girls ever bothered to watch me!)

Inventorying the Backyard

There certainly is a purpose for latent inhibition. This is a very important characteristic in evolutionary theory. If we were to process absolutely *everything* in our environment at *all* times, many times we would be unable to sort out conflicting information. As I watch the various wildlife that we have in our back yard interact, it is interesting to attempt to determine to what things they do and do not pay attention. Here are a few observations:

- The sparrows at the feeder don't pay attention to the cardinals—but will flee from the much bigger grackles.
- The male cardinals at the feeder don't pay attention to the sparrows or the grackles, but will readily assault another cardinal.
- The birds on the ground under the feeder don't pay attention to the squirrels next to them.
- The squirrels don't pay attention to the birds.
- The birds are aware of perches near the feeder that are available for when the feeder is overcrowded or in use by an unwanted rival.
- The squirrels are aware of all escape routes from the ground so as to avoid me and the dogs.
- The squirrels are not aware of perches they can't reach.
- Both the squirrels and the birds pay attention to a dog when one comes out.
- Both dogs pay attention to all squirrels regardless of location.
- One dog (Jake) pays attention to the birds; the other (Maya) does not seem to see them.
- Both dogs pay attention to the chew rope in the grass and will seek it out.
- The squirrels and birds do not acknowledge the existence of the chew rope.
- Both the birds and the squirrels pay attention to the state of the feeder and will even watch me come out to refill it. The dogs only think I'm going to play with them and the chew rope.

Consider that the important factors in the lives of birds, squirrels, and dogs are only those that are relevant to food, survival, and, in the case of the dogs, playing with the chew rope. Looking back through the list above and mentally checking off the relationships between entities as either relevant or not, we see that there are far more interactions that are *not* important than those that *are* important. For example, our dog Maya doesn't pay attention to:

- The location of birds
- The sizes and types of birds
- The locations of perches

- The location of the feeder
- The state of the feeder
- The potential escape routes for squirrels

She does, however, pay attention to:

- The location of squirrels
- The location of the chew rope

When looking for a place to lie down in the yard, Maya doesn't have to take into account the locations of the bird feeder, perches, or squirrel escape routes. She simply doesn't need or want to know about the location, sizes, and types of the birds. She has little use for the information on whether or not I need to fill the bird feeder. And, since she is now 15 years old (Lorne Greene would be quick to remind us that this is 105 in dog years), she may only be mildly interested in where the chew rope happens to be. If she sees a squirrel (at her age, she can't hear them any more) she will definitely pay attention and may, for a time, express a modicum of excitement. For the most part, however, this entire backyard inventory is not important to her. All she wants is soft grass in the sun. (Darn. I forgot to include "condition of grass" and "location of sun" in the above list. There is so *much* information to include!)

Statistical Overkill in Football

In our own life, we follow similar patterns. There is simply too much to worry about. A good portion of it is going to stay irrelevant most of the time. Most of it doesn't have anything to do with any particular decision we are making. And yet, it seems that humans try desperately to include this irrelevant information in their decision-making processes. They ascribe meaning where there isn't any. They see relationships where no relationship exists.

When I was working on a statistical handicapping algorithm for NFL games in 2002, I was amazed at how many things other handicappers took into account to predict the outcomes of games. Obviously, such things like "home field advantage" were relevant. However, some people went to great lengths to justify using statistics that were based on grass vs. turf, indoor vs. outdoor, good vs. bad weather, the month of the year, wearing normal vs. alternate home uniforms, and the entire history of one team against the other. Trust me, it doesn't stop there... there are even more esoteric and strange factors that people take into account in the holy quest for gridiron prognosticatory perfection.

Finding the flaw in using the above statistics takes only one little bit of information that many people overlook: The statistics are about the *teams* over the course of decades; the average tenure for the *players* with a team is measured in a few years. It doesn't matter if Team A beat Team B 10 straight times in the 1990s. Chances are, none of the players who participated in that lopsided rivalry are on either one of those teams any more. So, despite being really nifty information to look at and excellent fodder for sports bar trash-talking, is any of it relevant enough to take into account for *today's* game? How about just simply starting out with "is this team good or bad?" and building from there?

And yet, people are addicted to seeing connections in information. Literally. Scientific studies have shown that humans *want* to see order and connection. They *want* to determine cause and effect, but in their zealous pursuit of doing so, they see patterns that aren't there. How often, after seeing a coin land on heads five times in a row, have we said to ourselves—even momentarily—"The next one just *has* to be tails!"? We all know that those five tosses have nothing at all to do with this next one, but our mind tries to make the connection anyway. Thankfully, if asked what the odds are of the next coin flip being tails, we would probably be able to shake ourselves enough to still say "50/50," but decisions are rarely that simple.

IGNORING RELEVANT INFORMATION

Despite our obsession with ascribing meaning to information, typically it is not the act of being *over*-aware of possible considerations that becomes a problem. More often the failure happens when we decide that things are *not* important when they really are. By deciding—even subconsciously—that something is *not* relevant to the decision at hand, any calculations that would have included that information are either skewed to some degree or rendered completely null. This is typically the most problematic hitch that leads us to not act in a perfectly rational way.

The Monty Hall Problem

Excellent examples of people failing to calculate properly are exhibited in the way they make decisions when put on the spot on TV game shows. When I was a kid in the mid-1970s, I vaguely remember seeing *Let's Make a Deal*. At the time, I was more amused by the adults wearing ridiculous costumes to get the host's attention than I was by what has become an iconic statistical logic problem. However, one of the staples of that show has become a classic example of the way the human brain manages to neglect very important information needed for a calculation.

The **Monty Hall Problem** named after the host of the show, comes across as a deceptively simple decision. However, a staggering number of people get the actual answer wrong. Even when asked to explain their decisions, the respondents often offer a justification that shows they aren't acting in an entirely random fashion… they are simply wrong in their logic. Thankfully, plenty of studies have been done on Mr. Hall's challenge. Science has seemed to nail down exactly where people go wrong. Before I give away the answer, however, it is educational to approach the problem blindly.

The actual scenario presented predates *Let's Make a Deal* significantly. Variations on it can be traced back over 100 years. Joseph Bertrand proposed a similar question now known as "Bertrand's Box Paradox" in his book, *Calcul des Probabilités* in 1889. Another version is known as "The Three Prisoners." The Monty Hall version is a little easier to relate to, however, so we will use that as our example.

In the classic version of the problem, we (as the contestant) are presented with three doors. We are told that behind one of the doors is a valuable prize such as a car. Behind the other two doors are gag prizes such as a goat. We are asked by the host to select one of the doors behind which we believe is the car. Prior to opening the door, the host opens one of the two doors that we did *not* choose and reveals what is behind it. At this point, we are now asked if we want to stay with the door that we chose or if we would like to switch and take what is behind the *other* door instead. What should we do?

/* *I really have to point out here that when I presented this question to my wife, she responded, quite genuinely, "But what if I want the goat instead of the car?" I think it had something to do with not having to mow the lawn. Believe it or not, her comment was actually more helpful than you may think. We will cover the very important concept of the relative subjective worth later on in Chapter 9.*

For now, let's work from the premise that: car = cool; goat = lame. */

An overwhelming number of people to whom this problem is presented will stick with their original choice. Usually, the percentage is up around 80%–90%. Some people will switch, but the reasons they do so are based more on a "what the heck" attitude more than from any sort of logical deduction. The tragic thing about this is that, when presented with this problem, the best option is to *always* switch. It doesn't guarantee you the car, but it increases your odds of doing so.

"But how can that be?" we may ask. After all, with two doors left, we know there is a goat behind one and a car behind the other. Our odds of having already selected the door with the car are 50/50, right? This is the logic that is presented by the people who *do* switch as well. They figure that, with the even odds, switching makes as much sense as staying. Right answer, wrong reason.

Checking Our Premises

To find out what the actual probabilities are given our remaining two doors, we need to walk through the problem. When our decision time comes, there are two possible scenarios.

1. We picked correctly.
2. We did not pick correctly.

Before we let our 50/50 mentality lead us forward, we need to check the premises on which that 50/50 mentality is based. To do that, we have to understand what happened *prior* to the "keep or switch" decision. Somewhere between our initial choice of which door we wanted and our *second* choice of whether to keep or switch, something very relevant happened—but we have to know where to look for it.

As we know, the only event that happens in that time frame is that the host opens a door for us, showing us what is behind one of the doors that we did *not* select. As we have done before in Chapter 5, we need to now put ourselves in the role of the host. What decision is he making in that time? What information is he using to make that decision? And most importantly, what information does that convey to us for our keep or switch evaluation?

First, let us analyze what happens if we had picked correctly to begin with (Figure 6.4). At this point, the host is faced with two doors behind which are goats. It doesn't matter which one he elects to reveal to us. He could pick either one and it doesn't change the end result. We are, indeed, faced with a car (our door) and a goat (the door he left for us).

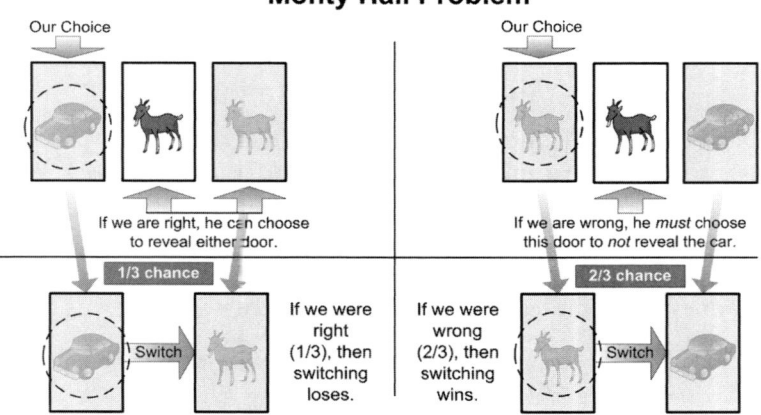

FIGURE 6.4 In the Monty Hall Problem, because the host knows where the car is, his selection of which door to reveal is more important than our initial, blind selection. Always switching doors nets us a two-thirds chance of winning the car rather than the expected one-half chance.

On the other hand, if we had picked a goat door to begin with, the host is now in control of two doors… one that hides the car and one that hides the other goat. The host is not going to reveal the car to us. Therefore, he *has to* open the door that hides the other grass-muncher. Logically, that means the door that he *didn't* open has the car.

At this point, our question may be, "But how do we know whether we selected correctly to begin with?" Well, we don't. However, the solution is for us to use some of the same simple probability math that we were willing to use before. Our error was not doing this probability math sooner.

Rethinking the Probabilities

Originally, there were three doors from which to select. That means a random choice (which was, in effect, what we were making) gives us a one-third chance of selecting the car and a two-thirds chance of selecting a goat. Again, for emphasis, we had a two-thirds chance of being wrong and only a one in three chance of being correct in the first place. When brought forward to our second decision, the same chances hold true. Regardless of what the host does in the interim, we still only have a one in three chance of currently claiming the correct door. We have a two in three chance of being the proud, temporary custodian of a domestic barnyard animal.

This is to our advantage, however. As we mentioned above, if we selected incorrectly (two-thirds chance), we forced the hand of the host. Of his two remaining doors, he *must* take the other goat off the table and leave the car on it (which is a fun metaphor, isn't it?). That means that if we originally selected one of the wrong doors, we now know that the *other* remaining door is the car. It has to be.

So, to sum up:

- We had a one-third chance of originally being right—we should stay with our door in order to win.

- We had a two-thirds chance of originally being wrong—we should switch doors in order to win.

If we rephrase slightly to see what happens if we *always* switch, we arrive at:

- With a one-third chance of originally being right—switching doors would *always* lose.

- With a two-thirds chance of originally being wrong—switching doors would *always* win.

Therefore, if we *always* switch, we win two-thirds of the time. The only time we would lose is if we had originally picked correctly—and that only happens one-third of the time. Notice how this is different from our original 50/50 premise?

What Did We Miss?

The question is, what information did we miss the first time that led us to the wrong conclusion? Research has shown that, for whatever reason, people seem to dismiss the host's selection of doors to reveal. They are so caught up in the randomness of their initial selection and the subsequent, seemingly random selection of whether to keep or switch that they neglect to consider the thought process that went into the host's decision. People seem to ascribe a similar random nature to the host's decision. They don't take into account the fact that the host *knows* where the car is. His decision is *not* random; he is trying to make you choose. After all, Monty Hall's game was not titled *Guess the Right Door*; it was called *Let's Make a Deal*. The attraction to the game was not seeing whether or not you got the car on the first selection. It was in the tension surrounding the decision of whether or not to switch. For that scenario to arrive, the host could *not* show you the car—and in doing so, tip his hand.

If we think back to the examples in Chapter 1, Monty was not the Blackjack dealer mindlessly dealing out random cards and following prewritten rules. Monty was in the role of the Poker player from Chapter 1, making his own decisions that directly affected yours. (Ironically, on any given show, he may have been the only person in the studio to *not* wear a stupid hat.)

So, it turns out that a puzzle that is certainly solvable from a logical, rational, mathematical standpoint fools most people to whom it is presented. Even people who get it right often do so for the wrong reason. Looking back at our normative decision theory criteria:

- Has *all* of the relevant information available
- Is able to *perceive* the information with the accuracy needed
- Is able to perfectly *perform* all the calculations necessary to apply those facts
- Is perfectly *rational*

We had all the relevant information *available* to make a decision. We were able to *perceive* the information accurately enough. Most people would be able to *perform* the very simple probability calculations with all the accuracy needed. And, with all of the above, we seemed to be acting in a perfectly rational fashion. The problem that slipped through was that, while we were *able* to perceive all the information, we *didn't* perceive it all. We simply left out the fact that Monty's decision on which door to open for us was a relevant fact. Somehow, we failed to take into consideration that *his* choice was not random—he knew where the car was and was intentionally avoiding showing it to us. More importantly, even if we knew that he was hiding it from us, we failed to take into account that this significantly skewed the odds in one direction. It was available and perceivable. We just didn't think it mattered.

The lesson here is that just because all the information is available to as and we know what to do with it, we won't necessarily think to use it. In short, humans fail… even with the simplest of decisions. Therefore, their quest for perfect rationality is bounded.

Rational Ignorance

While Monty Hall taught us that we often fail to take all the relevant factors into account when making a decision, there is a different reason we may not reach the pinnacle of rational decision making. Sometimes we may *elect* to not perform in a completely rational manner. This is different from what we explored above with the Guess Two-Thirds Game where we *decided* to not pursue a purely rational line of thought. In this case, by conceding to **rational ignorance**, we are making a rational decision to remain ignorant of all the relevant information. By doing so, we will be violating the rules of normative decision theory in that we will not have all the relevant information, may not perceive it accurately, or may not calculate it properly. There are certainly reasons for each of these.

The Cost of Information

Thinking back to Cutting the Cake in Chapter 5, as the Cutter, we knew that our opponent (the Decider) was going to select the biggest piece of the two. Therefore, it was in our best interests to cut as close to the middle of the cake as possible. However, short of laboratory conditions and a handy electron microscope, there is no way we could accurately ascertain the exact middle of the cake. Even as the Decider, after a less-than-perfect cut, we would have very little way of knowing which of the two pieces was bigger. In fact, the closer the cut is to being perfectly equitable, the harder it would become to make the correct decision. Given enough time and through painfully protracted measurements, we could eventually identify the biggest piece, but what would we have gained? And what condition would our confection be in after such a lengthy investigative process? That is, what is the cost of gathering all that information?

We face these decisions many times a day in our own lives. For example, imagine that at the grocery store, we see two cans of green beans from different companies on the shelf. While they are otherwise identical, there is a price difference of five cents between them. We could stand and ponder what would have caused the difference. Does the store have too much inventory of one and is trying to reduce it? Why is there too much inventory? Was it not selling? *Why* was it not selling? Perhaps the wholesaler of the more expensive brand is taking more profit? Or, turning to a factor that is likely more important to us, is there a quality difference between the two brands?

We could launch an investigation, interviewing the store managers and the wholesaler and researching the prices at other stores. We could jump out onto the Web to see ratings and reviews of other people's experiences and opinions with the two brands. We could pull the financial statements of both companies and examine their relative profit margins to see how much they are really making off their products.

Or we could just grab a can and continue shopping.

While all of that information could certainly be relevant to our decision, especially the quality difference, is it really worth the five-cent difference to go through all of the effort? We are far more likely to decide between the two based on a single factor: Is the possibility of a little extra quality in our beloved green beans worth five cents?

This would certainly be a different story if we were purchasing a new car and were looking at a difference of $5,000 instead. Why are those two seemingly similar automobiles priced so differently? In that instance, the information may be worth getting.

I'm not going to attempt to solve this problem now. We will attempt to quantify the costs of pleasure, pain, happiness, and even *time* in future chapters. The point is that by just grabbing a can of beans and moving on, we have made a *rational* choice to remain *ignorant* of facts that could possibly be relevant to us. The cost of that information is just too high for the benefit we would get out of it.

These decisions are common in the game world as well. Many times, the cost of the information is directly related to the computational power available to us. That is an external barrier that is not directly related to modeling of behavior, however. Even if we had more than enough processing power with which to compute things, there are times when it is more rational to *not* acquire information.

> **IN THE GAME**   **Scouting the Enemy**
>
> If we are playing a strategy game, we may be faced with a decision about what sort of units to build in an army. Do we want to construct melee units? Archers? Do we need fast units such as mounted ones? Do we need defensive, area-of-effect units such as catapults? Much of our decision is based on what the other player would be building. If he is constructing primarily melee units, for example, we may want to load up on archers so we can attack him at a distance before he gets the opportunity to close on our forces. But how do we know what he has built already or is building currently?
>
> One way of solving this problem would be to send scouting units to the enemy base. Once we discover him and spy on the make-up of his armies, we can better decide how to proceed with our own production.
>
> This approach has a few problems, however. First, we may incur a cost of time and material in creating a scout. We may *lose* that scout if it gets discovered. This is especially problematic if the scout is discovered prior to reaching the enemy base—we would get no information for our efforts. Additionally, we have to wait for the scout to reach the enemy base before any information can be gathered. That is time we could be spending producing an army but instead are electing to use waiting for the information to make the proper decision. And, on top of all of this, the scout could acquire incorrect information. In fact, our enemy may intentionally work to deceive potential scouts by building things differently initially and then changing later. Or, our enemy may hide the bulk of his *real* force and expose what he wants our scout to see—and for us to believe.
>
> All of these are things that can go wrong through us wanting to collect information with which to make a decision. We are costing ourselves valuable time and resources for what may be questionably useful information. At that point, most of us would be content to say "never mind" and simply start building an army with what we *believe* will be a correct balance. As we gather information later (and at less direct expense), we can change our plans or adapt accordingly.
>
> What we have elected to do is proceed with our plans in *rational ignorance*. We left ourselves ignorant of some of the information we could find useful simply because the cost of acquiring it would be too high.

THE COST OF CALCULATION

Another reason for adopting rational ignorance may be the cost of calculation. This is very similar to expending effort on the cost of information above. In this case, we are stating that sometimes the cost of calculating the relative merit of something is too high to justify the additional information it may provide us.

For the most part, humans are very accepting of generalized answers to questions. When we ask what time it is, we don't need an atomic clock on hand. When we ask how long it will take to drive to the store, we don't care to know down to the second. When figuring a tip at a restaurant, most of us shoot for the rounded-off dollar amount that represents whatever tip percentage we would like to bestow.

Imagine for a moment that you knew someone who *did* calculate this. Conveniently, I did know someone who did this, which makes for a wonderful, if hair-pulling example of this point. When splitting the bill with people, she would calculate the exact percentage of the bill that each person was responsible for (including the proper division of the total sales tax). Then, she would apply that percentage to an exactly figured 15% tip. When she was done, each of us knew not only what we owed for the meal, including splitting the sales tax, but exactly—*to the penny!*—what we should tip the waitress. (Don't bother e-mailing me with observations on how there was an easier way to do this… we tried to tell her.) The fun really began when she tried to collect money from everyone for each of their portions… down to the penny. She once had to ask the waitress for change so that she could give *us* change on our portions so that—you guessed it!—we could give the change back to the waitress.

Although we have never come to a conclusion on the exact pathology that caused her to do this (the cost of calculation was too high), we did come to the agreement that it wasn't worth it to go through all of that. Not one person in the arrangement—neither diner nor waitress—was all that interested in a penny here or there. We were all content to be *rationally ignorant* of the *exact* amount that each person owed or the *exact* amount that we should tip the waitress (which is a spectacularly arbitrary figure anyway). Just like in the above example of the cost of information, we were pleased enough to say, "Here… It's good enough. Take this so we can leave."

IN THE GAME   Counting the Enemy

In the previous example, we considered waiting until we knew the make-up of the enemy forces before we started trying to build our own. The hope was that we could then tailor our forces to match the type of units the enemy was building. One thing we overlooked for the sake of simplicity was that it was likely that the enemy would be building a reasonably balanced force. They were not likely to build all of one type of unit—archers, for example—and none of any other. Such homogeneity is, in and of itself, not very efficient. It would also lead to an answer that is not much more difficult than the decision matrix for Rock-Paper-Scissors.

If we are then to assume that the enemy forces are a cornucopia of varying unit types and strengths, how do we go about building our own forces to adequately match theirs? For example, if we were to discover that the enemy is building 60% melee units, is our decision going to be different from if they were building 70% melee units? Or 75%? What if they were building 60% melee units but also 30% mounted units? Is that different than 60% melee and 25% mounted? How much different? If there were five or six different unit types, the complexity mounts considerably. What if our archers are 80% effective against melee units but only 60% effective against mounted units? Is that much different from if the efficiencies were 70 and 50%, respectively? How much different?

Of course, this all comes with the caveat that we are able to perceive the numbers exactly. While this may be a simple task for a computer to do, it is somewhat more difficult for our senses to process. Humans can only handle counting so many objects at one time before we start to get a little bleary eyed. Unless the enemy is polite enough to line his army up in neat rows of 10 units each, simply getting an accurate count of the various units by type is a significant challenge. Oh... don't forget that this number is also likely to be continually changing as well.

The best we can hope to come up with is that the enemy is creating "more of A than of B and maybe twice as many A as C." Calculating with any greater accuracy than that may not only difficult, but, given the transient nature of any instantaneous count, it could also be a degree of specificity that is irrelevant. So what do we do? While we are still interested in the *general* makeup of the enemy army, we choose to be *rationally ignorant* of the exact order of battle.

COMBINING IT ALL

So what is the logical, rational conclusion of all of this? At the beginning of the chapter, we suggested that the human behavior that is presented by descriptive decision theory (i.e., what people *tend* to do) lies somewhere between the rigid perfection of normative decision theory (i.e., what people *should* do) and complete randomness. Let's review what we have explored.

- **Perfect Rationality Is Flawed:** While we can admit that acting under perfect rationality leads to decisions that are "right" in a theoretical sense, they often fail to yield realistic-looking decisions.
- **Not Everyone Is Rational:** The reason acting perfectly rational often does not yield good results is that we cannot expect superrationality—the perfect rationality of *all* other players.

- **Not Everyone Is Irrational:** Although we cannot expect superrationality, we can expect that at least *some* players will act in a rational fashion at least *some* of the time.
- **Pursuing Rationality Has Limits:** Even when people are attempting to be rational, they are often limited in their ability or desire to do so. This results in them acting partially rationally—often to varying degrees.
- **Acting Irrationally Can Be Logical:** Because we cannot expect *everyone* else to act either perfectly rationally or partially rationally, it is sometimes *logical* for us to act in a fashion that is not *perfectly* rational.
- **People Exhibit Bounded Rationality:** People are not perfectly rational because they often fail in their abilities to perceive and calculate the information correctly.
- **Pursuing Rationality Can Be Prohibitive:** Sometimes the costs of attempting perfect rationality are so high compared to the benefits we would gain that we can justify remaining in *rational ignorance* of the information.

The above observations lead us, not to a pinpoint solution of how to approach modeling human behavior, but rather to the notion that a range of behaviors is more appropriate. On one end of this range is the pure logic and math of perfect rationality; on the other end is the mindless chaos of randomness. Neither endpoint is acceptable as a solution that resembles the way "real people" think and act. But what lies in the middle?

Before we can proceed with modeling behaviors, we need to know what that range is. And before we can begin to map out what that range is, we need to determine how ranges like this are measured. That is, we need a measuring stick.

7 The Concept of Utility

One thing that was left unsaid in the analysis of the Prisoner's Dilemma was the reason behind making the decision. Perhaps this is obvious, but the underlying premise is that going to jail was something negative. It is an undesirable end—which is the reason it is considered a "loss." However, strange as this may sound, it is not a rigidly defined loss condition. Different people may have different beliefs about and weights for the negative aspects of incarceration. For instance, if you were quite certain that your wife would leave you if you were gone for five years but not if you were only gone for six months, it makes the six-month option look a lot better than the joint possibilities of either no time or five years. However, if even six months away would be horribly detrimental to your life, you may be more willing to take a chance on getting *no time* whatsoever by betraying your partner and hoping he doesn't do the same to you. What it comes down to is a matter of how you, as an individual, value the various factors involved.

There are other possible considerations. It is my understanding that there is an unwritten code among the criminal masses: You do *not* rat people out. Not only are there ramifications on the street for doing so, but there are ramifications from the other inmates while incarcerated as well. That adds another aspect of personal utility to the equation. How important is it—from a moral standpoint (and that term is used within the context of the criminal mind)—to *not* betray a partner simply on principle alone? These are all factors that provide the subtle shading of the decision process well beyond what we thought we had determined was the black and white of mathematics.

In economics, **utility** is a measure of the relative satisfaction from or desirability of consumption of goods. Put more simply, "How much does this mean to you?" Whether it is money, time, the value of building a tower, or the effectiveness of a razor blade, the problem with attempting to quantify the utility of an item is that different things are worth different amounts to different people.

111

For instance, in Chapter 6, in my introduction to the Monty Hall Problem, I mentioned that my wife suggested that getting the goat instead of the car wouldn't be too bad. I disagreed. She and I have a differing opinion on the relative merits of goats and cars. We put different utilities on them.

As a slightly less bizarre example, I put a differing value on a decent steak than does my wife. She, on the other hand will pay massive amounts of money for her particular favorite latte—which I view as paying money for coffee-flavored milk. I just don't get it. The technical restatement would be, *I have a different utility for lattes than does my wife*. It costs the same no matter which one of us buys it, so the *value* of the latte is the same regardless. This is something that we accept as part of human nature (and something we will attempt to quantify later).

To some extent, these differences can be modeled mathematically. While not accounting for everything, it gives us a starting point from which we can grow, tweak, and massage.

DECISIONS UNDER RISK

Probably one of the easier ways to examine utility is to do so in the realm of comparative values. By using ordinal rankings, we are able to achieve a sense of relation between objects or thoughts—that is, "This is *more* important to me than that." At that point, we can then begin the process of scaling things in a way that provides not only quantification but direct comparison—for example, "This is *twice* as important to me as that."

Blaise Pascal was one of the 17th century's more amazing minds. His contribution to mathematics came by way of trying to help out a French aristocrat kick his gambling habit. Despite Pascal's religiosity he did not preach to his friend about the evils of gambling. Instead, he provided mathematical advice on how to win at gambling.

He took up the question with Pierre Fermat, the wellspring of what we now know as modern calculus. In what was likely a series of conversations that included more numbers and symbols than actual words, it is likely that Pascal invented probability theory—and set in stone the underpinnings of today's casinos.

Pascal stated that when it comes to making bets, it is not enough to know the odds of winning or losing. You need to know what is at stake. For example, you might want to jump into a bet despite unfavorable odds if the payoff for winning would be really huge. (Which explains today's multi-million dollar lotteries.) Conversely, you might consider playing conservatively by betting on a sure thing even if the payoff is small. Of course, betting on a long shot wouldn't be terribly wise if the payoff is small. You might as well hand your money out.

If you have any awareness whatsoever of how gambling odds are set up in such things as horse races, you are familiar with this concept. The "favorite" horse generally has nothing to do with how congenial said steed is at parties. It is based entirely on the fact that many people believe he is the most likely to win. Naturally, if the aggregate opinion of the people can be trusted, we can assume that makes Mr. Horse a sure bet—and the payoff is low. However, if there is a horse that is considered a "long shot" in track parlance, the payoff is significantly higher. It can be… you aren't likely to win anyway. In a way, the excessive payout would be a reward for your foolhardiness.

Looking at Pascal's observations today, they don't seem terribly spectacular. It is something that is ingrained in us on many levels and in many areas of our lives. However, the premise does merit a closer look at some specifics, if only to help us identify the steps in the process that has become so intuitive. (We may even find some surprises.)

The essence of these sorts of decisions is that there is no way of knowing what the outcome is. Regardless, you have something of yours on the line—the wager. Given no control over the outcome for whatever reason (be it random chance such as a die roll or not enough knowledge of the situation such as in Matching Pennies), you are making what is referred to as a "**decision under risk**." Pascal was attempting to solve this problem in the realm of gambling, but it could be applied to everything from the stock market to whether or not to ask out a potential date to consenting to a potentially risky surgical procedure. ("As with any surgery, there is the risk of death.") The best you can do is collect knowledge of the situation, analyze your choices, and determine what the potential payouts might be. This is what Pascal brought to the table.

Pascal's Wager

After putting all of this thought into the mathematical laws of probability theory (and I assume passing on the advice to his gambler pal), Pascal applied his new concept back to his religious beliefs. What resulted is now known as "Pascal's Wager." Ol' Blaise wanted to justify, to himself mostly, his belief in God. More accurately, he wanted to justify his living his life *as if* God existed (which, naturally, includes believing in God).

He knew, as a good scientist, that it was impossible to *prove* the existence of God. In fact, he allowed that you couldn't even determine the *probability* that God existed. However, from his beliefs in the religious teachings, he could apply what was "at stake" in the wager… eternal life.

He created a decision matrix (Figure 7.1) much like what we have seen in Matching Pennies and Prisoner's Dilemma. In this case, one question was whether or not God does indeed exist. Admittedly, we cannot determine the probability for this—much like we couldn't determine the likelihood of our friend turning up heads or tails. As we will see, using Pascal's logic, this turns out not to matter all that much.

	God Exists	God Does Not Exist
Live As If God Exists	+ Infinite Heaven	– Nothing
Live As If God Doesn't Exist	– Infinite Hell	+ Nothing

FIGURE 7.1 The scoring matrix for Pascal's Wager. Pascal used these options and outcomes to determine that it was better to live as if God exists.

The other side of the grid involves "our play" in the game. We are trying to decide what to do. His two choices were:

- Live as if God exists (e.g., believe, follow the rules, etc.)
- Live as if God doesn't exist

His payoff matrix was based on his understanding of what was at stake. This speaks more to Pascal's reminder that we need to know what is being wagered and what is on the line.

Walking through the grid, we can infer Pascal's thought process. The most obvious possible outcome is the upper left. If we live as if God exists and it turns out that he *does* exist, we achieve eternal life in Heaven. That is, the payout is $+\infty$. On the other hand, if God exists and we life a... shall we say... less than exemplary life, we would be damned to hell for all eternity (or variations on that theme). The payout is $-\infty$. The interesting part comes in the right-hand column of the matrix. If God does *not* exist, then it doesn't matter. We lose nothing by living well; we gain nothing by living wild and free. For all intents and purposes those can be expressed by -0 and $+0$.

Pascal's Strictly Dominant Strategy

Looking at those potential outcomes, the strictly dominating strategy is not very coy. In fact, it kinda jumps right out at you. If we live well, the possibilities are $+\infty$ and -0. If we do not, our payouts are $-\infty$ and $+0$. Again, no matter what the probability of the fact that God exists—even if it is a 1% chance, we come out ahead by living *as if* God exists. (1% of infinite happy stuff beats 1% of infinite nastiness.) When you combine it with Pascal's premise that you gain and lose nothing if God doesn't exist, the solution is obvious.

However, much of the controversy surrounding Pascal's Wager stems from that last point. Pascal treated the two lifestyles in question as being equal. If they were not, Pascal could not have made the claim that you gain nothing and lose nothing if God does not exist. Apparently, Mr. P. found neither appeal in the benefits of loose living, nor restriction in the relatively conservative nature of piety. For all intents and purposes, the two rows of that decision matrix are no different in any sense *other* than as it applies to the question of eternal life.

Much like the blanket assumptions that were made in the Prisoner's Dilemma about how awful jail is, for Pascal's argument to be meaningful, we need to accept his views on a number of counts. What do we gain or lose by living in a Godly fashion? Exactly what does that mean for us? What are our "utility" values for lying, cheating, drinking beer, swearing profusely, and kicking puppies? For that matter, what are our views on the nature of Heaven and Hell? Do we have a way of quantifying our preferences for the proffered trappings of those two afterlife extremes? If we change those ideas based on our utility values, we also must change the payout matrix. This can occur even to the point where what we may believe a priori about whether God exists or not may come back into play much like we had to begin considering what our partner would do in the Prisoner's Dilemma.

What we must realize here is that the simple matrix is not so simple once we begin questioning the inputs themselves. Again, while the basics of decision theory can be expressed in such an uncomplicated manner, it also provides numerous hooks upon which we can attach more interesting and expressive statements. And when we do so, we inch ever closer on our quest for "interesting decisions."

No Pain, No Gain

Pascal cautioned us that we must know what is being wagered before we can make a decision. However, while that is certainly valid and wise, that is really only part of the issue. The other side to the equation when making a decision under risk is that we have to have a good idea of *why* we are risking.

In the case of Pascal's gambler friend, it was obvious that the point of the gambling was to win *something*. The odds and the amount wagered itself were only a means to an end. If the end is not accomplished, adjusting what it is you are willing to risk is no longer an issue. To frame things back into terms of Pascal's religious wager, if the terms of "living as if God exists" were structured such that it was impossible to accomplish, then even attempting that approach is no longer worth it. Put another way, if your risk-management strategy is not capable of producing the desired outcome, then it is not a viable solution. Therefore, why risk at all?

On the other hand, if your desired outcome is feasible if and *only* if you risk, then you will not accomplish your goal unless you enter into the risky behavior. If you elect not to risk, neither the odds nor the value of the prize will be of any importance. It's like multiplying by zero—nothing else in the equation matters at all. Therefore, at times, the utility that is present in a situation is specifically tied up in *taking* the risk in the first place.

A Monopoly on Preventing Monopolies

Many years ago, I had the opportunity to play the game Monopoly with some friends. All of the people involved had played the game numerous times. With that background, there is an assumption that people have an understanding of the core game mechanics. By this, I do not mean the mechanics of rolling the dice, moving around the board, and so on. I am referring to the fact that the overarching strategy of the game is "get more and better stuff so that you can charge your opponents lots when they land on it." Of course, the pinnacle of this concept is the titular "monopoly"—acquiring a collection of like assets so that their combined value is significantly greater than the sum of their parts.

One method of acquiring a monopoly is through the random chance of landing on the associated spaces (usually three of them) and purchasing them before anyone else does. The odds of this happening are generally slim—especially seeing that we had five or six players that night. Instead, it is a generally understood and accepted tenet that, if anyone is going to get a monopoly at all, there will have to be bartering of some sort. Sometimes this is straight up property-for-property, sometimes it involves cash, and sometimes there is a combination of transactions. Sometimes only two people are involved. Other times, there can be three-way transactions… or even more. The bottom line is, unless *some* sort of transaction takes place, the game stagnates quickly. Once all the properties are bought, the only action in the game becomes "roll and pay." And at the fees that are listed for the nonmonopolized, nondeveloped properties are relative loose change in the scheme of things.

In this particular game, one of the participants, Marci, exhibited a peculiar strategy. By the time the properties on the board were all bought up, she had managed to accumulate pretty much one of everything important. Of the nine main groups of properties (eight residential groups and the railroad group), she had one —*and only one*—property in five of them. At this point in the game, the transactions needed to start flowing if anyone was to get ahead at all. Because of the variety of Marci's holdings, she was a rather popular person to approach with deals.

At first, we thought she was taking full advantage of her position and holding out for better offers. Every different combination of offers was made. "I will give you A for X. No? How about A for Y? B for X? B for Y?" The solicitations were flying. However, after numerous turns and an exhaustive list of offers from all of the other players, it became clear to us that she simply was not selling. We began to query her as to why she wouldn't trade anything at all to any one of us. Her reasoning was, much to our amazement, staggeringly simple. She told us, "I don't want to give anyone *else* a monopoly."

Playing Not to Lose

While we conceded that she was certainly doing a bang-up job in that regard, we tried desperately to reason with her. We pointed out that, by trading someone a particular property, it wouldn't be giving them the *third* piece necessary to form a group... only the second. Her answer was that it would allow the *possibility* that they acquire the third item from someone else. We cajoled her by illustrating that, unless she traded, she would not be able to acquire a monopoly either—thereby weakening her own chances. To this she very simply asserted that she didn't care about winning by getting monopolies—she just didn't want to *lose* by allowing others to get them. Needless to say, her response elicited some significant confusion (and no small amount of frustration) in the rest of us.

For those of you who are curious, the game limped along in this fashion. It turned out that the assets were arranged such that no two people could directly trade so that each could acquire a monopoly without Marci's help. Likewise, any three-person deal (again sans-Marci) would have left one of the three severely wanting, and was therefore nixed. Slowly, there was some forced consolidation, however. Eventually, people started to gather power while Marci steadfastly held to her zero-risk strategy. As we had prophesied, with no means of reasonable income, she gradually bled out financially and succumbed to defeat. Of course, at that point, her properties were taken over one by one... and the game became the fast-and-furious trade-fest that it is generally meant to be.

What went wrong for Marci was that she had defined "risk" in a very different way than had the rest of us. Going back to her words, "I don't want to give anyone *else* a monopoly." At that, she succeeded, at least for a while. If you put her strategy aside for the moment and assume that her idea of winning was in line with the accepted definition of "winning" in the game of Monopoly (i.e., being the last one standing at the end), we can analyze the decision with all other things being equal.

Regardless of whether you elect to buy, sell, or trade properties in the game of Monopoly, winning is not a sure thing. At a very minimum, the random nature of the dice ensure that there isn't "one sure path" to winning. Therefore, a decision analysis such as the one we did for Pascal's Wager cannot include "winning the game" as one of the outcomes. The best we can hope for is to stay in the game and continue to have the possibility of winning. Of course, with that comes the possibility of losing as well, but that's why we play the game.

Marci, Meet Blaise Pascal...

We can analyze Marci's peculiar approach to Monopoly in a manner similar to how Pascal justified his own risk vs. reward scenario. If we construct a decision matrix similar to the one we used for Pascal's Wager (Figure 7.2), something *does* jump out at us. We can start by placing Marci's decision—trade or don't trade—along the left side of the matrix. Along the top, we list the possible *uncontrolled* outcomes. This represents the notion that, despite Marci's best intentions, people may or may not get monopolies without help from her. This is similar to the unknown existence of God that Pascal was facing. By analyzing the matrix as we have done often to this point, we can find the strictly dominating strategy... that of trading properties.

	Other People Don't Get Monopolies	Other People Get Monopolies
Do Not Trade Properties	Stalemate	Eventually Lose
Trade Properties	Possibly Win... Possibly Lose	Possibly Win... Possibly Lose

FIGURE 7.2 The scoring matrix for Marci's Monopoly strategy shows that the approach of trading properties is the only one where winning is possible no matter what the other players do.

There is a difference in this dominating strategy than what we have found in other analyses, however. In this case, it isn't dominating in that it guarantees a win, but rather in that it gives us a *chance* to win. After that, all the other factors of the game of Monopoly (including random dice rolls) take over. What we *do find* is that there is a selection that holds only negative consequences. If we do *not* trade properties with other players, the best we can hope for is a prolonged stalemate.

Worse still, if people manage to garner the monopolies without our help, we will almost definitely lose.

One lesson to learn here is that utility is often not inherent to a particular item—but in a particular *action* attached to an item. Marvin Gardens has a value as listed on the deed in the game. However, its utility in the game is in how it is used—which may have nothing to do with the values listed. In this case, if trading away Marvin Gardens could net you a property that you need to complete a trio, then Marvin Gardens' utility is worth something only in getting rid of it. If you don't do the action, then the utility is not realized.

To exercise this utility, however, Marci had to take a risk. She was correct in determining that, by trading, she was possibly giving someone else what they needed to eventually win. However, by focusing *only* on that aspect of the transaction, she hamstrung herself. She locked herself into the top row of Figure 7.2, but was only *looking* at the top left corner... stalemate. Notice that the stalemate result is the only one of the four possibilities that doesn't include the word *lose*. Of course, the top row is the only row that doesn't include the word *win*. That word *only* appears in the bottom row. It is that observation that very much sums up the entire point... in order to have the possibility of winning, you often have to accept the possibility of losing.

IN THE GAME The Tortoise and the Harried

Marci's approach in Monopoly is played out in the video game world as well, and it is often just as frustrating for the opponents. To dip into the vernacular of the players of our games, the term *turtling* is used both in strategy games and in team-based online first-person shooter (FPS) games. In both cases, it represents an approach of playing almost entirely defensively at the expense of the offense. Obviously, the metaphor is that of a turtle pulling into his protective shell and hoping to wait out his attackers. Much as was the case on that ill-fated Monopoly night in the early 1990s, this is an effective strategy (and frustrating for the opponents), but only if all you are trying to accomplish is to survive. For that reason, turtling is, more often than not, a pejorative term.

Certainly, depending on the game and the situation, there are times when it is more appropriate than others. In an online team game where the goal is for one team to capture the other's territory, then it behooves the second team to be entirely defensive. In a "capture the flag" scenario, however, the strategy of playing entirely defensively looks a lot like Marci's approach to Monopoly. In fact, if we put this scenario into a decision matrix such as in Figure 7.3, it will look strikingly like what we saw in Figure 7.2. If you elect to turtle and only defend, the other team may not get your flag, but you *certainly* are never going to get theirs.

	Other Team Only Defends	Other Team Attacks
Do Not Attack - Only Defend	Stalemate	Eventually Lose
Defend but Also Attack	Possibly Win... Possibly Lose	Possibly Win... Possibly Lose

FIGURE 7.3 The scoring matrix for a theoretical game of capture the flag shows that a turtling strategy (top row) may either prolong the game into a stalemate or eventually lead to a loss—but is not a valid strategy to win. The only possible way of winning is to attack at some point.

Again, depending on the game and genre, building armies or spawning soldiers is only part of the solution—just like holding on to Marvin Gardens. If the rules of the game dictate that a goal needs to be accomplished to win, and achieving that goal has an element of risk involved, then no amount of calculation will benefit you if you do not first elect to take the risk.

Now certainly, there are risks worth taking and those that are not. Much of the remainder of this book is designed to help with those calculations. However, the point made here is important. Just as Pascal posited that, in addition to the odds of the game, "you must know what is at stake," we must also know that there are times when putting things at risk actually *changes* the odds of the game. The question is not "Should I trade my properties in Monopoly?" The answer to that is "Yes." The question is actually "How should I trade my properties?" The answer to that involves more detailed calculation, as we shall see shortly. However, the assumption can be made that depending on how much and which properties you trade, the odds of winning will actually change significantly… for better or worse.

Similarly, in a capture the flag game, the question is not "Should some of my forces go on offense?" If your team ever hopes to win, again the answer is "Yes." The question would need to be "How many of my team members should go on offense?" Once again, this is a question that demands more calculation than a two-by-two matrix can provide. But, unlike betting on the fixed odds of a flip of a coin or the roll of a die, the amount of the wager (in this case, the team members committed to offense) actually changes the odds of success... again, for better or worse.

Of course, our next question—indeed, our next challenge—becomes determining the answers to those "how much" questions. And for that, we need more than vague ideas of none, some, more, or all. It's time to start putting values on the utility of our playing pieces.

Utility of Money

Part of our difficulty with Pascal's Wager was the inability to quantify the inputs. In fact, it was even made worse by using dissimilar measures such as Heaven and Hell vs. lifestyle. How do those compare? Is cheating on my wife or coveting my neighbor's ox worth even 20% of the value of the Heaven we may give up? Is telling the truth to my wife about how her new hairstyle makes her look like our neighbor's ox worth more than 14% of Hell? These are calculations that are near impossible to make because the comparisons themselves are so vague. (We'll give it a shot nonetheless a little later on.)

However, by making sure all measures are of the same type, our calculation process gets much easier. For the moment, let's follow a more intuitive approach by employing something that we use all the time as a universal quantifier—money.

Money has **value** that is hard to argue with. Most of the time, the actual value of any given item of currency is emblazoned right on it for all to see. A $20 bill is worth... 20 dollars. After all, it says so. The value of that currency relative to other currencies may change—that's what gives us fluctuating exchange rates. The value of a currency compared to what it can buy may even change—which gives us inflation and deflation. At that point all we are doing is comparing the *value* of that currency with the *value* of something else.

Value vs. Utility

Value is different from *utility*, however. As we mentioned at the beginning of this chapter, utility represents the relative satisfaction that we get out of something. Satisfaction, in this case, can also represent more than just happiness or pleasure. It can represent the usefulness of an item in achieving a goal.

In the case of Marci holding Marvin Gardens, the original *value* was represented by what she paid for it in the first place. As she held it, that value changed as people were willing to pay more and more for it. The reason for that shift is that Marvin Gardens had a *utility* over and beyond the face value of the property—other people *needed* it to improve their positions. For Marci, the utility of Marvin

Gardens was expressed in terms of her not wanting to lose. She had little hope of matching it with the other properties to get a monopoly—but she also did not desire that. To her (and to the rest of us), the utility of Marvin Gardens had nothing to do with its value. It had to do with power (such as it was).

When money is used as the example, many of us can relate to the difference between value and utility. We all have likely gotten into a discussion over whether or not something was "worth the price" that was set for it. The price the parties were discussing—the one on the tag—was the same for both people. Therefore, the *value* that would be paid for the item would be the same. The difference is in what we expected to get for that amount. Some people would be willing to pay that price for an object and others would not. They may have a greater notion of utility for their money than other people.

Even this example is complicated somewhat by necessarily including the opinions of value (and utility) that the people have for the item in question. If you were to remove *any* exchange from the process entirely, people's relative utility for the same value of money becomes a bit more apparent. For example, if you were to lose 20 dollars somewhere, would you try to find it? Ten dollars? Five? One? At what point is the utility of the money you lost so low that you no longer care?

Even this question is a little knotty in that we must account for the time spent looking for the lost money. If I dropped a dollar bill at my feet, I would bend down to pick it up. If I was told I dropped a dollar back in the parking lot, I wouldn't bother. While the value was still the same, my utility for a single dollar is not worth the time and effort to locate it.

What's It Worth to You?

In a different scenario, I was once caught behind a woman in the grocery store. Apparently a small can of peas had been scanned incorrectly—or at least different from the price she claimed she saw on the shelf. We were stalled waiting for the helpful grocery clerk to go and ascertain the validity of what she saw. I was standing behind her with a single item—mildly perturbed over having to wait. When I overheard that the difference between the scanned price and her claim was about 20 cents, I reached into my pocket, pulled out 20 cents and placed it on the counter between the customer and the cashier saying "here, I'll cover the difference."

The customer turned to me and (much to my amazement) explained with rather animated excitement that the store rules stated that if something was scanned incorrectly, you received it for free. It didn't take me but a moment to glance at the register and see that the can of peas had rung up at a whopping 78 cents. Knowing that I had plenty of change in my pocket, I reached back in and plopped what likely amounted to two entire cans of peas on the counter.

"Here," I said. "I don't know how much value you put on five minutes of *your* time, but five minutes of *my* time is worth more than the price of a can of peas."

There was a silent moment during which she displayed a thoroughly bewildered look (which was worth more to me than a can of peas). Collecting herself (but still probably uncomprehending that her time could possibly be worth more than 20 cents), she managed a brief nod to the cashier who, by this point, was beaming worshipfully at me like I was the grocery store equivalent of Charles Bronson in *Death Wish*. The price check was cancelled, the lady paid, and I left the store 30 seconds later.

What is the point of my reflective anecdote? While the *value* of the can of peas was the same 78 cents for both of us, the lady obviously had a higher *utility* for that 78 cents than did I. And the *utility* was the important factor in making the decision… not the *value*.

Utility vs. Risk

As we have discussed thus far, goals and tools can often be expressed in terms of utility. This may or may not equate to their stated value. Earlier in this chapter we also discussed the act of taking risks (or not taking them) in terms of utility. This becomes useful to us when we combine and compare the utility of the risk with the utility of the outcome. When we do this, we arrive at an expression that may yield an inequality of varying magnitude. It is this inequality that allows us to determine whether or not a risky activity is "worth it."

For purposes of keeping to a simple example, it would be best if we stay within the realm of a single, measurable unit. For now, we can construct an example that uses money as the manner of measurement for both the risk and the reward. To that end, let's begin with a scenario that is likely familiar to many of us.

Warranties and Risk

Imagine purchasing a computer for $1,400. With tiresome predictability, the salesperson offers you a warranty that offers free repair for your computer for a year at a cost of $300. (Yeah, I know… that's a little steep.) The question, naturally, is whether or not you should purchase the warranty.

Obviously, the decision as to whether or not to purchase a warranty is based largely on our expectation about whether the computer will need repair during the warranty period. (Repairs normally cost $200.) We are also going to consider the possibility that the machine could completely implode beyond repair and need to be replaced.

Given our vast experience with technology, we could apply what we believe are reasonable probability figures on this. We believe the odds of the computer continuing to work for the entire year are 70%. (Again, give me a break… it's a hypothetical.) We give it a 20% chance of needing a minor repair and a 10% chance of becoming a proverbial doorstop.

By applying the percentages and the associated costs for the various events, we achieve the figures shown in Figure 7.4. No matter what happens during the duration of the warranty, we are out the $300 we paid for it. If we *don't* buy the warranty and nothing goes wrong, then we don't lose anything. If the computer requires fixing, we have to pay $200 for the repair job. If something goes amiss and we must toss it on our ever-growing pile of defunct electronic equipment, we are out the entire $1,400 we paid for it. (May I suggest at this point that we *don't* replace it with a computer of the same model?)

Result:	Computer Works	Requires Fixing	Implodes	Estimated Utility of Warranty
Probability:	(p = 0.7)	(p = 0.2)	(p = 0.1)	
Buy Warranty	−300	−300	−300	−300
Decline Warranty	0	−200	−1400	−180

FIGURE 7.4 The prices for the computer and the warranty can be combined with the expected percentages of needing repair or replacement to determine whether or not to purchase a warranty for a new computer.

Similar to what we did with previous examples, we are going to attempt to calculate our expected utility for the prospective warranty. For a change, we now have solid numbers with which to work. As much as I don't want to make this a formula-laden book, I want to walk through the mathematics of this particular example.

For those of you not familiar with reading statistical and logical notation, I will explain a bit of terminology. First, we will define W as meaning the purchasing the warranty. The symbol "$\neg$" means "not." So $\neg W$ would mean "not W"—or in this case, "not purchasing the warranty."

To calculate the relative benefits of each of those two paths, we need to calculate the **expected utility** (E) of each of either purchasing ($E(W)$) or not purchasing ($E(\neg W)$) the warranty. This involves taking into account the cost of the three possible outcomes in a manner that also respects the likelihood of those outcomes occurring.

/*
In these examples, the math may seem somewhat redundant or excessive. For example, when buying a warranty, in all three cases the cost is 300. Multiplying 300 by 0.7, 0.2, and 0.1 only to add them back together to arrive at 300 may seem a little silly. The reason that I do this is to keep in mind that we do have three possible outcomes that we may need to treat separately. While in this case those three outcomes were the same (i.e., paying $300), in other examples that we will use shortly, this will not be the case. Please bear with me until then.
*/

The expected values for the two actions are:

$$E(W) = 0.7(-300) + 0.2(-300) + 0.1(-300)$$

$$E(W) = -300$$

In English, the expected utility of purchasing the warranty is to lose $300 over the course of that year, which is the cost of the warranty no matter what happens.

In the case of not purchasing the warranty:

$$E(\neg W) = 0.7(0) + 0.2(-200) + 0.1(-1400)$$

$$E(\neg W) = -180$$

Again, in more readable terms, the expected utility of *not* purchasing the warranty is a cost of $180 for the year. This reflects the 20% chance of needing a $200 repair and the 10% chance of replacing the $1,400 computer.

Because $E(\neg W) > E(W)$, this means that the value of *not* purchasing the warranty is greater than the value of purchasing it. However, the result of –180 leads us to expect that we will have to pay about $180 on repairs over the course of the year.

Different Inputs, Different Outputs

The example above is not a proof that *all* warranties are rip-offs. Given that we performed a mathematical analysis of the problem, our solution is only as good as the numbers we used. Some of the figures were established in a concrete fashion. For example, the price of the computer and the price of the warranty are values that we can point to as being known quantities. Other figures in the example were estimates. We would have to estimate the likelihood that the computer we are purchasing is going to need repair work or be cast into the bowels of hell. The question then arises: What happens when those estimates change?

The happy part is that, once established, these formulas can be applied to any values we want to use. For example, simply changing the percentages of computer failure will change the results significantly.

Figure 7.5 shows a slightly different scenario. In this case, the computer is a complete piece of garbage and only has a 50% chance of surviving that first year. It will need a repair 30% of the time (remember, those cost you $200 without the warranty), and 20% of the time it will need to be replaced. By changing those figures, we get the following:

$$E(W) = 0.5(-300) + 0.3(-300) + 0.2(-300)$$

$$E(W) = -300$$

$$E(\neg W) = 0.5(0) + 0.3(-200) + 0.2(-1400)$$

$$E(\neg W) = -340$$

In this case, we find that $E(W) > E(\neg W)$. Therefore, the expected value of buying the warranty is greater than the expected value of not purchasing it. (Has anyone yet considered not purchasing this computer at all?)

Another scenario, shown in Figure 7.6, takes into account the possibility that the warranty is simply over-priced. Let's return to the original assumptions about failure rates (20% = needs repair, 10% = boat anchor). However, we are going to reduce the price of the warranty from $300 to $150. (Apparently there's a half-price sale on warranties for junky computers.)

Result:	Computer Works ($p = 0.5$)	Requires Fixing ($p = 0.3$)	Implodes ($p = 0.2$)	Estimated Utility of Warranty
Buy Warranty	−300	−300	−300	−300
Decline Warranty	0	−200	−1400	−340

FIGURE 7.5 By increasing the percentage chances that the computer requires repair or replacement, the expected utility of purchasing the warranty increases as well.

Result:	Computer Works	Requires Fixing	Implodes	Estimated Utility of Warranty
Probability:	(p = 0.7)	(p = 0.2)	(p = 0.1)	
Buy Warranty	−150	−150	−150	−150
Decline Warranty	0	−200	−1400	−180

FIGURE 7.6 By reducing the price of the warranty, the expected utility of purchasing the warranty is better than what we can expect by not purchasing it.

The math works out to:

$$E(W) = 0.7(-150) + 0.2(-150) + 0.1(-150)$$

$$E(W) = -150$$

$$E(\neg W) = 0.7(0) + 0.2(-200) + 0.1(-1400)$$

$$E(\neg W) = -180$$

Now, with our half-price warranty in hand, the expected value of the whole shebang is a negative $150. However, as we saw before, *not* purchasing the warranty will cost us about $180. This time, despite the fact that the computer is just as reliable as it was in the first example in Figure 7.6 (for whatever *that's* worth), we see that $E(W) > E(\neg W)$. The difference in the price of the warranty made it more worthwhile to purchase. More accurately, it made it less of a drain than the *potential* of the computer breaking and us *not* having the warranty.

Generalizing the Formulas

Remember, however, that we are assuming that the failure rates are static and accurate. We have only "solved" the situation for those figures. It would behoove us to formalize the formula (so to speak) so that we can apply it to all combinations of parameters just by plugging in the numbers.

The above equations show that this is actually a simple process. Once we have the different variables that we need laid out in the proper arrangement, calculating the two utility values is rather straightforward.

Given the following variables:

- c: The cost of the computer
- x: The cost of the warranty
- f: The likelihood of complete failure
- b: The likelihood of a breakdown needing a repair
- r: The cost of a repair

Our formulas for the estimated utility of both purchasing a warranty and not purchasing one are as follows:

$$E(W) = (1 - f - b)(-x) + b(-x) + f(-x)$$

$$E(\neg W) = b(-r) + f(-c)$$

If we wanted to decide whether we should purchase or not, we would then just need to determine whether $E(W) > E(\neg W)$.

Putting It in Code

Of course, to get this calculation into a game-type environment, we will need to arrange it in terms of code. Once we have arranged our formulas in such a way that we are solving for the utility values that we need, this is actually a rather straightforward process.

When we were solving this problem "by hand" above, we had two formulas and a comparison of their results. Similarly, we will lay out two functions—one for calculating the utility of the warranty and one for calculating the utility of *not* purchasing the warranty. A third function will compare them and return a Boolean as to whether or not we should purchase the warranty with the given numbers.

For purposes of simplicity, we are assuming that the appropriate numbers are calculated elsewhere and stored as member variables in our class. Note that the function WorksOdds() simply returns the percentage chance that the computer works based on what is already set by mRepairOdds and mReplaceOdds.

```
float MyGame::UtilityWarranty()
{
    // Returns the utility value of purchasing the warranty.
```

```
    float Utility;

    Utility =
        ( WorksOdds() * -mWarrantyPrice )
        + ( mRepairOdds * -mWarrantyPrice )
        + ( mReplaceOdds * -mWarrantyPrice );

    return Utility;
};

float MyGame::UtilityNotWarranty()
{
    // Returns the utility value of not purchasing the warranty.

    float Utility;

    Utility =
        ( mRepairOdds * -mRepairCost )
        + ( mReplaceOdds * -mComputerCost );

    return Utility;
};

bool MyGame::PurchaseWarranty()
{
    // Returns the decision on whether or not to purchase the
    // warranty based on the relative utility values returned from
    // the two functions.

    if ( UtilityWarranty() > UtilityNoWarranty() ) {
        return true;
    } else {
        return false;
    }
};
```

Given the above functions, we could set the appropriate values and call the function `PurchaseWarranty()` to get our answer at any time. In this case, we are using the values from the original example.

```
// Set the appropriate values
mComputerPrice = 1400;
mWarrantyPrice = 300;
mRepairCost = 200;
mRepairOdds = 0.2f;
mReplaceOdds = 0.1f;
bool ShouldWeGetWarranty;
// So, should we purchase the warranty
// with the values set above?
ShouldWeGetWarranty = PurchaseWarranty();
```

Relative Utility

As simple and comprehensive as the above solution seems to be, there is another factor we have yet to consider with our warranty purchase. We have left out the notion of the *utility* that an individual may place on a working computer. How much is it worth to us to avoid downtime on a computer? How much is that computer an integral part our lives? If it breaks and we cannot fix it, are we in dire need?

I know that if my computer were to break, my entire life would be on hold until such time as it was repaired or replaced. A warranty is a necessity for me. (In fact, I happen to have next day, on-site with accidental damage coverage… I can get my computer repaired or replaced faster than I can get in to see my doctor.) On the other hand, my mother would probably not even realize something was wrong with her computer for months. She can spend that money elsewhere on things that she can actually get usage out of.

These sorts of ruminations get a little beyond the scope of this chapter. We will attempt to approach this level of depth later on in the book.

 IN THE GAME **Protecting the Barracks**

While the above scenario is a familiar one to us in real life, I am not aware of too many games where the AI agents purchase a computer, much less have to decide whether or not to purchase a warranty for it. However, by using a little creativity it is not hard to envision a scenario in which the concept is easily applied.

In our computer plus warranty example, the values we used were either based on the cost of something (i.e., money) or the percentage chance that something would happen. By limiting the value references to money, we don't have to concern ourselves with converting between two different types of values. For the sake of continuity, we will stick with that formula here to best mimic the warranty example.

It is a staple of real-time strategy (RTS) games to construct buildings of some sort for whatever reason. These buildings cost money to produce and are, therefore, a valuable commodity much like the computer. Once we have spent the money for the building—let's just say it is a barracks—we would rather not lose the building by having it damaged or destroyed by the enemy. Put simply, we want to keep our investment intact. To do so, it may behoove us to protect our investment against damage or destruction.

One common method of protecting buildings in a game such as this is to build defensive structures such as towers. A tower could repel invaders that would seek to damage our building. Of course, towers also cost money to build. Spending money on a tower is a big decision because the money could be spent elsewhere, for example, on more military or on other, more productive buildings. So, what sorts of factors must go into our decision to build an accompanying tower hovering over our beloved barracks?

Certainly, we must have a value associated with the construction of our barracks. How much did it cost us? We can assume that a total destruction of the barracks would require a replacement cost that is equal to the original construction cost. We can also assume that there is a cost of repairing any damage that is done to the barracks. Therefore, we should be able to assign a cost of repairing the damage done to the barracks with or without the tower present. Of course, for all of this benefit that the tower provides, we need to know what the cost of building a tower is.

Once the values of building and repair are established, we also need to know what the likelihood of the barracks being attacked is. We will assume that the barracks could be attacked by a small force, a large force, or not at all. If the tower is present, the difference between the two sizes of attacking forces is reflected in the amount of damage done. If there is *no* tower, a large force will destroy the barracks, whereas a small force will only damage it heavily before they are driven off.

We must note that this is different from our warranty example in that, with a warranty in place, we paid *nothing* for a repair or replacement. The only cost was that of the warranty itself. In this case, some of the entries represent the cost of the tower *plus* the cost of damage done despite the presence of the tower.

Laying out some hypothetical costs:

Building a Barracks	500
Building a Tower	150
Repair Small Damage with Tower Present	100
Repair Small Damage without Tower Present	250
Repair Large Damage with Tower Present	250
Repair Large Damage without Tower Present	500 (new Barracks)

And some hypothetical probabilities of attack:

No Attack:	30%
Small Attack:	50%
Large Attack:	20%

If we lay out the possibilities as we did in the case of the computer warranty scenario (Figure 7.7), we arrive at two utility values. Note that they are negative utilities because, in this case, they represent costs to us. With that in mind, we are looking for the *highest* utility, that is, the *least* cost. Using the figures above, we find that it would be better for us *not* to build a tower.

Result:	No Attack	Small Attack	Large Attack	Estimated Utility of Tower
Probability:	(p = 0.3)	(p = 0.5)	(p = 0.2)	
Build Tower	−150	−150 − 100 = −250	−150 − 250 = −400	−250
Do Not Build Tower	0	−250	−500	−225

FIGURE 7.7 In this situation, we are not assuming a great probability of receiving a large attack. Therefore, when we figure the cost of building a tower plus the benefit that it provides, the utility is less than the utility of not having one (and rebuilding the barracks if necessary).

For the sake of completeness, let's lay out the formulas themselves. We are now solving for $E(T)$, the estimated utility of building a tower.

$$E(T) = 0.3(-150) + 0.5(-250) + 0.2(-400)$$

$$E(T) = -250$$

Compare this to the estimated utility of *not* building a tower.

$$E(\neg T) = 0.3(0) + 0.5(-250) + 0.2(-500)$$

$$E(\neg T) = -225$$

Again, we find that $E(\neg T) > E(T)$. Therefore, the estimated utility of *not* building the tower is greater than that of building it.

Many factors go into this determination, so the decision is rather tenuous. Certainly, the building costs of the barracks and the tower have a lot to do with the determination. However, one of the major components is our *assumptions* about the likelihood of attack. In this example, we are using what is probably a rather naïve assumption that there is a 30% chance that our barracks won't be attacked at all. Likewise, we are assuming only a 20% chance that it will suffer a large attack. This may be the case if the barracks is well back behind our lines deep in our city. In that case, by simply using some nonmathematical reflection, we could agree that not having a tower over the barracks would be justified.

However, if we were to change these assumptions about the susceptibility to attack—perhaps by assuming the barracks would be along the front lines—we would expect the utility of an accompanying tower to shift as well. For instance, let's use the same costs for the buildings and the damage estimates but change the attack probability figures to something that is more in line with a typical "in the thick of things" RTS scenario.

No Attack:	5%
Small Attack:	60%
Large Attack:	35%

As we can see by the updated figures in Figure 7.8, by simply changing the expected percentages of attack, the utility functions have swung significantly in favor of building a tower. The equations themselves would now be as follows:

$$E(T) = .05(-150) + .6(-250) + .35(-400)$$

$$E(T) = -297.5$$

Result:	No Attack	Small Attack	Large Attack	Estimated Utility of Tower
Probability:	(p = 0.05)	(p = 0.6)	(p = 0.35)	
Build Tower	−150	−150 − 100 = −250	−150 − 250 = −400	−297.5
Do Not Build Tower	0	−250	−500	−325

FIGURE 7.8 In this situation, we are assuming a greater probability of receiving an attack. Now, the benefits provided by the tower in case of attack are more prevalent—making the utility cost for building one much greater.

Compare this to the estimated utility of *not* building a tower.

$$E(\neg T) = .05(0) + .6(-250) + .35(-325)$$

$$E(\neg T) = .05(0) + .6(-250) + .35(-325)$$

Now, we find that $E(T) > E(\neg T)$. The utility of building (−297.5) is greater than the utility we achieve by *not* building (−325). Based on the numbers provided, our decision should now be to build the tower.

PUTTING IT IN CODE

Just as we did with the computer warranty example before, the act of converting this example to code is relatively simple. In fact, the functions and flow look strikingly familiar. Again, we have one function for the utility of building a tower, one for the utility of not building a tower, and a third that does a simple comparison of those utilities to advise us. The numbers used for the building costs, the repair costs, and the odds of attack can be set elsewhere in the game (which is important, as we shall see in a moment).

```
float MyGame::UtilityTower()
{
    // Returns the utility value of purchasing the tower.

    float Utility;
```

```cpp
    Utility = ( OddsNoAttack() * -mTowerCost)
        + ( mOddsSmallAttack * -( mTowerCost + mSmallDamageTower ) )
        + ( mOddsLargeAttack * -( mTowerCost + mLargeDamageTower ) );

    return Utility;
};

float MyGame::UtilityNoTower()
{
    // Returns the utility value of not purchasing the tower.

    float Utility;

    Utility = ( mOddsSmallAttack * -mSmallDamageNoTower )
            + ( mOddsLargeAttack * -mBarracksCost );

    return Utility;
};

bool MyGame::BuildTower()
{
    // Returns the decision on whether or not to purchase the
    // tower based on the relative utility values returned from
    // the two functions.

    if ( UtilityTower() > UtilityNoTower() ) {
        return true;
    } else {
        return false;
    }
};
```

At any point in our game we could call the `BuildTower()` function, and it would process whatever values we had in place for the necessary variables and yield a Boolean value as to whether the expected utility of building the tower was greater than the expected utility of not building it… that is, is it worth it to build a tower over our barracks or not?

Again, using the values from the original example:

```
// Set the appropriate values
mBarracksPrice = 500;
mTowerPrice = 150;
mSmallDamageTower = 100;
mSmallDamageNoTower = 250;
mLargeDamageTower = 250;
mOddsLargeAttack = 0.2f;
mOddsSmallAttack = 0.5f;
```

The code to make the decision would simply look like:

```
bool ShouldWeBuildTower;
// So, should we build the tower
// given the values set above?
ShouldWeBuildTower = BuildTower();
```

When Changing Changes the Changers

There is one thing that we have not yet considered in this calculation that may be of interest in our utility functions. It is possible (if not likely) that simply building a tower next to the barracks may change the probability that it will be attacked at all. An undefended building is an almost irresistible target for even small forces to take on. On the other hand, the presence of the defensive structure provides a deterrent—especially to those lighter squads. To reflect this, we may want to work with *two* layers of probability of attack—one that reflects an undefended barracks and one that takes into account the fact that enemies may more carefully consider attacking a building with a tower hovering nearby. Needless to say, the complexity of our calculations goes up significantly at this point.

To see this effect in action, we need to define two different sets of expectations for the likelihood of attack based on the presence of the tower. First, let's assume that without a tower present, we can expect:

No Attack:	10%
Small Attack:	50%
Large Attack:	40%

Next, let's assume that with a tower present, the probabilities change to the following:

No Attack:	50%
Small Attack:	10%
Large Attack:	40%

The differences in the above figures represent what would likely be reluctance on the part of the enemy to attack a protected barracks with a small force—perhaps electing instead to only attack when it can commit the larger force that would be necessary. The resulting figures are shown in Figure 7.9.

Result:	No Attack	Small Attack	Large Attack	Estimated Utility of Tower
Probability:	($p = 0.5$)	($p = 0.1$)	($p = 0.4$)	
Build Tower	−150	−150 − 100 = −250	−150 − 250 = −400	−260
Probability:	($p = 0.1$)	($p = 0.5$)	($p = 0.4$)	
Do Not Build Tower	0	−250	−500	−325

FIGURE 7.9 By including the idea that the presence of the tower may discourage attack, we must change the probability numbers—which, in turn, change the way the utility costs are applied.

Note that to visualize this new wrinkle, we need to change the way we are laying out our table. Before, we were putting the likelihood of attack at the top of each column. Now, these figures change based on the row as well. For clarity, I have broken the table into two parts—one for building the tower and one for not building it.

If we calculate the utility of *not* building the tower ($E(\neg T)$) using the probabilities that we have in place for building it (i.e., 50%, 10%, 40%), the resulting utility is −225. The utility of building the tower ($E(T)$) is −260. $E(\neg T) > E(T)$. Therefore, the utility of *not* building it is greater—that is, it would not be worth it to build.

However, once we adjust for our "deterrent factor," the utility of *not* building the tower ($E(\neg T)$) becomes −325. That means $E(T) > E(\neg T)$. Without changing any of the figures, including the cost of building the tower itself, we find that the deterrent factor alone is enough to justify building the tower.

Of course, a major disclaimer over all of this is that the numbers we have selected for the likelihood of attack may not be accurate. A change of even 5% on one of those figures could make a significant change in the decision about whether or not a tower is worth building. Additionally, we may want to vary what our estimates are of the damage that would result from the differently sized forces. What's more, we may have more than those two sets of attack probabilities that we want to use. For example, we may want to have different assumptions based on where the barracks is in relation to enemy territory or other buildings that we have already constructed. We may even want to create a separate function that determines those factors for us in a different part of the AI code.

 ## Putting It in Code

Thankfully, if we wanted to include this very specific decision into our game, we could package everything we have done into a few small functions that simply return whether or not, based on our estimates, building a tower to cover our barracks has a utility value that makes it worthwhile.

In this case, rather than holding the odds of there being a large or small attack in external variables that we access from the utility functions, we actually pass the variables into those utility functions. That way, we can send it whatever we want. Of course, that means our base function `BuildTower()` needs to have all the values passed in as well so it can distribute those values appropriately. Therefore, we will change `BuildTower()` to ask for the four odds values that represent the likelihood of a small or large attack depending on the presence of the tower. (Note that the odds of *no* attack is simply the percentage left over after the odds of the small and large attacks; you will see the function call for this in the code below but not the very simple function itself.)

```
float MyGame::UtilityTower( float OddsLargeAttack, float OddsSmallAttack )
{
    // Returns the utility value of purchasing the tower using
    // alternate attack odds

    float Utility;
    float NoAttack = OddsNoAttack(OddsLargeAttack, OddsSmallAttack);
```

```
    Utility = ( NoAttack * -mTowerCost )
            + ( OddsSmallAttack * -( mTowerCost + mSmallDamageTower ) )
            + ( OddsLargeAttack * -( mTowerCost + mLargeDamageTower )
);

    return Utility;
}


float MyGame::UtilityNoTower( float OddsLargeAttack, float
OddsSmallAttack )
{
    // Returns the utility value of not purchasing the tower using
    // alternate attack odds

    float Utility;

    Utility = ( OddsSmallAttack * -mSmallDamageNoTower )
            + ( OddsLargeAttack * -mBarracksCost );

    return Utility;
}


bool MyGame::BuildTower( float OddsLargeAttackTower,
                         float OddsLargeAttackNoTower,
                         float OddsSmallAttackTower,
                         float OddsSmallAttackNoTower )
{
    // Returns the decision on whether or not to purchase the
    // tower based on the relative utility values returned from
    // the two functions - including the different odds of attacks
    // on the barracks based on the presence of the tower.
    float thisUtilityTower;
    float thisUtilityNoTower;
```

```
            thisUtilityTower =
                UtilityTower( OdcsLargeAttackTower, OddsSmallAttackTower );

            thisUtilityNoTower =
                UtilityNoTower( OddsLargeAttackNoTower, OddsSmallAttackNoTower );

            if ( thisUtilityTower > thisUtilityNoTower ) {
                return true;
            } else {
                return false;
            }
        }
```

As before, this could be called from code at any point that we needed to make a determination as to whether or not we should build a tower over our barracks. We are still ignoring where we are getting the numbers for the attack odds—assuming that they are being set elsewhere.

UTILITY OF TIME

Money certainly is an obvious and reasonably measurable commodity to which we can ascribe value and utility. Even items on which we can hang a price tag, such as a computer of questionable quality, can be converted to be expressed in terms of the value of money.

Another commodity, however, is important to consider when discussing the concept of utility—especially as it corresponds to decision theory. The idea of *time* as having measurable utility is not a foreign concept. After all, we often utter musings to ourselves or to others along the lines of "if I only had the time to *spend*," "but I don't want to *waste* the time," "it's not *worth* my time," and "could you *buy* me some time?" Notice that the emphasized words are all ones that can be used in similar sentences regarding money. Just as we can say we *spend* money and *waste* money, that our money is *worth* something, and we can even *buy* it, we have internalized a measurement of time as being a measurable quantity against which we can judge other items.

Even the direct comparison of time to money is something that is a given in our mental approaches to life. We often get paid a specific rate of money per hour. We rent cars, apartments, and carpet steam-cleaners in dollars per day. Even without being explicitly addressed, people will make the comparison. For example, paying $50 for a video game that has only two hours worth of gameplay content and zero replayability would likely make a few people grumble. If they took the time to think about it, they have paid $25 per hour for the privilege of playing the game. However, a role-playing game (RPG) that managed to offer up 50 hours' worth of gameplay drops the rate to $1 per hour… a much more respectable number.

Notice that the above rates are all expressed in the form of the amount of *money* spent per a fixed amount of *time*. It would seem that, when the two forms of measurement are in the same formula, we naturally tend to think in terms of the money spent. Is this simply a result of the fact that our society thinks in terms of money as the universal measuring stick? Perhaps not.

PRODUCTION OVER TIME

Even when dealing with issues of production, for example, the amount of time seems to get reduced to the role of denominator in the ratio. For example, we may think of how many widgets we can produce in a fixed amount of time. Chuck can churn out six widgets *per hour*, whereas Ralph can only produce five *per hour* (Figure 7.10). It would seem that Chuck is more of a widget-meister than is Ralph. It is perfectly viable to think the other way around, of course. We could have said that it takes Chuck 10 minutes to produce a single widget, but it takes Ralph 12 to do so. The math works out the same, but it seems strangely uncomfortable. We feel almost drawn to do the mental flip-flop to convert it once again to "widgets per hour." Why is that?

	Widgets per Time	Time per Widget
Chuck	6 / hour	10 minutes / widget
Ralph	5 / hour	12 minutes / widget

FIGURE 7.10 Depending on what problem we are trying to solve, production over time can also be expressed in terms of time per unit of production.

Often, it comes down to what we are measuring. What is important? Of course, one thought process is that we are measuring *widgets,* not time. Therefore the widget measurement should be in the position of importance. In the above example, the reason for this way of thinking may be that it seems more intuitive to think in terms of "widgets per hour" because we are expecting that lying around nearby is a measurement of how much we are *paying* our widget-making pair. After all, if we are paying them the same amount (per hour), and all widgets have the same value, then it isn't a stretch to determine that Chuck is more productive (per hour) than is Ralph. Notice how we didn't even bother to compare how much we are paying Chuck or Ralph *per widget?* It's always in terms of widgets *per hour* and dollars *per hour*.

Even when money is not involved, time seems to get the back seat. Giving another, more personal, example… When I entered into the agreement to write this book, I gave my publisher a wild guess as to an expected number of pages (at the time of this writing, we have penciled in a figure of 500). In turn, we also agreed that I would have the book completed within six months. Only after that point did I come to the startling realization that I would have to write about 20 pages per week. I even subdivided it further to about three pages per day. Notice that my thought process was in *pages* over *time.* At no time did I bother to think in terms of how long it would take me to write a single page. Why is that?

Again, it comes back to what is important. In the case of writing the book, I was not calculating how many pages I *could* write per day. I was determining how many I *needed* to write per day. There's a subtle difference there. In my case, I realized that I needed to work the book writing around the rest of my life. I could tell myself, "I need to manage to work in my three pages today." However, while this approach makes for a great mental bookmark, it doesn't do me much good for making decisions. For that, I *do* need to start to calculate things in terms where *time* is the important factor.

Putting Time at the Top

For instance, if I were to try to decide what my plans for the evening were on any given night, I would look at the available time. Let's say that after getting home from my "day job" of doing AI consulting, I determined that I had five hours into which to work all of my evening routine. Dinner would take one hour to cook and eat. Spending some time with the wife and kids would take another hour. That brings me down to three hours available for that evening. The question then arises, "Can I afford to watch a one-hour TV show and still get my three pages in?"

The only way I can answer this question is to know how much time it would take me to write those three pages—which is directly related to the value of *time per page.* I am able to assign time expenditures to dinner, time with the family, and even to the TV show that I am pondering. The only thing I don't know is the time value to assign to the three pages of writing. The rest of this decision exercise is not terribly relevant (let's just say I'm spending as much time as I can this weekend trying to catch up on the writing that I didn't get done during the week). The point is, however, that there are two separate measurements in play.

Originally, I had calculated how many *pages per day* I would need to write to finish the book on time (three). That differs significantly, however, from the calculation of how long I would have to leave in each day to accomplish the three-page goal. In that case, the value and utility of *time* as the primary measuring device becomes important. "Can I *spend* time watching the TV show and still have enough time to *spend* writing my book?" Notice the emphasis on *spending* time. How important is that TV show to me that I would spend time on it—perhaps in exchange for something that is not as important to me later in the week so that I can make up the time on my book?

IN THE GAME **Settlers and Warriors**

Similar sorts of gymnastics are often necessary when doing calculations for games. At times, it is not enough to know how long it takes to create something. You need to know how many *somethings* you can create in a particular amount of time.

Imagine that we are calculating a build order in a turn-based strategy (TBS) game. (We could do the same with an RTS game, but thinking in terms of "turns" instead of seconds or minutes is easier for this example.) In our game, we know that it takes three turns for a city to create a warrior. We also would like to use the production of these cities to create a new settler unit so we can expand our empire —as soon as possible. The settler takes five turns to create. Additionally, creating the settler unit is useless unless we can send a warrior along to protect it.

We also know that we could expect an attack in as few as 20 turns. We want to be able to defend our city with a minimum number of four warriors. The four warriors must be built and in place on that twentieth turn when the attacks could begin to occur.

One approach would be to build the four warrior units *first* and, once the city is suitably defended, proceed with building the settler and the escort warrior. However, because expanding our empire is a high priority, we want to begin that as soon as possible. The question is, can we afford to build the settler unit and its accompanying escort warrior *right away*, send them off in search of the promised land, and *then* begin cranking out our defenses? Will we have the four defensive warriors in place by the time the twentieth turn arrives?

Now, most of us will recognize this exercise as not much more than the word problems that were so maligned back when we were in math classes in school. (I never understood why people griped about the word problems so much. I kinda liked them! But then again, here I am writing a book on the mathematics of game AI.) Just like those word problems, the trick is putting things into their proper frame of reference.

For instance, we know by the rules of the game that a warrior takes three turns to produce. We also know that it takes five turns to produce our settler unit. For the sake of visualization, let's assign those to variables.

Time to produce a warrior: TW = 3
Time to produce a settler: TS = 5

If we were to produce our settler and warrior exploration team, it would take us eight turns:

$$T_{W+S} = T_W + T_S = 8$$

Subtracting that from the 20 turns during which we know we are going to be safe from attack leaves us with 12 turns. If we were to take the remaining 12 turns and build nothing but warriors, could we make our quota of four to have a suitable defense when the attacks come? I don't mean to be pedantic about this. I know we have all done this in our heads about three paragraphs ago. I'm merely trying to express a point… bear with me.

To do that, we need to express the equation not in terms of turns per warrior, but in terms of warriors per turn. Knowing that it takes three turns to produce a warrior, we know that we can produce one-third of a warrior per turn. Twelve turns of producing one-third of a warrior each gives us the following:

$$W = 12 \times \left(\frac{1}{3} warrior\right)$$

$$W = 12 \times \frac{1}{3} = \frac{12}{3} = 4$$

So, it would seem that we will be able to complete our four warriors in time for that magical twentieth turn deadline.

Certainly, we could have done the math the other way around—dividing the remaining 12 turns by 3 turns each—and arrived at the same result. The point was the mentality shift involved in putting things in terms of how much can we do *per time period* rather than in terms of how much time *per action*. This is important because it helps us frame time as a valid and useful *component* of utility rather than simply a *measurement* of utility. That is, we are "spending time" doing something rather than doing something "over a period of time."

When viewed as a whole process, building five soldiers and a settler takes 20 turns no matter which way we do it (Figure 7.11). However, we know that the settler unit has another job to do—that of starting a city. When he starts the city, the city will grow over time. The longer the time the city is established, the more it will grow. Therefore, *time* has a *utility* with regard to cities. If we want to maximize this utility, we want to maximize the time the city has to grow, which means that we want to start the city as soon as possible—that is, in the *least amount of time*. Therefore, the utility of time that is so important to the city is transferred to the settler itself. Any time *saved* in the process of building the settler has a valuable utility in our overall process.

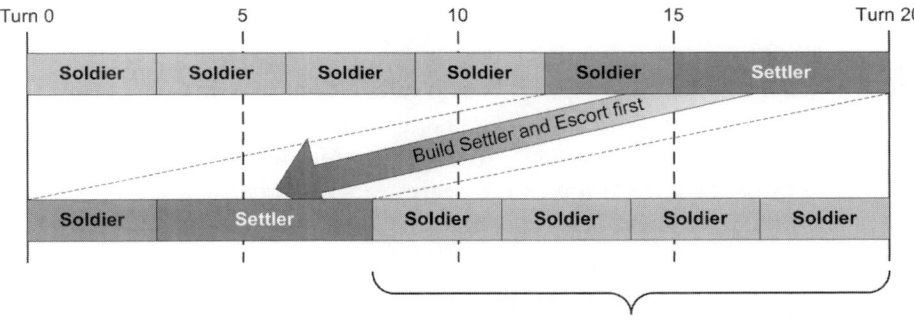

FIGURE 7.11 In terms of the number of each type of units produced, the end result of each build order is the same. If the settler has another job to do (presumably starting a new city), the time saved by building it with its escort first has a utility value.

DISTANCE OVER TIME

Another very important aspect to take into account when designing game AI is the relative value of time when attached to travel distance. If we had an agent deciding between two available cover points (see Figure 7.12), one consideration would be how far away those cover points are from the current location. All other things being equal, the closer cover point is a more attractive option. The further away the cover point is, the longer it would take to get there and, we would assume, the longer the agent is exposed to the threat from which he is trying to get cover.

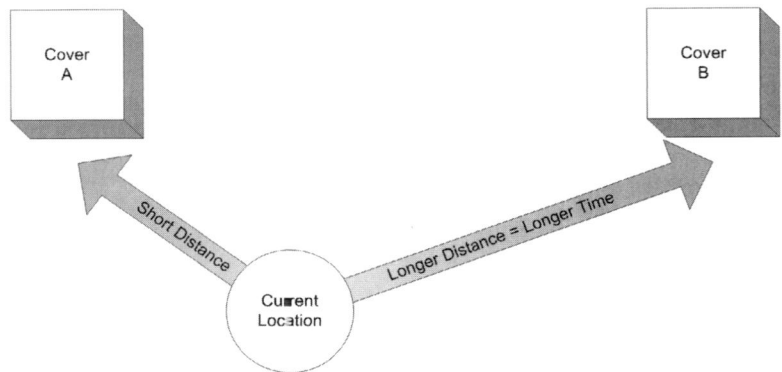

FIGURE 7.12 A common consideration for the utility of time is when it is calculated as a result of a traveled distance. In this case, the longer distance to cover B would require being exposed for a longer period of time.

This is hardly a surprise. We do calculations like this all the time. In fact, when constructing an AI that would take this into account, we likely wouldn't bother with converting the distance to time. It would be easier to simply sort the cover points by distance and pick the nearest one. As we discussed above, this is relegating time to the back seat once again.

Other considerations could be in play that may make us start to think about the value of time, however. For instance, if the path to cover point A is tougher terrain that would cause you to move slower, now we are thinking in terms of time. The distances may be the same, but it takes a longer time… that is, we are *spending* our time in traveling the rougher terrain. If we were using a pathfinding algorithm that incorporated terrain types or another such method of representing traversal time, this is a calculation that can be performed through those numbers. Regardless, the distance-time relationship is still somewhat interlinked.

There are times, however, when the time required to travel a distance would have to be compared to something less closely related. In the above example of cover points, the assumption was that all cover points are created equal. However, game agents are often presented with two objectives that are not only *not* the same thing (i.e., cover = cover) but are actually two *different* goals entirely (e.g., "raze *this* building" or "destroy *that* army"). When this occurs, the time involved must be included in whatever decision we are making regarding those goals.

If we were in a situation where the distance to each goal was the same (Figure 7.13), then the time factor would not be important (assuming there are no other factors to consider). We could make the decision based entirely on the relative values (V) of the two goals. Likewise, if the values of the goals were the same, such as in our cover point example, then we could rely solely on the distance comparison to make our decision. The situation is slightly more complicated when the distances and the values of the goals are different.

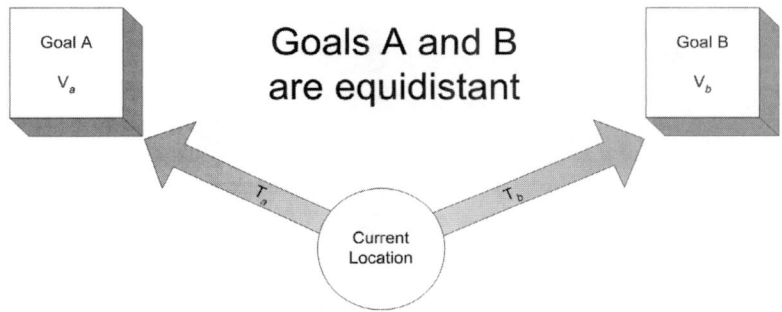

FIGURE 7.13 If the distances to the goals are the same, the values of the goals would be the deciding factor. On the other hand, if the values of the goals are the same, the distances to them may be the deciding factor.

Unequal Times to Unequal Goals

Let's assume that our agent is deliberating between accomplishing goal A and goal B (Figure 7.14). Each of those goals has a value (V) that we have calculated with other criteria. In addition to this, let's assume that the agent is currently closer to goal A. We now have a number of factors to consider. First, how much closer are we to goal A than to goal B? Second, what is the difference in importance of accomplishing goal A vs. goal B? Third, and perhaps most evasively, what is the *relative* importance of time compared to the values of the goals themselves?

Let's deal with the distance question first. For purposes of this argument, let's assume there are no terrain issues, so that distance can be directly related to time. It is not a difficult proposition to determine which distance is greater. The value we will need to determine, however, is *how much* different the distances are. After all, if the difference is negligible, there isn't much to lose by tackling the further goal. Just for the sake of putting it out there, however, let's show the formula.

$$T_n = T_b - T_a$$

We are simply calculating the difference (T_n) in the time it would take to reach goals A and B (T_a and T_b, respectively). For purposes of this example, we are assuming that we had already determined that B was the most distant—this way I don't have to clutter things up with absolute values and so on.

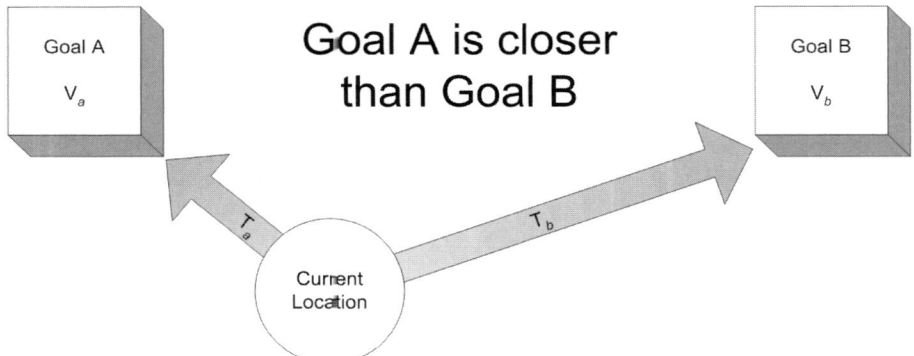

FIGURE 7.14 In this example, goal A is closer than goal B. We must consider both the values of the relevant goals as well as the time it takes to get to the goals.

At this point, T_n is simply a **linear difference**. We have only determined what the difference between them is numerically. For example, if $T_a = 10$ and $T_b = 25$, then T_n would be 15. While that is valid mathematically in that it allows us to compare the two values, it doesn't tell us as much about the *relationship* between them. For instance, if the distances to A and B were 1,000 and 1,015, respectively, T_n would still be 15. At that point, the difference of 15 is not terribly relevant. Obviously, that difference of 15 doesn't mean as much as the difference of 15 when the values were 10 and 25.

The solution, as we shall see throughout this section and indeed throughout this book, is to normalize the result against one of the values. We need to determine not what the *linear difference* is, but rather the **relative difference**. In other words, we want to express one of the values in terms of the other one. In this case, let's specifically compare all time values to that of the shortest time, T_n. Therefore,

$$T_n = \frac{T_b}{T_a}$$

If we insert the values $T_a = 10$ and $T_b = 25$, we find that $T_n = 2.5$. That is, traveling to goal B (T_b) is going to *cost* us two and a half times as much as we would spend getting to goal A (T_a).

All of this is fairly simple so far... no surprises yet. In fact, we can do much the same calculation with regard to the value of the goals themselves. Without getting too deep into what the goals are and how we arrived at the values (we'll tackle this problem later on in the book), let's assume that the value of goal A (V_a) is 50 and the value of goal B (V_b) is 75. Performing the same sort of calculation as we did with the time expenditures, we could determine that the difference in the values of the goals is:

$$V_n = \frac{V_b}{V_a} = \frac{75}{50} = 1.5$$

In English, the value of achieving goal B is one and a half times more valuable than what we secure by achieving goal A. Putting numbers like this into the form of relative difference helps us put things into perspective when comparing unlike types of values. For instance, if the difference in the value of the goals was 50% (such as above), but the difference in the time was only 1%, then the time difference isn't nearly as significant as the goal value difference.

All of that is well and good, but the question still comes up: Which goal should we pursue? Goal A is closer but not worth as much. Goal B is farther away but worth more. The only way we can solve this equation is to find a way of equating the value of *time* and the values of the *goals* themselves. We need to place some sort of algorithmic translation between the goal values and the time values. To do this, we need to have an idea of what their relationship is. The problem is very context specific, of course. The values would depend largely on the game design. Some examples might be:

- Destroying an army before it can attack
- Destroying a building before it can be completed
- Destroying a building before it can finish producing something
- Arriving at a defense location prior to the arrival of opposing forces

Of course, there may not be a particular reason that it is important to even pay attention to the time factor. However, if there is no time pressure involved in completing either goal A or goal B, and if we know that we could do both if we want to—and only need to select which *order* in which to do them—this problem is no longer a big deal. Naturally, the course of action would be to accomplish goal A first since it is nearby and then proceed to goal B when we are finished with A (Figure 7.15).

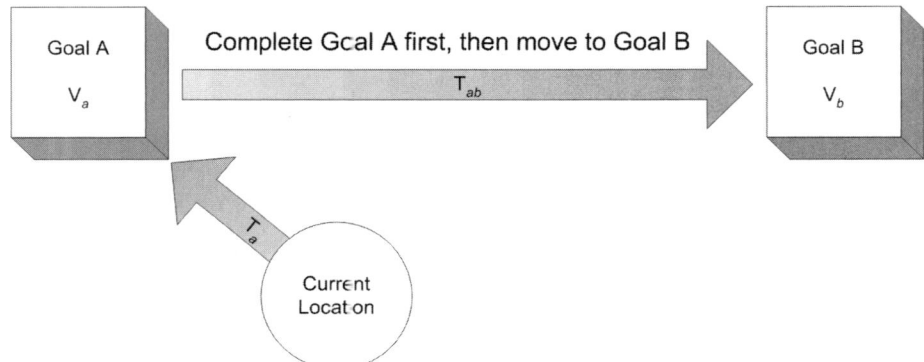

FIGURE 7.15 If the respective values of goal A and goal B are equal, there are no time restraints and no other considerations, then it is more efficient to complete goal A first and then proceed to goal B.

Regardless, if there is no detriment to putting off goal B (or goal A for that matter) until we can get around to it, there is really nothing to consider. In fact, what is to stop us from taking the scenic route and going all the way over to goal B first and then backtracking to goal A? Of course, if there is no time limit, then the value of the time spent getting there is not really relevant. So let's make it relevant…

CHANGES IN UTILITY OVER TIME

To make this problem *far* more interesting, let's assume that the values of accomplishing goals A and B will diminish over time. For simplicity's sake, let's assume that the rate of decay (r) for the goal values is the same for both A and B. This change causes an inherent utility in the time spent (or saved) in traveling to goals A and B. We can no longer take a leisurely approach. Again, this puts us back in the mindset of taking the shortest route through the two goals. There is one caveat, however… what if goal B was so important that it couldn't wait? Is there a point where accomplishing goal B quickly is urgent enough that we would postpone accomplishing goal A until later despite the fact that we are relatively close to it? Let's construct our formula and test a couple of cases.

The components that we need to consider are:

V_a The value of goal A
V_b The value of goal B
V_{ab} The total value of goals A and B
T_a The time to move to goal A
T_b The time to move to goal B

T_{ab} The time to move between A and B
r The rate that the values of goals A and B decay

The entire formula that we need for calculating the value of going to A first and then to B would be:

$$V_{ab} = V_a(1-(r \times T_a)) + V_b(1-(r \times (T_a + T_{ab})))$$

Let's restate that in English (left to right):

1. The total value of accomplishing A and B—in that order (V_{ab})…
2. is the value of A (V_a)…
3. after reducing it by the decay over the travel time ($1-(r \times T_a)$) …
4. plus the value of B (V_b)…
5. after reducing it by the decay over the travel time to A and from A to B ($1-(r \times (T_a + T_{ab}))$)

In step 5, it is important to note that we have to include the time it took to get to A and then from A to B. After all, the value of B was decaying that whole time. That's why we have to multiply the decay rate by ($T_a + T_{ab}$).

If we want to calculate the value of doing things via the reverse path (V_{ba}), which we need to do to compare them, we simply flip the As and Bs accordingly. (We can assume for now that the distance from A to B is the same as from B to A.)

$$V_{ba} = V_b(1-(r \times T_b)) + V_a(1-(r \times (T_b + T_{ab})))$$

To decide which route we should take, all that remains for us to do is to compare the values of V_{ab} and V_{ba} to see which one provides us with the highest value.

To test our scenario, let's plug in some numbers (Figure 7.16). First, let's see what happens when the goal values are the same. Let's use the following values.

V_a	The value of goal A	100
V_b	The value of goal B	100
T_a	The time to move to goal A	10
T_b	The time to move to goal B	25
T_{ab}	The time to move between A and B	45
r	The decay rate	1% per time period

Putting those values into the formula above, we arrive at:

$$V_{ab} = 100(1-(.01 \times 10)) + 100(1-(.01 \times (10+45))) = 135$$

$$V_{ba} = 100(1-(.01 \times 25)) + 100(1-(.01 \times (25+45))) = 105$$

As we can see, V_{ab} = 135 and V_{ba} = 105. That means, of the original combined value of goals A and B (200), we could achieve 135 by visiting A first (then B) and 105 by going the long way to B first and proceeding back to A. Put another way, by performing A first, we will achieve 68% of the possible total score, whereas we would only get 53% the other direction. (As these values change, it will be increasingly important for us to express the outcomes in terms of percentages.) This intuitively makes sense to us. At that point, we would expect that the greatest value lies in the path that takes the shortest time to execute... A first and then B.

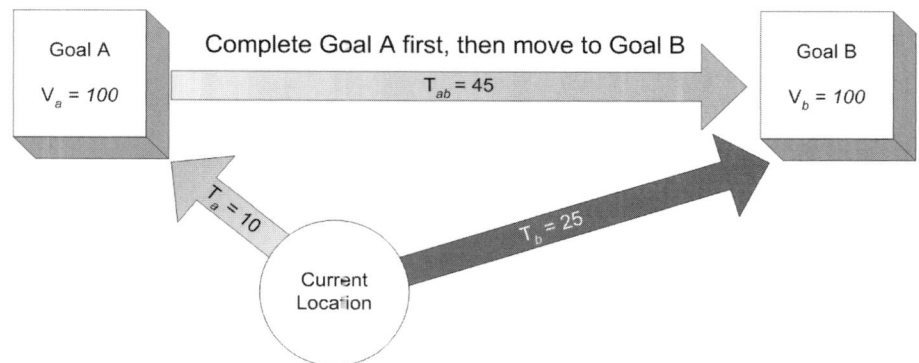

FIGURE 7.16 If the values of goal A and goal B start the same and are both decaying at the same rate, we should complete the closest goal first—in this case, goal A.

However, what if we raise the value of goal B to 200, for instance? We now have 300 potential value points between A and B. Leaving the distances the same as in the first example, we would arrive at:

$$V_{ab} = 100(1-(.01 \times 10)) + 180(1-(.01 \times (10+45))) = 171$$

$$V_{ba} = 180(1-(.01 \times 25)) + 100(1-(.01 \times (25+45))) = 165$$

We still have a situation where $V_{ab} > V_{ba}$, although the margin is a little tighter. The 210 out of 300 possible points is only 70%. We have lost 5% of the value that we accomplished in the first example. However, it is still greater than the 65% that we would achieve by going to B first. The best decision is still goal A, then B.

The fact that the margin of importance is decreasing tips us off to something. As the relative value of goal B increases as compared to goal A, we are no longer quite as sure of our decision to take on goal A first. What would happen if this trend were to continue?

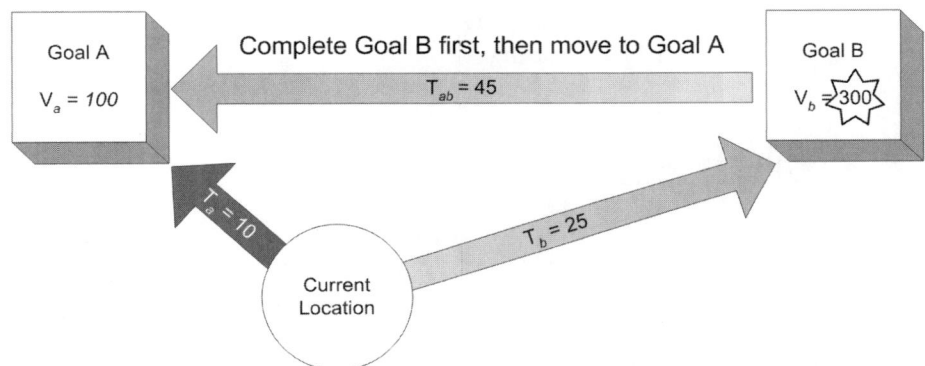

FIGURE 7.17 If the value of goal B is significantly greater than goal A, it becomes more worthwhile to travel the extra distance to goal B first to accomplish it as soon as possible before the value decays too much. We can then backtrack to goal A.

Let's try a third example (Figure 7.17). This time, we will increase the value of goal B to 400. All other values remain the same as before. This means the total value of all goals is now 500.

$$V_{ab} = 100(1-(.01\times 10)) + 300(1-(.01\times(10+45))) = 225$$

$$V_{ba} = 300(1-(.01\times 25)) + 100(1-(.01\times(25+45))) = 255$$

This time, $V_{ba} > V_{ab}$. We have passed a threshold where the importance of goal B has increased enough to warrant us going out of our way to accomplish it and only afterward backtracking to touch on goal A. In fact, if we were to put the equations up against each other and solve for V_b, we would find that when $V_b = 300$, the two solutions are equal… it wouldn't matter in which order you visited them.

The only reason the order was a factor in this decision is because there was a mechanism in play that caused *time* to be a factor—namely the decay rate (r) of the values of goals A and B. In the final example, goal B was not only worth more but, due to the 1% decay rate, was losing value four times as fast as goal A. In layman's terms, we "didn't have time to waste" in dealing with the lesser objective of goal A.

So, as we can see, the *time* one spends in travel is a valuable commodity. Similarly, the amount of time that may be spent in performing an activity also needs to be considered. If we were in an RTS environment, for example, goals A and B could be constructing buildings. Not only would the travel time to the locations need to be considered (such as we did above), but the time spent in the actual building process would need to be added. The process is much the same—the only difference being that we would have to include two more variables, one for the construction time of each building.

PUTTING IT IN CODE

Just as we did with the warranty and tower examples above, we can create a simple utility function to calculate the utility values of accomplishing the goals at various times. In this case, we can create a function, `GoalUtility()`, that calculates the utility of a particular goal. This is based on the value of the goal itself, the time spent traveling to the goal, and the decay rate at which the goal value will be reduced over that time. This function is the business end of the process in that it is the sole place where the utility of the goals is being calculated.

```
int MyGame::GoalUtility( int ValGoal,     // value of the goal
                         int Time,        // time to the goal
                         float Decay )    // decay rate %
{
    // Calculate utility of a goal based on the value of the
    // goal, the time traveled to get to it,
    // and the decay rate

    int Utility; // Temporary local utility value

    // Utility is the value of the goal reduced by however
    // much the value decays during the time over which
    // the distance is traveled
    Utility = ValGoal * ( 1.0 - ( Time * Decay ) );
```

```
    // Make sure the utility is a minimum of zero.
    if ( Utility < 0 ) Utility = 0;
    return Utility;
}
```

Then, in the function `SelectGoal()`, by calling that function with the appropriate values, we can determine which of the two approaches is going to yield the greatest utility. Note that for clarity, we have declared a type, GOAL_TYPE, which enumerates which of the two goals we are returning as our decision.

```
typedef enum {
    GOAL_A,
    GOAL_B
} GOAL_TYPE;

GOAL_TYPE MyGame::SelectGoal( int ValA, int ValB,
                              int TimeA, int TimeB, int TimeAB,
                              float Decay )
{
    // Process the utilities of going to goal A first then goal B
    // and going to goal B first then A.

    float UtilityAB; // Utility of going to goal A first
    float UtilityBA; // Utility of going to goal B first

    // Get utility of going to A then B
    UtilityAB = GoalUtility( ValA, TimeA, Decay )
              + GoalUtility( ValB, ( TimeA + TimeAB ), Decay );

    // Get utility of going to B then A
    UtilityBA = GoalUtility( ValB, TimeB, Decay )
              + GoalUtility( ValA, ( TimeB + TimeAB ), Decay );

    // Compare the two utilities to determine which is preferable
    if ( UtilityAB > UtilityBA ) {
```

```
            return GOAL_A;
    } else {
            return GOAL_B;
    }
}
```

There is nothing magical about the `SelectGoal()` function. Its purpose is simply to arrange the values appropriately for the `GoalUtility()` function to calculate the utility. If the scenario in which we are working changes, those changes would be reflected in `SelectGoal()`—or any other function that we want.

For example, if we were to change the scenario to include *three* possible goals from which we wanted to select the best two to combine, we could write a function that arranged and passed the appropriate values to `GoalUtility()`. This is a standard function pattern that, if you have done programming, you will likely recognize. Accordingly, you will see similar patterns throughout this book. For now, the point is that we have to get used to treating *time* as a parameter that has an inherent utility all its own.

IN THE GAME   **Taking Fire**

The consideration of the utility of time becomes clearer once we put it into a common game example. In keeping with a similar two-goal example like we have used above, imagine the following all-too-common shooter scenario.

We are in a firefight, currently wounded and pinned down behind some cover (Figure 7.18). On one side of us is some available Armor that, once used, reduces the rate of damage we take from enemy fire. On the other side is a Health Kit that, as one would expect, increases our total health. Both of them are exposed to enemy fire. As soon as we step out toward either one, we are going to start taking damage. We would like to acquire one or both of them and then return to our place of cover with more health than when we left. There are a few questions to solve:

- Is it even possible for us to arrive back at cover better off?
- Can we acquire the Armor as well as the Health Kit and have at least some of it remaining when we arrive back at cover?
- Does it matter in which order we acquire the items?

As with our previous examples, we need to know a bit about the world before we can process these decisions. Let's use the following variables to define the relevant items we will be using in the example.

Current Health	H_0
Ending Health	H_n
Value of Health Kit	V_h
Value of Armor	V_a
Time to Health Kit	T_h
Time to Armor	T_a
Time between Health Kit and Armor	T_{ha}
Rate of damage from enemy fire *without Armor*	D
Rate of damage from enemy fire *with Armor*	D_a

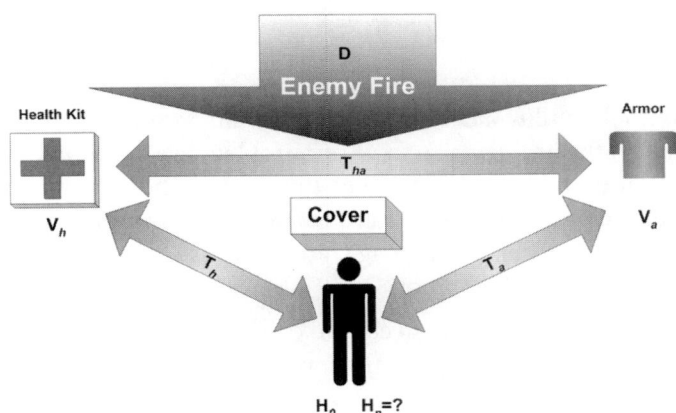

FIGURE 7.18 The agent needs to decide whether or not it can acquire the Health Kit, the Armor, or both and arrive back behind the cover better off than it left. The utility value of the time spent traveling under enemy fire is the greatest consideration.

As we are starting to get more complex in our calculations, at this point it would benefit us to break this process down into manageable sections. First, we need to establish formulas for how much damage we would take both with and without armor. We know the *rates* at which we will take damage, but how much damage we take is based entirely on the time we will be exposed. For example, if we run to the Health Kit, we would take damage as follows:

$DamageToHealth = T_h \times D$

Similarly, if we run to the Armor, the formula would be:

$$DamageToArmor = T_a \times D$$

And, if we ran between the Health Kit and Armor (assuming we did not yet have the armor), we would incur:

$$DamageHealthToArmor = T_{ha} \times D$$

The common thread here is that it is always the damage rate multiplied by the *time spent*. Assuming the values of the items themselves never change, the whole decision would be based on the *time* we are exposed to enemy fire and under what conditions (e.g., armored or not). Therefore, it is a simple and logical next step to condense the above three functions into a more generalized one that provides us the amount of damage we are going to incur in a period of time given a damage rate.

$$DamageTaken = Time \times DamageRate$$

With this utility function, we can throw any combination of time and damage rate we want at the problem. To solve our problem, we need three of these combinations —one for each leg of the trip. The times would be dependant on the distance and any other considerations we need to take into account (e.g., running slower while wearing the Armor). The damage rate, of course, would be based on whether or not we had picked up the Armor.

To test our theory, we need to try a couple of examples. Since the rate of damage taken on different legs of the journey is a factor, it would be best to have our first examples expose that as the deciding factor. Therefore, let's assume that the time to get to the Health Kit and the Armor are the same—five seconds. The long run from the Health Kit to the Armor (or vice versa) is eight seconds.

In the first test, let's assume that we are going to retrieve the Health Kit first and then go to the Armor. Using our damage utility function above, we arrive at the following results for each leg of the foray:

Leg	Time	Rate	Damage
Cover to Health Kit	5	2	10
Health Kit to Armor	8	2	16
Armor to Cover	5	1	5
Total	-	-	**31**

The total amount of damage that would be taken is 31.

If we were to reverse this path, getting the Armor first, the data would be:

Leg	Time	Rate	Damage
Cover to Armor	5	2	10
Armor to Health Kit	8	1	8
Health Kit to Cover	5	1	5
Total	-	-	23

In this case, the total amount of damage taken is only 23 points. This intuitively makes sense to us in that the difference in the second case was the fact that the long run across the middle was done *after* acquiring the Armor. Therefore, only half damage was taken during those eight seconds.

We can now run a couple of new tests with one of the objects being significantly farther away than the other. In this case, let's make the two cover runs 10 and 5, respectively. The run across the middle will have to be longer as well—we will make it 20. Once again, we will do two examples with this configuration—one with the Health Kit on the long side and one with the Armor there. The data ends up as follows:

Leg	Time	Rate	Damage
Cover to Health Kit	3	2	6
Health Kit to Armor	8	2	16
Armor to Cover	7	1	7
Total	-	-	29

The total amount of damage we would take is 29.

Again, if we were to reverse this path, getting the Armor first, the data would be:

Leg	Time	Rate	Damage
Cover to Armor	7	2	14
Armor to Health Kit	8	1	8
Health Kit to Cover	3	1	3
Total	-	-	25

That is, by getting the Armor first and *then* going to the Health Kit we would take a total of 25 points of damage. Once again, the results "feel right" to us. The best solution, given these circumstances, is to get the Armor first—even if it is farther away from cover. The reason for that is that while we may take a lot of damage running to get the distant Armor, we are very exposed for a long period of time running all the way across the zone. It would be better to have the Armor on for those 8 seconds than to not have it.

Of course, if we arranged the scenario so that our starting health was at or below 25, we would not be able to make it to the Armor and all the way back to the Health Kit before we died. In that case, every health point would matter significantly until we increased it. Therefore, it would be better to get the Health Kit first. But we shall explore those sorts of factors in the next chapter.

PUTTING IT IN CODE

As we discussed above, the *utility* function we used multiple times in this example is simply one of *time* and *rate* (of damage). Expressed in code, this function is as simple as it sounds.

```
int MyGame::Damage( int Time, int Rate )
{
    return ( Time * Rate );
}
```

The rest of the decision is based on how and when we use the utility function. By using it multiple times with the relevant data, we can construct a total amount of damage taken. All of this action is performed in the function `GetBestAction()`.

In this function, we have put a slightly different spin on how we arrive at the result. We start with our current health (`mMyHealth`) and then reduce that health value by the damage that is taken on each leg of the trip. The result is stored in `HealthFirst` or `ArmorFirst`, respectively. The reason we do this becomes clear at the bottom of the function. If our starting health is greater than *both* of the results, then it is clearly in our best interests to not leave the cover spot at all! (Note that I did not check for the possibility of running out of health along the way. That logic is not the point of the example and will actually be handled in a far more interesting way in the next chapter.)

Once again, for visual clarity in returning a value from the function `GetBestAction()`, we use an enumerated type, `GOAL_TYPE`. This is, of course, entirely cosmetic for purposes of this example.

```
typedef enum {
    GOAL_NONE,              // Do not get either
    GOAL_HEALTH_ARMOR,      // Get Health Kit first
    GOAL_ARMOR_HEALTH       // Get Armor first
```

```cpp
} GOAL_TYPE;

GOAL_TYPE MyGame::GetBestAction()
{
    // Calc our remaining health if we get the Health Kit first
    int HealthFirst = mMyHealth
                    - Damage( mTimeToHealth, mDamageRate )
                    - Damage( mTimeHealthToArmor, mDamageRate )
                    - Damage( mTimeToArmor, mArmoredDamageRate )
                    + mHealthKitValue;


    // Calc our remaining health if we get the Armor first

    int ArmorFirst = mMyHealth
                    - Damage( mTimeToArmor, mDamageRate )
                    - Damage( mTimeHealthToArmor, mArmoredDamageRate )
                    - Damage( mTimeToHealth, mArmoredDamageRate )
                    + mHealthKitValue;


    // If both methods would leave us WORSE off than we started
    // then do neither.

    if (    ( mMyHealth > HealthFirst ) &&
            ( mMyHealth > ArmorFirst ) ) {
        return GOAL_NONE;
    }


    // Return which of the two approaches will leave us with
    // the most remaining health.

    if ( HealthFirst > ArmorFirst ) {
        return GOAL_HEALTH_ARMOR;
```

```
        } else {
            return GOAL_ARMOR_HEALTH;
        }
    }
```

The above function is now able to decide based on any values we throw at it. No matter what the travel times are or what the damage rate is, we will find out which of the three approaches is best.

One More Factor Couldn't Hurt

Upon further examination of the details of this adventure, we can prove that getting the Armor first is always the correct thing to do. The reason is that the sum of the lengths of two sides of a triangle is always longer than the length of the third. Given the parameters of our situation, it is better to be wearing armor while running two sides rather than running only one.

However, this is a visitor from the realm of cold geometric theory. If we could guarantee that all our scenarios ONLY had those components in them, that would be, as they say in certain geometric circles, *peachy*. However, trying to teach our bots basic theories and getting them to apply them at the appropriate times is a bit outside the scope of game development. Our job, instead, is to provide them with tools they can apply in any situation.

If we add one more component to this example, we ruin the simple triangle theory. Let's assume the value of the Health Kit declines over time at a rate of 1 point per second. Therefore, the quicker we get to it, the more benefit we get from it. Now we are dealing with two different changes over time. The amount of change in our health from taking fire and the amount of benefit we get from the Health Kit.

Tweaking our example once again, let's assume that a Health Kit starts at 100 points and declines by 1 point per second.

Leg	Time	Rate	Damage	Health Added	Net
Cover to Health Kit	3	2	−6	+97	
Health Kit to Armor	8	2	−16		
Armor to Cover	7	1	−7		
Total	-	-	−29	+97	+68

We would sustain 29 points of damage and gain 97 health. This results in a net gain of 68 points.

Again, if we were to reverse this path, getting the Armor first, the data would be:

Leg	Time	Rate	Damage	Health Added	Net
Cover to Armor	7	2	−14		
Armor to Health Kit	8	1	−8	+85	
Health Kit to Cover	3	1	−3		
Total	-	-	−25	+85	+60

By adding this one simple factor, we have reversed our original decision. If we had proceeded on our original route of getting the Armor first, we still would have taken 25 damage points over that time. However, the Health Kit that *was* worth 100 when we started was only worth 85 by the time we reached it 15 seconds later. Our net gain for the three legs of the triangle would be 60. On the other hand, when we go to get the Health Kit first, it only loses 3 points, down to 97. We still take 29 points of damage from fire during our brief stroll, but we end up with a net of 68 points greater than when we started.

In this example, if we were to *only* consider the (very relevant) factor that it is better to be wearing armor when running out in front of enemy fire, we would have decided to get the Armor first—and we would have been worse off in the end. However, by recognizing the fact that the utility of time counts in *two* ways, we were able to make the correct decision.

PUTTING IT IN CODE

To reflect the fact that the value of the Health Kit is *not* static, we need to simply replace the line where we added the Health Kit with a call to a function. This function acts much the same way as our damage function does.

```
int MyGame::HealthKitValue( int Time, int Rate )
{
    int HealthKitEndingValue;

    // Calculate the ending value of the Health Kit
    HealthKitEndingValue = mHealthKitValue - ( Time * Rate );

    // A Health Kit can never be less than 0
    if ( HealthKitEndingValue < 0 ) HealthKitEndingValue = 0;

    return HealthKitEndingValue;
}
```

Notice that we have trapped this function so that the value of the Health Kit can never be negative. No matter how late we are in arriving at the kit, it will never actually *damage* us.

Our resulting decision code would then be:

```
GOAL_TYPE MyGame::GetBestAction2()
{
    // This implementation includes the fact that
    // the value of the Health Kit decays over time

    // Calc our remaining health if we get the Health Kit first
    int HealthFirst = mMyHealth
                    - Damage( mTimeToHealth, mDamageRate )
                    - Damage( mTimeHealthToArmor, mDamageRate )
                    - Damage( mTimeToArmor, mArmoredDamageRate )
                    + HealthKitValue( mTimeToHealth,
                                      mHealthKitDecayRate );

    // Calc our remaining health if we get the Armor first

    int ArmorFirst = mMyHealth
                    - Damage( mTimeToArmor, mDamageRate )
                    - Damage( mTimeHealthToArmor, mArmoredDamageRate )
                    - Damage( mTimeToHealth, mArmoredDamageRate )
                    + HealthKitValue(mTimeToArmor + mTimeHealthToArmor,
                                      mHealthKitDecayRate );

    // If both methods would leave us WORSE off than we started
    // then do neither.

    if ( ( mMyHealth > HealthFirst ) &&
         ( mMyHealth > ArmorFirst ) ) {
        return GOAL_NONE;
    }
```

```
        // Return which of the two approaches will leave us with
        // the most remaining health.

        if ( HealthFirst > ArmorFirst ) {
            return GOAL_HEALTH_ARMOR;
        } else {
            return GOAL_ARMOR_HEALTH;
        }
    }
```

The differences from our earlier version is that we replaced the variable `mHealthKitValue` with the function call `HealthKitValue(mTimeToHealth, mHealthKitDecayRate)`.

If we wanted to, we could continue to add factors to this decision. What if we want to consider the likelihood that the Health Kit or Armor will still *be there* by the time we arrive? All we need to do is add additional variables or functions to calculate the various utilities and apply them to the decision equation itself.

Additionally, we could extend this function to accommodate many possible end decisions. For example, perhaps it is best to go out and get *only* the Armor? Or *only* the Health Kit? What if we included a third potential stop along the way—such as a nifty weapon. We would only need to process our different utility values and compare them at the end. Theoretically, we could have many different possibilities stored in an array or a list and, after processing them all, sort them by the result value and see which one is the best. But now we are really getting ahead of ourselves. We will revisit this later on. (Aren't you excited?)

OUR UTILITY OF UTILITY

What we have covered in this chapter is what amounts to a core building block of decision making. It is the measuring stick with which we determine how important the different sides of a problem are to us. In the Prisoner's Dilemma, this was the length of time in jail. In Cutting the Cake, our utility for cake was what made us *want* to make sure we got the biggest piece possible.

In the Ultimatum, Dictator, and Trust Games, utility was measured in terms of money—and yet there a few other things sneaking into the equation... Guilt? Fear? Altruism? These factors prevented us from electing to purely maximize our utility for money. In the Pirate Game, money was certainly a factor, but fear was definitely on our minds. We wanted to avoid getting tossed overboard!

We found out that, despite our fears, you have to sometimes risk utility to gain utility. Pascal was afraid of risking eternal damnation—whatever he believed that entailed. He apparently put a pretty negative utility value on it. He was willing to risk changing his lifestyle to avoid that and garner the infinitely positive outcome.

Making the decision to buy a warranty on our seemingly doomed computer was a simple calculation—until we pondered how much the utility of having a working computer was really worth to us. In a similar vein, how much is it worth to protect our barracks with a tower? Is the utility more than the simple value of building the tower? It seemed like it was—especially when we considered that there may be a deterrent factor to simply *having* one around. Even if it never gets used, if it prevents the enemy from attacking simply because it is there, that is of great utility to us.

Marci wanted to win the game of Monopoly (I think) but her utility of winning wasn't as high as her utility of *not losing*. She didn't want to take the risk, so she kept her properties to herself. That drove up the relative utilities of the properties she held in *other* people's eyes. Those utilities made the asking price *far* more than what was printed on the Monopoly board. Getting those properties meant *potential* for the future. Just like building the tower could reduce the *potential* of an attack, getting a matched property in Monopoly gave us the *potential* for more income later on.

And time… we spend it, we waste it, we take damage under fire during it. Time has a utility that often needs to be taken into consideration. The actual passage of time, in and of itself, is a powerful factor that needs to be measured and pondered.

So… with all of the above, we seem to have found a way of placing concrete numbers on factors in our environment. *This* is worth *that*. *This* is worth far more than *this other thing*. On the other hand, *this* is nowhere near as important as *those things over there*. However, another caveat is lurking about. The utility of an item may change. Not just from one day to the next, but from one *moment* to the next. From one *item* to the next—even if they are the exact same type of item.

Even from one chapter to the next…

8 Marginal Utility

In Chapter 7, we discussed how objects or actions can have relative merits that may differ from their values. Different items have different utilities to different people or even in different situations. However, going a bit further, the same item may have a *different* utility to the same person at a different *time*. This complicates our calculations significantly. We cannot simply count on something having a particular utility any time we encounter it. We experience a constant ebb and flow in the relative utilities of those items. How, then, can we use utility in our calculations? If the utility is always changing, what is something *really* worth? That is the struggle with trying to quantify utilities.

For instance, when I get up in the morning, having a can of caffeinated pop is pretty high on my priority list. I have to admit that, at that point in my day, even the idea of my wife's coffee-flavored milk (latte) is almost attractive to me (although still a little peculiar). That early in the day, caffeine of *any* sort has a higher appeal. I figure I'm not alone in this assessment. At a different time of the day, however, my utility for caffeine is not as great. The can size is the same, the milligrams of caffeine per ounce are the same—everything about my intake of the product is the same. The difference is that it's just not that important to me at that time. The utility has changed simply based on the time of day.

Moving one square further down this path, even the changes in the amount of something that someone *already has* in an item can represent different increases in utility. As I mentioned, I like that first can of pop in the morning. In fact, I like it about as much as I can like any can of pop during the day (100% value). I like the second shot of caffeine quite a bit as well. It isn't the same as getting that first dose, however. There has been a drop-off in the utility that I have for it. As the day progresses, each additional can of pop has a smaller utility for me (Figure 8.1). I am still gaining utility from each can, just not as much as the one before, and certainly not as much as I received from the first can. Eventually, I get to a point where the utility of a can of pop is next to zero. I am not getting any utility out of it at all. I could take it or leave it.

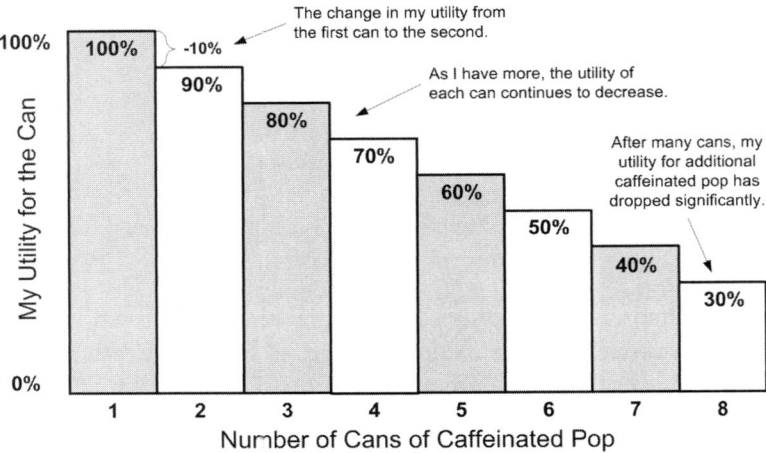

FIGURE 8.1 After I have had my first can of caffeinated pop in the morning, the utility that I get from each additional can drops. Eventually, that utility drops to almost nothing—that is, I'm not really getting anything out of it any more.

Each additional can does not mean the same as the one before it. The amount of pop that each can adds (the value) is the same. Similarly, each additional can provides me with utility. However, it is simply not as useful to me. The change in utility from one can to the next is the **marginal utility** that I have for that next can.

VALUE VS. UTILITY VS. MARGINAL UTILITY

As we discussed earlier in Chapter 7, the notion of "value" is generally linked to something concrete. However, "utility" is usually somewhat more ephemeral. Even something as simple as a $20 bill has a somewhat amorphous utility. Its value is based on the two and the zero emblazoned on it for all to see. Its utility can be more of an "eye of the beholder" function, however. What makes marginal utility tick, however, is that the beholder himself can change his perception of the exact same value... much like me and my morning pop. As the perception of the value changes, the utility changes. The change from one point to the next is the marginal utility.

For instance, a starving person on the street would find the $20 bill extraordinarily attractive, would covet it greatly, and do whatever he could to acquire and protect it. That $20 bill has a large utility for this person. For that matter, a second $20 bill would have a fairly large marginal utility as well—only slightly smaller than the first. Note that marginal utility works both ways. Just as gaining that first $20 was very important, losing it would be tragic.

A person of moderate means (such as a game developer) would find the $20 bill at least interesting and likely wouldn't turn it down if offered. On the other hand, that same person may be of the mind to part with it if someone were in need. The marginal utility of $20 has tapered off somewhat. In this case, gaining $20 is moderately attractive and losing $20, while not pleasant, is only moderately distressing.

For someone who has plenty of twenties lying around, the utility of any given one of them is low. Getting an additional one is likely not worth the calories you would burn in raising an eyebrow about it. Likewise, giving one away is just as uneventful. In fact, I'm sure that there are people who would not be terribly concerned if one fell out of their pockets and landed on the street in front of the aforementioned starving person. After all, what is twenty bucks when you're sitting on twenty million?

The differences between how these three people view that $20 bill is a function of how many twenties they already have. The more twenties they have, the smaller the marginal utility of each individual one that they gain or lose. When placed into the equation of decisions such as purchasing the warranty on a computer or buying a $5 latte, these differences in the utility that person places on both the money and the purchase come into play.

CHANGES IN MARGINAL UTILITY

The very fact that utility *can* change is the reason utility is important. If utility never changed no matter where we were on the scale against which we were measuring it, it would be far easier to calculate. We could often simply apply a ratio between the value of an item or action and its corresponding utility. However, the changes in utility that take place over that scale are what justifies treating utility as a separate entity from value in the first place. Therefore, much of the discussion about utility revolves around *marginal utility*—that is, the changes in utility.

The reason marginal utility is important is that it can change as well. In the example of the $20 bill above, the utility of the $20 bill was different for the poor person, the average person, and the rich person. Because of that, the marginal utility of an additional $20 bill was different for them as well. However, there are not simply three categories of people—poor, average, and rich. There is a continuous transition between someone who has nothing and someone who has everything. So at what point does the utility (and likewise the marginal utility) of those $20 bills change? The answer is that there is a *continuous* change happening. Each additional $20 bill has a utility. As we move from one bill to the next, the utility changes.

Decreasing Marginal Utility

Returning to my caffeine example, in Figure 8.1 we graphed the utility of each can of pop and the utility that each can provided me in terms of caffeine. Each additional can provided less and less utility. If we were to graph this in terms of my total caffeine intake, we can see how the changes in the utility of each can are reflected in my overall utility for caffeine (Figure 8.2). For clarity, we have made the graph continuous instead of per can. (Think in terms of milligrams of caffeine instead of cans.)

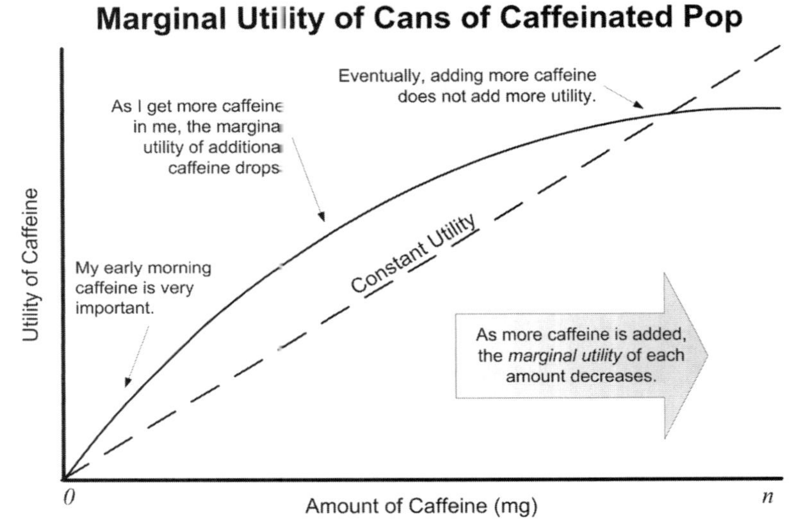

Marginal Utility of Cans of Caffeinated Pop

FIGURE 8.2 As additional milligrams of caffeine are added, the utility I gain from them still increases but at a slower rate. The change in utility from one milligram to the next is the marginal utility for that milligram.

As we can see, each milligram of caffeine adds more utility. The amount of utility it adds changes depending on how many I already have in me. Initially (left side of the graph), each unit increases the total utility by a large amount. This is the same as what is shown in Figure 8.1—the first can of caffeine was the most important. This is apparent from the initial slope of the graph in Figure 8.2.

By the time we get to the right side of Figure 8.2, it is similar to what we saw with the last can in Figure 8.1. Utility is being added, but not as much. Again, this is evidenced in Figure 8.2 by the slope of the graph being almost horizontal. Not much utility is added by increasing the amount of caffeine.

The slope of the graph is particularly important. At any given point along the graph, it is that slope that represents the marginal utility. As the marginal utility between any two points changes, the slope of the line between those two points changes as well. If the slope is changing as we progress along the line, we can identify the very important features **decreasing marginal utility** and **increasing marginal utility**.

Figure 8.3 shows a small segment of a utility curve. As the value changes from x to y on the graph, the utility changes by a. Therefore a is the marginal utility of the change in value from x to y. Likewise, as we change from value y to z, the utility changes by b. The marginal utility of y to z is b. When we compare the marginal utilities a and b, we find that $b < a$. Therefore, as our value moves from 0 to n, we see *decreasing* marginal utility.

Decreasing Marginal Utility

- a is the marginal utility of going from x to y.
- b is the marginal utility of going from y to z.
- $slope_a = \dfrac{a}{i}$
- $slope_b = \dfrac{b}{i}$
- Because $b < a$, marginal utility is *decreasing* as value moves from 0 to n.

FIGURE 8.3 A segment of a utility curve. Despite the fact that the total utility is increasing, the *marginal utility* of each additional unit is *decreasing*.

| IN THE GAME | **Building Soldiers** |

Marginal utility has a very important part in game mathematics. Remember that utility represents the "importance" of something. Naturally, decision making involves deciding what things are important, which things are more important than others, and even *how much more* important things are. However, the importance of something is not static—just as the importance of the $20 bill is not static and the importance of any given milligram of caffeine is not static. Things change.

Marginal utility represents the *change* in importance of something. Accordingly, the factors that go into our agents' decision making may change in importance. By taking into account not only the importance of something but the *change* in importance, we can craft our agents with more realistic, dynamic decision-making ability.

Plenty of examples can be invoked of times when a linear approach would look inefficient or even silly compared to one that respects marginal utility. An example of utility gone awry would be building units in a strategy game (Figure 8.4). When you build your first military unit, that unit has a utility that may even be *greater* than its value. (Remember the "deterrent effect" of the tower in Chapter 7?) After all, it is important to us to have *something* there to defend our city. However, as we build more and more units, the *marginal utility* of each one diminishes. We could lose one and not even really care. At some point, our build manager might want to say "enough is enough" lest we end up with a ridiculously sized army that is an essay in overkill. If we were to *not* take decreasing marginal utility into account, the build manager may continue to crank out units assuming that each one is just as important as the first.

This becomes even more important if there are multiple uses for the same resources. There is probably never a point where we could say that building another soldier is *not* valuable. However, once our army is "big enough," that is, the *marginal utility* of an extra unit is negligible, the *value* of the resources that would have been spent on that unit could be spent on something else that had a *higher* utility. That is, as the importance of building a soldier decreases, it may look less important than

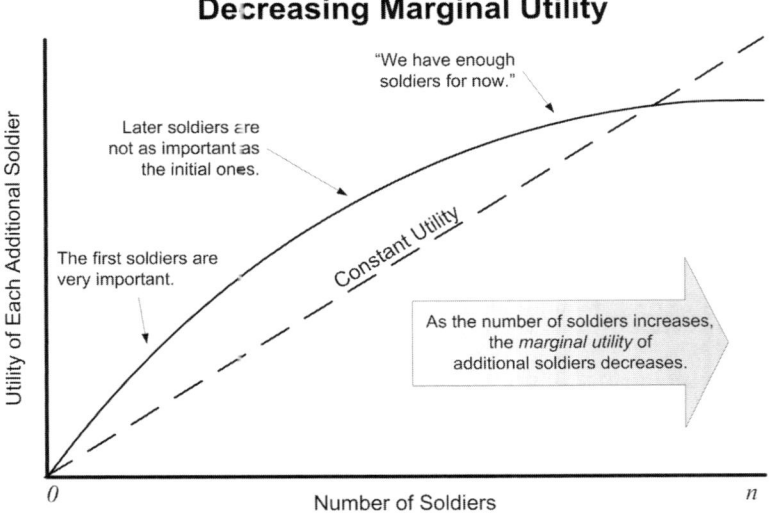

FIGURE 8.4 The first soldiers built are very important. As we build more units, the marginal utility of each additional unit decreases until we arrive at a point where we have "enough."

building other things. A more colloquial way of saying this is that you could spend your resources where you get the most "bang for your buck" at any given time.

Constructing the Formula

There are a number of different ways that we could construct formulas to express the changing marginal utility of building the soldiers. Which one we choose depends largely upon how we want our build manager to view the relative importance of the soldiers.

For a simple example, we will use a linear function. This is similar to our caffeine example at the beginning of the chapter (Figure 8.1). There is a steady decline from the first unit to the last. Let's assume we want to build 10 soldiers. As we discussed earlier, we are more interested in building the first soldier then we are in building the tenth. If we were to start with a maximum utility of 100 for the first soldier and reduce the utility by 10 points for each additional soldier, the utility of the 10th soldier built would be 10. This could be expressed with the following formula (in terms of the utility of the nth soldier):

$$U(S_n) = ((11-n) \times 10)$$

This would yield the following utility values for the soldiers:

Soldier	Utility
1	100
2	90
3	80
...	...
9	20
10	10

Just as we have seen in our previous examples, the utility of the first soldier is high. The second soldier is also important. While the 10th soldier does have a positive utility, it is relatively insignificant compared to the respective utilities of the earlier soldiers. The marginal utility of each subsequent soldier decreases; the importance of building each soldier after the first decreases.

One problem with this approach, however, is that it continues on in this fashion beyond the 10th soldier. The 11th soldier would have a utility of zero, which is probably interpreted as being useless. Worse still, the 12th soldier would have a utility of −10. The marginal utility has become negative. In other words, the importance of acquiring this next soldier is actually detrimental. The implication is that we would be better off if this soldier had never been built. While that may sound like something a particularly abusive drill sergeant may scream at a recruit, it doesn't make much sense in what we are trying to accomplish.

Certainly, there are times when marginal utility could turn negative. In my caffeine example, having too much is probably not a good thing. This effect is far more noticeable with beer. Eventually, having that next one *is* going to be detrimental. Having one more beyond that is going to even be *more* injurious. The next one beyond that... well, you get the point.

In this case, the problem we encountered was that we assumed that 10 soldiers are all we would need. (As we will see a little later, this approach *does* have its benefits in certain circumstances.) A better solution is to construct a formula that reduces the marginal utility of each soldier as we acquire more yet allows that marginal utility to stay positive.

For example, consider the formula:

$$U(S_n) = \frac{100}{n}$$

The values we are arrive at are:

Soldier	Utility
1	100
2	50
3	33
4	25
...	...
9	11.1
10	10
11	9.1
...	...
15	6.7
...	...
20	5
...	...
50	2
...	...
100	1

We are certainly showing decreasing marginal utility in the above table. Also, as we wanted, the formula will yield a positive marginal utility for any positive number of soldiers. However, the curve is significantly different from what we achieved from our original formula. Notice that there is a very large drop-off between the first and second soldiers. In our original example, the second soldier had a marginal utility of 90. It was almost as important to us as the first one. Likewise, the third soldier had a marginal utility of 80, whereas in this example, it is 33.

This seems to run counter to what we originally intended... concentrating on building initial soldiers. What we need is a formula that supports n soldiers without giving a negative utility but keeps to the spirit of the original formula—that the marginal utility should stay high initially and drop off later on once a reasonably sized force has been built.

Let's change to this (somewhat contrived) formula:

$$U(S_n) = 100\left(.95^{3(n-1)}\right)$$

Our results would now be:

Soldier	Utility
1	100
2	86
3	74
4	63
...	...
9	29
10	25
11	21
...	...
15	12
...	...
20	5
...	...
50	0.053
...	...
100	0.00002

This is a bit more in line with what we originally intended. The marginal utility of the second and third soldiers is still high, that is, it is still important for us to build them. Additionally, as we look toward the 9th and 10th soldiers, we see that the values are much lower than those of the initial soldiers. We have also solved our problem of negative utility. While the marginal utility continues to decrease, it approaches but never reaches zero. Even the 100th soldier has *some* marginal utility to us, albeit a very small one.

The difference between the three formulas is apparent when we graph them together (Figure 8.5). In the case of the first, linear formula (the solid line), the marginal utility decreased but was destined to cross into negative territory shortly after the 10th soldier. The dashed line shows the undesirable rapid drop-off in marginal utility that the second formula provided.

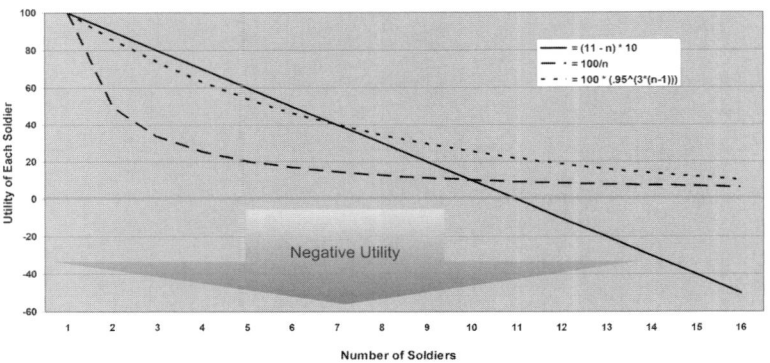

FIGURE 8.5 All three of the example formulas show decreasing marginal utility yet exhibit very different characteristics such as the rate of decrease or eventually intercepting the *x*-axis.

The dotted line is the result of the third formula. Its curve is in the same neighborhood as the original, linear formula. Even by simply eyeballing the graph, we can tell there is a different characteristic, however. It approaches the axis but at a steadily decreasing rate. As we saw from the data, even if we extended this line out to 100, it would not have reached a marginal utility of zero. Constructing curves that exhibit this characteristic is a key to building suitable algorithms in behavioral mathematics. We will get into more detail on how to approach these issues later in the book.

INCREASING MARGINAL UTILITY

In the above case, the marginal utility decreased as a certain point was approached. Contrary to that, sometimes marginal utility can *increase*. In this case, something that may not be important originally may become *more* important as the situation changes. As the other end of the scale is approached, the marginal utility increases, making each additional unit more and more important.

Often, increasing marginal utility is tied to goals. For example, the minimum purchase price of an object is a goal that must be attained. If we wanted to purchase a new video game at a price of $60 (I may have just unwittingly dated this book), the first dollar we save is not very important. We do not have much money, and the goal is distant. In fact, we may not be certain that we are ever going get to the goal of $60. On the other hand, if we have $59, we know we are almost at our goal. We find ourselves saying, "Just one more!" The marginal utility of that last dollar is far greater to us than the early ones.

Another example of increasing marginal utility is accumulating properties in Monopoly. In Chapter 7, I related how Marci would not accumulate properties through trading. She did not realize the value of how each additional property she acquired gave her more leverage than the one before.

In Monopoly, it is important to continue to acquire properties. This is evidenced by how one single property does not provide much income. Similarly, having two properties—even if they are the same color—does not provide a utility that is much greater than the stated values on the deeds. Acquiring the third property in a group, however, greatly increases the amount of income that can be collected from an opponent landing on any one of the three properties. The marginal utility of acquiring the *third* property is greater than the utilities of purchasing either the first for the second property. It's because of this increased marginal utility of acquiring the third property in any given set that the other players and I were so desperate and willing to trade so heavily to acquire those properties from Marci. We found ourselves saying, "Just one more!"

In fact, identifying scenarios that involve increasing marginal utility is often as simple as finding situations in which the phrases "just one more" and "almost there" are appropriate. Those phrases highlight the relative importance of the steps that are necessary to finish a task or achieve a goal.

 IN THE GAME **Declining Health**

In our Health Kit and Armor example in the previous chapter, we alluded briefly to a caveat that could possibly affect our interest in pursuing the Health Kit. Specifically, the lower we are on health, the more important the Health Kit is to us—despite the fact that the *value* of the Health Kit does not change. If we have 80% health and are only loosing it at the rate of two points per second, getting a 50% Health Kit isn't a very high priority. If we have 50% health and are losing it at the same rate, we might want to keep an eye out for one. If we only have 20% health, it becomes a top priority. The reason for this is that the last 20 points of health we lose—those between 20 and 0—are *far* more important than the first 20 points of health we lose —from 100 down to 80. That is, the marginal utility of each health point increases as our health drops lower.

In that example, we considered that the utility of a single point of health was static. Fifty percent is fifty percent. However, we may not have been comfortable letting our health get too low in the interim even if the outcome would have been better in the end.

This phenomenon is more apparent if we compare the importance of the *first* health point (e.g., from 100 to 99) lost to that of the *last* health point we may lose (Figure 8.6). Obviously, losing that first point of health is not important. Losing the last one is… well… *fatal.* By extension, losing the *next*-to-last one is pretty darn important as well. On the other hand, going from 99 to 98 isn't anything to fret about. The same could be said for going from 98 to 97. Someplace in the middle ranges of health, however, these two views on the importance of a single point of health are going to have to meet. Eventually, as we continue to lose health point by point, we are going to have to be more concerned about bleeding all over the place. Accordingly, the importance of each health point lost is gradually going to increase. That is, the marginal utility of each health point *increases* as we approach zero health.

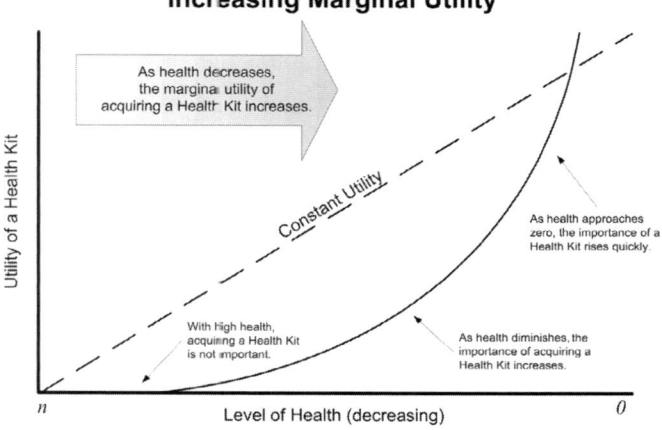

FIGURE 8.6 As our level of health decreases, marginal utility of the Health Kit increases. The lower we are on health, the more important it is to find a Health Kit to replenish our supplies.

If we had taken that into consideration as we decided whether to acquire the Health Kit or the Armor first, our outcome may have been different. The solution to that problem may have been to assign a utility to the Health Pack that differed from its "face value." That is, treat it as *less* than 50 if we have high health, but *more* than 50 if we are running low. That way, when we considered our health status at the end of each leg, we may have revised our decision as to whether or not to get the Armor or the Health Kit first. To repeat, if our health is low (e.g., 20), 50 points of added health mean more to us than adding the same 50 points when our health is high (e.g., 80).

Increasing Is Not Always the Inverse of Decreasing

It is worth noting that the Health Kit example could have been expressed in terms of *decreasing* marginal utility as well. However, caution must be exercised in transposing the utility curve. In Figure 8.6, our level of health is expressed as decreasing as we move from left to right. Consequently, the utility of the Health Kit is *increasing* as we moved from left to right as well. On the left side, we express very little utility for the Health Kit, as our health level is high. On the right, as our health nears zero, the Health Kit is of great utility. When dealing with marginal utility, however, the shape of the curve is important. It is not enough to simply say "low utility when health is high; high utility when health is low." How the marginal utility changes over the course of the progression is important as well.

Again referring to Figure 8.6, there is no movement in the utility of the Health Kit when our health is high (the left side). Only at the end (when health gets critical) do we see major movement in the *marginal* utility of the Health Kit. The rate of increase in the utility (the marginal rate) is at its greatest just as our health value approaches zero. This makes sense to us—the urgency of acquiring a Health Kit gets significant as we are about to die.

When we reverse the axis so that health is now *increasing* from left to right, we want to represent the marginal utility of the Health Kit as *decreasing* from left to right (Figure 8.7). However, we must take care to replicate the same progressive effect on the marginal rate. Both lines in the graph represent decreasing marginal utility. The difference between them is *when* that change is at its greatest rate.

If we were to duplicate the effect in Figure 8.6, we would need to use the solid line in Figure 8.7. This is best examined by working from the right side of the graph (n) and back toward zero at the left. Traversing the graph in this direction gives us the same result as that illustrated in Figure 8.6: The utility for a Health Kit stays small and then slowly increases until the urgency rises significantly close to zero.

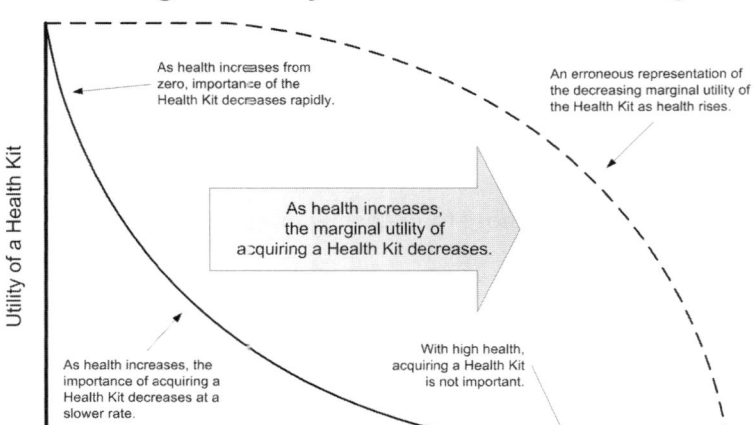

FIGURE 8.7 We can restate increasing marginal utility as decreasing by changing the direction of the axis. Because both curves are descending, they both show decreasing marginal utility. They exhibit different characteristics, however. Care must be taken to represent the effect in the desired way.

In contrast, both the solid line and the dashed line in Figure 8.7 show decreasing marginal utility while moving from left to right (i.e., health increasing). The effect is very different, however. In the case of the dashed line, the utility for a Health Kit would start high when the agent's health is zero. It would stay high until moderate health was reached, at which point it would slowly begin to decrease. As the level of health approaches the maximum, there is a rapid change from one point to the next. In fact, most of the change in utility on the dashed line takes place over a span of health where the solid line's utility is already close to zero, that is, not important.

If we were to put this into practice in an example of an agent incrementally *losing* health (i.e., moving right to left on the graph), we would notice an almost immediate jump in the utility of acquiring a Health Kit. The first small wound would assign great importance to finding a way to heal. This is not the original behavior that we had constructed in Figure 8.6. The dotted line is incorrect. The lesson to learn here is that when we converted an expression of increasing marginal utility into terms of decreasing marginal utility by flipping the axis, we had to make sure that our resultant utility curve was the same as well.

Many more subtle caveats can trip up the unwary designer when dealing with curves in this fashion. And yes, keeping track of the difference between value and utility makes for magnificent headaches. (Of course, this increases the *utility* of pain killers compared to their *value*.)

/* *We could have addressed this without flipping the axis as we did above. The same idea can be represented by going the opposite direction on a marginal utility curve. If moving left to right on a graph gives us decreasing marginal utility, then moving right to left represents increasing marginal utility. Often, the choice of which direction to express a utility curve will depend on what the predominant usage of it will be.* */

Marginal Risk vs. Marginal Reward

Marginal utility is used for more than just determining the relative importance of things we are either acquiring or already have (such as the soldiers and health). Marginal utility can also be used to weigh things that we are either giving up or putting at risk.

For example, each additional dollar of our money that we spend has an increasing marginal utility. While we may be willing to spend our first or second dollar, we may not be as enthusiastic about spending our last dollar. Along the way, each additional dollar that we spent meant more and more to us.

In the example of purchasing the warranty for a computer in Chapter 7, one question that was never addressed but is relevant in an intriguing sort of way is "How much money do we have in the bank?" We aren't simply talking about whether we can afford to purchase the warranty in an absolute sense, that is, whether we have that extra $600 over and above the cost of the computer itself. We are addressing something a little more ephemeral. We want to know what that extra $600 *means* to us.

When Pascal cautioned us that we "need to know what is at stake," there was more to it than a simple value measurement of the wager alone (in this case, the dollar amount of the warranty). Not only do we have to consider the relative value of the wager to the potential outcome, but we must consider the value of the wager itself relative to what we can *afford*. If money is tight, a person may opt to not take the extra cost of the warranty and instead take his chances on getting through that first year unscathed. The value of the money saved by not buying the warranty might be needed elsewhere. To use a rather obvious example, rather than purchasing the warranty to guard against the *possibility* that we might need it, we may choose to keep the money to fund the *extreme likelihood* that we will want to purchase food in the next 12 months.

Conversely, a multimillionaire would probably not bother with the hassle of a warranty on this computer. To him the replacement cost is negligible. (One could make the case that a multimillionaire should be buying a better computer than the hypothetical brick-to-be that we have been using in the example.) For that matter, maybe the multimillionaire should just buy the warranty and be done with it. After all, the cost of the warranty is loose change to him.

It all comes down to how important that money is for a person—not so much in an absolute sense ("there is enough money in my account to cover the warranty…"), but more so in a relative one ("…but ensuring a working computer in the future is not *as important* to me as having beer money right now"). What we have witnessed is the application of marginal utility to something that is being given up (or even potentially given up). This is the marginal utility of risk.

The St. Petersburg Paradox

The phenomenon of marginal utility of risk was illustrated in spectacular, yet controversial, fashion by Swiss mathematician, Daniel Bernoulli, in 1738. In introducing the St. Petersburg paradox, Daniel showed that using a purely mathematical approach of probability theory to determine decision theory can cause problems. (Credit where credit's due: The original problem was conceived by Daniel's cousin, Nicolas Bernoulli. Daniel just presented it and got it published in *Commentaries of the Imperial Academy of Science of Saint Petersburg*.)

The St. Petersburg paradox is based on a lottery concept of a very simple sort. The pot starts at one dollar. You then repeatedly flip a coin. On any given round, if the coin shows tails, you win the pot. If it shows heads, you get to flip the coin again. Therefore, if you flip tails on the first toss, you would win the initial value of the pot: $1. However, if you were to flip heads first and your *second* flip showed tails, you would win $2. If you showed heads on the second flip and tails on the third, you would win $4. Skipping ahead a bit, if you got on a roll and threw ten heads in a row before tossing tails, you would win $1,024 ($2^{10}$). The big question is, "How much would you be willing to pay to enter this lottery?"

The question makes for an interesting twist on Pascal's charge that we need to determine what is at stake. In this case, we are going to try to determine what it is that we want to *put* at stake. The temptation is to look for the purely mathematical solution to this question. After all, that approach worked admirably for us in determining how much we should pay for a warranty on our (less than stellar) computer.

The starting point involves trying to figure out how much we are likely to win. This part, at least, is relatively straightforward mathematically. All of the information we need was given to us in the rules of the game. A single flip of a coin is a 50/50 proposition. The pot doubles with each "successful" flip of a head. Let's bust out the math.

On the first flip, we have a 50% chance of winning the $1 pot. So our expected winnings after one round (E_1) are

$$E_1 = \frac{1}{2} \times \$1 = \$.50$$

We can expect to win an average of 50 cents on the first round. If we were to be betting *only* on one flip of a coin, we would be done now. We can expect to win 50 cents on average, so we would be willing to bet 50 cents on the game. In theory, over time, we would hope to break even with this. If we are allowed to wager less than 50 cents, that's a bonus, as we would most likely come out ahead in the long run. A wager over 50 cents is not in our best interests, as we are going to be bleeding cash the longer we play. (Although that doesn't seem to stop people from lining up at casinos, does it?)

Our little lottery game doesn't stop there. If we pass the first flip (50% chance), we then have another 50% chance of winning $2. Therefore,

$$E_2 = \left(\frac{1}{2} \times \$1\right) + \left(\frac{1}{4} \times \$2\right) = \$1$$

Third flip?

$$E_3 = \left(\frac{1}{2} \times \$1\right) + \left(\frac{1}{4} \times \$2\right) + \left(\frac{1}{8} \times \$4\right) = \$1.50$$

Or, to simplify,

$$E_3 = \frac{1}{2} + \frac{1}{2} + \frac{1}{2} = \$1.50$$

So now we can expect to win $1.50 on average after three flips. It seems that, if we were to stop here, we should wager $1.50 because we have a chance of winning that after three flips.

The peculiarity comes into play when we extend things out to infinity. After all, in theory, we could flip heads an infinite number of times in a row before throwing that tail and collecting our winnings. Looking at it in a formula,

$$E_n = \sum_{n=1}^{\infty} \frac{1}{2} = \infty$$

Translated into English, this reads: The estimated payoff on n tosses (as n goes to infinity) is an infinite accumulation of 50 cents, which, of course, is an infinite payoff. Following our premise that we are willing to wager what we are likely to win over time, we should be willing to put up an infinite amount of money for the privilege of playing the St. Petersburg lottery. But is that necessarily feasible?

On one hand, who would be willing to put up an infinite amount of money to play this lottery? Certainly, none of us has an infinite amount of money, so we should be a little more reasonable and suggest that we could put up everything we own for this lottery. Doesn't this sound a little silly? It doesn't matter how many times I tell you that you could win an infinite amount of money, or even that it is possible that you could at least win all your assets back. You are still probably not going to take me up on this deal.

On the other hand, if there is a potential for such a massive payoff, who would offer this lottery in the first place? Even if the players are wagering massive sums of money, there is always the possibility that you are going to pay out far more than what has come in. Jokes of governmental debt aside, I can't even see a city, state, or country being able to back the potential "infinite" payoff.

So what went wrong? Why won't people be willing to put up massive amounts of money to play the St. Petersburg lottery? Why won't anyone offer it anyway? The problem came into play when the nasty little concept of infinity got involved. The trouble you can get into when infinity is involved is actually worthy of its own book. (In fact, *To Infinity and Beyond* by Eli Maor is a fun read about the cultural effect that the notion of infinity has had over time.) However, the lesson we have learned actually has gone beyond the pitfalls of limitless numbers.

By using infinity, Bernoulli unwittingly crafted a problem that can be posed to any person, regardless of their personal wealth. The hidden factor that makes this possible is the underlying question of "how much is this worth to you?" That is a question that each of us would be forced to ask ourselves as we pondered how much we would be willing to put on the line in the St. Petersburg lottery. The complicating factor is that there is not *one* factor to consider (and one corresponding question to ask). There are actually *two*. Both of them involve marginal utility. In fact, they are actually almost reciprocals of each other.

Marginal Utility of Reward

First, we must consider what value we would put on the money won. Sure, we would like to win a few bucks. That's always nice. However, as the money goes up, it starts to look the same. The increase from $1 to $2 on a wager is rather substantial. We have doubled our money! In fact, the increase from $2 to $4 is just as attractive. Again, we have doubled our money. The case can be made that having $4 is twice as good as having $2, just as having $2 is twice as good as having $1. However, as many psychological studies have shown, there is a sort of leveling out point. Once a certain threshold is reached (although that threshold is fairly vague), extra money isn't as important as it was earlier on in the acquisition process.

In similar fashion to the caffeine I ingest so ravenously in the morning, after a certain point, people tend to say, "I have enough" with other things as well. Let's say you have reached approximately $2 million in winnings from your coin-flipping adventure in the St. Petersburg lottery. Is 4 million really *twice* as good as only 2 million? What about 8 million? Is that really *twice* as good as having only four million? If you were sitting on $150 million, is your life going to be *twice* as good if you double it to $300 million?

The quandary would be a little more obvious if we were working with a fixed value of money rather than doubling each time. For instance, increasing from $100 to $200 is nice. Increasing from $1,000 to $1,100 isn't as big of a deal. Increasing from $1,000,000 to $1,000,100 is loose change. Certainly, the effect is more obvious with this example—particularly because we can see the *percentage* change that each additional $100 has. Is it doubling the first hundred? Is it a 10% addition to $1,000? Or is it a miniscule 0.01% increase when tacked on to a million? However, while it is more obvious when expressed this way, even doubling the *value* each time translates into a diminishing utility at some point. It's simply a matter of scale.

Regardless of scale, we can represent the concept of diminishing marginal utility with a curve such as the one on the left side of Figure 8.8. Note that, despite being the same width as the areas represented by *a*, margins *b* and *c* show significantly less of a vertical increase. In other words, despite the fact that the face *value* of a prize in a lottery increases, each additional amount of increase begins to mean less and less in terms of the *utility* that we would have for that prize.

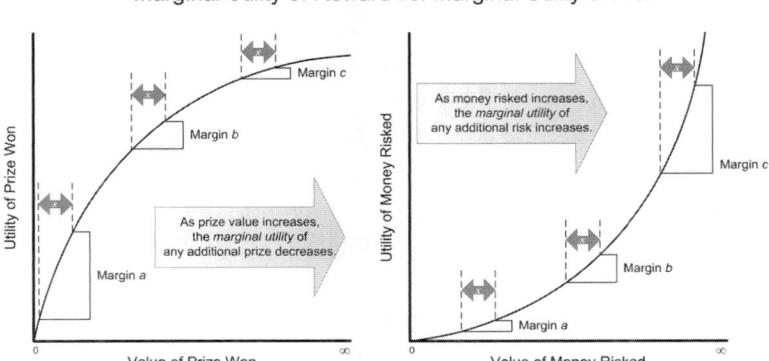

FIGURE 8.8 As the value of a prize goes up, the marginal utility of each increase gets smaller. As the value of a wager goes up, the marginal utility of each increase gets larger.

Marginal Utility of Risk

As interesting as the mental exercise of pondering "how much is too much?" can be, it is still a little difficult to see what is at stake. After all, we can win an *infinite* amount of money. Who wouldn't want that? Why artificially limit it? Well, things become a little more sobering when the other side of the wager is analyzed. How much are we willing to *risk* in this lottery? The reason this isn't quite the same problem is that the scale of the *x*-axis is a little more defined. After all, most of us don't have an infinite amount of money to plop down on a wager. In fact, we usually have a maximum net worth with which we can work. And that draws the proverbial "line in the sand" on making our decisions.

As we discussed earlier, marginal utility can increase. Just as with the curve for the reward, we can envision a similar curve for risk such as the one on the right side of Figure 8.8. In this case, the utility change of the initial money is not that big of a deal for most people. Wagering a dollar is fine for most of us. The second dollar as well. As the *value* changes early on, the *utility* difference is not all that significant. However, there's a point where we start to raise our eyebrows a bit. Perhaps not if we go dollar by dollar... but more likely if, as above, we go $100 at a time. Naturally, if we start doubling the values, things get out of hand quickly.

Maximizing the Difference

Either way, there comes a point where the respective utilities of the money we are risking and the money we could win are moving in opposition to one another. Any additional money we stand to lose means more and more to us, that is, the marginal utility goes up significantly. On the other hand, the marginal utility of any additional money we stand to win gets smaller. Eventually, we arrive at a conflict in which the additional risk is not worth the additional reward.

The answer to the St. Petersburg lottery question—"How much would you be willing to wager?"—is, therefore, highly subjective when expressed in terms of *value* (which is, after all, what the question is asking). The secret is for each person to find the "sweet spot" where there is a maximization of the ratio of the *utility*—not *value*—that would be gained over the *utility* of what is being risked.

If we were to overlay the utility curves from Figure 8.8, we would see, in a very abstract sense, this point illustrated in Figure 8.9. There is a point where the two curves are the furthest apart. In English, "For *that* kind of payout, I can risk this much!" That is the maximization point. Accordingly, there is a point where the two curves cross. Once again, in lay terms, "It's not worth the risk."

Given the scenario of the St. Petersburg lottery, I wouldn't be willing to wager more than a dollar. (Perhaps a by-product of running the numbers too much?)

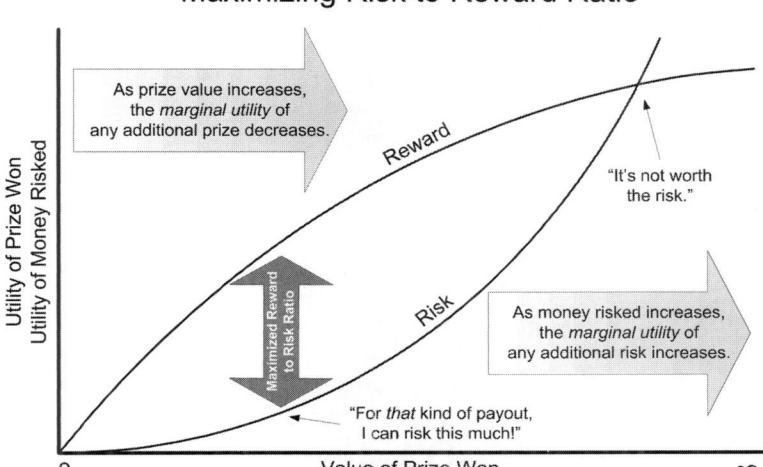

FIGURE 8.9 As the value of a prize goes up, the marginal utility of each increase gets smaller. As the value of a wager goes up, the marginal utility of each increase gets larger.

DEFINING THRESHOLDS

Of course, as with many of the concepts that we discuss in the book, trying to mathematically describe "enough" is a bit more art than science. In the St. Petersburg paradox, the graphs we used were indistinct in that our scale of value ran from zero to n, infinity, or generally "somewhere over there someplace." The utility axis was even more hazy in that it really only expressed "more" or "less" utility. In a sense, that was by necessity since the entire dilemma dealt with "personal preference in the space of possible infinity." If that isn't vague, I don't know what is.

In the examples we have shown so far, some of the thresholds we have set have been concrete. In the case of declining health, reaching zero health is a fixed point. There is nothing subjective about it. The same could be said for spending our last dollar. Some thresholds are defined by the rules of the environment. In Monopoly, the rules of the game state that three properties of the same group have more utility when combined than they do individually. Therefore, it is an inherent property of the game that three properties is an important threshold for determining marginal utility.

On the other hand, some of the thresholds we suggested were somewhat more flexible. In the case of building soldiers to defend our town, we arbitrarily decided that four soldiers was enough. We made a design decision. The same could be said for deciding that we need six soldiers before we send out our patrol. Those thresholds were entirely up to us to set. We needed to consider what would look and feel realistic.

Generally, thresholds are set at a fixed number. How we arrive at that fixed number, however, could be determined in many different ways. In fact, the threshold target could continually be changing. From the standpoint of calculating utility and *marginal* utility, however, we need to know what the threshold is *at that moment*. Once we have that fixed number, we can begin to include it in our calculations.

Also, as we mentioned earlier, thresholds could represent different approaches in the way our marginal utility behaves. Marginal utility could change as we move toward a threshold or it could change as we move away from a threshold. Marginal utility could either decrease or increase as a threshold is neared. There are no magic solutions for how thresholds are either defined or constructed. What is important is that we recognize that they exist so that we can start thinking in terms of them. We will explore methods of calculating utility, marginal utility, and thresholds later in the book.

MULTIPLE UTILITY THRESHOLDS

Up until this point, we have been envisioning utility curves as being somewhat asymptotic. That is, they curve in a single direction, approaching either a specific value or a particular slope. There are times when utility curves—both for risk and reward—may reverse themselves. This has the effect of making the extra value risked "worth it" again.

The quandary posed by the St. Petersburg paradox is a staple of many of the game shows that we see on TV these days. Games like *Who Wants to Be a Millionaire* and *Deal or No Deal* have a component to them that encourages the players to weigh the marginal utility of the money they could win by continuing. There is an assumption that, as we saw in Figure 8.9, a person will reach a point where it is "no longer worth it" and will quit (if he hasn't failed already). There is a subtle flaw in this premise.

Interestingly, examples of this behavior are evident in those shows if you know where to look for them. Often, players in those games and others like them change their minds about whether to risk more money for achieving a greater reward. We will use *Who Wants to Be a Millionaire* as an example.

Who Wants to Be a Thousandaire?

According to the rules of the game, if players get to the $32,000 level in *Millionaire*, they are also guaranteed that if they lose over the next few questions they will still receive that $32,000. There are a few of those safety net values in the game that guarantee that, once you achieve those levels, you won't go home empty handed.

Imagine that you are a player who is at a prize level of $125,000. Obviously, you have passed the $32,000 safety net—you are guaranteed that you will take home that much. The next prize level is $250,000—*if you get the question right*. If you risk going forward by attempting the next question, you *could* win another $125,000 for a total of $250,000. On the other hand, you could also risk losing $93,000—dropping you back to the $32,000. So, if your odds were 50/50 on winning $125,000 or losing $93,000, which would you choose? Also, remember that your third option is to *not wager* any more and simply walk away with the $125,000.

Solving this mathematically from a strictly value standpoint (which is the only thing numbers can convey without context) is fairly simple. Working with the assumption that we have a 50/50 chance of selecting the right answer (which, in fact, one of the "lifelines" will guarantee you) makes things even easier. We have a 50% chance of winning $125,000 and a 50% chance of losing $93,000. We'll shave the zeros off for simplicity.

$$E(W) = (.5 \times 124) - (.5 \times 93) = 16$$

This equation says that our estimated winnings ($E(W)$) are statistically likely to be a gain of $16,000. Of course, that is based entirely on the odds being extended over time. According to the rules of the game, there is no way that after this single decision we could actually walk out with $16,000 more than the $125,000 we have at the moment. The formula only shows us that the advantage is slightly in our favor... and would be statistically more accurate if we were to make this bet numerous times over the long term. Because we are only making this wager one time, however, the bottom line is that we will either have $32,000 or $250,000. But what about *not* wagering? We still *do* have the option of not continuing on and simply taking our $125,000 off the table.

Given those three values—$250,000, $125,000, and $32,000, many of us have an opinion about the *utility* of the three prizes relative to their face values. Most of us would be quite pleased to walk away at this point. You often hear players or their families saying, "That's good enough—I don't want to risk it anymore." Taking home $125,000 is "enough" to make us happy about our little adventure. On the other hand, for others, simply knowing that the *minimum* that they could leave with was 32 Big Ones is fine with them—they would be willing to risk losing that $93,000 to try for *another* $125,000. But why the difference? Aren't the numbers clear?

Enough Is Enough Until It's Not Enough

Much of it comes down to the individual perception of wealth. Some of this is a psychological factor. A number of studies have shown that once certain plateaus are reached, people are satisfied. Interestingly, these plateaus are often in tiers (Figure 8.10). That is, people might be satisfied for some time at one tier so that the marginal utility of additional wealth drops as it does in Figure 8.10. As that wealth increases for a while, however, another perceived "level of wealth" is approached so that the marginal utility increases rapidly once again.

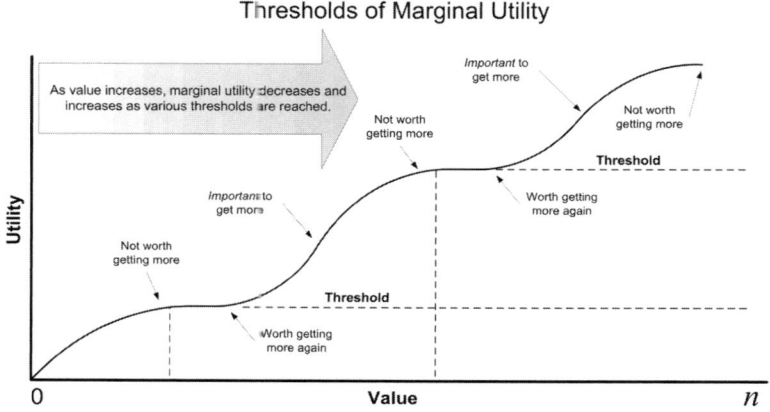

FIGURE 8.10 As the value of a prize goes up, the marginal utility of each increase gets smaller. As the value of a wager goes up, the marginal utility of each increase gets larger.

I can't provide firm figures on where these tiers are since they differ wildly based on the cost of living, the mentality of the society, and obviously the current value of the dollar. However, the function seems to be tied up in the perception of lifestyle changes that could happen at those tiers.

If a lottery prize is less than $100, it might buy you a nice dinner for the family —or a single AAA game title. It's not going to cause a significant lifestyle change, however (unless you lock yourself in your house to play that AAA game 16 hours per day for weeks on end… but I digress). Prizes in the hundreds of dollars are intriguing because they could help you pay off some bills or buy a new next-gen console. Prizes in the thousands get a little more fun, as do those in the tens of thousands. At that point, people are beginning to think "new car," for example. However, those sums aren't going to put you on *Lifestyles of the Rich and Famous*.

When you get to six figures, however, people start thinking about entire new houses. (At least here in the Midwest, six figures gets you a nice house.) And that seems to be a magic number on shows such as *Millionaire* and *Deal or No Deal*. That tier is enough of a lifestyle change to make a difference to people. When you are sitting on $125,000, an extra 10 grand isn't going to be that much of a deal. Even the extra $125,000 in the example above isn't as important because the threshold of "nice new house" has already been reached.

The next threshold seems to be in the area of a million, which is not surprising given the popularity of the term *millionaire*. In fact, it is not a coincidence that the TV show *Who Wants to be a Millionaire?* is named the way it is. Can you envision answering the titular question any *other* way than "Uh… I do!" However, using the standard rules of both that show and *Deal or No Deal*, the top edge of the game is the million dollars. Therefore, along the way most people end up asking themselves the question "Do I want a hundred thousand dollars?" Usually, when they get to that point, they go home. If you were to extend those games to include *tens* of millions, I suspect we would see another tier at the one-million mark. The statements by the players and families would then be, "We've got our million, that's enough. Quit now."

Sometimes, that is good advice. Even Fast Eddie should have taken Charlie's advice in the movie *The Hustler*. When Eddie was up $11,400 on Minnesota Fats, Charlie tried to get him to quit for the night saying, "You wanted ten thousand? You got ten thousand." Eddie didn't quit and proceeded to lose it all.

IN THE GAME   How Many Troops?

The phenomenon of multiple thresholds can be applied to games as well. Earlier, we used an example of the marginal utility of building extra units in a strategy game. Once a certain number of troops is reached, the marginal utility of building additional units begins to decrease—we simply have "enough." However, as we have been examining above, having "enough" is often tied to context. With the prize money, we theorized that people could be thinking in terms of a nice dinner, a new video game, a new game console, a new car, paying off a mortgage, buying an entire new house, and so on. Each of those was a milestone that defined *enough*— at least temporarily. Once that landmark was reached, the marginal utility of receiving additional value dropped somewhat. However, as the next milestone was neared, the frame of mind changed so that additional value was now thought of in terms of "if we only had a *little* more." When this happens, the marginal utility of additional value increases again. Getting additional value is important if the next goal is to be attained.

In our example of building units, "enough" can be relative to certain thresholds or goals as well. For example, rather than the lifestyle changes that the prize money can help us attain, let us frame building units in terms of game-contextual goals. We may think of counting our units in terms of having enough to:

- Defend our base against a small raid
- Defend our base against an attack
- Defend our base *and* harry a small enemy outpost
- Defend our base *and* destroy a small enemy outpost
- Defend our base *and* destroy a medium enemy outpost
- Defend our base *and* destroy a well-defended enemy base

Each of those goals would require a specific number of troops. As we reach the number, we would be temporarily satisfied with that number. While we may not stop building troops entirely, the urgency of building them isn't as great as it was when we were just short of the required number.

A Few Good Men

Let's work from the top down (or bottom up in terms of troop levels). Early in a real-time strategy (RTS) game, we may decide that we want to have four soldiers in our fledgling base just in case the enemy sends a couple of soldiers of his own over. If we haven't built any of them yet, the utility for the first soldier is fairly high. We really *need* that first one finished so we don't have to worry. If someone comes, we can at least slow them down a little. Once the first soldier is built, the second one is a little less urgent, but important nonetheless. Three is certainly better than two, but it is no great tragedy if an attack were to come prior to the third one being finished. The fourth soldier may very well be our insurance policy. The utility it provides is less than the third—and certainly far less than the utility of getting that first soldier out the door. Once we reach that minimum of four soldiers, we may have a comfort level that allows us to concentrate on other things such as training more workers, erecting other buildings, and so on. Note that those other concerns also have utility values that would be taken into consideration as well… but let's not complicate things just yet. (Yes, that sort of fun comes later in the book.)

So, because we have achieved that threshold of four soldiers, building a fifth one doesn't provide us with much utility at all—*at this time*. This is hardly a permanent solution, though. It should be obvious that we aren't going to accomplish much in a typical strategy game with only four soldiers. In fact, we will likely continue cranking them out, but only if other more immediate priorities (i.e., those with higher utility values) don't get in the way.

Eventually, we are going to be concerned about defending against a larger attack, and to do so, we will need more units. For that contingency, let's assume we feel that 16 soldiers is the right number. While the numbers—and even the *scale* of the numbers—may have changed, the pattern is similar. If we only have 9 or 10 soldiers, we are going to place a great deal of importance on the 11th and 12th. Once we arrive at 14 or 15, the urgency starts to fade—as expressed by the marginal utility of each individual unit dropping slowly once again. The pattern will repeat as we move down our list of goals, although its character may change somewhat.

Are We There Yet?

As we discussed earlier in this chapter, marginal utility can *increase* as a threshold is approached. This generally occurs when we have specified a *minimum* for a project rather than a preferred level that makes us feel safe. For example, let's assume we have our 16 defenders and accomplished anything else on our nonmilitary list. We may want to construct a patrol dedicated to finding (and subsequently annoying the heck out of) nearby enemy outposts (Figure 8.11). If we decide, through whatever algorithmic crystal ball we employ for this sort of decision, that this patrol needs to be comprised of six units—and we aren't leaving until we have six—then that becomes another threshold. Building the fifth and sixth units is of great importance. Why would we build the other four if they are going to be left waiting?

Notice how this differs from the prior examples of the defending force. In those examples, if we were one short, we were still rather comfortable. Three instead of four initial defenders was not a great setback. The same could be said about 15 instead of 16. If there was a priority to do something else, we could have stopped

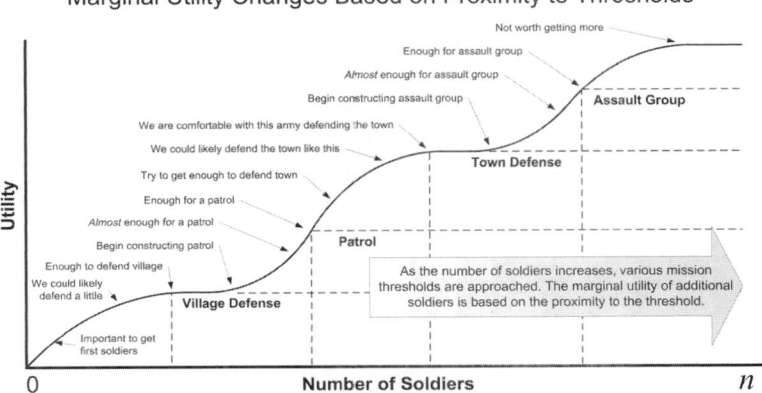

FIGURE 8.11 As we approach and reach various thresholds in building our army, the marginal utility of each additional soldier may increase and decrease.

without building the 16th soldier for a time. The first 15 could do the job almost as well as if they had waited for that 16th one. Likewise, the value we spent on those first 15 would not have been wasted or left sitting idle. However, by specifically defining that we want a patrol of *six* soldiers, it does us no good to build the first five and then quit. In that case the marginal utility per soldier actually *increases* as we near the goal, rather than leveling off the closer we get.

THE UTILITY OF MARGINAL UTILITY

As we have seen, marginal utility can assist us in expressing some of the subtlety in how an agent could perceive the world. Just as utility allows us to give an object or an action a level of importance that was different than its value, marginal utility allows us to vary that level of importance as the number of objects or actions increases or decreases.

Also, as we saw with Bernoulli's St. Petersburg paradox, marginal utility can assist us in analyzing the differences between two utilities such as risk and reward. By thinking in terms of the differences in utility rather than differences in value, we can solve problems that would otherwise yield irrational results such as betting an infinite amount of money.

We explored the idea of thresholds as anchors for these utility judgments. By finding places where we say, "That's enough!" we establish targets and goals for our marginal utility to approach. However, we also saw that the thresholds themselves may not be as much of an anchor as we thought. Sometimes, a threshold may be "good enough for now," only to change to a different one later on.

In the end, we have found that marginal utility can be a powerful tool in expressing shifting opinions about things. And, because most decision makers are not purely rational, opinions are a major component of the decision process. As we continue through this book, we will encounter numerous places where marginal utility plays an important role in constructing realistic and dynamic behaviors.

9 Relative Utility

There is still one problem that we have yet to solve with regard to utility and marginal utility. While we can now express differences in importance between one item and another item of the same type, the numbers that we have been using so far have often been abstract. What does a utility of 100 on my first can of pop mean? We know that it is twice the utility of my sixth can of pop (50), but what does it mean when compared to my utility for salsa, for instance?

As we examined the potential uses for multiple thresholds when building our armies in Chapter 8, one of the reasons we cited for pausing the building of soldiers was so we could potentially build *other* things that were more important at the time. How do we know if something is more important? How much more important is it? Would we have built the tower over our barracks in Chapter 7 if we had needed the resources to finish one final soldier for our patrol? For that matter, would we have built the relatively unimportant final soldier in our town defense force if we needed those resources to build the tower?

Utility and, by extension, marginal utility are only valuable when they are put into a comparative context. As we have discussed, to compare things, we need to be able to measure them. More importantly, we need to measure them in such a way that they can be compared to other measurements. The advantages of money and time are that they can be measured in some form—for example, dollars and cents or hours, minutes, and seconds. Production of a manufacturer can be measured in the number of units—and compared to the dollars we are paying the manufacturer and the price we are receiving for the unit. The efficacy of a fertilizer can be measured in the growth of the plant in inches or in the output of a crop in bushels. This can be compared to the price we pay for the fertilizer and the price we receive for the bushel. Many things can be empirically measured in some form or another. However, plenty of considerations go into making a decision that can't necessarily be counted up and compared. Some things just don't lend themselves to being measured in so distinct a fashion. People have certainly tried it before, however, and those attempts merit a closer look.

HEDONIC CALCULUS

In the late 18th century, the English utilitarian philosopher Jeremy Bentham developed what came to be known as the **felicific** or **hedonic calculus**. He developed an algorithm that was formulated, in his mind, to help in calculating the degree or amount of pleasure (i.e., hedonism) that an action was likely to cause. Likewise, it could be used to calculate the amount of pain that said action would cause—perhaps doing one or the other to two different people—or even doing both to the same person.

By rating any given action, he posited that you could determine whether an action was worthwhile—or even moral. In fact, by using his algorithm and the various weights he applied to actions, Bentham constructed arguments in favor of individual and economic freedom, the separation of church and state, freedom of expression, equal rights for women, the end of slavery, the abolition of physical punishment, animal abuse laws, the right to divorce, free trade, the interest charged on loans, and even the decriminalization of homosexual acts (and remember, this was the 18th century!).

Although this may be presumptuous, his methods were definitely crafted in such a way as to make life easier for game artificial intelligence (AI) developers. As a unit of measurement (i.e., a common "utility" value), he reduced everything to "hedons" and "dolors"—positive and negative, respectively. He rated actions using a combination of variables, which he called "elements" or "dimensions." What they amounted to was vectors of pleasure (or pain) that could be added together to combine into one final result. These dimensions included:

1. **Intensity:** How strong is the pleasure?
2. **Duration:** How long will the pleasure last?
3. **Certainty or Uncertainty:** How likely or unlikely is it that the pleasure will occur?
4. **Propinquity or Remoteness (Time Distance):** How soon will the pleasure occur?
5. **Fecundity:** How probable is it that the action will be followed by sensations of the same kind?
6. **Purity:** How probable is it that the action will *not* be followed by sensations of the *opposite* kind?
7. **Extent:** How many people will be affected?

The first six of these were designed to be applied to the individual in question, whereas the seventh was meant to encompass others as well.

By analyzing any given situation or decision and applying what should ostensibly be an objective rating to the various facets involved, he believed you could arrive at a score that was descriptive of what should or should not be done. The decisions themselves could be of low importance such as selecting a flavor of ice cream, or they could be of great weight such as selecting the benefit of one human life over another during a deadly medical outbreak.

Bentham Goes to Dinner

To show how the formula works, we can toss all sorts of anecdotal examples at it. If I were to try to decide how to spend money on a night out with the family, for example, I would likely want to weigh the pros and cons of various activities. If we were to go to dinner, I may be presented with a wide variety of choices of where to go. If I were to analyze certain components of the dining experience, however, we may be able to sift through the possibilities a bit easier. By using Bentham's seven criteria, I can at least get a better idea of how these choices stack up.

- **Intensity:** There may be a significant difference in the quality of the food from one establishment to another (intensity of the pleasure). On the other hand, that can easily be countered with a significant difference in the amount of money I would need to pay (intensity of displeasure). Of course, that necessitates me weighing the relative utilities of the pleasure from the food and the displeasure of spending money.

- **Duration:** Do we enjoy spending time at an eating establishment? If so, we may include the value of how long the pleasure lasts. Driving through a burger joint and inhaling their wares in the car doesn't provide a long duration of pleasure; sitting down in a restaurant with a pleasant atmosphere and taking our time may be an important part of the experience for us.

- **Certainty:** If we are familiar with a restaurant, and know what our favorite dishes are there, we can be more certain of the pleasure than if we were to go to a new, unfamiliar establishment where we don't know what we are getting into. In that case, if we aren't feeling experimental—such as a night when we are treating company to dinner—we may want to play it safer and avoid the uncertainty involved in visiting a new restaurant.

- **Remoteness (Time Distance):** If we are very hungry or are concerned with time, we may be more inclined to select a place that is closer to our house than to drive across town. The delay in the pleasure would be a significant factor to us. The same could be said for the expected waiting time. If we know that we can expect to wait an hour before we get served, it may greatly affect our decision.

- **Fecundity and Purity:** If, despite liking the food that a place serves, we are aware that there is a possibility that our digestion will suffer for the remainder of the evening, we may not be enamored with the purity of the experience. Do we really want to take a chance on feeling ill later on?

- **Extent:** How many people in the family are going to enjoy this experience? Is it something that most people can agree on or is it going to alienate the wife and kids? This addresses Bentham's last point—how many people are going to be affected by my decision?

The trick to the whole process (and unfortunately its major sticking point) is trying to determine what the utility values should be. Even ranking things within one category can be hard—do I like pizza more or less than tacos? Or steak? Or pasta? How much more? Still worse is comparing things across categories. For example, is the difference in how much I like pizza compared to tacos worth more than the difference between a 20-minute wait and a 5-minute wait?

To score things appropriately, we would need to have more than an ordinal ranking such as pizza > tacos > pasta. We would need to know *how much* greater pizza is than tacos and *how much* greater tacos are than pasta. And that scale would need to be directly comparable to the scales used elsewhere... the duration, the wait, the certainty of the experience, the likelihood of potential indigestion, and whether I have to put up with my family griping that they don't like my choice of restaurant. Arranging all of these disparate factors into a framework that can help us make one decision is no small task (yet we will take a crack at it later on in the book).

MULTI-ATTRIBUTE UTILITY THEORY

Bentham's hedonic calculus attempts to combine multiple scores in such a fashion so as to create a single score. For the goal for which hedonic calculus was intended, those categories were reasonably adequate. In fact, there could possibly be game situations where those categories would be appropriate. Of course, not all of Bentham's categories would necessarily fit in a game environment decision. However, most game environments have a constellation of factors that can be taken into account to weigh the available choices that an agent might have. These factors are very decision-dependent. That is, no one set of criteria or factors works in all situations.

The important thing to learn from Bentham's approach is that decisions can be composed of many different pros and cons. Not only do each of the individual pros and cons need to be scored or weighted, but the relationship between them needs to be defined. Eventually, we can arrive at one value that represents the total utility that the agent would derive from the action. This concept is known as **multi-attribute utility theory** (MAUT).

MAUT is used in many industries as a decision tool, although it may go by different names (e.g., multi-criteria decision analysis, multi-criteria decision making). The business world presents an overflowing cornucopia of formalized methodologies available to assist decision-makers in processing massive amounts of data. A quick search even turned up the *International Society on Multiple Criteria Decision Making,* which claims to have over 1,400 members in 87 countries. On their Web site (www.terry.uga.edu/mcdm/), they define their field as follows:

> "MCDM can be defined as the study of methods and procedures by which concerns about multiple conficting (sic) criteria can be formally incorporated into the management planning process."

Aside from the egregious spelling error, that definition pretty much sums up what we are trying to accomplish with game AI. Working backward, "management planning process" is a buzzword for making a decision. To arrive at that decision, we need to "formally incorporate" a number of "conflicting criteria." That sounds strikingly like what Bentham had in mind.

This approach is also at the core of designing and programming game AI. If we look back over the examples we used earlier in this book, we find that MAUT would have been appropriate in many of them. They use many, possibly conflicting criteria that we need to formally incorporate into a unifying algorithm to arrive at a decision. For example:

- When my daughter was formulating her strategy for running for VP of the fifth grade, she identified many criteria that would have led to decisions about whether to run for president or vice president, whether or not to make stickers and posters, and if she should tailor her speech to be more kid-friendly.

- When my son was considering raising prices in his zoo, he pondered the perceived value of his zoo based on how many exhibits he had already created and the balance between more visitors at a lower price and fewer visitors at a higher price.

- When I analyzed my decision to use the next razor blade in the pack, I took into account how many blades were left, the cost of purchasing more blades, my comfort in shaving with a used blade, and how much I had already used prior blades.

Even some of the examples in the previous chapters on utility were based on some assumed premises that could have been further explored and defined with MAUT. For instance:

- Pascal was far to simplistic when he relegated "live as if God exists" and "live as if God does not exist" to equal status. I'm sure that Mr. Bentham would have been more than happy to point out to the conflicted Mr. Pascal that those two choices carry a significant amount of complexity in and of themselves.

- When we built our tower over the barracks, we assumed that the barracks was important to defend. Why is it important? What if we already had three barracks buildings and this was a fourth that we were building for insurance? What if we were currently beating back our opponent so badly that the likelihood of having our barracks attacked was nil?

- When we decided to build our settler and his escort soldier first, we worked from the premise that sending out a settler earlier was better than doing so later. Why? How much better? Is this as important if we are *not* concerned with expanding our empire? Why would we be concerned about expanding our empire? Are two smaller cities worth more than one slightly larger one? How much more?

All of these factors could be defined in terms of a utility attribute. We would then be able to score the factors appropriately and include them in our decision.

In the Game   The Engagement Decision Revisited

In Chapter 3, we showed a brief example in which we took multiple criteria into account to construct a decision about whether or not an agent should engage the enemy. In this case, the seven categories that Bentham defined would not be appropriate. Instead, we identified eight factors that we thought we should consider. Those were:

- Agent's health
- Enemy's health
- Agent's weapon
- Enemy's weapon
- Number of enemies
- Proximity to a leader
- Proximity to an important location
- Agent's "anger" level

If we define each of those factors as a utility, the process of combining them into a single utility function is an instance of MAUT (Figure 9.1). Specifically, we are taking multiple, disparate attributes and blending them together to arrive at a single, deciding factor—in this case, should we attack, hide, or flee?

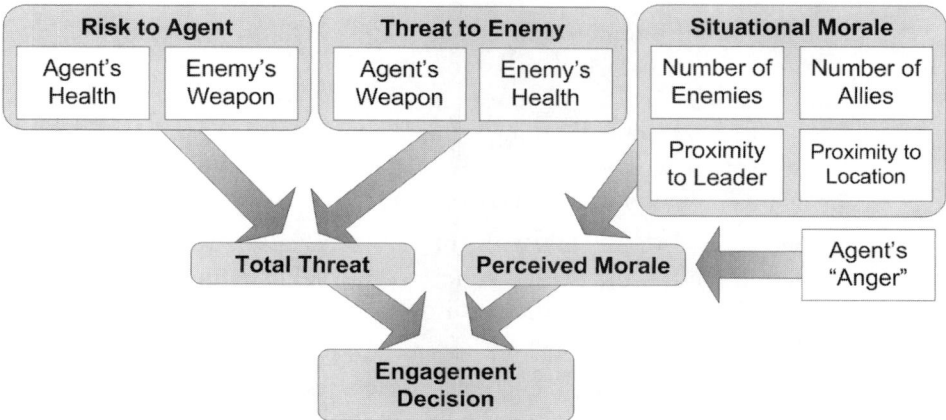

FIGURE 9.1 The engagement decision from Chapter 3 is an example of MAUT.

Analyzing the Attributes

To show how the thought process is similar to hedonic calculus, we can step through each of the attributes above just as we did with our dining decision. For each, we can list what we believe the relevant factors are.

- **Agent's Health:** How healthy are we? Are we fully healed? Damaged? If we are almost dead, taking any additional damage would be a serious concern. (Remember the increasing marginal utility of declining health from Chapter 8?)
- **Enemy's Weapon:** What sort of weapon does the enemy have? How much damage does it do in one hit? How much damage does it do over time? This is important because it needs to be considered in direct relation to our current health. While a stronger weapon would be dangerous at all times, a weaker weapon would still be dangerous if we were low on health. Therefore, the enemy's weapon is not an isolated factor.
- **Enemy's Health:** We need to consider the current state of the enemy. How damaged is he currently? It would be a shame for us to run away if our foe was only barely clinging to life.

- **Agent's Weapon:** What sort of weapon do *we* have? Are we packing something serious like the rocket launcher from Chapter 5, or are we stuck with the equivalent of a military issue peashooter? How much damage could we do in one hit? Over time? What is the accuracy? Is it area of effect or direct fire? All other things being equal, how long would it take us to dispatch our horrible nemesis?

- **Number of Enemies:** How many baddies are out there after all? Is it just this one dude with dark glasses and a stupid hat, or are there many shade-wearing, ridiculously crowned nemeses that we have to deal with? If it is more than one, is it still a reasonable enough number that we would feel confident in our abilities, or are we counting on the art department to provide our character with a change of pants after this encounter?

- **Number of Allies:** How many of our own chaps do we have around to assist us? We certainly would feel far more comfortable taking on the enemy if we had some support. Are we alone, or do we have strength in numbers?

- **Proximity to Leader:** Is our fearless and inspiring leader within visual range? Is he the type who would encourage us to press on into the battle—either through positive reinforcement or the threat of his boot to our head? If he is close by, we may feel more comfortable (or more afraid of him than the enemy). If he is distant—or dead—we may begin to feel that all is lost.

- **Proximity to Location:** Is our pitched battle taking place near an important location we need to claim? Or near one we absolutely *must* defend? Are we near a safe fall-back point, or is our back up against a wall?

- **Anger:** How clearly are we thinking about all of this? Is our morale artificially heightened to an irrational level by a sense of vengeance? Do we just want to "get even" regardless of our situation?

All of these issues need to be addressed and codified in some manner. When we do that, each of them can be represented as a utility value. Constructing some of them will likely use the principles of marginal utility as well.

As utility values, they become our core building blocks. As such, everything that follows from this point on will be based on what we determine to be the appropriate interpretations of these factors. If we are inconsistent or flawed in our approach to creating them, these inconsistencies will be cascaded throughout the rest of the decision algorithm.

Assembling Our Blocks

Additionally, as is illustrated in Figure 9.1, we can begin combining these individual factors into intermediate concepts. Each of these concepts, once created, can stand on its own as a new attribute that can then be combined with other attributes.

For example:

- **Risk to Agent:** Our current health combined with the enemy's weapon constitutes a risk to us. Is his weapon so powerful that a single hit can take us down? If not, how long would it take?
- **Threat to Enemy:** In the reverse of Risk to Agent, how much health does our enemy still have left? How does that compare to our weapon? Can we take him out in one hit? If not, how long would it take?

These two attributes can then be combined into yet another attribute that represents an aggregate of the two of them.

- **Total Threat:** Given the risk that the enemy poses to us and the threat we pose to the enemy, who holds the upper hand? All other things being equal, who would die first in a firefight?

By looking carefully and perhaps changing a few words, we start to recognize similar patterns to problems we have addressed in previous chapters. For example, in determining the "total threat" utility, we included the *risk* that we are undertaking and the *threat* we pose to the enemy (i.e., our reward). The respective utilities of risk and reward are concepts that we dealt with in previous chapters. In Chapter 5, we pondered the risks and rewards of running out to grab the rocket launcher. In Chapter 7, we addressed the risks and benefits of building a tower over our barracks and whether we should grab the armor or boost our health first. In Chapter 8, we put risk and reward directly opposed to each other to help us analyze the St. Petersburg paradox.

In this case, we have constructed the concept of "Total Threat" from two other utilities—each of which was constructed from two other utilities, which, in turn, we created as measurements of utility. Assuming that we have confidence in the choices we have made in the process so far, we can express similar confidence that Total Threat represents an accurate assessment of whether or not our agent is in a position of power in the engagement.

When the Heart Rules the Mind

Total Threat is only part of the total decision, however. It is a very mechanical "my gun is bigger than your gun" question. Not a lot of subjectivity is involved in the analysis of whether or not the rate of damage I can deal is going to be enough to counter the rate of damage he is dealing to me. The inputs are fairly concrete numbers yielding an equation that can be solved by some simple algebra. The other side of the problem, however, involves some speculation and subjectivity.

We started by combining the respective number of allies and enemies that were present, our proximity to our leader, and the proximity to a point of interest into a concept of "Situational Morale." While the actual count of allies and enemies nearby is concrete, how those results factor into morale is not. How many allies is enough? Is the morale we gain from allies a linear function? Are we *twice* as secure if there are four allies as we were when there are only two? Is there decreasing marginal utility? What is the threshold?

Additionally, the conversion of the proximity distances into utility functions is not something that immediately leaps into the realm of the obvious. What does proximity mean? Within sight? Unobstructed sight? Within a certain radius? Is it a linear function of distance, or does it exhibit marginal utility as well? Which direction? Does the utility start flat but then drop off when we get to a certain distance? Does the utility drop off quickly as soon as we move away a little and then slowly trickle off from there?

There is another consideration in the complexity of interaction. What if the state of one utility affected another? For example, let's say the distance from our leader inside which we can still feel comfortable is dependant on how many enemies there are. The more enemies, the closer we need to be to our leader to feel emboldened. The examples of how these factors can be combined together are infinite. Certainly, many of those infinite answers would not make much sense—but that doesn't make our problem much easier to address.

Regardless, at some point, we could craft a method for combining those four factors into a notion of Situational Morale. As we noted on our diagram and in the descriptions, this morale as a whole could be colored somewhat by our anger state. If we are angry, the morale that is implied by the four factors could be thrown out the window—at least for the duration of our anger. (Snapping back to reality after acting angry can provide for tragic—or humorous—situations… "Oh heck… now what have I got myself into?") By factoring in our anger level, we are potentially skewing our model of Situational Morale into one of "Perceived Morale."

The Final Connection

We have rolled up our original nine utility factors into two factors: Total Threat and Perceived Morale. These two variables need to be glued together in the same manner that we have done others up to this point. What is the relationship between them? Anecdotally, we could say that if our morale is higher, we are more willing to stick around despite a less than preferable threat level. In fact, we could say that there is a direct relationship between the two. The higher our morale is, the better our tolerance for threat; the lower our moral is, the lower our tolerance.

The goal, therefore, is to construct an equation that reflects this relationship. Is that equation linear? Exponential? Does it approach an asymptote at some point? What is that asymptote?

It's worth stressing (and believe me, we will stress it repeatedly over the next 200+ pages) that the only thing we should have to consider at this point is the relationship between the threat level and our perceived morale. All the other considerations that are present in our model have been included already. At any point in the process, we should be able to trust our underlying assumptions and decisions that we made based on them. If we find ourselves questioning the validity of either of these two factors—or, worse yet, making accommodations for them—then we need to return to the previous levels and address our misgivings there.

If we have done our work properly to this point, and if we find a relationship between our last two factors, then the result of that last step would provide us with the decision utility that we need to determine whether we should attack, hide, flee, faint, or simply suffer a massive psychological trauma and collapse into a quivering pile of wimpiness. By using MAUT on our nine factors, we have reduced a relatively large state-space into a single decision.

Yes, I know that we have provided no fun specifics yet. We're all dying to see real numbers and formulas! Don't worry. We'll get there—in Ryan Seacrest's pop-culture staple—"after the break."

INCONSISTENCIES

As we saw in our musings about both the dining out and engagement decisions, there is a lot of undefined "wiggle room" in how we could determine the weights of and associations between the factors. Much of the problem is due to the very fact that we are trying to quantify ideas that are not necessarily quantifiable.

The effect of this problem often becomes exposed when people are polled about something that should be common knowledge. Even when faced with the exact same situation, different people can come away with different views on what something actually is. This is not a surprise to any of us; we have all experienced it. Differences in perception, understanding, and opinion are the staple of crime dramas, romantic comedies, and reality shows alike. It isn't that we all just come to different conclusions; often we are all working with a completely different set of *perceived* facts or *conceived* understanding about the situation. It is these differences in the *input* of data that start to skew the subsequent processing of that data for purposes of making decisions. In short, we are using different measuring sticks.

PROBLEMS WITH PERCEPTION

Often, the way people perceive and process things is the major bottleneck to establishing a sorting of how we would prefer things. One of these problems is the actual *perception* of a stimulus. While this may seem obvious, it is an important facet of the process to cover. At the very core, a stimulus must be perceived to be included in consideration. This is somewhat different than the simple fact of whether or not the stimulus *exists*. Plenty of stimuli exist and yet are either below a threshold of detectability (e.g., too quiet to hear) or outside the sphere of awareness (e.g., happening behind or around the corner from the intended observer). In those cases there is a legitimate argument that, despite the very real occurrence of the trigger event, the agent was simply not able to be aware of it. If the agent was not aware of it, he couldn't use it as part of the decision-making process.

The science of **psychophysics** is an area of study that deals with a much more subtle and even scientifically intriguing area. It deals with the way that we psychologically process differences in stimuli. For example, if someone were to hand you two objects of similar weight—one in each hand, could you tell if they were different weights or the same? Could you tell how much different the weights were. If one weight was five pounds and the other one was six, would you be able to tell that the difference was the same as if they weighed four and five pounds respectively? In both cases, the difference is one pound, yet they may feel significantly different. How much different would the weights have to be before you were able to accurately determine which of the two was heavier?

If we are modeling the sense of hearing for an agent, we would likely want to take into account what level of sound would be perceptible to that agent. We also may want to take into account how loud that sound is compared to other sounds in the area—that is, the relative sound level. It is entirely possible that a loud sound could go unnoticed when it is heard in concert (so to speak) with other loud sounds. Also, could the sound be mistaken for something else? My wife swears that there is a stairwell door in the hospital at which she works that squeaks in a manner that sounds remarkably (and eerily) like our cat that died in 2005. It is not a case of feline reincarnation as a fire door; it is a matter of flawed perception.

Likewise, different people can perceive visual stimuli in dramatically different ways. My dad is red-green color blind, for example. If he isn't specifically looking for it, he will not see a red traffic light in a background of a green tree. (Or a green light in a background of a red tree, I suppose.) If he were to visit a city that flipped their traffic lights upside down, he would really be in trouble!

Problems with Categorization

Difficulties also arise when you are trying to categorize things. Often, the definition of a category is entirely subjective. In our color example, people may have different understandings of what a color "should be." My ex-wife used to ridicule me for claiming that one of the four colors of tiles in our Rummikub set was orange. She asserted that it was yellow. In fact, neither of us was "right." Orange and yellow are examples of invented classifications that we humans have devised for the sake of simplicity. By being able to say "orange" or "yellow" we spare ourselves the headache of trying to communicate color through an expression of relative wavelengths of light. (On the other hand, there is a growing portion of the computer-graphic-savvy population that can speak quite fluently in red-green-blue [RGB] triads.)

My ex and I were looking at the same color wavelengths. For the sake of argument, let's assume that our eyes worked well enough to perceive those wavelengths properly. The problem arose because we likely had differing opinions of where yellow ended and orange began (or vice versa). In fact, the color was somewhere in between the commonly accepted definitions of those two colors. However, not having a box of Crayola crayons handy to help us negotiate a compromise such as "sunglow," "dandelion," "goldenrod," or even simply "yellow orange," neither one of us was willing to back down on our assertion about the color of the tile.

(Full disclosure: Wikipedia lists the color as yellow, but the instructions on the official Rummikub site list it as orange. I feel better about myself now. Kinda vindicated, ya know?)

This concept is surprisingly important to modeling not only perception systems in games, but decision systems as well. Let's look back over some of the classifications we have to make for our engagement decision: What is "low health?" How many enemies need to be present before we begin to get nervous about being "outnumbered?" What is the actual linear distance away from our leader that no longer constitutes "close enough to feel safe?" These are examples of decisions we would need to make if we wanted to measure and compare attributes in a meaningful way.

Problems with Understanding

The issue that generates the most inconsistency and subjectivity when people address attributes is based more in psychology than perception, however. Even when observation and measurement can be exact, therefore taking the vagaries of perception out of the loop, there are other issues in play. Extensive studies have shown that not only do different people put differing values on things, but the same person may put differing values on things based on their understanding of the situation. By stating the situation another way or in terms of another scale of measurement, the answers that people give may change significantly. The facts don't change, but the meaning people ascribe to them may differ significantly.

When Is Dying not Dying?

One of the more famous examples showing how people's decisions can be greatly affected by their perceptions was offered up by Daniel Kahneman and Amos Tversky. Incidentally, despite being a psychologist, Kahneman won the Nobel Prize in economics in 2002. (Tversky had died a few years prior to that; otherwise he would have been the co-recipient.) The point is that there is an increasingly significant and accepted link between psychology and the realm of economics.

In their experiment, they presented the following choice to one group of people:

Imagine that the U.S. is preparing for the outbreak of an unusual Asian disease, which is expected to kill 600 people. Two alternative programs to combat the disease have been proposed. Assume that the exact scientific estimates of the consequences of the programs are as follows:

- If program A is adopted, 200 people will be saved.
- If program B is adopted, there is a ⅓ probability that 600 people will be saved and a ⅔ probability that no people will be saved.

Which of the two programs would you favor?

Additionally, they presented the same scenario to a second group of people but with different choices:

- If program C is adopted, 400 people will die.
- If program D is adopted, there is a ⅓ probability that nobody will die, and a ⅔ probability that 600 people will die.

Which of the two programs would you favor?

It may take a bit of looking at the question, and maybe a pencil and paper, but closer examination shows that the choice between A and B is the same as the choice between C and D. If we were to show the various choices in terms of expected *deaths*, without regard to wording, we are able to cut through the clutter somewhat.

$$E_A = 400 \text{ people will die}$$

$$E_B = \frac{1}{3}(0) + \frac{2}{3}(600) = 0 + 400 = 400 \text{ people will die (statistically)}$$

$$E_C = 400 \text{ people will die}$$

$$E_D = \frac{1}{3}(0) + \frac{2}{3}(600) = 0 + 400 = 400 \text{ people will die (statistically)}$$

In the first group, most of the people chose A—that is, to save one-third of the people (200) for *certain* rather than roll the proverbial dice and gamble about saving everyone yet risk losing *everyone* in the process. On the other hand, the second group chose program D—apparently thinking that the odds of saving everyone were preferable to heartlessly letting two-thirds of them (400) die. The contradiction is clearly irrational, given that there is no mathematical or statistical difference between the two courses of action: A/C vs. B/D (Figure 9.2). The only difference was in the *perception* of the situation based on the carefully chosen language of the questions. The words we used played upon people's feelings—the horror of losing 400 people when they could have been saved.

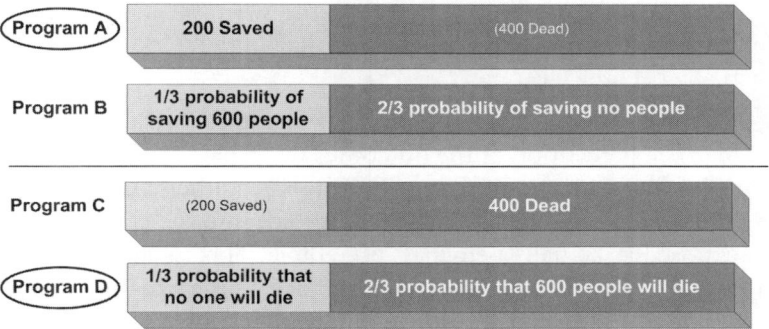

FIGURE 9.2 In Kahneman and Tversky's outbreak problem, people overwhelmingly selected different choices based entirely on the wording of the question despite the fact that the meaning of the words was exactly the same. (The selected answers are circled.)

If flawed (or at least skewed) judgments like these were used in constructing mathematical ratings for Bentham's hedonic calculus, the results of any given calculation would be all over the map. The premise that he had begun with, that his method would cut through all the complexity of making multivariate decisions, was hamstrung by the very fact that most of the variables are next to impossible to define.

Put another way, it isn't the solving of the equation that is the problem; it is the determination of what values to use when we are solving the equation that is the most important part. When approaching the task of constructing behaviors, many people stop at the point of coming up with an algorithm without considering the fact that the numbers they are feeding into the algorithm may have been subjectively skewed—even slightly—in such a way as to not yield the outcome they would like.

Furthermore, they may look to place the blame on the algorithm itself without analyzing and testing the validity of the components. The point is that both the construction of the algorithm and the values and weights that are used in the algorithm are of equal importance. Later on, we will address both of these components in more detail.

APPARENT CONTRADICTIONS

Another interesting issue to consider is the possibility that there might be times when it is actually *preferable* to select a *less attractive* option. I use the preceding sentence with the disclaimer that both the terms *preferable* and *less attractive* are entirely subjective. As in the deadly outbreak example, when we analyze what is truly happening at a mathematical level, a statement that initially looks like a contradiction may actually become clearer.

This is different from the outbreak example above, where the options were the same. The perception of the outcomes was what was flawed. In this case, we face a choice where, on the surface, one option is mathematically superior to another—in the short term. Once we place the choice into the entire framework, however, it is exposed as actually being *less* preferable. This issue can be even more apparent when placed in a continuum. For instance, as the situation changes, it would seem that one choice would become *more* advantageous. Yet surprising results can occur.

GIFFEN GOODS

Interestingly, it seems that we humans often confuse ourselves by making situations overly complex. Animals often seem to "get it." One example that showed how animals can grasp the sometimes elusive complexity involved in hedonic calculus was an experiment conducted by Raymond Battalio and John Kagel. They showed that laboratory rats were perfectly capable of analyzing the relative merit of controlled supplies of pleasure and discomfort and making the correct decisions with that information.

The experiment involved placing rats in a box equipped with the equivalent of two vending machines. Each machine would dispense a measured amount of liquid for the rats to drink for each press of the lever. They also changed how many lever presses were available to the rats in each session in the box. With a moment of reflection, you can see how the variables in play correspond to familiar terms in the world of economics. By capping the number of lever presses available to the rats, they were setting the *income* level, that is, the most the rats had available to spend in any one period. By adjusting the amounts of liquid that the respective lever presses dispensed, they were setting prices for the liquid, that is, how much bang the rats were getting for their buck.

After some time learning how the levers worked, the rats had a pretty good handle on how much liquid was dispensed by each one. Invariably, they would head for the one that gave them the most liquid. This doesn't seem important in and of itself. In fact, even without a lever-press limit, we can all see that it would make sense to patronize the establishment that was dishing out the most liquid.

Root Beer for Rats

The next change, however, gave the rats something a bit more complicated to ponder in their quest for quenching their thirst. The experimenters modified the box so that one lever produced root beer—apparently a favorite beverage of lab rats—and the other one dished out water flavored with quinine. Since rats do not seem to appreciate the bitter taste of tonic water, it made for an appropriate counterpoint to the tasty root beer. All other things being equal, a rat would choose root beer over quinine. However, not all other things were equal!

The dispensers were set so that the amount of root beer provided was significantly less than the amount of quinine. Again, without a limit on lever presses, this decision is only slightly more complex. If you are a rat willing to work for it, the root beer is still available to you… you just have to press more often to get it. However, the researchers *did* set a maximum number of times that you could press the two levers during a single session. (Note that this was *total* lever presses—each lever counted against the single total.) With that limit in place (your fixed income), however, you now have to decide how to spend wisely.

Enter the final criteria… you are a rat who gets thirsty—more thirsty than you can satisfy by simply selecting the small doses of root beer. You are going to have to satisfy your thirst with some combination of quinine and root beer. And *that* is what gives us our decision to make. How much quinine should we put up with when we really would prefer root beer?

Over time, the rats would work out a balance that satisfied both their individual levels of thirst and their preferences for root beer relative to quinine. For each rat, there would be a slightly different level. In the end, however, equilibrium would be established. They learned that they would have to quench much of their thirst with the quinine and only occasionally dip into the root beer for a marvelous taste holiday.

Again, that the rats established an equilibrium that balanced their desires is not a surprise. The math is similar to that of purchasing the warranty, selecting workers based on productivity, and deciding which goal is the most important when you consider how long it takes to get there. The calculation is intuitive for the most part.

If I were to ask, though, what you would do (or what the rats would do if you want to stay out of it) if the researchers were to cause the price of the quinine to go up—that is, decrease the amount of quinine per lever press—what would your answer be?

Too Much of a Good Thing

Analyzing it at a purely surface level, our initial instinct may be that we would have to drink *less* quinine per session… perhaps even increasing our intake of root beer. (And what a tragedy that would be!) However, this is not what the rats did. When the price of the quinine was increased (less per press), the rats actually *increased* their intake of the bitter liquid by selecting the quinine lever more often. Of course, that also meant that they drank less root beer as a result. But why would the rats use *more* of something after the price went *up*?

The answer to that question is what lies at the heart of a concept called "**Giffen goods**." In his 1890 book, *Principles of Economics*, Alfred Marshall named the concept after the 19th century British statistician and economist Robert Giffen, to whom he attributed the original idea. A Giffen good is an inferior product or commodity whose usage defies the principles of demand in that its usage increases as the price goes up and goes down as the price lowers. There are only a few examples of Giffen goods, yet studies of microeconomic mathematics show how this phenomenon certainly can exist. In fact, the example used by Marshall of staple foodstuffs is remarkably similar to that exhibited by our thirsty rodents.

To find where the core principle kicks in, let's break down the issue mathematically. With all the talk of the prices of the various drinks and the amounts that are dispensed for each press, it is easy to get caught up in just those two issues. After all, it was the "price" of the quinine that changed, so the answer must lie close to that particular facet. There are two *other* important factors to remember, however. More importantly, they seem to be the factors that get forgotten first:

1. The rats have a fixed level of need (i.e., the amount of thirst per session).
2. The rats are on a fixed income (i.e., the number of lever presses per session).

When the price of the quinine was raised, neither of these two factors changed. Our parched pests still needed to drink *something* to satisfy that need. Also, they knew that they only had a limited number of presses available to them regardless of what they chose to drink or how much of each drink they were granted. It is these *fixed* values that sets the boundaries for the possible decisions made when the *variable* values change. What the rats realized was that to slake their thirst for the duration of the session, they were going to have to spend *more* of their (hard-earned?) lever presses on the quinine than they used to get the *same amount* of liquid. Therefore, if they were using *more* lever presses to get the quinine, they had *fewer* lever presses left to "splurge" on the luxury of root beer.

Doing the Rat's Math

Put into a utility formula similar to what we have used earlier, we can express it as follows. First, let's define our terms and the initial settings of the levers:

P_r Number of root beer lever presses

P_q Number of quinine lever presses

P_{qr} Number of lever presses per session

A_r Amount of root beer per press

A_q Amount of quinine per press

A_{qr} Amount of quinine and root beer to be consumed per session (thirst)

We also need a few formulas. Let's start small. We can glue them all together later.

The amount of liquid consumed is the number of presses for each multiplied by how much liquid is dispensed for each:

$$A_{qr} = (P_r \times A_r) + (P_q \times A_q)$$

The number of lever presses for root beer and quinine respectively add up to the total number of lever presses:

$$P_{qr} = P_r + P_q$$

We need to put everything in terms of quinine. Therefore, we are trying to eliminate references to root beer in our equations. Obviously, the number of presses for root beer will be the maximum number of lever presses minus how many are used for quinine. To express this, we just need to flip the terms around:

$$P_r = P_{qr} - P_q$$

Substituting into the original formula, we get:

$$A_{qr} = ((P_{qr} - P_q) \times A_r) + (P_q \times A_q)$$

Jumping through the hoops to solve for the number of presses of the quinine lever () gives us:

$$A_{qr} = A_r P_{qr} - A_r P_q + P_q A_q$$

$$A_{qr} - A_r P_{qr} = -A_r P_q + P_q A_q$$

$$A_{qr} - A_r P_{qr} = P_q (A_q - A_r)$$

$$P_q = \frac{A_{qr} - A_r P_{qr}}{(A_q - A_r)}$$

In its current form, that looks a little cryptic. Let's plug in some numbers. Note that in all of our examples, the only number that we will change is the amount of quinine that is bestowed per lever press (A_q).

P_{qr}	Number of lever presses per session	25
A_r	Amount of root beer per press	1
A_q	Amount of quinine per press	100
A_{qr}	Amount of liquid to be consumed	200

Placed into the formula above, we arrive at:

$$P_q = \frac{200 - (1 \times 25)}{(100 - 1)} = 1.77$$

This means that we only need 1.8 presses of the quinine lever to give us all the liquid we would need for our thirst. We can spend the other 23 presses splurging on root beer. At a rate of 100 per press, quinine is incredibly cheap compared to root beer. We could buy a lot of it, but we don't have to. With just under two presses, we have satisfied everything we need from the less-than-pleasant quinine. When it comes to root beer, we rats can go hog wild, so to speak.

As we reduce A_q dramatically (to 36, for example), we start to see a significant difference (Figure 9.3). Now the quinine is getting more expensive. (Nothing about the root beer has changed.) However, we now have to spend more of our presses on acquiring quinine. When $A_q = 36$, P_q climbs to five. That still leaves 20 presses for root beer. It's not really time to panic.

Continuing the trend of raising the price of quinine to the point where we are only getting 10 per press, we find that we now need to press the quinine lever over 19 times to get what we need to survive. Despite the fact that the *relative* value of root beer to quinine has gotten significantly better, we can actually afford *less* of it. We are spending too many presses just getting enough liquid to survive. We can only afford to tap into the root beer keg five times.

When A_q reaches 8, it is obvious that root beer is now completely out of the picture. Our 25 presses at 8 each will just get us enough to satisfy our thirst. Root beer is tantalizingly similar in cost to the annoying tonic water—at least compared to what it used to be—and yet we can't bother ourselves with it.

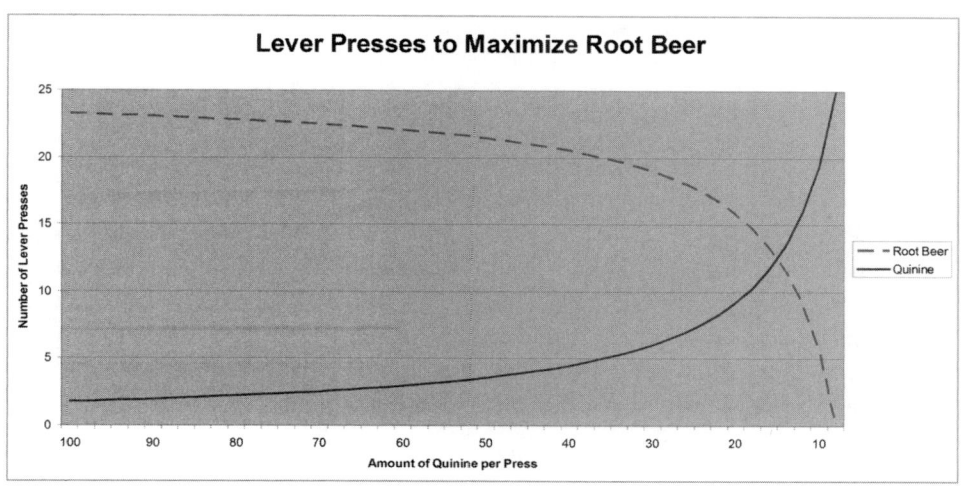

FIGURE 9.3 Because the number of lever presses per session is capped at 25, as the amount of quinine dispensed per press goes down, the number of quinine level presses must increase for the rat to quench its thirst. The rat can no longer "splurge" on the tasty root beer.

Bentham vs. the Rats

There are a few lessons to be learned here. One is that utility levels aren't always obvious and aren't always simple. It would be difficult for Bentham to have ascribed values to the root beer and the quinine that would have, without other considerations, allowed us to rank them appropriately in his hedonic calculus. Let's look again at Bentham's seven criteria:

1. **Intensity:** In this case, the root beer is far more pleasurable than the quinine. This much is simple.
2. **Duration:** This is similar to how much liquid is being dispensed per lever press.
3. **Certainty or Uncertainty:** The rats learned over time that the liquid was a *certain* outcome of a lever press, rendering this issue irrelevant.
4. **Propinquity or Remoteness (Time Distance):** The dispensing was immediate —irrelevant.
5. **Fecundity:** Irrelevant
6. **Purity:** Irrelevant
7. **Extent:** Irrelevant

Looking at the list, we would think that the only things that mattered were the intensity and duration (amount) of the pleasure. However, the one thing that was missing in Bentham's list was the notion of *context*. The decision in question did *not* happen in a vacuum. It was not entirely stand-alone. Some ramifications were not covered by the seven parameters.

The second lesson is that utility values don't always ebb and flow the way we would expect them to. Or at least not in a way that is as simple and clear-cut as we would like. Everything that we have internalized about the laws of supply and demand tells us that as a price goes up, we should consume less of it. However, that outlook is simplistic in the sense that it doesn't take into account all of the other laws that are in effect at the time… notably that we were working between the bookends of finite quantities and finite demands.

The third lesson is that lab rats are a lot smarter than we give them credit for.

IN THE GAME   Wizardry and Wands

The reason the rats even had a decision to make in the first place was that they were on a budget. They had a limited number of level presses available to them. We can think of that limit in terms of "income." Additionally, they had a fixed amount of thirst. They had a set amount of liquid (of any type) that they wanted to consume. This is analogous to "expenses." Given the juxtaposition of those two limits, we have a very simple income vs. expense comparison. That's what Giffen goods were originally designed to analyze.

The question of income vs. expense is no stranger in the game world. Obvious examples come from the strategy game world, where purchasing decisions are common. Examples abound in which we must decide how to distribute a fixed amount of a resource between two or more options with differing costs. However, there are other game choices that involve income and expense transactions that aren't quite as obvious simply because they don't use the familiar "buy and spend" terminology.

Imagine we are a spell-casting character in a role-playing game (RPG). We have the ability to cast a fireball spell but with only moderate results—dealing a paltry five points of damage. However, we are packing a magic wand that casts a blizzard spell that does 60 points of damage. The drawback of the wand, however, is that it only has a limited number of charges. We are reluctant to use it unless it is absolutely necessary. With our own spell-casting, for all intents and purposes we can cast spells as many times as we want. Given the choice, we would prefer to use our fireball spell and save the wand's blizzard for urgent situations. Regardless of whether we are casting a spell or using our wand, it takes us five seconds to perform either action.

We encounter a massive foe that will take 260 points of damage to kill. Additionally, we determine that this foe is so powerful that it is likely it will kill us within about 60 seconds. Therefore, at five seconds per action, we only have 12 total actions that we can perform before our time is up. With all that in mind, we decide that this certainly qualifies as an "urgent situation" and pull out our trusty blizzard wand.

Before we proceed any further with this pending altercation, let's lay out the numbers that we have established so far:

Our fireball spell:	5 points of damage
Our blizzard wand:	60 points of damage
Maximum total actions:	12 (i.e., 60 seconds at 5 seconds each)
Damage we must deal:	260 points

We can, of course, drop these into the same formula that our mathematical rodents used to determine their choice of beverage:

$$C_b = \frac{D_{bf} - D_f C_{bf}}{(D_b - D_f)}$$

where:

C_b Casts of blizzard
C_{bf} Total casts of blizzard and fireball allowed
D_b Damage from blizzard
D_f Damage from fireball
D_{bf} Damage necessary to defeat the enemy

This would yield the following:

$$C_b = \frac{260 - (5 \times 12)}{(60 - 5)}$$

$$C_b = \frac{200}{55} = 3.6$$

Remembering that we want to limit the number of uses of our blizzard wand, our optimum course of action would be to use the wand four times, dealing 240 points of damage, and then cast four fireball spells to deal the remaining 20 points.

(Note that 3.6 is the minimum, and since we can't cast partial spells, we need to round up.) That only amounts to eight spell casts. However, there is no more efficient way of doing it that would save our precious wand charges. If we were to only use three blizzards, we would do 180 points. The remaining time allows for nine spell casts and, at five points each, we could only do another 45 points of damage—bringing the total to only 225. Therefore, the four and four distribution is best.

Getting the Cold Shoulder

Just before we begin the combat, however, our foe pulls out a ring of cold resistance. With our vast mental repository of magical lore, we know that the ring will provide a 20% resistance to our blizzard wand. Therefore, each usage of the wand will only do 48 points of damage rather than 60. How do we proceed?

Originally, the blizzard wand dealt 12 times the damage that our pathetic fireball did. Now, the ratio is less than 10 to 1. In a relative sense, our fireball is more powerful than it was before our enemy donned the ring of cold resistance. Likewise, the blizzard wand is now *less* effective. At first glance, at 48 points of damage, we are getting less bang for our buck (or gore for our gold, I suppose) than we were when we were doing 60 points of damage. If we were to base our decision *only* on how powerful our two attacks were *relative to each other*, we would be less inclined to use the blizzard wand charges and lean more on the usage of the fireball.

The lesson of Giffen goods taught us differently, however. As with the rats and their root beer, when the cost of an undesirable selection goes up—in this case, using the precious wand charges—it sometimes is necessary to use it *more* often. To confirm this, we place the new numbers into our formula. The only one that has changed is the first number in the denominator—from 60 to 48.

$$C_b = \frac{260 - (5 \times 12)}{(48 - 5)}$$

$$C_b = \frac{200}{43} = 4.7$$

With the amount of blizzard damage per cast reduced to 48, we now have to use it *five* times instead of four. (The remainder of the damage can still be dealt by two fireballs.)

Continuing down that trend (Figure 9.4), if the damage from the blizzard was reduced to 40, we would have to use it six times. At 30, we would need to cast it eight times. If the effectiveness was reduced to 25—only five times greater than our piddly little fireball spell—we would have to use it *ten times!* What went wrong?

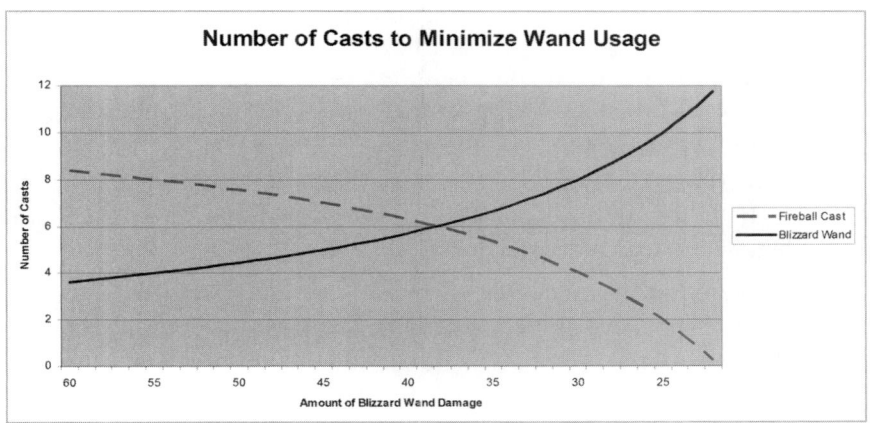

FIGURE 9.4 Because the number of attacks is limited to 12 and the amount of damage we need to do is fixed, as the damage dealt by the blizzard wand decreases, the minimum number of usages increases.

Originally, the factors that went into our decision seemed only to be how much damage we could do with each weapon and which one we preferred to use (our never-ending fireball spell). However, just as in the Monty Hall Problem, we must be careful to take into account *all* the parameters that affect the equation. In this case, the reason we can't simply use the relative strengths of the two weapons as our guide is that other factors are in play. First, we have a limited number of actions we can take in the time allotted to us (12). Second, we have a minimum amount of damage we need to do (260) in that amount of time. Therefore, as the efficiency of our more powerful, yet less desirable, weapon goes down, the necessity of its usage goes up.

The moral of our story is that like the rats and their root beer, our agents need to be able to identify situations where a change in one factor may require a corresponding change in action that seems contradictory to what we would expect. The problem often results from not taking every factor into account.

Another stumbling block is an assumption that some things are equal when they are not. For the moral of *that* story, we turn to a story about morals.

Moral Dilemmas

In the outbreak problem, the decisions were exactly the same—people simply didn't realize it because their perceptions were colored by the emotionality conveyed by the ideas of saving people and letting them die. Because of this, the issue isn't as relevant in the realm of hedonic calculus. People who would choose group A over B but not C over D would do so not because A was more *moral* than C—they would do it because they *perceived* that there was a moral difference when there was not. There was a mathematical equivalency there that they did not understand. In plenty of situations, however, a perceived mathematical equivalency can actually resonate deeply on a moral level, and this is the sort of quandary that Bentham was after when he constructed his hedonic calculus.

There is a famous series of "moral dilemma" problems that have various versions and spins. All of them center on a runaway trolley and are, with another nod to Sir Occam, starkly simple. Taken as individual choices, they make for interesting discussion. The real intrigue comes when they are taken as a series, however. That way, they are not being judged as the simple A vs. B questions that they are. Instead, we are forced to deal with why option A in one question is better or worse than option A in another one.

When Is Killing not Killing?

In the initial question—the one that sets up the series as a whole—we are given the following scenario:

> An unmanned, runaway trolley is heading down a track. In its path are five people (who are either unaware of the approach of the trolley or, in a more dramatic version, tied to the track by some nefarious dude) who will be killed by the trolley if it reaches them. Thankfully, you are by a switch that will send the careening trolley onto a siding. On the siding, however, is a single person (also either blissfully unaware or tragically trussed) who will be killed if you were to send the trolley onto the siding. What should you do?

It would seem, given the relative simplicity of the scenario that the answer is clear—you must throw the switch, saving the five people on the main track despite killing the one on the siding. Tossed up against Bentham's criteria (particularly the seventh one), this makes sense. The extreme negativity of death is multiplied by the five people in the first choice and only by the one in the second. Five is greater than one. Throw the switch. Divert the trolley. Save five people. (Sorry buddy....) Done.

Let's put a spin on this issue (Figure 9.5). Imagine that we are now on a bridge over the track with a large weight available nearby. If we toss the weight onto the track, we can stop the trolley before it hits the five people. Once again, this much is simple: Toss the weight. Stop the trolley. Save the people. Done.

But what if the trolley-stopping weight on the bridge was a rather obese man who just happened to be minding his own business? Should we toss him off the bridge to stop our horrible trolley from killing the five people? This is something more problematic, as most of us would agree, although we can't seem to put our fingers on exactly why. If you were to approach it mathematically, it would seem to be similar to the original solution: One person dies so that five may live. That doesn't seem satisfying—or even comfortable to us, though. Bentham's seven rules don't seem to address anything that would make this scenario different from the original siding-based one, either. So what is the issue?

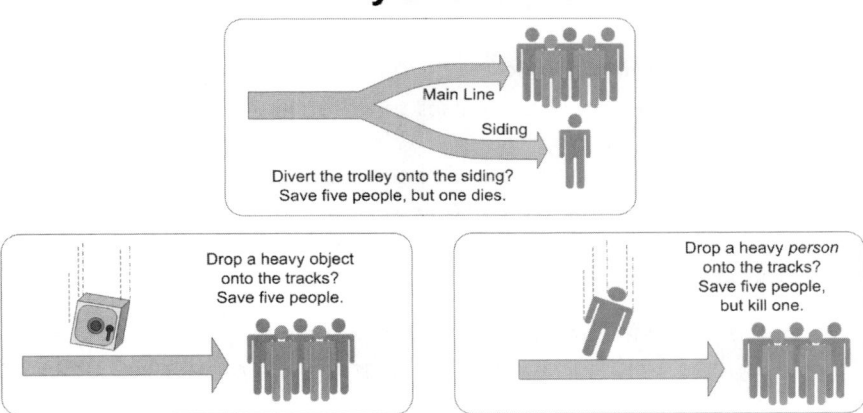

FIGURE 9.5 In its various forms, the Trolley Moral Dilemmas provide different insights into not only relative tragedy but the morality of active vs. passive roles in a tragedy. For example, *allowing* one person to die to save others is different from *killing* one person to save others.

Looking back at the two examples, there is a difference between the original man on the siding and the one on the bridge. In the latter, we are actually using the man (presumably against his will) to stop the trolley. He would not be involved at all if it weren't for us bringing him into the problem through our decision. In the former, we are not using the individual to save the five people on the main line— we are using the *siding* to save them. The hapless human on the siding just *happens* to be on the siding. It's not *our* fault. The five people on the main line would have been saved by utilizing the siding whether the single person was present or not. The difference, therefore, is the fact that we chose specifically to cause the death of the man on the bridge as a tool rather than as a side effect of an action.

Of course, the case could be made that, if the track is currently set to run on the main line toward the five victims, by doing nothing at all, we are not really killing them—the trolley and track configuration is doing that. However, if we were to throw the switch to the siding, we would be *selecting* to kill the one person on it. He would not have died if we had not been involved, whereas the five people would have died regardless of whether we were present or not. The deaths of the five people are not our responsibility; the death of the one person would be.

Despite being constructed for the purpose of determining dicey propositions such as those we refer to as "the lesser of two evils," this form of instinctive morality does not seem to get covered in Bentham's calculus. Somehow, we would need to quantify the relative tragedies of their deaths.

When Is a Victim More of a Victim?

Absent from the above problems is any differentiation between the people. They are all just "victims" in our example. While this makes for simpler calculations—five deaths is greater that one, for instance—it does seem rather impersonal. We don't know anything about these people whom we are using as markers in our morbid decision equation. Are there factors that we have not considered that may make our simple calculation more complicated? Consider the following:

- The five people are all in a van that became stuck on the tracks while transporting them to a critical care facility for treatment of short-term, terminal illnesses. Are they less valuable than the person on the siding?
- The single person on the siding is a nine-year-old child in perfect health. The five people on the main line are in their 50s and 60s. Do you sacrifice the one child to save the five older people?
- The five people are all criminals who have committed heinous crime for which they are serving life sentences. The person on the siding is an average person. Are the five felons less valuable than one free man?
- The one person on the siding is a wealthy, philanthropic benefactor who has dedicated his life and fortune to helping the poor, sick, and unfortunate. Do you sacrifice the saint to save the five normal people?
- The one person on the siding is a doctor who is the only person who can stop an outbreak of a deadly virus. Do we sacrifice five people so that the doctor can potentially save hundreds?
- The five people on the main line already have a deadly virus. There is a two-thirds chance that they may all die anyway—but a one in three chance that they may all survive. Do we consider the likelihood that they will die and save the one person for sure?

- The five people are regular folks, but the obese person on the bridge is a convicted murderer? Do you now feel better about using him as a trolley-stopper?
- The person on the siding is a prodigious and talented artist—Mozart, for example. Do you now feel worse about silencing him forever?

By personalizing the potential victims somewhat, we have made the decision more complicated. We are now including factors that aren't as simple as raw mathematics (e.g., five is greater than one) and further distorting the already confusing issues of morality (e.g., a intentional victim vs. an unfortunate bystander). Yet, to make a decision, these are factors that we must consider, and to consider these factors, we need to quantify them in some way.

Bentham's hedonic calculus can provide some support in this effort. However, it can only go so far as to identify that we *should* consider certain factors. It doesn't offer guidelines as to the exact weight that we should put on those factors. For example, citing the "duration" rule, Bentham may have suggested that the life of a healthy young person is more valuable than the lives of five people who are likely to die soon. One method of scoring this factor would be to count the years. If the one person likely has 50 more years of life left and the five people likely have only one year each, then we would be more inclined to save the young person. Although saving five lives is greater than saving one, saving 50 years of life is greater than saving only five. Of course, there is the possibility that the young person may *not* live for 50 years. But that is how actuaries make their money.

And what about the lives that would be touched indirectly? Assume that each person has the same number of family members who would grieve their loss. Assume as well that grief lasts for one year. If we let the one person die, a small circle of people will grieve. By letting five people die, we would be causing great emotional trauma to *five times* as many people for a year each.

As we have discussed numerous times in the past few chapters, there are factors that aren't quite as comparable. How much pleasure would the artist bring to how many people? If the artist (such as Mozart) has the capacity to "touch" millions of lives for hundreds of years, is that worth sacrificing five otherwise nondescript people? Certainly, purveyors of eugenics would claim that the artist's long-term benefit to society outweighs the loss of the five "normal" people that the decision would incur. Of course, extreme genius and talent often come packaged together with mental illness. Does *that* change our position on saving the artist?

As we have suggested numerous times throughout this book, deciding how to assign utilities to all of these disparate factors is more art than science. More specifically, it is an art that is often driven by the game scenario that we are trying to fill out. Some aspects of decision making are more relevant in certain game genres or game situations than in others. In a first-person shooter (FPS) game, for example, we need to consider a different constellation of factors than we would be concerned with in a real-time strategy (RTS). Similarly, there will be different considerations in an RPG than there would be in a sports game. For purposes of illustration, however, we can conjure up an example that is similar to our moral dilemmas above.

| IN THE GAME | **Hippocratic Morals** |

Imagine that we are a medic for a platoon of soldiers. We have a number of seriously wounded squad-mates. Three of the injured are normal combatants. One of them, however, is the only demolitions expert in the group. Given the arrangement of the situation and the relative severity of the wounds, we must choose between saving the lives of the three normal soldiers *or* the life of the demolitions expert. We are also aware that the demolitions expert has the ability to destroy the enemy forces that are massing for a final assault that will assuredly wipe out the entire platoon. As the medic, who should we tend to?

At first, the exercise seems strictly mathematical: Three people are more important than one. However, we are also aware that there is another layer involved. We must consider that by saving the demolitions expert, we are actually doing a greater good (by preventing an inevitable greater loss). The unfortunate loss of the other three soldiers is a by-product. We are not *choosing* to kill them; we are choosing to save *many* people over and above the four injured soldiers that are in our immediate care. By realizing that extra layer of abstraction in the problem, we avoid the apparent contradiction that saving *one* person is more important than saving *three* people.

To arrive at the solution to this problem, we would have to assign utility to the people. For example, we can assign that value based on the number of other lives they would save. This could either be direct, such as by healing another medic so he can assist others, or it could be indirect, such as in the scenario above where demo dude is going to prevent the enemy from killing *more* of our own side than are in jeopardy at present. Of course, there are other considerations. The three soldiers may have the ability to do some damage as well. If we were to heal them, they could start reaping vengeance upon our enemies… but *how much* vengeance? How does it compare to what the demo man can do?

This example still comes down to a question of "how many?" Instead of stopping merely at "how many lives can I save *right now*?" it becomes "how many lives will be saved *eventually*?"

Other scenarios may have more abstract considerations. Regardless of the form they take, however, if we can convert them to a utility value, we can measure and compare them. Through those comparisons, we can determine which course of action is the most preferable. On a simpler level, they may seem contradictory. When we put the considerations into the entire framework of the scenario, however, we can determine that an apparent moral tragedy is actually the lesser of two evils.

THE RELATIVE BENEFIT OF RELATIVE UTILITIES

In the end, the benefit of utility theory depends on not just ascribing utility to an object or an action, but framing it in a manner that we can compare to the utilities of all other objects or actions. We may find that this process is clear and simple, or we may find that we must apply a liberal dose of situational subjectivity.

Once we have determined those utilities (regardless of whether they are static or dynamic), we can proceed with the delicate and often equally subjective task of applying them in some meaningful manner. Using hedonic calculus as a model, we can determine a way of combining the factors through MAUT practices so that each receives a proper weight in the final decision.

However, as we have shown, caveats abound. Human perception and understanding does not lend itself well to firm measurement, categorization, and interpretation. Messy things such as the emotional content of words such as *save*, *live*, *die*, and *kill* can place a smoky, distorted filter over comparisons that should yield equality. Worse still, things that should be obvious *inequalities* in one direction can tip in the *opposite* direction by simply putting them into a larger context.

Despite all the vagaries, relative utility is the foundational building block from which all of decision theory is constructed. It is an extraordinarily powerful and flexible building block as well. For much of the remainder of this book we will focus on what you can build with this magic toy.

Part III
Mathematical Modeling

When constructing decisions for game artificial intelligence (AI), it is important to tap into various types of statistical modeling and probability math. Part III explains some of the basic mathematical constructs that we will use throughout the remainder of the book.

Chapter 10, "Mathematical Functions," shows examples of some of the common mathematical functions that we can use in the modeling of behaviors.

Chapter 11, "Probability Distributions," explains the terminology of distributions of data, shows how we can model different distributions of populations, and gives examples of their usage.

Chapter 12, "Response Curves," shows we can construct data structures that allow for simple creation, manipulation, and retrieval of activation functions and probability distributions.

Chapter 13, "Factor Weighting," explains considerations and methods in the process of codifying, scaling, and combining utility values.

10 Mathematical Functions

It's no secret that mathematical functions are integral (Oooh… a calculus pun!) to game development as a whole. This is especially true in the subspecialty of game artificial intelligence (AI). In Part II, we explored the heady world of decision theory. Much of the discussion, however, was theoretical rather than practical. Even as we delved into the mathematics of utility, much of what we explored was relatively straightforward. If we are to convert that theory into practice, we need to explore the language necessary for expressing those theories.

A good example is that of marginal utility. In Chapter 8, we discussed how utility can change over a range such as time or quantity. Simply *knowing* that it can change—or even which direction it is changing—is not enough. We need to define what that rate of change is. We may need to even define the rate of change of the change! There are numerous ways of accomplishing this task, the selection of which depends on exactly the effect that we desire.

As we have repeated throughout this book so far, the best approach is for us to lay out the tools and make note of some convenient examples of their usage. In that pursuit, this chapter will consist of a reference guide to these basic tools.

SIMPLE LINEAR FUNCTIONS

 The most basic function we will use is the **linear function**—named as such due to the result forming a straight line. We usually see this early algebraic staple defined in the **slope-intercept** form,

$$y = mx + b$$

 where m is the **slope** of the line and b is the y-intercept (the point where the line crosses the y-axis).

We can also use a version that is solved in terms of x instead:

$$x = \frac{y}{m} + c$$

In this case, c is the x-intercept rather than the y-intercept.

There are a number of other variations on how to express a line. However, many of them are slightly more difficult to work with from a programming standpoint in that they have more than one term on the left side of the equal sign. For example, rather than a slope, we could substitute in values that result in the slope of the line:

$$m = \frac{(y_2 - y_1)}{(x_2 - x_1)}$$

Note that in the above equation x_2 cannot be equal to x_1 lest we encounter a "division by zero" error and cause a catastrophic and untimely end to our faux universe.

There is really only one simple rule to remember about the linear function. If $m < 0$, the line is descending. If $m > 0$, the line is ascending. (For that matter, if $m = 0$, the line is horizontal.) Because the slope is, for all intents and purposes, the only defining characteristic of the linear function, m is the only value that changes the *effect* of the function. Changing the value of b merely moves the line around in space. We can see examples of these changes in Figure 10.1.

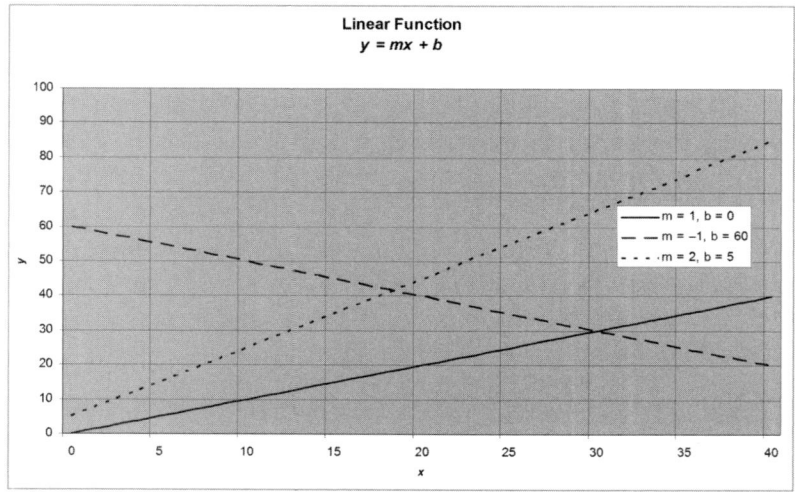

FIGURE 10.1 The graph of three linear functions with different values for m and b. Note that a negative value of m creates a descending line.

QUADRATIC FUNCTIONS

We can create another common and useful function in a similar fashion to the linear function above. By inserting an exponent into the formula, we create one of the veritably plethoric varieties of **quadratic functions**. Rather than being a straight line, the quadratic family exhibits parabolic curves. The most simple of these equations is the familiar

$$y = x^k$$

This function creates a parabola centered on the *y*-axis whose **vertex** (the point where the parabola changes direction) crosses the origin. The exponent (k) can be any non-zero real number. For simplicity's sake, however, let's restrict ourselves to $k = 2$ over the next few examples. (A little further on, we will see why different values of k can complicate things.)

Most of us are used to thinking of equations with exponents as exponential *functions. That term, however, has a very specific meaning. Technically, functions with a squared component (or higher) are referred to as* quadratic.

Additionally, while quadratic *specifically refers to equations whose highest exponent is 2, it gets a little clumsy to refer to* cubic, quartic, *and* quintic *functions for exponents of 3, 4, and 5, respectively. This will get even more confusing when we use non-integer exponents. Therefore, when I refer to a* quadratic *function, please take it to mean simply one with parabolic characteristics.*

We can perform numerous manipulations on this base equation to shape it to our liking and move it to our desired position in the graph space.

SHIFTING THE QUADRATIC

First, we are likely going to get more use out of the line produced by the quadratic equation if we can position it in different locations. To move the line vertically, we must add a value to it in a way similar to what we did with the linear equation above. In fact, we will term this value b since it performs a similar function to the *y*-intercept value of a linear equation. This causes the resulting function to be

$$y = x^k + b$$

Positive values of b move the curve up the graph; negative values move it down. It is important to note, however, that b is *not* necessarily going to be the point where the line crosses the *y*-axis. If we move the parabola horizontally, the same function will cross the *y*-axis in a different place. Therefore, it is better to think of *b* in terms of shifting the vertex of the parabola up or down by *b*. That is, if *b* = 5, then the vertex will be at *y* = 5 regardless of what the *x* value is.

To shift the vertex (and the entire parabola) horizontally, we *subtract* the value from *x* before raising it to the exponent. In keeping with the terminology established above, we will term this value *c* (although it is *not* necessarily the *x*-intercept). The equation for this is

$$y = (x-c)^k$$

If we set *c* = 5, the curve is shifted to the right by five units. Therefore, the vertex would be located at the point (5, 0).

Combining the two adjustments into one equation, we would arrive at

$$y = (x-c)^k + b$$

By using this formula, we can generate a simple parabola with a vertex at the point (*c*, *b*). We can see three examples of shifted parabolas in Figure 10.2.

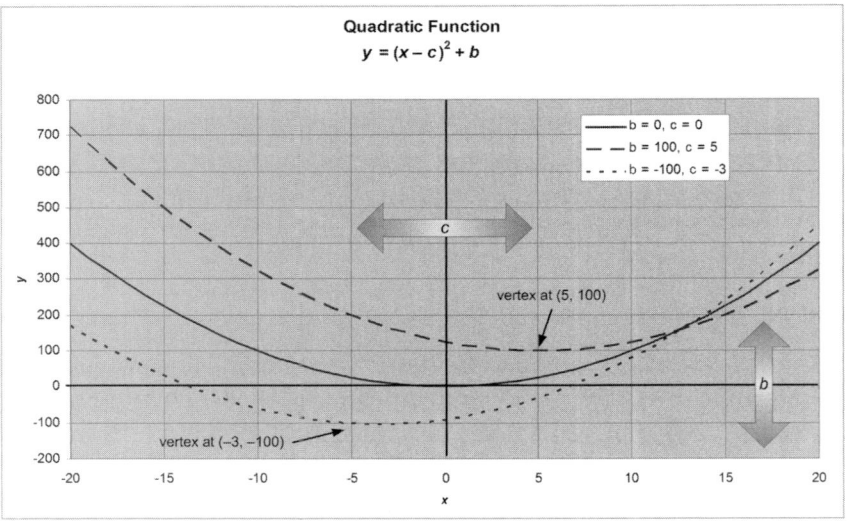

FIGURE 10.2 Three examples of quadratic functions of the form $y = (x - c)^2 + b$. The value of *b* shifts the curve vertically, and *c* shifts it horizontally. The vertex of the parabola is located at (*c*, *b*).

TILTING THE PARABOLA

By adding the value of x without an exponent, we can "tilt" the parabola one direction or the other. For example, assuming $x > 0$, the following formula will tilt the parabola slightly to the left:

$$y = x^2 + x$$

By adding a coefficient to the first-degree component (the one without an exponent), we determine the magnitude of the effect. For example, the formula

$$y = x^2 + 10x$$

generates a parabola that tilts significantly further to the left than does the one from the original equation above (Figure 10.3).

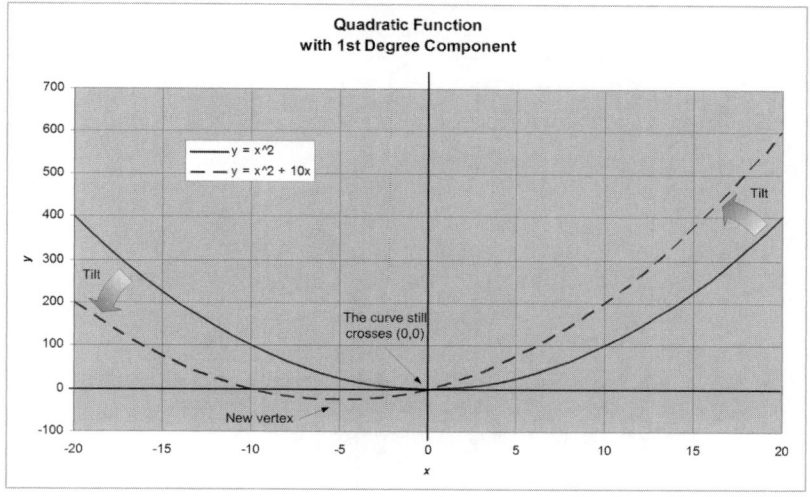

FIGURE 10.3 By adding a first-degree component to the otherwise second-degree function, we can "tilt" the parabola. In this case, the addition of 10x to the basic parabola tilted the curve to the left.

Note that the addition of other components will also change the vertex locations much like the inclusion of the b and c parameters. In the case of the formula in Figure 10.3, the new vertex is at (−5, −25). When $x = -5$, the original x^2 portion of the equation still wants to be at $y = 25$. The new 10x portion yields a −50, however, which pushes that side of the curve down. Similarly, positive values of x push the right side of the curve *up* by adding 10x to it—thus the "tilt" effect. Note that you can't tilt the parabola such that you can have two y values for the same x value. (Parabolas wobble, but they don't fall down!)

Reshaping the Parabola

As elegant as the above parabola is, it is unlikely that its shape will exactly fit our needs. We may want to make it wider or narrower, or skew it slightly one direction or the other. The formula can be modified a number of ways to affect the shape of a parabola. Many of them come with caveats, however, that we must be aware of.

Increasing the Exponent

The first major modification that we can make to a quadratic equation is to change the exponent (k). Doing so changes the rate at which the slope of the parabola changes. That is, it makes the parabola narrower or wider.

One thing we must remember, however, is that odd exponents (e.g., 3, 5) will cause the portion of the parabola to the left of the vertex to curve *downward* (Figure 10.4). The reason we note this as "to the left of the vertex" rather than "below 0" is that if we shift the parabola horizontally using the techniques above, the x location of vertex may be greater than or less than 0. The inflection change happens at the vertex… not at the y-axis. We can avoid this effect by taking the absolute value of the function. In that case, both arms of the parabola still extend in the same direction.

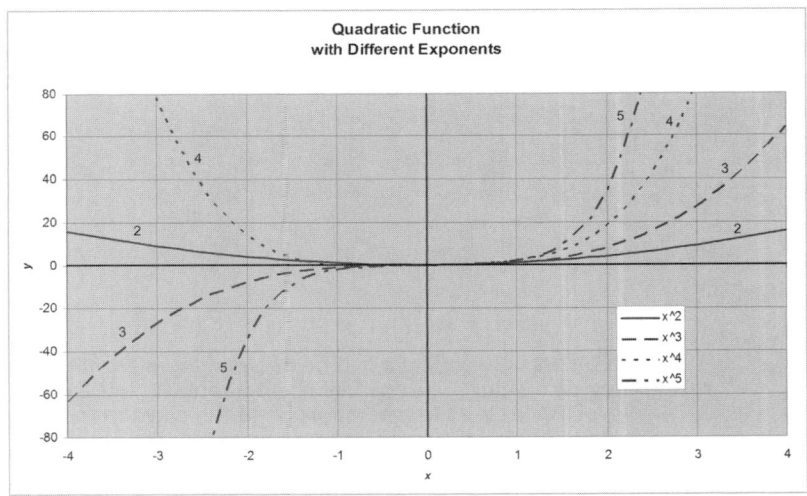

FIGURE 10.4 The quadratic function $y = x^k$ with the values of k as 2, 3, 4, and 5. As the exponent increases, the parabola narrows. Also, odd exponents cause the portion of the curve below 0 to descend rather that ascend. (Note that we can avoid the negative y effect by taking the absolute value of the function.)

This is not an issue if we are only concerned with the portion of the parabola that is to the right of the vertex. In fact, by focusing only on that side of the parabola, we can open up another bag of tricks with regard to the exponent.

By dispensing with the possibility of *x* values less than 0, we are allowed to raise *x* to fractional exponents (Figure 10.5). The result of doing this is the same as increasing the exponent by whole numbers—the higher the exponent, the steeper the resulting parabola. However, by allowing real numbers rather than integers, we have much more flexibility in the exact shape of the curve.

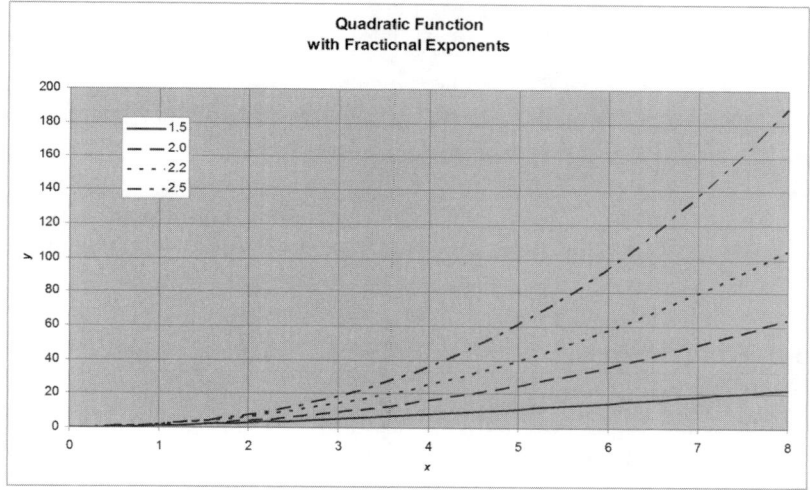

FIGURE 10.5 The quadratic function $y = x^k$ with the values of *k* as 1.5, 2.0, 2.2, and 2.5. As before, as the exponent increases, the bowl of the parabola narrows.

Rotating the Curve

Another convenient manipulation is to use values of *k* that are between 0 and 1. Remember that another way of writing the square root of *x* is $x^{0.5}$. Therefore, by raising *x* to *k* values between 0 and 1, we are actually taking a root of *x*. The resulting curve is a parabola whose axis of symmetry is parallel to the *x*-axis rather than the *y*-axis (Figure 10.6).

As with exponents greater than 1, we can change the shape of the parabola by modifying the magnitude of the value of *k*. In this case, when we make the exponent smaller, the parabola narrows. An easier way to remember this is for us to think in terms of *closer to* or *farther away* from 1. Just as with $k > 1$, the farther away from 1 we move, the narrower the curve.

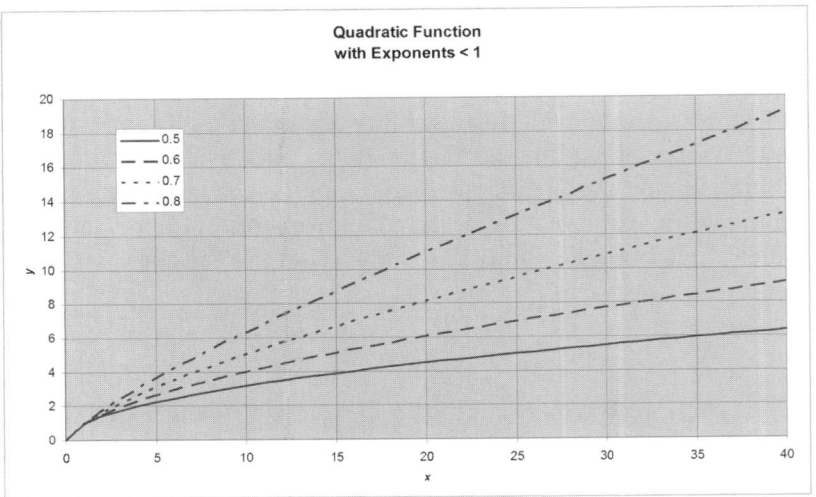

FIGURE 10.6 The quadratic function, $y = x^{0.5}$ (or the square root of x), yields a parabolic curve with its primary axis horizontal rather than vertical.

SIGMOID FUNCTIONS

One of the more useful, and therefore oft-used, functions is the **sigmoid function**. Specifically, the name *sigmoid* refers to a function with an "s-curve." Therefore, sigmoid functions are actually an entire family of curves. We will examine some of the more common ones below.

THE LOGISTIC FUNCTION

The most common of these is the **logistic function**. It pops up in a variety of applications ranging from biology, economics, probability, statistics, and (strikingly relevant to us) the mathematics of behavioral psychology.

The formula for the logistic function is

$$P(t) = \frac{1}{1 + e^{-t}}$$

Because logistic functions are often used for population and time-based calculations, the value P stands for *population*, and t stands for a specified point in time. Therefore, we would read the function above as "the population at time t equals ...." However, this is simply a naming convention.

Converting it to our standard notation, we could rewrite the formula as

$$y = \frac{1}{1+e^{-x}}$$

We can attribute the usefulness and popularity of the deceptively simple-looking logistic function to the presence of that ever-so-mystical value e. The value e (also known as Euler's number) is the base of the natural logarithm. Like the constant *pi*, the value of e extends off to unfathomable lengths. For our purposes, a reasonable approximation is 2.718281828. In fact, we can usually get away with something less precise such as 2.718.

The tails of the logistic curve asymptotically approach 0 and 1 (Figure 10.7). Given the rate at which they close, when we are using the value e, there really isn't much need to calculate the logistic curve outside the x range of $[-10...10]$. At those points, the function is within 0.0001 of the respective bounds. We can even define cutoffs at -6 and 6, respectively, and not lose much resolution. For example, at $x = 6$, $y = 0.9975$.

If we want, we can use other, non-negative numbers besides e for the base in this function. The greater the number, the narrower the shape of the logistic function. Regardless of the base that we use, however, the values still approach the asymptotes 0 and 1.

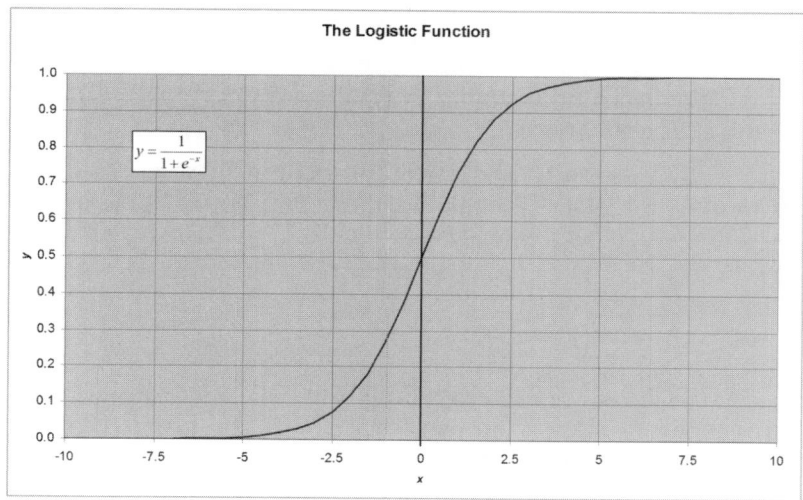

FIGURE 10.7 The logistic function is the most commonly encountered member of the family of sigmoid functions.

One of the advantages of the vertical range of the logistic function being [0...1] is that it works very well as an expression of percentage. Despite being apparent on the graph in Figure 10.6, it's worth noting that the function crosses the "50% mark" at $x = 0$. If we think in those terms, we can see how the curve would be advantageous in applications of psychology such as subjective utility functions.

For instance, if we were to say that we were "50% satisfied" with something when it was "normal" (i.e., 0), we could then make the further observation that, as that thing improved (i.e., $x > 0$), we would be *more* satisfied with it. Eventually, if the improvement continued, we would approach a point where we were almost 100% satisfied with the object or action. Likewise, as the quality of the object or action grew worse (i.e., $x < 0$), we would be *less* satisfied with it until such time as we had almost 0% satisfaction.

In both cases, the further that the quality of that thing moved away from "normal," the less dramatic the effect is. This is reminiscent of marginal utility… but in *both* directions away from the starting point. Unlike the root-based quadratic equations that continued on to infinity in both directions, the asymptotic nature of the logistic function provides the natural boundaries of 0% and 100%. After all, we can't be *less* satisfied than "not at all" or *more* satisfied than "perfectly so."

Also, because the vertical range of the curve is neatly defined, we can flip the curve upside down quite easily by changing the formula to

$$y = 1 - \frac{1}{1 + e^{-x}}$$

Using the above formula, we find that the curve now starts near 1.0 when $x < 0$ and ends near 0.0 when $x > 0$.

We can also shift the curve left or right in a fashion similar to the way we did with other functions above. Using the same notation as before (the variable c), our new function would look like this:

$$y = \frac{1}{1 + e^{-x+c}}$$

Because the line extends infinitely in both directions, using the point where y crosses the 0.5 mark is our best landmark. In the unshifted curve, when $x = 0$, $y = 0.5$. If we include a value for c, we know that y will cross the 0.5 mark where $x = c$. As we noted before, the differences in value get insignificant outside the range of about –6 to 6. Therefore, if we wanted the curve to start with $x = 0$, $y = 0$, we could set $c = 6$. Accordingly, y would be within the same margin of 1.0 at about $x = 12$.

THE LOGIT FUNCTION

Close kin to the logistic function is the **logit function** (pronounced *low-jit*). We can think of a logit curve as a logistic curve rotated 90 degrees. Where the logistic curve approached $y = 0$ and $y = 1$, the s-curve defined by the logit function approaches the asymptotes of $x = 0$ and $x = 1$. The formula for the logit function is

$$y = \log\left(\frac{x}{1-x}\right)$$

As with the logistic function above, we can define any base to the logarithm that we wanted, although our good friend e is typically used (Figure 10.8). By increasing the value of the logarithm base, we can "flatten" the s-curve horizontally.

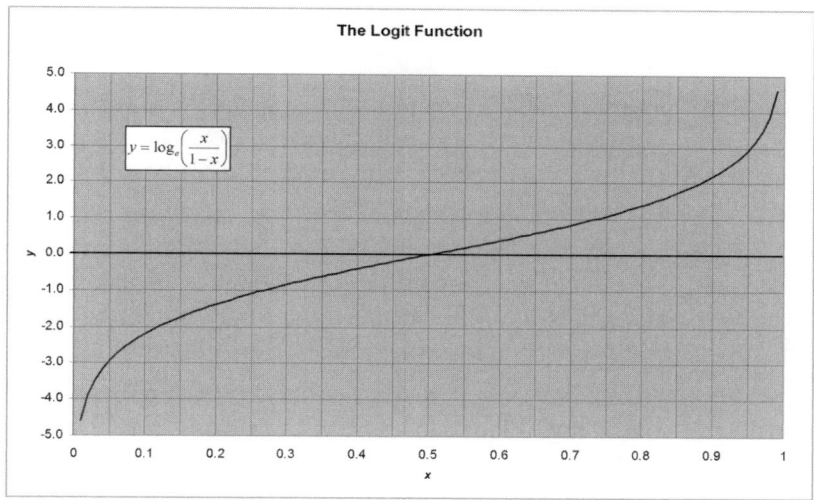

FIGURE 10.8 We can think of the logit function as a rotated version of the logistic function. The curve approaches but does not reach $x = 0$ and $x = 1$. Therefore, we must take care not to attempt to solve for those values of x.

As with the logistic function, we can use the logit function in numerous applications with regard to behavioral and psychological perceptions and reaction. For example, rather than resembling the notion of *decreasing* marginal utility like the logistic function, as we move from the "center" point ($x = 0.5$), the logit curve resembles *increasing* marginal utility.

Because the value of y approaches infinity the closer x gets to 0 and 1, there truly are no upper and lower bounds. However, as you can see from Figure 10.8, the shift is so dramatic that the actual boundaries are based on the decimal precision that we use for *x*. If we are not using very precise values of *x*, those extreme values of *y* do not come into play. For example, using *e* as the root (as shown in Figure 10.8), $y < -5$ only when $x < 0.0057$. Therefore, if we only concerned ourselves with two decimal places, we would never see values of *y* less than −5 or greater than 5.

Because of this, one common shift we can perform is to move the curve up by five points. This means the effective range of the logit function becomes 0 to 10 rather than −5 to 5. For completeness, the formula would be

$$y = \log\left(\frac{x}{1-x}\right) + 5$$

AD HOC FUNCTIONS

By no means are the above functions an exhaustive list. What they do provide is a number of core building blocks from which to work. By using the basics, tweaking them with coefficients, and even combining multiple types into the same equation, we can create many very distinct curves.

As we will see over the next few chapters, fine-tuning a function to fit a need is a skill that is core to constructing proper behavioral mathematics. Often, constructing the right curve takes a lot of trial and error. I very much recommend using a tool such as Excel to construct formulas and examine the resulting graphs.

When all else fails, there are ways of handcrafting data points that break completely out of the formula-based approach. We shall cover those in Chapter 12.

11 Probability Distributions

As we discovered in earlier chapters, there are many reasons for the gulf between the one "should be done" solution that normative decision theory provides and the myriad possibilities that are summarized by descriptive decision theory—that is, what people as a whole tend to do. The suggestions and guides that descriptive decision theory provides often are based on observation and collection of information. This data is necessarily an aggregate. As such, we have a picture of the population as a whole rather than any individual member of that population.

The end result is that, while we know that people do different things, we don't know *why* they do them. While we can ascertain to some degree some of the possible *non-optimal* solutions that people may provide to a particular decision, often the reasons *why* they do so get lost in the background noise of human individuality.

The other shortcoming of the descriptive decision theory approach is that, for obvious reasons, the game development world doesn't have data on the behaviors we would like to model. We simply don't have enough data on how often orcs elect to use their hand axes or the accuracy with which demons from hell can toss balls of flaming plasma. Even in cases where we *do* have data from which to work, it may not provide the sort of behavior mix that makes for a believable, engaging *game* character. Therefore, to model these behaviors, we must be able to assemble our own substitutes for the data that we believe is representative of the population as a whole.

/* *Throughout this section, the term* population *may represent a group of data points rather than simply the typical definition of "a group of people." In large part, these concepts can be interchanged. For example,* population *could signify many people each making one decision about* X *or one* person *making many successive decisions about* X. */

IDENTIFYING POPULATION FEATURES

To artificially model a population, we need to identify the key components of that population. We need to make some broad assumptions about the decision that the population faces and use those conjectures as both building blocks and constraints as appropriate. Much like setting out stakes and lines defines where we will build a house, identifying, measuring out, and fixing in position the important features of our population is a necessary step in the process of constructing an accurate model of a population. From that model, we can then make the assumption that any one sample drawn from that population is representative of a randomly selected member of that population. The **law of large numbers** suggests that the more samples we draw from that model, the more the aggregate of our selections begins to mimic the population as a whole.

For example, if we fill a bag with five red balls, three blue balls, and two green balls, and then select randomly from the balls in the bag, we have no idea which color ball we are going to select on any given draw. We can say nothing about the individual selection. While we can suggest that we may select a red ball about as often as a non-red ball, we can't exactly predict which color we are going to select *next*. We also can't say *why* we picked the color we just did. We didn't follow a rule that said, "You will pick a green ball this time." However, over time (and assuming that we replace the selected ball each time), we will find that we are selecting red balls 50% of the time, blue balls 30% of the time, and green balls for the remaining 20% of the time.

By artificially defining a distribution of colored balls, we can model an eventual distribution of those colors without necessarily prescribing the color of any individual draw. Similarly, by defining a distribution of any behavioral trait or decision, we can model an eventual distribution of these traits or decisions without prescribing any individual event or agent.

In Chapter 4, we glibly recalled the marketing staple "four out of five dentists surveyed recommended sugarless gum…." This does not mean that any given dentist recommends sugarless gum to 80% of his patients. This means that if we were to select a random dentist, we are 80% likely to have selected one who recommends sugarless gum. The statistic as a whole tells us nothing about any individual dentist. However, if we were to attempt to model that population in a game, we could leverage that one number. It wouldn't be difficult to create a game ("Dental Prophylaxis Simulator") wherein the player would discover that 80% of the dentists he encounters recommend sugarless gum. That experience would mesh with what we know of the real world (or at least what the marketing folks have told us about the real world).

Numbers such as the "four out of five" statistic not only tell us about the behavior of populations, but they offer us useful tools with which we can reconstruct the behavior of populations. If we were to construct a histogram about the dentists the same way we did with the number guessers, it would look like the one in Figure 11.1.

"Four out of Five Dentists" Histogram

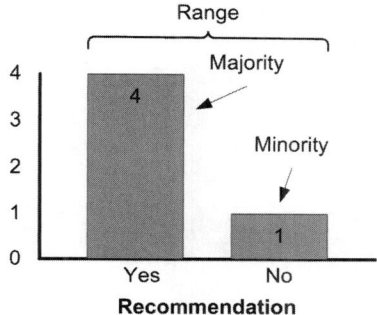

FIGURE 11.1 A simple histogram showing how the marketing adage "four out of five dentists surveyed" would look.

Based on this histogram, if we were to ask what was the percentage chance of randomly selecting a dentist who answered "yes," the answer would be four out of five. Therefore, if we were to build an agent pretending to be a dentist, and we wanted this dentist to answer the "sugarless gum" question, we could use this exact same histogram as a source. In this (admittedly simple) case, we would leverage that same mathematical proportion—four out of five… or 80%.

Turning the Tables

The trick is in turning the statistics back upon themselves. By looking at the survey data, we can realize that we are 80% likely to encounter a dentist who recommends sugarless gum. Therefore, when we create a random dentist, we make him 80% likely to recommend sugarless gum. We are taking survey data from *five* dentists and boiling it down into collection of probabilities that we can use to construct *one* dentist at a time.

To reiterate, in this case we created the histogram from the knowledge we had of dentists (i.e., "four out of five"). By using that histogram as a decision tool for our dental agent, we applied the process in reverse. We gave a four in five chance that he would respond "yes" and a one in five chance that he would respond "no." If we change the numbers, the histogram would change. Of course, if we changed the numbers, the odds of the two potential outcomes would change as well. The histogram is representative of the odds. As such, the shape of the curve that it exhibits is an important tool in determining what outcomes we can draw from its data.

/* *Throughout this book, I will use the word* curve *often in regard to graphs of data. While the line implied by the data may or may not be curved, I will use* curve *regardless. Please do not get out a straight edge to determine if a line that looks straight to you actually has a curve to it simply because I referred to it as such.* */

SEGMENTING THE POPULATION

In the Guess Two-Thirds Game in Chapter 6, we identified some general categories of people. There were the random guessers who we termed Index 0. We saw a spike in the number of people who guessed 33 (Index 1) and a spike in the number who guessed 22 (Index 2). Those were three distinct categories for which we could make a reasonable case as to *why* they selected what they did. However, a significant majority of the population guessed plenty of answers that were neither mindlessly random nor calculatingly centered on the magical numbers of 33 and 22. Why did those people guess that way? The distribution of guesses showed that it wasn't completely random, but it wasn't completely rational either. So how do we get into those people's heads?

The truth is that we don't really need to get inside their heads as to exactly why they chose the way they did. If we were to ask 100 members of that large majority of people what their rationale was in choosing their number, chances are we would get 100 different answers. Everyone has a different thought process that may or may not be based on logical premises. It may even be based *partially* on a logical premise but has been obscured or adulterated by an interloping, *non*-logical thought. In Chapter 6, we covered many potential pitfalls that, if they don't completely ensnare a person's train of thought, can at least make it stumble somewhat. Each of the individual person's perceptions and thought processes may be composed of a different cocktail of truth, falsehood, error, and subjective coloring. Trying to model all of those individual rationales is not only prohibitive but usually largely irrelevant.

We must ask ourselves, what problem are we trying to solve? If we were (for some obscure reason) trying to simulate people trying to play the Guess Two-Thirds Game, we would have to include three different approaches (Figure 11.2). First, we would have to model the intelligent calculators. This is actually a fairly straightforward process of determining what percentage of people picked those two numbers (33 and 22).

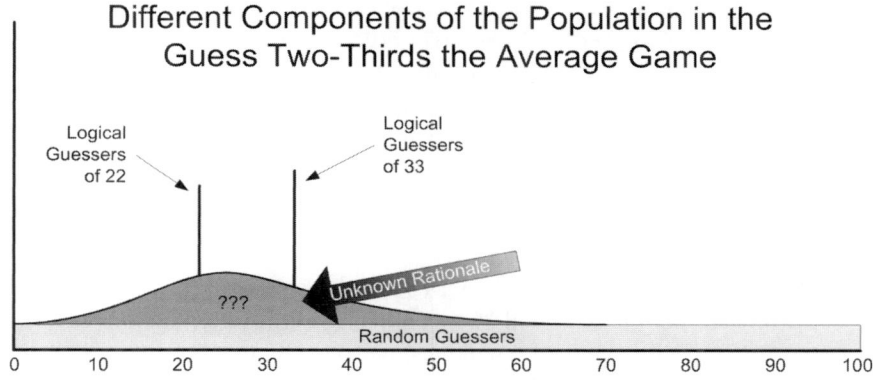

FIGURE 11.2 The Guess Two-Thirds Game had three types of participants: the random guessers, the logical guessers, and a group of individuals who each had their own methodology. Without knowing the rationale of each individual, we can still identify where those people tended to guess and in what concentrations.

Glancing at the data from Chapter 6, we see that about 6.5% of the population picked 33, and just over 6% guessed 22. However, we must take note that only about half of those two populations stuck up "above the crowd." We would be reasonable in making the assumption that only those people above the rest of the nearby population *specifically* selected those numbers for a reason. The others selected 33 or 22 with as random a process of the people who selected 31, 34, 21, or 23. Let us assume that 3% of the guessers selected 22 in a logical fashion, and 4% of the guessers selected 33 in the same manner. That accounts for 7% of our population total.

Second, we would have to model the random guessers. Likewise, this is a relatively simple task. By determining the number of people who are guessing randomly, we can then spread them evenly across the entire range of possibilities by simply selecting a random number from 0 to 100. For example, we could say that 30% of the population guessed randomly. Evenly spread, this would mean about 0.3% would pick each of the 101 possibilities from 0 to 100.

The third task is slightly more involved and certainly less definable. We would have to come up with a method of representing the 63% of the players who weren't *random*, but weren't *logically* calculating. Because we *can't* model the very personal, unique thought processes that went on in each person's mind, we have to look at them as an aggregate. Using the terminology from descriptive decision theory, "What do people tend to do?"

Regardless of their motives, people playing the game pick numbers. We need to find a way of modeling those picks. We do not start from the lowest level of *why* they pick the way they do, however. We need to generate the equivalent of what the descriptive decision theory would show us—that four out of five dentists recommend sugarless gum, for example. If we were to look at the histogram of the guesses that the players offered, we could identify the populations we mentioned above.

Looking at Figure 11.2 again (which has been grossly simplified from the original histogram from Chapter 6), we have identified our three groups. Spread across the entire spectrum from 0 to 100 are the random guessers. Those are the small number of people who will guess anything without rhyme or reason. Additionally, we saw that there were two spikes of people who guessed 33 and 22, respectively. In Chapter 6 we showed why people would have guessed those particular logical answers. The darkened section in the figure represents our mystery population. There was an obvious bulge in the lower half of the histogram. Many people guessed those semi-logical answers—far more so than guessed randomly. Unlike the random guessers and the targeted 33/22 folks, we have no idea what these people were thinking. We only know that they tended to be between approximately 10 and 50, with a distinct bulge between 20 and 30.

Re-Creating the Bulge

Turning to artificial intelligence (AI), if we wanted to model an agent that would play the game *the way humans do*, we would have to take *all* of these populations into account. Creating an agent that generated purely random guesses wouldn't create the histogram that the Denmark study yielded. Creating an agent that logically solved the answer would generate the same answer every time—entirely dependant on the single logical formula we devised. Neither of these solutions, when repeated enough times to resemble a large population of people would mimic the results that 19,000 *very real* people gave us in the Denmark study.

The solution is to incorporate three approaches. If we were to assume that a small portion of the population *did* guess randomly, we could allow some of our agents to do that. If we were to assume that a small portion of the population *did* guess logically, we could allow some of our agents to do that. However, the remainder of our agents fall into that shadow zone. What we need is a way of creating the guesses that those agents would offer. That process requires us to do more investigation on the characteristics of *only* that population.

ANALYZING A SINGLE SEGMENT

To analyze *only* the population of semi-logical guessers, we will isolate them from the graph in Figure 11.2. If we look at the counts of the guesses of the people who are in this category, we may see something like what is in Figure 11.3. Note that unlike the random guessers, who were equally probably all across the range from 0 to 100, and unlike the targeted guessers who focused *only* on the numbers 33 and 22, these guessers exhibit certain characteristics. Let's describe the observable features of this group one by one.

- Their guesses range from 0 to about 70.
- The majority of people guessed between about 15 and 35.
- There was a minority who guessed from 0 to about 15.
- There was a minority who guessed from about 35 to about 60.
- There were some rare "outliers" who guessed above 60.
- Significantly more people guessed any given number in the majority range (e.g., 27) than guessed any given number in the minority ranges (e.g., 50)—as much as three or four times as many.

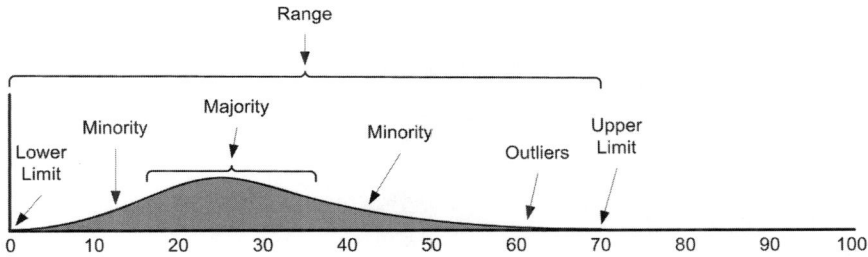

FIGURE 11.3 The guesses of the semi-logical guessers shown are spread over the range from 0 to 70. The majority of the guesses are clustered between approximately 15 and 35.

Even without the graph, from that list of descriptive characteristics, we can begin to generalize what the population of semi-logical guessers looked like. We can then start to construct an artificial curve using those characteristics that we could use to represent the population. But what would we do with this information?

Reconstructing a Guesser

In the case of the Denmark experiment, each possible selection from 0 to 100 has a number of people who selected it. Focusing *only* on the segment of semi-logical guessers again, we don't care *why* they selected the number that they did. After all, there are probably 15,000 of the initial 19,000+ respondents in that category. However, by analyzing how many picked each number, we can remix those exact figures and turn them into *likelihoods* that any one person would pick those numbers.

For example, if 2% of the people picked the number 29, we could assume that any random person had a 2% chance of picking 29. If 1.3% of the people picked 15, we could assume that any random person had a 1.3% chance of picking 15. If 0.3% picked the number 70, we can assume that any given person has a 0.3% chance of picking 70 as well.

Selecting the Proper Tool

While the curve that defined the dentist's recommendations was relatively simplistic, and the curve that resulted from the respondents in the Guess Two-Thirds Game was slightly more involved, there *are* plenty of standard curves that fit many situations. Additionally, we can tweak, adjust, and even combine each of the standard curves with each other to build in subtle nuances. We can use these results just as we did above—to model the likelihood of any given person from a population in proportion to that type of person's occurrence in the population. If we do this process carefully and correctly, we can model a startlingly deep array of behaviors.

But first, we must learn about some of the common tools of the trade. At the end of this chapter, we will use some of the tools to address the Guess Two-Thirds population problem above.

UNIFORM DISTRIBUTIONS

For the sake of completeness and of setting a base from which to work, we must first at least pay a passing recognition to **uniform distribution**. As the name implies, it is a probability distribution that is... well... *uniform*. Every item in the population has an equal chance of being selected. Examples are not hard to come by. If we were to flip a coin, the odds of heads or tails showing would be uniformly distributed between the two options. If we roll a fair die numerous times, we would find the result of the rolls to be uniformly distributed among all the sides. Each of the 52 cards in a deck has an equal opportunity to be picked; therefore, the probabilities of each card being selected would be uniform. When we ask the computer for random numbers (yes, I know they are actually *pseudo*-random numbers), we receive results that are theoretically uniformly distributed between 0 and some maximum value. Certainly, we have made the point by now.

This sort of random selection is probably the most leaned on by game developers as well. Very often, programmers simply ask for a random number between two values. If we have three options in a decision, it is perfectly legitimate for us to generate a three-possibility random number and select the associated option. Uniform distributions of this sort are also delightfully extensible. If we add a fourth potential option to our decision, it is a simple matter to change the random number call to add a fourth result.

There are those who say that a person's greatest strength is also their greatest weakness. Whether or not that holds true for people, it is definitely the case with uniform distributions. Their biggest weakness is that they are… well… *uniform*. There are plenty of phenomena that we can't model with them.

IMPORTANT DISTRIBUTION TERMS

A number of terms apply to distributions as a whole. While not directly related to our endeavor, they are important to recognize nonetheless.

- **Cumulative distribution function (CDF):** The CDF represents the sum of all the probabilities equal to or less than a given value x. That is, rather than the probability of x alone, it represents the probability that a random number will be $\leq x$.

- **Discrete random variable:** A probability distribution is considered discrete if there are one or more places where the distribution function is not continuous. For example, while there are probabilities of rolling a 3 or a 4 on a die, there is no corresponding probability of rolling a 3.5.

- **Continuous random variable:** A probability distribution is considered continuous if its cumulative distribution function is continuous. A continuous function is one that has a solution for *all* real numbers in the range specified.

- **Probability mass function (PMF):** The probability that a discrete random variable is equal to some value.

- **Probability density function (PDF):** Because a continuous random variable can be subdivided into infinitely small segments, the probability of any one value is likewise infinitely small. The PDF expresses the probability that a continuous random variable will occur within a specified range. As such, it is based on integral calculus.

Referring back to our Guess Two-Thirds example, the group that we had identified as random guessers seemed to be a uniform distribution across the range from 0 to 100. We could get away with modeling their guesses as random numbers from 0 to 100. However, the distribution of the slightly more thoughtful group was certainly *not* uniformly distributed (Figure 11.2). If we wanted to model the guesses that group would yield, we would need a slightly more involved approach.

NORMAL (GAUSSIAN) DISTRIBUTIONS

Perhaps the most well-known of all probability distributions is the **normal distribution**. People often refer to it as a **Gaussian distribution** after Carl Friedrich Gauss, the 19th century German mathematician and scientist. Most of us best know this function, however, by its colloquial name of the **bell curve**. The reason for this is purely visual coincidence—in its standard form, it looks like a bell.

We find the hallmark of the bell curve in all its shapes and sizes all throughout nature, science, sociology, astronomy, and behavior. Even in just observation of humans, much of what we can measure ends up on a bell curve somewhere. Height, weight, strength, speed, and intelligence (IQ) are measurements that tend to lie in a bell curve. Even statistical processes as simple as flipping multiple coins or rolling multiple dice churn out bell curves. It is this connection that makes normal distributions one of the most valuable components in modeling behavior… and, therefore, one of the ones we will examine in greater detail.

PROPERTIES OF NORMAL DISTRIBUTIONS

Every normal distribution has key components (Figure 11.4). These properties reflect the size and shape of the distribution—and therefore the population it represents. If we know these properties, we can make assumptions about the population. Additionally, and more importantly to AI developers, we can also reasonably recreate the curve that the distribution shows.

Range

The **range** of a distribution is a measurement of the distance between its lowest and highest members. Sometimes, this is a function of the parameters of what we are trying to measure. For example, in the Guess Two-Thirds Game the minimum guess was 0 and the maximum was 100. The range could not be any wider than 101. As long as at least one person guessed 0 and one guessed 100, the range would be 101.

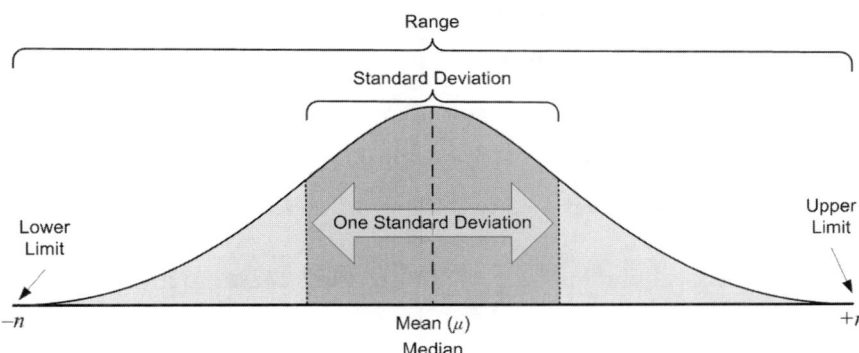

FIGURE 11.4 A generic representation of a normal (Gaussian) distribution showing the range, mean, median, upper and lower limits, and one standard deviation.

Of course, it could certainly be *smaller* than 100. We must make certain to not confuse the parameters of the scenario and the reality of the sample. If no one in our sample guessed 100, the uppermost bound would not be 100. In our example subset illustrated in Figure 11.2, the range was about 71—from 0 to 70. In this case the *actual* range differed from the theoretical maximum that the parameters of the scenario defined.

There are times, however, when there are no parameters that would artificially constrain a range. For example, the distribution of people's heights has no theoretical maximum—or at least not one that we have found. Therefore, the uppermost limit of the distribution is the height of the tallest person. Similarly, the lower limit of the range is pinned at the height of the shortest person in the sample. The resulting range is the difference between those two extremes.

We must remember that the range is specific to the population. Two different populations may have completely different ranges. An obvious example would be the distribution of the heights of NBA players compared to the heights of the general population. They each have their own maximums and minimums which, in turn, yield different ranges.

Mean, Median, and Mode

Another major player in defining a normal distribution is the relative locations of the **mean,** the **median,** and the **mode**. The mean (represented by the Greek letter *mu*: μ) is the average value of all the items in the population. The median is the point where there are as many items greater than it as less than it. The mode is the point in the range that has the most samples.

In its purest (and most cited) form, the bell curve is symmetrical. That means that the mean, median, and mode values are identical. They are also co-located exactly in the middle of the range. In a normal distribution with a range of [0...100], all three figures would be 50. Therefore, we could assert that:

- The average of all the values is 50.
- There are as many items *below* 50 as there are *above 50*.
- The number 50 is the most common value in the population.

As we will find out later, these assertions come in handy.

Skew

When mean, median, and mode are *not* aligned we call that **skew**. If the "tail" of the curve is longer in the positive direction, we call that "positive" skew. Naturally, if the "tail" is longer in the negative direction, we say that the distribution is "negatively" skewed. We can look at the features of this a different way. In a positively skewed distribution, the bulk of the population (and therefore the mean) is on the left half of the range (i.e., left of the median). In a negatively skewed distribution, the bulk of the population is on the right side.

A convenient example of a skewed distribution is national household income. The curve has a significant skew in the positive direction. That is, the tail extending to the positive end of the range is longer than the one to the negative side. For the sake of example, let us place the median household income at $50,000. That means that half the households make more than $50,000 and half make less.

The lower limit of the range is necessarily $0—there are people with *no* income whatsoever. (For the sake of saking, ignore the fact that people can actually have *negative* income.) On the other hand, there is no limitation on how much money you can make. That is, there is no upper limit to the range. The current upper limit is the income of the household making the most money. Because people on that long positive tail can make millions of dollars, the *mean* income is well above the median $50,000—for purposes of example, let's say $70,000. The mode, on the other hand, is below the median. Again, pulling numbers out of the air, let us assume that the *most common* household income is $40,000.

When a distribution is skewed, the mean, median, and mode are no longer co-located. They do have tendencies, however. In a positively skewed distribution such as the one showed in Figure 11.5, the mode will be less than the median, which will, in turn, be less than the mean. In a negatively skewed distribution, the opposite will be true: *mean < median < mode*.

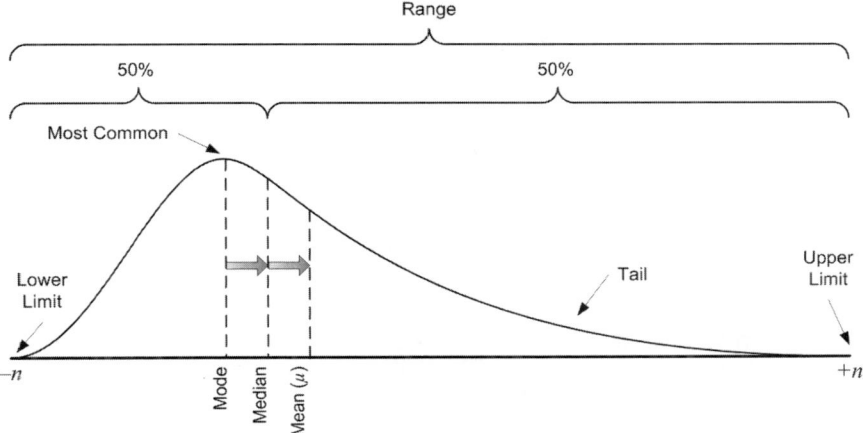

FIGURE 11.5 A skewed probability distribution has the bulk of the population on one side and a tail on the other. As a result, the mean, median, and mode are no longer co-located.

Standard Deviation

Another measurement that gives us valuable information about the makeup of the distribution is **standard deviation** (represented by the Greek letter *sigma*: Σ). It tells us how spread out the bulk of the population is—also known as "dispersion." A probability distribution can have exactly the same range, mode, median, and mean, and yet many different standard deviations (Figure 11.6). This is important to remember because it is the standard deviation that determines the "character" of the population. When most of the population is clustered tightly around the mean, the standard deviation is small. If the standard deviation is high, then we can assume that there is a wide dispersion of the population. A normal distribution with $\Sigma = 1$ is considered a **standard normal distribution**.

There are actually multiple layers of standard deviations for the same curve. They lie outside each other. For a normal distribution, about 68% of the data is within the **first standard deviation**—34% on each side of the mean. The **second standard deviation** is significantly wider than the first—encompassing 95% of the population. For any normally distributed population, 99.7% lie within **three standard deviations** of the mean. It is important to note that this is the case for *all* normal distributions. No matter what the shape of the curve, 68% of the population will be within that first standard deviation. This is known as the **68-95-99.7 rule**—the rule being that, in a normal distribution, almost all the data is within three standard deviations of the mean.

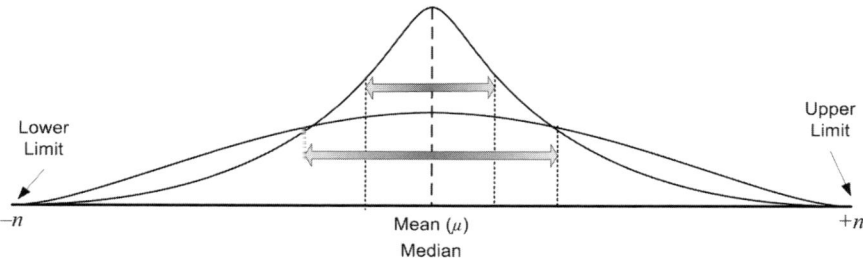

FIGURE 11.6 The standard deviation of a normal distribution determines the characteristic of the population. A small standard deviation makes a narrower, higher bulk of the population. A higher standard deviation leads to a broader, flatter curve.

GENERATING NORMAL DISTRIBUTIONS

The formulas for generating true normal distributions are delightfully cryptic and involved. The following formula, the Gaussian function, generates the continuous probability density function of the normal distribution:

$$\varphi_{\mu\sigma^2}(x) = \frac{1}{\sigma\sqrt{2\pi}} e^{-\frac{(x-\mu)^2}{2\sigma^2}}$$

In the above equation, Σ (sigma) is the standard deviation, e is our friendly natural logarithmic constant (≈ 2.71828), and the parameter μ (mu) is the *expected value*... a fun little term used in statistics. And of course, π (pi) is, well... *pi*. All of this squished together gives us a value for θ (theta) that shows the density of the curve at or around x. Now isn't *that* pleasant?

As you can see, dealing with this function is a little messy. Also, for the most part, it doesn't do us a lot of good in the game development world. After all, we aren't using these functions for analyzing existing data; we are trying to re-create data. Certainly, if we knew the exact figures needed to model a population's behavior, we could plug those into a normal distribution curve and churn out figures. These calculations can be fairly processor-intensive, however—and processor time is not a luxury producers often grant us AI folks in the trenches of game development.

Even more importantly, we aren't trying to model things exactly. There is a point of diminishing returns where the minutia of hundredths of a percent gets lost in the shuffle. Our job is to generate something *similar to* what it is we are trying to replicate. Close enough for the effect but not so involved as to grind the process to a halt.

Thankfully, we have plenty of techniques at our disposal for generating normal distributions of all sorts of sizes and shapes. Interestingly, many of us "older folks" were introduced to these techniques in the form of hunks of acrylic or hardened plastic—dice.

A Fantasy RPG Introduction to Real Statistics

The pen-and-paper role-playing games (RPGs) in the mold of Dungeons & Dragons (D&D) were many people's unwitting introduction to probability and statistics. This phenomenon became so ingrained in the gaming culture that many people still refer to probability curves in terms of combinations of dice. If I write terms such as "2d8" and "3d6," there is no shortage of people that recognize them as "the sum of the rolls of two eight-sided dice" and "the sum of the rolls of three six-sided dice," respectively. In fact, the latter was a D&D staple for generating the six character "ability scores" —strength, intelligence, wisdom, dexterity, constitution, and charisma. This is not a coincidence.

As we mentioned before, we often find normal distributions in nature. Traits such as the six listed above are natural candidates for us to plot on normal distributions. Using strength as an example, most people are going to have a strength that is near a concept of "average" strength. The farther away from that average we go, the fewer people we will find who fit the description. There will be a very select few who are at the extremes—those who can barely lift their own hands and those that can heft small planetoids. This fits with what we know of the characteristics of a normal distribution. The same can be said for intelligence; most people are fairly close to average, with very few at the extremes. These characteristics of population distribution are why the creators of D&D elected to generate ability scores in the fashion that they did: "Roll 3d6" (Figure 11.7).

Perusing the D&D literature, there is a veritable cornucopia of die-roll combinations in evidence. Although I am not willing to invest the time to prove it, I believe the creators used every possible combination of dice at least once. (That is *not* a small number, either.) Die-roll instructions have their own formalized protocol that is very expressive. Using simple operators, you can instruct someone on exactly the way to use those tumbling tools to generate the distribution that you are trying to achieve. Some examples are:

1. d20
2. 3d4
3. 2d6 + 1
4. d6 + d10
5. 3d8 + 2d4 + 10
6. d10×10 + d10 (for generating numbers from 0 to 99)

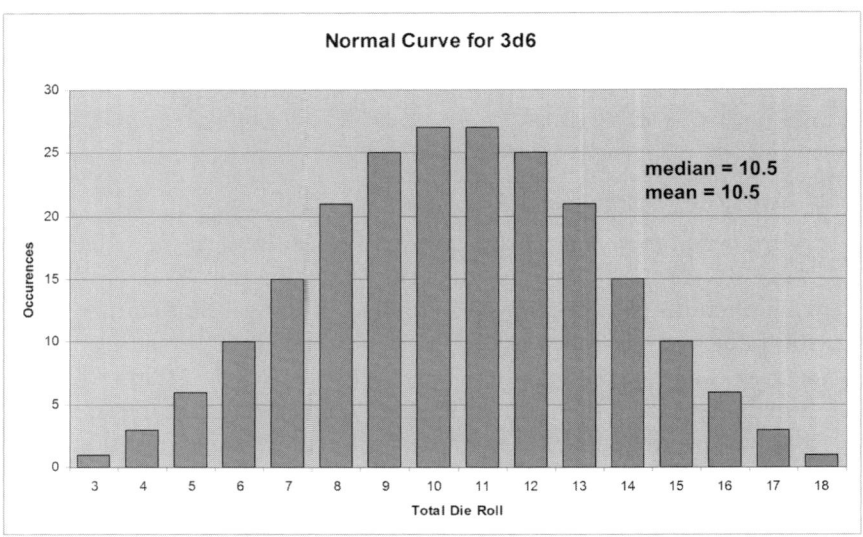

FIGURE 11.7 The result of adding the results of tossing three six-sided dice generates a normal distribution.

In the above list, the first entry is a simple flat probability. Each of the 20 possibilities is equally probable. We can say the same for number 6. It yields a flat probability from 1 to 100. Numbers 2 to 5, however, all create some variant of a normal distribution. We can ascertain characteristics of the resulting curves by looking for some key features of the die-roll equation. By isolating those features, we can learn how to utilize them in constructing our own probability distributions.

Generating a Simple Curve

For purposes of example, we will standardize on curves that produce a range of [0...30]. Additionally, we are *not* going to limit ourselves to the Pythagorean solids (and the 10-sided die) that make up the holy relics of D&D dice. We will allow random numbers to be generated in the spirit of dice of any number of faces. For example, 0–15 will be a perfectly legitimate die roll for our purposes, although making a fair 16-sided die would be an interesting feat of engineering.

Given all of those options, there are plenty of ways that we can generate random numbers from between 0 and 30. The simplest, of course, is by simply rolling a d31. (Note that a d30 would only generate either [0...29] or [1...30].) This would give us a uniform probability distribution. The probabilities would be even across the entire range.

Another method would be to roll 3d11 (each of which allows the results 0 to 10). If we were to graph the probability distribution of this method (Figure 11.8), we would see the familiar bell shape of a normal distribution. The median and mean are both 15. Naturally, the mode is 15 as well, with 6.84% of the rolls adding up to it (91 of 1,331 possible combinations).

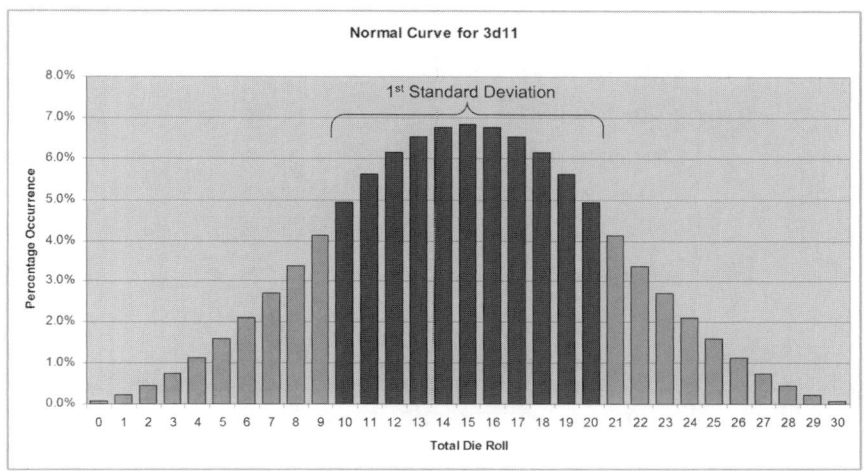

FIGURE 11.8 This chart shows the random numbers from 0 to 30 that would be generated using the distribution 3d11. The standard deviation of 5.48 means that the middle 11 selections ranging from 10 to 20 (in black) encompass ≈ 68% of the possibilities.

The sample has a standard deviation of 5.48. That means that the data entries ±5.48 from the mean of 15 (e.g., 10 to 20) are in the first standard deviation. Therefore, approximately 68% of the sample is between 10 and 20 inclusive.

 ## PUTTING IT IN CODE

 For convenience, the die-rolling code in this chapter is on the Web site at http://www.courseptr.com/downloads. It is contained in a single class, `CDie`. *By inserting this class into your projects, you can use it to simulate a variety of die-roll combinations.*

We can create a simple function for generating normal distributions by first creating one that parameterizes a die roll. For example, the following code block simulates one die roll.

```
unsigned short CDie::SingleDie( unsigned short NumSides,
                                bool ZeroBased /*= true */ )
{
    unsigned short ThisRoll = rand() % NumSides;

    // if the die roll is not 0-based,
    // add one to it.
    if ( !ZeroBased ) {
        ThisRoll += 1;
    } // end if

    return ThisRoll;
}
```

By calling the function with the desired number of sides as the parameter, we will get a random number simulating the roll of the single die.

```
unsigned short RollResult = SingleDie( 11 );
```

Note that the parameter `ZeroBased` allows us to determine what the starting number of the die will be. If `ZeroBased` is true (the default), then the die roll will start with 0. For example, a d6 roll would generate the numbers 0 to 5. If `ZeroBased` is false, then a d6 roll will generate the numbers 1 to 6 like the six-sided die we are familiar with.

If we wanted to simulate the 3d11 roll from our example above, we could call the function `SingleDie()` three times, passing in the number 11 each time, and add the results together. On the other hand, since we may be finding ourselves doing plenty of multiple-dice calls, we can create a function that condenses all of this into one package.

```
unsigned short CDie::MultipleDie( unsigned short NumDie,
                                  unsigned short NumSides,
                                  bool ZeroBased /*= true */ )
{
    unsigned short TotalFoll = 0;
```

```
   for ( unsigned short i = 1; i <= NumDie; i++ ) {
      TotalRoll += SingleDie( NumSides, ZeroBased );
   } // end for

   return TotalRoll;
}
```

The call to the function `MultipleDie()` takes an additional parameter for the number of dice we want to roll. In this way, we can get our random 3d11 roll through a single function call:

```
unsigned short RollResult = MultipleDie( 3, 11 );
```

Changing the Shape

If we change our number generator from 3d11 to 5d7, it still generates numbers from 0 to 30. The curve exhibits some different characteristics, however (Figure 11.9). The range of the distribution is still 0 to 30, but the center of the chart is taller and narrower than the one in Figure 11.8. This is because the standard deviation of this distribution is only 3.4, rather than the wider 5.48 of the prior curve. The result of this is that the 68% of the population that is in the first standard deviation is condensed into a smaller range— from 11 to 19. In plain English, this means we can more reliably expect numbers nearer the mean of 15.

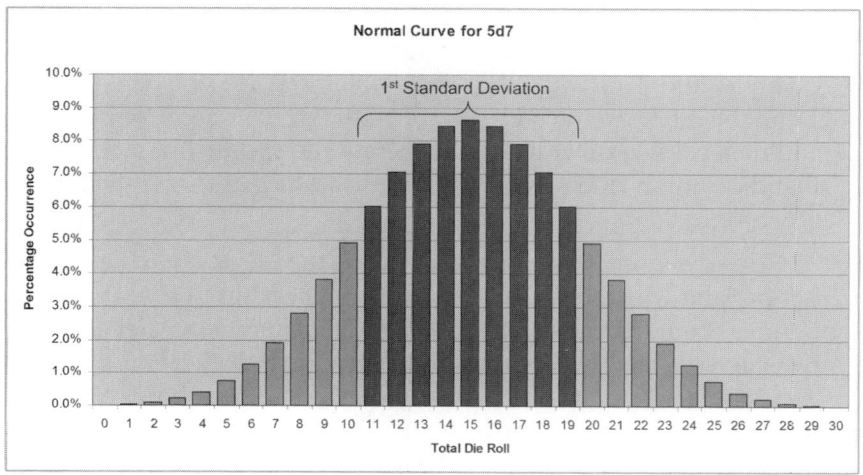

FIGURE 11.9 The random numbers generated using 5d7 create a taller, more condensed curve. The standard deviation is only 3.4. Therefore, only the selections from 11 to 19 (in black) are in the first standard deviation.

Laying the two curves over each other (Figure 11.10) makes it easier to see the differences between them. The first thing we notice is that the 5d7 curve is taller than the 3d11 distribution. The reason is that the combination of five dice makes for more possibilities for the middle numbers than 3d11 makes. Specifically, when using 5d7, 1,451 out of the 16,807 possible combinations (8.63%) yield our median value of 15. With 3d11, only 91 out of the 1,331 combinations (6.84%) give 15.

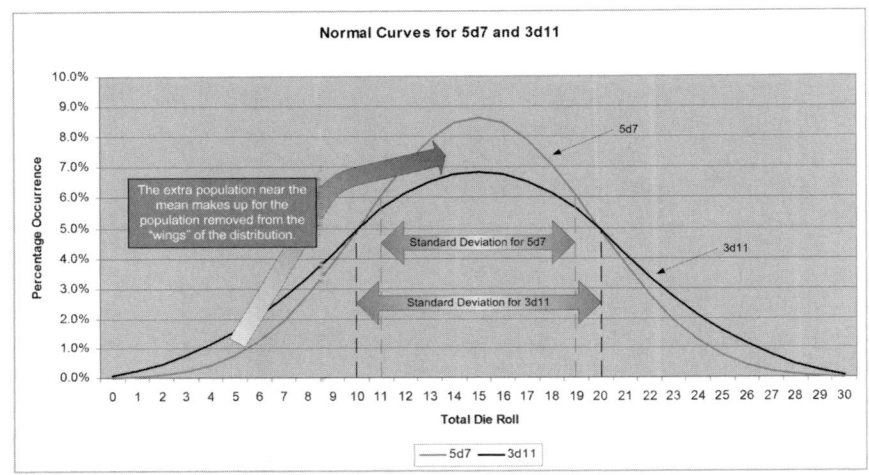

FIGURE 11.10 The distribution of numbers generated by 5d7 is narrower and taller than the one generated by 3d11. Accordingly, the tails of the curve are flatter.

On the other hand, with more dice involved, it is significantly harder to get them all to play nicely together and roll extreme numbers such as 1 or 30. For example, to roll a 1 with 3d11, you would need any one of your dice to come up a 1 and the other two dice to show 0. With 5d7, you need to show a 1 on one die... and then get *four* other dice to cooperate and show a 0 as well. It is my experience that dice simply don't work well together when you want them to be all nice and synchronized.

This dynamic is not only what causes the 5d7 curve to be taller in the middle, but explains why the "bulge" is narrower. The additional probability of the middle numbers comes at the expense of the extreme numbers. After all, the area under the two curves is identical. Both of them represent 100% of the possible outcomes. If we add somewhere, we need to take away from somewhere else. We can see evidence of this in the difference between the two standard deviations. The 5d7 curve has a narrower range for its standard deviation because more of the population is compressed in the middle.

Skewing the Curve

The two examples that we created above were similar in that they were symmetrical. That is, the mean, median, and mode were all 15. If we wanted to generate a probability distribution that did *not* have the bulk of the population in the middle, we would have to take a slightly different approach.

For example, instead of rolling 3d11, we could use 4d11 and, once rolled, drop the lowest from consideration. We add the remaining three together just as if they were the only three that we rolled. We can see the result in Figure 11.11. The median of this curve is now 19 rather than 15. The standard deviation is almost the same as it was with 3d11, but it has been **skewed** to the right by four places. Now, the first standard deviation (68% of the possible outcomes) is in the range of 19 ± 5.2.

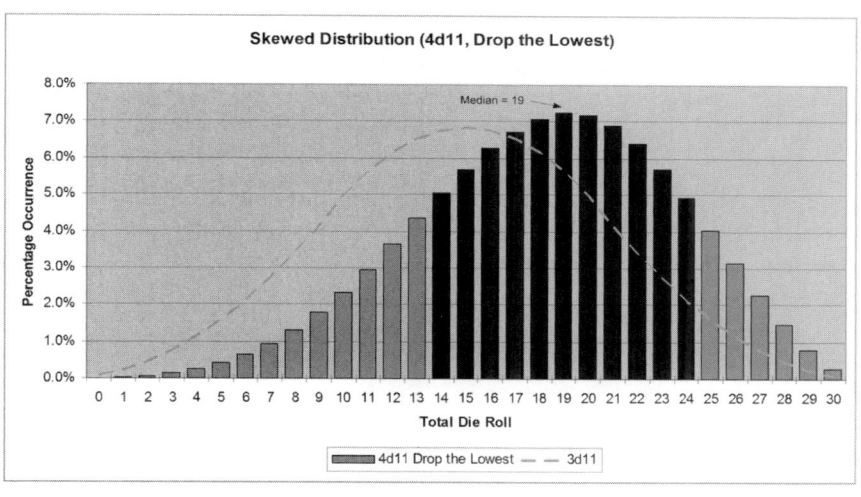

FIGURE 11.11 By rolling 4d11 and dropping the lowest die, we skew the curve to the right (i.e., negative skew). Now, the higher results (around 19) are more likely than the middle ones from the original (around 15). The original 3d11 roll is shown by the dashed line.

Note that we could have skewed the curve in the opposite direction by dropping the *highest* of the four dice rather than the lowest. Additionally, we could have made the skew *more* pronounced (in either direction) by rolling five dice and dropping two of them.

The last thing to note—something that has almost been forgotten in the shuffle—is that these distributions have the same range… [0…30]. In all the cases, skewed or not, we can legitimately claim that we are generating a random number between 0 and 30. This is important to remember. When faced with a situation that calls for a random number between 0 and 30, we must ask ourselves the question, "How do we want that distribution to look?"

Why Skew?

Arranging a probability distribution this way allows for very expressive characteristics. As I mentioned, in the original D&D, the prescribed method for generating the six character stats was 3d6. That created the bell curve that we saw in Figure 11.6. However, if the definition of the numbers 10 and 11 for traits was "average," then we were generally creating average characters. In a game such as D&D, playing an average character is hardly the point. In fact, it is rather unlikely that the average peasant would be the type to foray out into the wilderness to dispatch all sorts of baddies and perform the requisite "noble deeds." That sort of adventure was more the purview of people who were inherently *above average.* But how could a D&D player create an above-average character worthy of such mighty endeavors?

One method, of course, is the tried and true "brute force" method. Roll up a character. If you don't like it, discard it and try again (or just give it to your little brother). However, many house rules started cropping up that made for slightly better than average character generation but still kept the spirit of randomness. Similar to our solution above, rather than roll 3d6, players would roll 4d6 and drop the lowest one. (Around *our* house, we rolled 5d6 and dropped two!) Just as we saw above, doing this skews the curve to the right (Figure 11.12). In the context of the game, this curve made for slightly above-average characters while still allowing for the occasional abysmal score on one attribute.

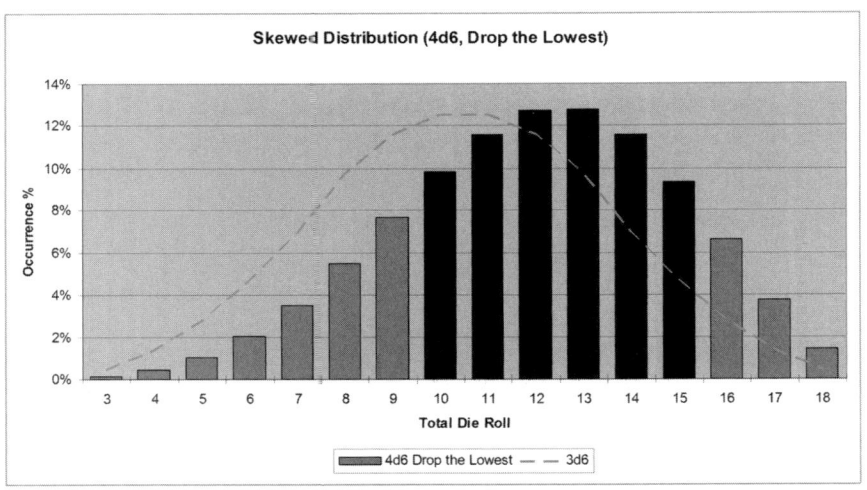

FIGURE 11.12 By rolling 4d6 and dropping the lowest die, we skew the curve to the right. The stats of our D&D character will *generally* be better but still allow for the occasional low score. The original 3d6 roll is shown by the dashed line.

Naturally, we can skew curves in the other direction as well. If we need to recreate the example of household income mentioned earlier in this chapter, we would create a distribution curve that is heavily skewed to the left. This would indicate that the bulk of the households have a relatively low income but still allow for the likes of Bill Gates and Warren Buffet on the extreme right end.

PUTTING IT IN CODE

The code necessary to roll multiple dice and then remove one or more is slightly more complicated. The reason for this is that we need to keep track of *all* the roll results until the end. We can't simply add them together as we go. If we know that we are only going to be removing one die result, we can keep track of the highest or lowest roll (depending on which direction we are skewing the curve), add the rolls as we go along, and then add or subtract the stored value from the total of the rolls. While this will certainly work, we would be limiting ourselves to only skewing by *one* factor. For example, we could perform "4d6, drop the lowest" but not "5d6, drop the lowest *two*."

By extending our multiple dice function above, we can make it account for situations where we want to skew the curve. It will handle skews of both directions (or no skew at all) and an arbitrary number of dice.

```cpp
typedef enum {
    SKEW_NONE,
    SKEW_RIGHT,
    SKEW_LEFT
} SKEW_TYPE;

unsigned short CDie::MultipleDie(
                    unsigned short NumDie,
                    unsigned short NumSides,
                    bool ZeroBased /*= true */,
                    SKEW_TYPE SkewDirection /*= SKEW_NONE*/,
                    unsigned short SkewCount /*= 0*/ )
{
    // Vector container to hold our die rolls
    std::vector<unsigned short> vRolls;
```

```cpp
// Current die roll
unsigned short ThisRoll;

// Total number of dice to roll
unsigned short TotalToRoll = NumDie + SkewCount;

// Get as many die rolls as we need
// including the ones to drop for the skew
for ( int i = 0; i < TotalToRoll; i++ ) {
    ThisRoll = SingleDie( NumSides, ZeroBased );
    vRolls.push_back( ThisRoll );
} // end for

// Total of all dice
unsigned short TotalRoll = 0;

// Array indexes of endpoint dice to consider
unsigned short iFirstDie;
unsigned short iLastDie;

// Determine if we need to drop dice —
// if so, sort and set the range of the ones to consider.

// Remember that the vector indexes are 0-based, thus we
// subtract one from the number of dice to roll to get the index.

switch( SkewDirection ) {
    case SKEW_NONE:
        iFirstDie = 0;
        iLastDie = TotalToRoll - 1;

        break;
```

```
        case SKEW_LEFT:
            std::sort( vRolls.begin(), vRolls.end() );
            iFirstDie = TotalToRoll - NumDie - 1;
            iLastDie = TotalToRoll -1;

            break;

        case SKEW_RIGHT:
            std::sort( vRolls.begin(), vRolls.end());
            iFirstDie = 0 ;
            iLastDie = NumDie - 1;

            break;

        default:
            break;
    } // end switch

    for ( i = iFirstDie; i <= iLastDie; i++ ) {
        TotalRoll += vRolls[i];
    } // end for

    return TotalRoll;
}
```

To handle any number of dice, we create a `std::vector` container. This will be our temporary die-roll storage location. The number of dice that we are going to roll is set by the number that we want to consider for our result (`NumDie`) plus the number that we need to accomplish the skew (`SkewCount`).

After filling this vector with all the die roll results by calling our original `SingleDie()` function, we sort the results. Depending on which way we are skewing the curve, we then move the endpoints of the dice that we are going to consider. For example, if the results of 4d6 rolls are [2, 3, 5, 6] and we are only going to be dropping the lowest, we would only want to consider the second through fourth positions in the array. (Note that the vectors are zero-based arrays, so we would be using array indexes 1 through 3.) Likewise, if we were going to be dropping the highest, we would use the first three positions (indexes 0 through 2). We accomplish this by setting `iFirstDie` and `iLastDie` accordingly based on the `switch` statement.

The last portion of the function simply iterates through the vector between `iFirstDie` and `iLastDie` and adds the results together as if they were the only dice.

As an example of calling this function, the "4d6, drop the lowest" call would be passed as:

```
RollTotal = MultipleDie( 3, 6, true, SKEW_LEFT, 1 );
```

Reading this in English: "roll 3d6, zero-based, skewed to the left by one die."

Note that on the Web site at http://www.courseptr.com/downloads, this function has the third, fourth, and fifth parameters set with defaults as follows:

```
unsigned short MultipleDie(
        unsigned short NumDie,
        unsigned short NumSides,
        bool ZeroBased = true,
        SKEW_TYPE SkewDirection = SKEW_NONE,
        unsigned short SkewCount = 0 );
```

Therefore, by not passing those parameters, we can use this same function even if we do not want to skew the distribution.

Shifting the Curve

Looking back at the D&D example in Figures 11.6 and 11.12, we will notice that the lower bound is 3. This is an artifact of using three dice with the numbers one through six on their faces. Mathematically, it is impossible to generate the number two by rolling three dice constructed in that fashion. Likewise, we arrived at the maximum of 18 in the same way. There is no way to achieve a 19 with these three, standard-issue dice.

There *are* ways at arriving at numbers such as these, however. If we decide that we like the *shape* of the curve generated by 3d6—namely the range of 16 and standard deviation of about 3, we can pick that shape up and move it to many other places. For example, by using the formula (3d6 – 10) we could generate the numbers –7 to +8. The resulting curve would share the same probability characteristics as our original 3d6… just in a different location on the number line. Similarly, we could generate numbers from 50 to 65 using the equation (3d6 + 47). Again, the only difference is the numbers generated. The functional performance of the numbers relative to each other is the same. The range is the same (with different endpoints), the relative locations of the mean, median, and mode are the same, and the standard deviation is identical to the pre-shifted version of the distribution. This is going to be an important feature to remember as we move through the remainder of this book.

The Distribution Checklist

By arranging the tools above, we can create a massive variety of normal probability distributions to serve a variety of needs. Each feature of a normal distribution has an associated factor that we can adjust to generate it. When constructing a distribution, we need to ask ourselves how we want these features to look and take the related steps to accomplish that.

- **Range:** What is the range of the distribution? That is, how wide is the "footprint" going to be? This range will determine what the sum of our die rolls needs to be.
- **Standard Deviation:** How clustered or spread out should our population be? This will determine how many dice we will use to create the desired range. The more dice we use, the more compact the population will be.
- **Skew:** Will the distribution be symmetrical or skewed to the positive or negative direction? This will determine how many dice we will roll initially, keeping only the number necessary to generate our desired standard deviation.
- **Position:** This will determine the lower and upper bounds of the range. By adding or subtracting a number from our die rolls, we slide the resulting distribution left or right.

If we have in mind the sort of distribution that we would like to generate, we only need to adjust these four parameters to craft our curve.

Putting It in Code

There is a function on the Web site at http://www.courseptr.com/downloads that simplifies the generation of normal distributions. The declaration of this function is:

```
int RandomFromNormalDist (
    int LowBound, // lower boundary
    int HighBound, // upper boundary
```

```
                 unsigned short Pinch = 0, // extra die to narrow bulge
                 SKEW_TYPE SkewDirection = SKEW_NONE, // side tail extends to
                 unsigned short SkewFactor = 0); // extra die to skew curve )
```

Rather than manually calculating the number of dice needed, this function allows us to pass in a lower and upper bound for our range. This feature will also shift the curve to a final location for us. For example, setting the boundaries to −10 and 10, respectively, would generate a range from 0 to 21 and then shift it down by 10.

When the range requested is not an exact multiple of the number of dice, the function adds an extra die roll for the remainder. For example, 3d11 (0-indexed) generates the range 0 to 30. If we wanted the range to be 0 to 32, the die roller would use 3d11 and add the result of an extra d3 (0 to 2). We could have also dealt with this by rolling 2d12 and a single d11, which yield the ranges of 0 to 22 and 0 to 10, respectively. Adding them together results in the range 0 to 32. Please note that this is *not* the method that is on the Web site at http://www.courseptr.com/downloads.

The pinch parameter changes how narrow the standard deviation will be. This parameter actually adds additional dice to the minimum of three. Therefore, pinch = 2 would divide the range up in five dice rather than three. As we saw before, this raises the center of the curve and flattens the tails.

The last two parameters, SkewDirection and SkewFactor, are the same as we encountered before.

We could call this function similarly to these examples:

```
RollTotal = RandomFromNormalDist( 0, 10 );
```

The above line returns a random number from a symmetrical normal distribution with a range from 0 to 10.

```
RollTotal = RandomFromNormalDist( -50, 50, 0, SKEW_NONE, 0 );
```

This call returns a random number from a symmetrical normal distribution with a range from −50 to 50.

```
RollTotal = RandomFromNormalDist( 20, 100 , 2, SKEW_LEFT, 2 );
```

The above function returns a random number from a normal distribution with a range of 81, skewed to the left (the bulge is on the right). The bulk of the population will also be in a relatively narrow range due to the "pinch factor" of 2 in the third parameter.

This function is included as a part of the class `CDie` on the Web site at http://www.courseptr.com/downloads. We can easily add the class to any project.

TRIANGULAR DISTRIBUTIONS

A **triangular distribution** is, in essence, a stripped-down form of a normal distribution. It shares some of the same characteristics, but without some of the additional complexity. For example, a triangular distribution has a mean, median, and mode just like its fancy cousin. Naturally, it also has a range in which its values lie. Triangular distributions, however, have some special qualities that make them useful in decision generation and simulation.

SIMPLIFIED NORMAL DISTRIBUTIONS

Triangular distributions can be used as a simple, slightly faster version of normal distributions. To see why, let's go back to our repeated efforts at generating a number from 0 to 30. We showed two different methods that produced different curves: 3d11 and 5d7. If we had continued to increase the number of dice used, the curve would have continued to get taller in the middle, with more of the population clustered tightly around the mean. The curves in the curve (if you will pardon the expression) became more pronounced as the population sample had to ramp up from a large span of very small values to very large ones, top off, and then plunge back toward 0% again.

However, if we were to reduce the number of dice from three to two (i.e., 2d16), we would find that something very interesting occurs. There are *no* curves in the curve whatsoever. In essence, we are left with two straight lines that meet at a peak (Figure 11.13). Just as in the symmetrical normal distribution, the peak of an unskewed triangular distribution is the mode, median, and mean.

Using a triangular distribution as a substitute for a normal distribution is often an acceptable practice. While we may lose a little of the subtlety of the normal distribution's shape (specifically, the tapered tails), we gain quite a bit in the rapidity of calculation. Obviously, using the above example of reducing a 3dx to a 2dx curve, we are cutting the number of random number calls by 33%. In heavily used decision models, that can add up to a substantial savings of processor time.

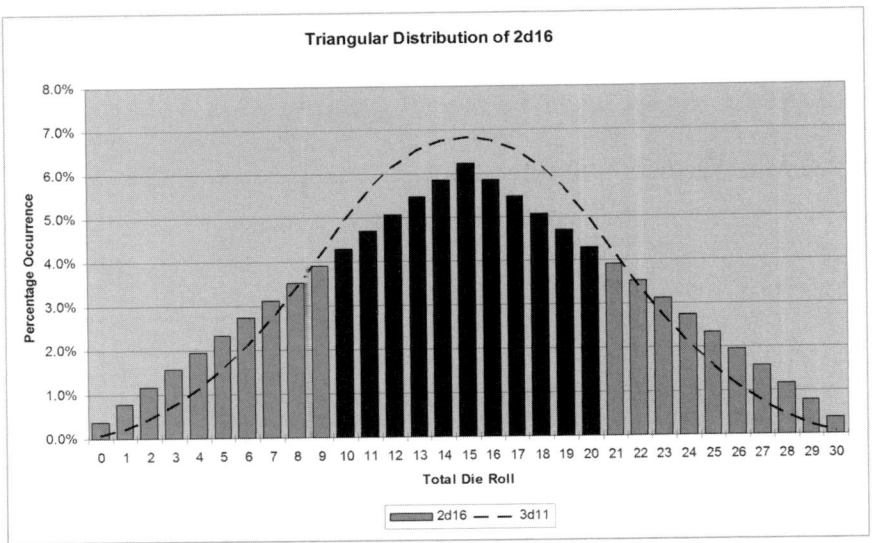

FIGURE 11.13 By using 2d16 to generate numbers between 0 and 30, our bell curve becomes a triangular distribution. The range, mean, median, and mode are all the same as the 3d11 distribution (dashed line). The standard deviation (black bars), however, is slightly greater due to the slightly flatter spread of the population.

PARAMETRIC BUILDING

While the above is merely a simplification of the normal distribution, there is another method that we can use to create triangular distributions that is enormously powerful and flexible. By setting only three parameters, we can automatically generate a continuous triangular distribution. The first two parameters are simply the upper and lower bounds of the range. The third parameter is the peak of the triangle. We can actually think of these three items as "worst case," "best case," and "likely case." Looking at a sample triangular distribution in Figure 11.14, we can identify these points.

If a and c are integers, then for any integer value x between the points a and c, we can determine what the percentage of the total sample under the curve x is by using one of the following formulas. The formula we use is based on whether the value x is above or below c. The value of x must be within the range specified by a and c. Therefore, the actual deciding factors and their formulas are:

If $a \leq x \leq c$ then:

$$f(x|a,b,c) = \frac{2(x-a)}{(b-a)(c-a)}$$

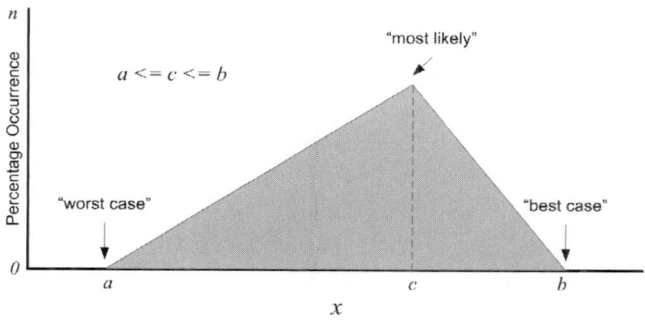

FIGURE 11.14 By setting the variables *a*, *b*, and *c*, such that $a \leq c \leq b$, any triangular distribution can be created quickly and easily.

If $c \leq x \leq b$ then:

$$f(x|a,b,c) = \frac{2(b-x)}{(b-a)(b-c)}$$

By programming the formulas and their constraints, we can yield quick probability distributions for all *x* between *a* and *b*. For example, by using the relatively arbitrary numbers 6 and 53 for *a* and *b*, respectively, and 41 for *c*, we get the probability distribution shown in Figure 11.15.

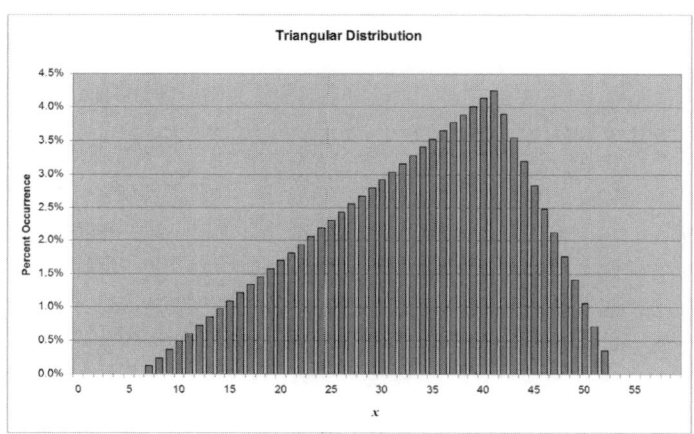

FIGURE 11.15 The triangular probability distribution generated by $a = 6$, $b = 53$ and $c = 41$. Note that because the curve crosses the axis at *a* and *b*, the value at these points is 0%.

Most distribution formulas are polite enough to give us either the number or the percentage of occurrences for a given value of x. However, unlike using the "dice-rolling" method, we can't turn the function back around and give us a randomly selected x out of the distribution. This is a problem we will encounter throughout the remainder of this chapter. We will discover how to turn a distribution function into a random selection method in the next chapter.

Uneven Distributions

 Another simple probability curve to create is an **uneven distribution**. While not technically a recognized form of probability distribution, we can still find it useful. In a way, it is a variant of the triangular distribution above, but with the c point co-located at either a or b. Rather than use the triangular distribution method, however, we can lean on the linear function we examined in the previous chapter: the formula, $y = m(x) + b$ where m is the slope of the line and b is the y-intercept.

The probability distribution that results from a linear distribution has very simple but identifiable characteristics. First, we can easily determine the "more likely" options compared to the "less likely" ones. In fact, due to the linear nature of the formula, we can assert that as x moves in one direction, the probability y will always move in one direction as well. In the distribution shown in Figure 11.16, for example, as x increases, y always decreases. Not only does it always decrease, but it does so at a constant rate. The decrease in y over the range x_a to x_{a+1} is the same as the decrease in y from x_b to x_{b+1}.

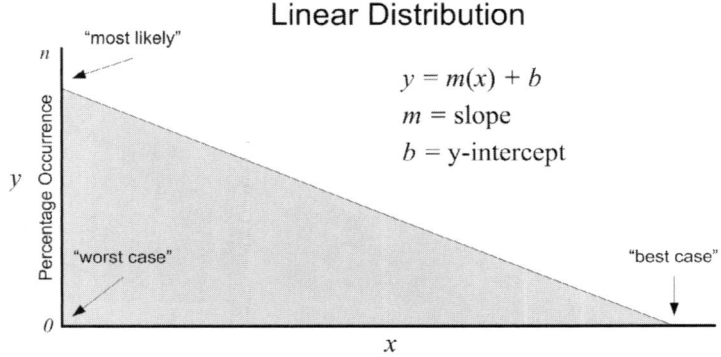

FIGURE 11.16 A linear distribution is constructed from a simple equation-based line such as those of the form $y = m(x) + b$ with which we all became so familiar with in school.

Second, if we haven't determined a range artificially (for example, stating that we are only concerned with x values between 5 and 15), we can easily identify the range of the distribution as the areas where $y > 0$. Through some painless algebraic yoga we can solve any equation for the point $y = 0$ to determine the exact point at which this occurs along the x-axis.

Some variations to linear equations merit mention. Not all lines will intercept the x-axis in the range that we are concerned with. In Figure 11.17A, for example, the probability increases over the range between x_{min} and x_{max}. At no time, however, is that probability 0.

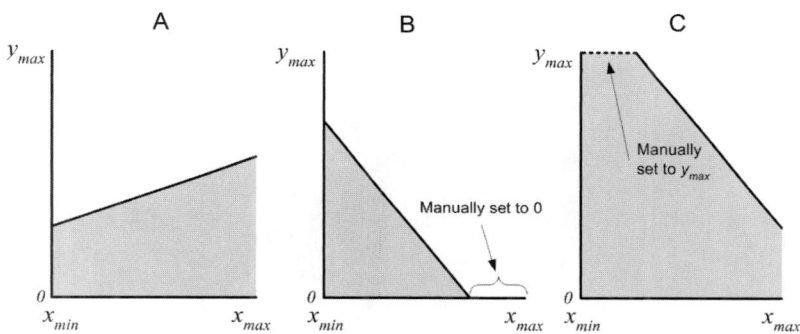

FIGURE 11.17 (A) A linear distribution that does not reach 0 within the range. (B) A linear distribution that reaches 0 within the range. Values below 0 must be clamped to 0. (C) A linear distribution that extends beyond a defined maximum must be clamped to the maximum.

If we have established a range for the possible events (e.g., x_{min} to x_{max}), we may encounter a situation where the probability line proceeds below 0 (Figure 11.17B). We need to be careful to trap our code to avoid the possibility of *negative* probability. In those circumstances, overriding the formula to set y to 0 is a simple solution.

Similarly, if we set a maximum value for y, we need to be aware of another potential problem. In the graph shown in Figure 11.17C, we see that the line proceeds above the maximum value that we have set for y. In these cases, we must be careful to cap the value returned by our formula to y_{max}.

The bottom line on linear distributions is that they are a simple yet elegant solution to crafting increasing or decreasing probabilities. It certainly makes for a nice change of pace from uniform distributions but without time-consuming clutter. As mentioned above, we will soon show a method for selecting random numbers out of this distribution.

Parabolic Distributions

We can create another common and useful distribution in a similar fashion to the linear distribution above. By inserting an exponent into the formula, thus making the formula a quadratic function such as we discussed in Chapter 10, we create one of the veritably plethoric varieties of **parabolic distributions**. The linear distributions have a subtle advantage of expression over the uniform distributions in that the probability value changes over the range. Similarly, a parabolic distribution is slightly more expressive than a linear distribution in that the *rate* of change in probability changes over the range (Figure 11.18).

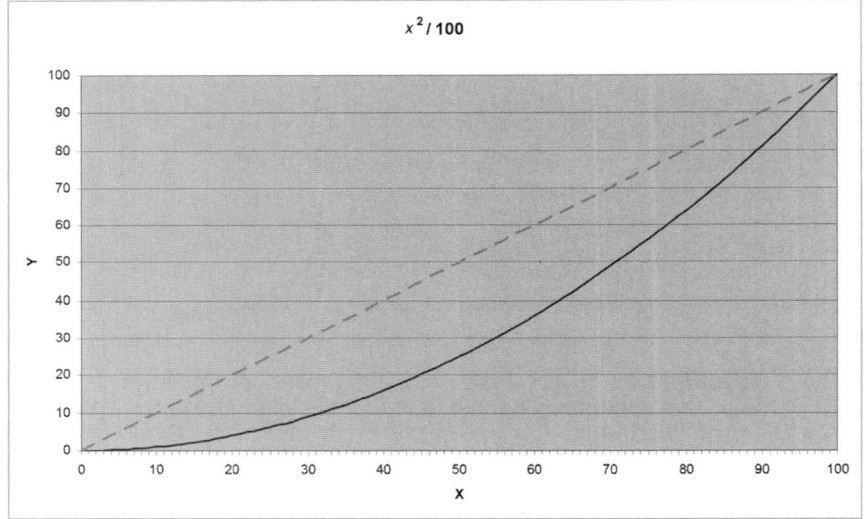

FIGURE 11.18 Despite starting and ending at the same pair of locations as the linear function $y = x$ (dashed line), the parabolic probability distribution $y = x^2/100$ shows significantly different characteristics.

We can manipulate parabolic distributions in the ways that we covered in the previous chapter. First, by changing the exponent, we can dramatically change the inflection of the curve. For example, raising x to the power of three rather than two causes a more pronounced "corner" to appear. We can also utilize non-integer exponents (e.g., $x^{1.7}$) to fine-tune the shape of the curve.

By using exponents less than one, we can reverse the inflection of the curve. For example, the formula $x^{.5} \times 10$ (Figure 11.19) starts by climbing quickly and tapering off. This curve is reminiscent of some of the decreasing marginal utility curves that we discussed in Chapter 8.

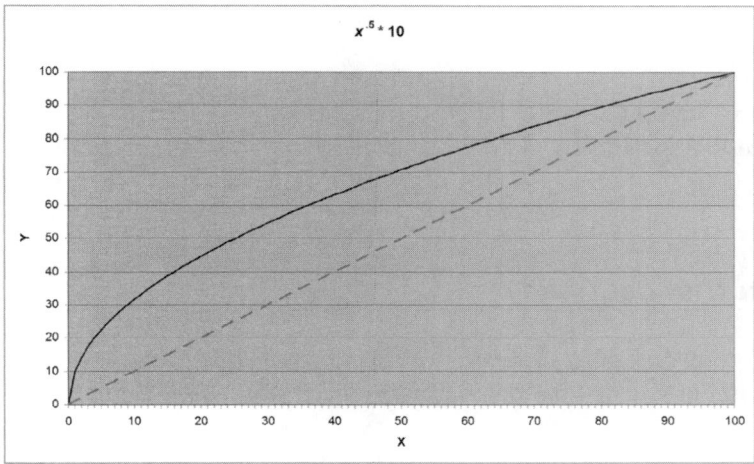

FIGURE 11.19 Exponents less than 1 create a curve with a downward inflection. The graph above shows the formula $x^{.5} \times 10$ (which could also be referred to as the square root of x times 10).

Again, by changing the exponent, we can dramatically or subtly affect the shape of this curve. However, if we are trying to get the values to fit into a certain range (such as how the curve in Figure 11.19 ranges from 0 to 100), we will need to change the rest of the formula to accommodate the massive shifts that changing an exponent will cause.

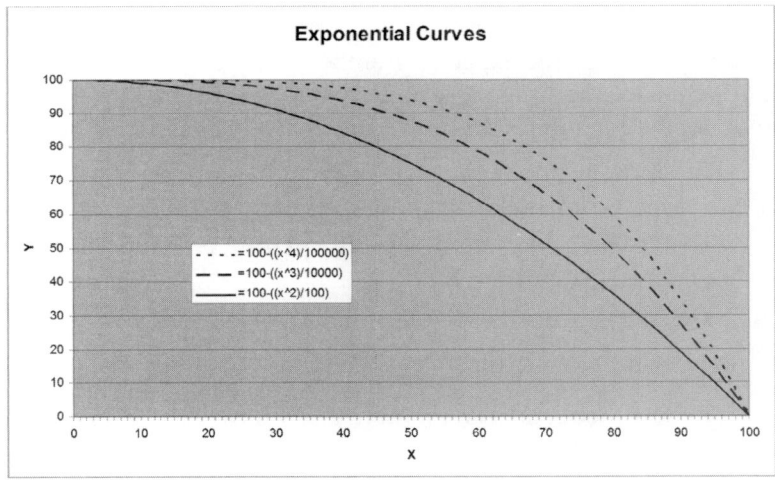

FIGURE 11.20 By using three different exponents, we have crafted three different curves. We divided the formulas by different numbers so that the y values remained between 0 and 100 over the range $x = [0...100]$.

In Figure 11.20, we show three similar parabolic curves being subtracted from 100 and arranged such that when *x* reaches 100, *y* reaches 0. The paths that the three curves follow to get there are different, however. The shapes of the curves themselves are different because the exponents are different: 2, 3, and 4. However, because the results expand so rapidly, we needed to divide the equation by 100, 10,000, and 1,000,000, respectively. By doing that, we ensure that when $x = 100$, $y = 0$.

POISSON DISTRIBUTIONS

Another useful, if slightly more esoteric, probability curve is the **Poisson distribution**. Siméon-Denis Poisson originally developed it in 1838 as a way of expressing the probability of events happening over time. Accordingly, we can use it in game AI to generate events that occur at average intervals but without resorting to predictable time periods. On the other hand, we are not limited to using the Poisson distribution in connection with time-based events. We can benefit from using the unique properties of the Poisson distribution in other areas as well.

The formula for a Poisson distribution is:

$$f(k;\lambda) = \frac{\lambda^k e^{-\lambda}}{k!}$$

The values in the equation are a little counter-intuitive at first and merit explanation. The value k (the equivalent of x on the graph) represents the number of occurrences of an event over a time period. The value λ (lambda) is a positive, real number equal to the expected number of occurrences over a given time period. The familiar value e is the base of the natural logarithm (approximately 2.71828). The result of the equation is the probability that k events will happen in that time period.

For example, if we know that an event happens five times in a minute on average ($\lambda = 5$), the Poisson distribution suggests that 17.6% of the time we can expect it to occur exactly 25 times (5×5) times in exactly five minutes.

$$f(5;5) = \frac{5^5 e^{-5}}{5!} = \frac{3125 \times 2.718^{-5}}{120} = 17.6\%$$

On the other hand, if we want to know how often we could expect it to happen 25 times (5×5) in *six* minutes, we would find:

$$f(6;5) = \frac{5^6 e^{-5}}{6!} = \frac{15625 \times 2.718^{-5}}{720} = 14.6\%$$

As we can see, it is less likely that the 25 events would be distributed over six minutes than the usual five. Similarly, plugging $k = 7$ into the equation yields 10.4%; it is even *less* likely that 25 events would be spread over seven minutes. Each value for λ produces a distinct curve that expresses the probability of λ events occurring in each discrete value of k. Figure 11.21 shows three examples for λ values of 5, 15, and 30.

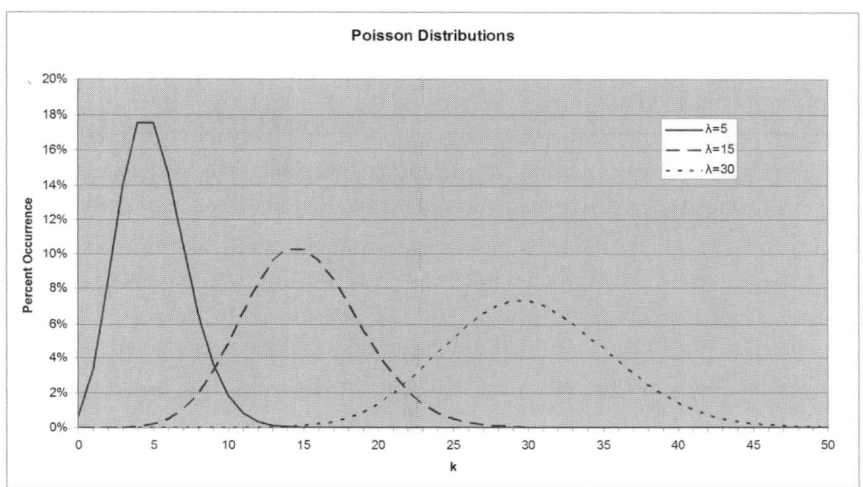

FIGURE 11.21 If we change the value for λ, the resulting curve spreads out to account for the different probabilities.

Another Use for Poisson

We can also use a Poisson distribution to model an event that happens once every k minutes instead of λ times per minute. We use the same equation but simply change our mindset. Referring again to Figure 11.21, we could use the curves shown to represent events that happen every 5, 15, and 30 minutes. In this case, the probabilities are the probability that the event happens during the specified time period.

For example, if we are expecting an event to happen *on average* every 15 minutes, ($\lambda = 15$), we would find that the actual recurrence of the event would be distributed to values *around* 15 minutes. It *may* occur at the 15-minute mark, but it also may occur at 14 or 16 minutes. For that matter, it may occur at 5 or 30 minutes. The odds of those results are significantly less likely than 14 or 16, however. We can observe this result easily by examining the associated curve.

The shapes of the curves are directly related to the value of λ. Loosely described, the Poisson distribution takes an average interval and "fuzzies it up" a bit. The longer the interval, the more room for variation there is. That is, the longer the average interval, the more possibility for "spread" we can experience. For instance, if the average interval was 5 minutes, it is very unlikely that we would encounter an interval of more than 10 minutes. The reason for that is an almost necessarily mathematical symmetry that is necessary for generating an average. That is, with an average of five minutes, every six-minute interval can be balanced by a four-minute one, every seven-minute interval can be balanced by a three-minute one, and so on. While an interval of 10 minutes or more is certainly *possible*, to maintain the 5-minute average it would require more than one corresponding interval of *less* than 5 minutes.

The result of this balancing act is that as the average interval decreases, the range of the distribution narrows. As the average interval increases, the range widens. It is worth noting that because of this balancing problem, the distributions are right-skewed—that is, the median and mean are to the right of the mode. The tails are longer on the positive side than they are on the negative side.

Another artifact of this characteristic is that the likelihood of the average interval occurring decreases because the distribution is spread over more intervals. This is similar to the effect we saw with the normal distributions. The wider the bulk of the curve (i.e., the standard deviation) is, the fewer occurrences of the result at the mode.

This distribution is excellent for randomizing the times between events that otherwise would occur at regular intervals. For example, if we want an agent's action to occur every 15 seconds, we can generate a Poisson distribution with $\lambda = 15$ to determine in which second the event should occur.

Computational Drawbacks

One of the drawbacks of the Poisson distribution is the computational overhead involved in calculating factorials. From a calculation time standpoint, factorials are relatively inexpensive to compute. We can determine them from a simple loop. If we *did* want to speed up this calculation, we could use a lookup table instead.

Of more concern is how quickly the *size* of factorial results increases. $10! = 3,628,800$. $11!$ checks in at just under 40 million. Likewise, we face some significantly large intermediate calculations with λ^k in the numerator of the equation. With $\lambda = 15$ and $k = 15$, that single calculation is $437,893,890,380,859,375\ldots$ and we haven't even multiplied it with e^{15} yet! I know the graphics folks like to brag about how many calculations and big numbers they push around, but we don't need to try to out-gun them quite *this* much!

As percentages, the actual results of Poisson distributions are not terribly large. Therefore, if we know the ranges of the potential λ and k values that we want to use ahead of time, they can be calculated offline and stored in a lookup table. (As we will see soon, storing probability values in an array-like structure will come in handy anyway.)

Substituting Normal or Triangular Distributions

If the above calculations are prohibitive, we can obtain much the same result by using a normal distribution. If we set the range to be slightly more than twice what we would normally be using for λ (that is, half of the curve would be on either side of λ), position the mode at λ, and slightly skew the curve to the right (i.e., make the positive portion of the tail longer than the negative), we can achieve a similar distribution. We can even generate very similar results without the skew on the normal distribution. What we end up with is a normal distribution that amounts to λ, +/− half of λ, centered on λ.

DISTRIBUTING THE DISTRIBUTIONS

To tie off a loose end that we left dangling earlier in the chapter, we will revisit reconstructing our Guess Two-Thirds participants. We had identified three different types of guessers. We are going to break that into four types for purposes of this exercise. We also identified the rough percentages of the whole that each of these groups of people represented. To recap:

Group	%
"33" guessers	4
"22" guessers	3
Random guessers	30
Semi-logical guessers	63

When generating a random guesser, the first thing we need to determine is which of the four categories the guesser is in. The result of that will determine our next course of action. Once we know the *type* of guesser we are working with, we then select what process we want to use to generate their actual guess. In the case of the "33" and "22" guessers, the answer is simply 33 and 22, respectively. The random guessers (30% of the population), as we determined earlier, would divide their guesses up across the entire range from 0 through 100.

As we discussed before, the semi-logical bunch requires a bit of special treatment. We noticed that they fall roughly into a normal distribution with a range from 0 to about 70. The distribution has a slight right skew that shifts the bulge of the population from its natural center of 35 to a new mode of about 25. However we construct it, we know that 63% of the time, our guesser needs to pick a guess from that distribution.

So… let's throw this model into some code using the tools we laid out earlier.

Putting It in Code

For clarity, we will define an enumerated type GUESS_TYPE to represent our four possible types of guessers.

```
typedef enum {
    GUESS_33,
    GUESS_22,
    GUESS_RANDOM,
    GUESS_SEMI,
} GUESS_TYPE;
```

To generate a guess using the complete model, we only need call the function GetGuess(). The first order of business in GetGuess() is to call GetGuessType().

GetGuessType() is a function that will, using the percentages laid out above, identify which type of guesser we are modeling.

```
GUESS_TYPE CGuesser::GetGuessType()
{
    int index = DieRoller.SingleDie( 100, false );

    if ( index <= 4 ) return GUESS_33; // 1..4 = 4%
    if ( index <= 7 ) return GUESS_22; // 5..7 = 3%
    if ( index <= 37 ) return GUESS_RANDOM;   // 8..37 = 30%
    return GUESS_SEMI; // 38..100 = 63%
}
```

Note that we are using the object DieRoller that is an object of type CDie that is declared in the header of CGuesser. We are asking for a number from 1 to 100. (By leaving the second parameter, ZeroBased, as true, we would have received one between 0 and 99.)

Once we have received a type of guesser back from GetGuessType(), we can select the appropriate manner in which to generate the guess.

```
unsigned short CGuesser::GetGuess()
{
    GUESS_TYPE GuessType = GetGuessType();
    unsigned short Guess;
```

```
    switch( GuessType ) {

        case GUESS_33:
            Guess = 33;
            break;

        case GUESS_22:
            Guess = 22;
            break;

        case GUESS_RANDOM:
            Guess = DieRoller.SingleDie( 101 );
            break;

        case GUESS_SEMI:
            Guess =
                DieRoller.RandomFromNormalDist( 0, 70, 0,
                                        SKEW_RIGHT, 2 );
            break;
    } // end switch

    return Guess;
}
```

The `switch` statement is fairly self-explanatory. If GUESS_TYPE is GUESS_33, then the guess is 33. Likewise, if the guess type is 22, the guess is set to 22. In the other two cases, we generate random guesses based on the parameters shown.

For example, if the guesser is one of those who is guessing randomly, we simply ask our number generator for a number between 0 and 100 via the call `DieRoller.SingleDie( 101 )`. This returns a uniform distribution. All of the possibilities are equal.

If the guesser is one of the semi-logical guessers we identified earlier in the chapter, we ask for a random guess from the normal distribution called for by the parameters:

LowBound	0
HighBound	70
Pinch	0
SkewDirection	Right
SkewFactor	2

As we can see, this distribution has a range of 70 and is skewed to the right—meaning that the "tail" extends more to the right than it does to the left. This description fits the curve that we identified in Figure 11.2.

By calling the function GetGuess(), we are creating random guessers of all four types in the percentages that we laid out. That means that each call to GetGuess() could generate a 33, a 22, a random guess between 0 and 100, or a random guess between 0 and 70 with a bias toward about 25. If we call this function many times and examine a histogram of the results (Figure 11.22), we see a distribution similar to the one we found in the original data from the Denmark experiment.

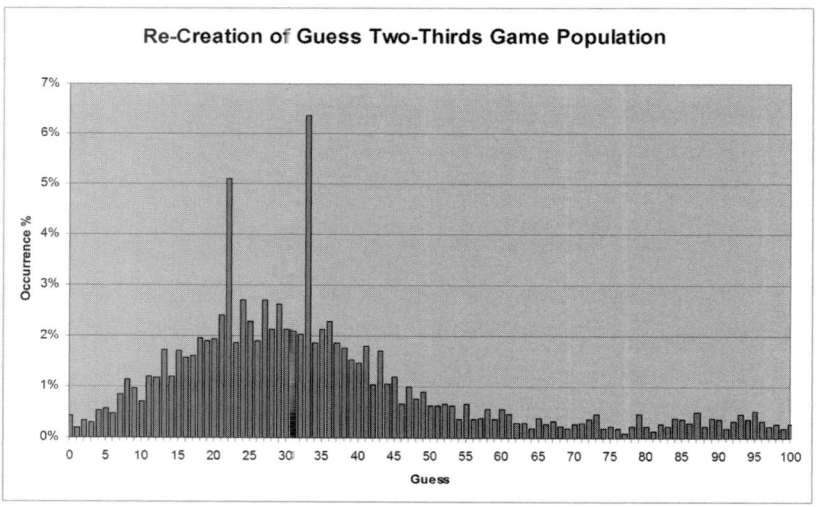

FIGURE 11.22 The histogram of 3,000 random guesses using the GetGuess() function. Aside from the two specific guesses of 22 and 33, we created the rest using two different types of probability distribution: a uniform distribution from 0 to 100, and a right-skewed normal distribution from 0 to 70.

With some analysis of the population (which we performed earlier in the chapter), some planning, a little tweaking of our percentages, and a few calls to our probability distribution functions, we are able to replicate the population that entered the

Guess Two-Thirds contest in Denmark. Notice that while we certainly *understood* some of the logic involved in people's guesses (especially that of the "33" and "22" guessers), we didn't necessarily need to *apply* that logic in reconstructing our somewhat complex population distribution.

If we were to hook this function up to a research project similar to the one that the chaps from Copenhagen did, we would likely be hard-pressed to determine the difference between the real guessers and the simulated ones. We could even be so bold as to suggest that our Guess Two-Thirds simulation passes the Turing test... and yet we did it without actually modeling the mindset behind any given guess. In fact, our function knows nothing of the rules of the game. The major drawback of this is that if the rules of the game change (such as becoming "Guess 70% of the Average"), our function does not know how to respond. What's more, *we* don't know how to change it until we either see empirical evidence of how real people play or translate some of our understanding of the original game into the new rule set.

Regardless, we have shown that by using various forms of probability distributions, we can simulate a relatively complex population. This skill will play a part throughout much of the remainder of the book—in both large ways and small.

12 Response Curves

One of the drawbacks of some of the functions we looked at in Chapter 10 is that we are entirely at the mercy of the mathematics. Even if we could construct a function that gives us *close* to the shape that we wanted, we are still stuck with every bit of it. We have no way of tweaking a portion here or there to be "just a *bit* higher" or "not quite as steep in *this* part." More importantly, there are plenty of situations where no mathematical function—no matter how convoluted—is going to give us anything close to what we need.

Similarly, in Chapter 11, some of the probability distribution functions we examined allowed us to construct pretty curves but did not offer a way for us to extract a random number from them. Being able to do so is important if we are to use those probability distributions to construct decisions and behaviors. It doesn't matter if we know that choice x should occur y% of the time if we can't cause x to occur at all. For example, while we know that a coin should land on heads 50% of the time, until we actually *toss* the coin, we won't know who wins the coin toss. We know that rolling a 7 on 2d6 occurs 16.7% of the time—and yet the nice man running the craps table will be very annoyed with us if we never actually *throw* the dice.

To address both of these problems, we need to introduce a new method of dealing with functional data. To solve the problem of customizability, we need a way to store the results of a function, tweaking those results at will, and extract what we need out of it. To solve the problem of extracting a random number x, y% of the time as determined by a continuous probability distribution function, we need to do something very similar: store the results in a data structure that allows for retrieval in the appropriate proportion of occurrences. **Response curves** handle both of these situations admirably.

CONSTRUCTING RESPONSE CURVES

One of the advantages of implementing response curves is that it gives us a new way of looking at data. By changing our vantage point, so to speak, we are able to process this data in ways that are more conducive to manipulation and selection.

We will start with a simple example from the previous chapter… our helpful dentists. As we have recalled a few times, rumor has it that "four out of five dentists recommend sugarless gum." If we were to generate random dentists from this data, we would want to make sure that 80% of the time, the dentist was of the mind to recommend sugarless gum. According to what we've been told, that's realistic, right?

Certainly, there are plenty of ways that we could generate a sugarless dentist 80% of the time. It is actually a rather simple exercise. However, for purposes of this example, let's look at the histogram from Chapter 11. On the left side of Figure 12.1, we see the histogram representing the dentist data.

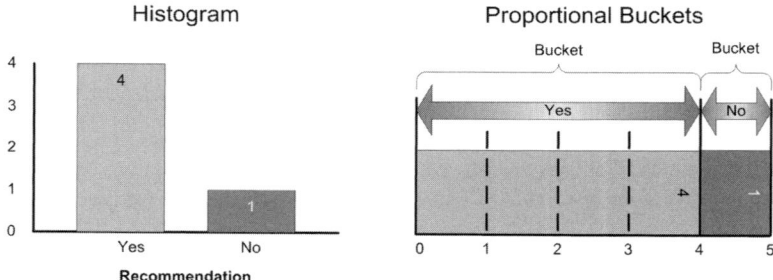

FIGURE 12.1 By laying the histogram bars end-to-end, we lay the results over a number line. This allows us to mark the beginnings and ends of each range.

I don't mean to wander into pedantic territory here, but there is an aspect of this histogram that we should make a note of. By the very nature of histograms, we know that the "yes" bar is four times the size of the "no" bar. After all, another way of expressing the recommendations of the dentists is "dentists recommend sugarless gum at a 4-to-1 ratio over gum with sugar in it." It logically follows that a representation that measures ratios should be ratio-based in its portrayal. However, these two vertical bars don't do us much good for randomly selecting which camp our prospective dentist is in.

From Bars to Buckets

If we were to turn the bars on their sides, however, and lay them end to end, we change our perspective. The bars are still in the same proportion as they were before: 4 to 1. By placing them in this orientation (Figure 12.1, right side), we can see how they lie across what is now an *x*-axis. In this example, the "yes" answers run from 0 through 4 and the "no" answer is the single unit between 4 and 5.

We can refer to these ranges as **buckets**—a name that makes sense when you extend the metaphor slightly. Imagine a game of randomly dropping a ball into these buckets (not too dissimilar from the game Plinko from the game show, *The Price Is Right*). If the ball drop is truly random, it would have a 4:1 chance of landing in the "yes" bucket. This is a result of the "yes" bucket being four times as big as the "no" bucket.

Now, because these are *not* real buckets and we are *not* dropping a real ball, we have to *simulate* dropping a ball into the buckets. To do this, we generate a random number between 1 and 5. By referring to the number line below our buckets, we can determine which number corresponds to which bucket. For example, if we were to roll a 2 (using our dice terminology again), we would let that signify that our random ball has fallen into the "yes" bucket. In fact, if we were to roll a 1, 3, or 4, our ball would have landed in the "yes" bucket as well. On the other hand, if we were to roll a 5, our ball would have landed in the "no" bucket. The difference is that the ball landed on the other side of the **edge** that defines the separation between the buckets—in this case, the edge is 4.

In such a simple example, all of this seems rather obvious. However, as we shall see, there is a lot of potential wrapped up in this method of approaching random selection.

Adding More Buckets

For a slightly more involved scenario, let us return to another example from the previous chapter. When we were trying to re-create the results of the Guess Two-Thirds Game, we identified four segments of the population that had distinct characteristics. Each of those four types of guessers had their own method of approaching the game. We also identified what we believe to be the relative occurrence percentages of the four groups. To reiterate:

Group	%
"33" guessers	4
"22" guessers	3
Random guessers	30
Semi-logical guessers	63

We can lay out this data in a similar fashion as we did with our dentist data. Just as we based the sizes of the "dentists' recommendation" buckets on the ratio of those recommendations, we construct our buckets based on the relative sizes of the four segments of the "guesser" population. When we lay them end-to-end, the total width is 100. Because the figures were percentages of the whole, and we have accounted for all of the groups that make up the whole, it makes sense that they add up to 100. (We will find later that this is not a necessity.)

Once again, by laying the buckets side-by-side over our *x*-axis, we can determine the edges of the buckets (Figure 12.2). By dropping our metaphorical ball into the buckets (by generating a random number between 1 and 100), we determine which population segment our next guesser is going to represent. Theoretically, 63% of the guessers are going to be semi-logical, 30% will be random, and so on. While the relative frequencies of the "33" and "22" guessers are small, there still is a possibility that our ball will find its way into one of those two buckets.

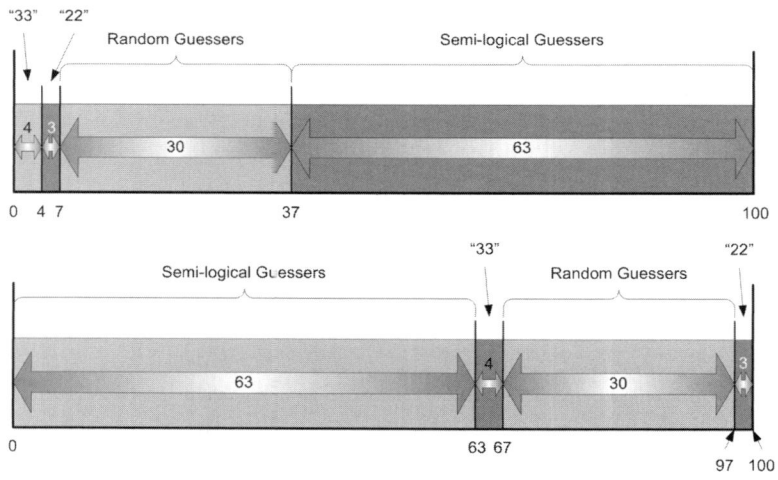

FIGURE 12.2 The buckets created by arranging the relative population segments of the Guess Two-Thirds Game. Note that the proportional sizes of the buckets persist regardless of in what order we place them.

Notice that the order that we place the buckets in doesn't matter. In the bottom half of Figure 12.2, we moved the buckets into a different arrangement. However, because the sizes of the buckets haven't changed, the odds of our random ball dropping into any one of them do not change either. For example, there is still a 4% chance of a "33" guesser appearing.

The locations of the edges of the buckets *do* change, however, and this is where our focus must lie.

BUILDING BUCKETS

The numbers at the bottom of each of the two depictions in Figure 12.2 represent the *cumulative* sizes of the buckets that we have added. For example, in the top group, the first bucket we added was the probability of the group that guesses "33." We had determined that the size of that group was 4%. The edge of this bucket is, therefore, 4. If our random number is 1, 2, 3, or 4, we pick the first group.

It is important that we notice that the right edge of a bucket is inclusive. For the bucket above, the edge is 4, not 5. We can think of this as being "anything in the 4s is still fair game… but 5 is on the *other* side." This will be an important distinction to remember as we write our code later.

The second group that we add—the "22" guessers—occurs 3% of the time. We add this 3% to the original 4% from the first group. Therefore, they would occupy the next three slots on the number line—5, 6, and 7. The bucket edge for this group would be 7. As we will explore later, we only need to store one edge for each bucket. We can infer the other edge by the bucket immediately to the left.

The third group, the random guessers, represented 30% of the whole. As above, we add 30 to the edge of the preceding group (7). Therefore, the edge of this bucket would be 37. If our randomly generated number falls anywhere in the range of 8 to 37, we select the third bucket.

Naturally, we repeat the process for the fourth bucket, the semi-logical guessers. The width of their bucket is 63; their bucket spans the range from 38 to 100. It is important that we do not simply *assume* that anything that doesn't land in the first three buckets lands in the fourth. We need to make sure that we keep track of the actual width that we intend the last bucket to be. The reason this is important is that we do not want to *assume* the total width for the combined buckets. We shall revisit this issue in a moment.

PUTTING IT IN CODE

In the previous chapter, we laid out some code for selecting which of the four groups of guessers we were going to generate. The code for that was relatively simple.

```
GUESS_TYPE CGuesser::GetGuessType()
{
    int index = DieRoller.SingleDie( 100, false );
```

```
    // 1..4 = 4
    if ( index <= 4 ) return GUESS_33;

    // 5..7 = 3
    if ( index <= 7 ) return GUESS_22;

    // 8..37 = 30
    if ( index <= 37 ) return GUESS_RANDOM;

    // 38..100 = 63
    return GUESS_SEMI;
}
```

By looking closely, we can see some familiar numbers. In each of the `if` statements, we were checking to see if the random number was less than a specified number. The first one, `if ( index <= 4 )`, is testing to see if `index` lands in the first bucket (the "33" guessers). Likewise, the second statement, `if ( index <= 7 )`, is testing to see if our random number lands in the second bucket—between 5 and 7 inclusive. This continues to the third `if` statement, checking to see if the number is between 8 and 37 (inclusive). If we have not exited the routine after the third statement, the number is above 37, and we return `GUESS_SEMI` from the function.

This arrangement is a very familiar construct to most programmers. While it is certainly functional, it has one serious drawback. If we want to change the bucket widths—even just *one* of them, we have to change some (or even *all*) of the `if` statements. Specifically, we have to change the statement for the bucket we are changing the size of and all the ones that occur *after* it. The worst-case scenario occurs if we want to change the first bucket. That means we have to change *all* of the `if` statements in the entire function. For example, if we decide that the "33" guessers occur 5% of the time instead of 4% (at the expense of 1% of the semi-logical guessers), our new code would look like this:

```
GUESS_TYPE CGuesser::GetGuessType()
{
    int index = DieRoller.SingleDie( 100, false );

    // 1..5 = 5
    if ( index <= 5 ) return GUESS_33;
```

```
    // 6..8 = 3
    if ( index <= 8 ) return GUESS_22;

    // 9..38 = 30
    if ( index <= 38 ) return GUESS_RANDOM;

    // 39..100 = 62
    return GUESS_SEMI;
}
```

As we can see above, we had to change all three `if` statements, increasing the test number by one in each case. It is easy to see that this is *not* a very flexible way of laying out code. Trust me: As I was fine-tuning this example in the last chapter, I changed those numbers a few times… it's not fun. (The process was made even more annoying by the fact that I had to change my comments as well.)

There are a few considerations over and above the time consumption argument. First, it is ridiculously prone to errors. For example, if we forget to change one of those numbers, we are going to skew the probability of *two* occurrences rather than just the one that we are changing. Second, the difficulty in keeping track of our problems increases with the number of possibilities. The above example had only four selections (which gives us three `if` statements. If we have dozens… or even *scores* of possible actions, managing the bucket edges efficiently gets prohibitive quickly.

Perhaps the most problematic issue in constructing the probabilities in this manner is the fact that it is hard-coded, however. We have no way of changing the edges during run time. This goes beyond the ability to have data-driven code such as probabilities based on a difficulty setting that a designer sets beforehand. We have no way of efficiently changing these values *on the fly*. We will address the myriad uses for this later on in the book.

The solution to this is to store the edge values in a data structure. For example, we will create a `struct` named `sGUESSER_BUCKET` in our project that represents a bucket. Each bucket represents one type of guesser. The components of `sGUESSER_BUCKET` are simple: a width, an edge (both of type `USHORT`), and a `GUESS_TYPE`.

```
typedef enum {
    GUESS_33,
    GUESS_22,
```

```
        GUESS_RANDOM,
        GUESS_SEMI,
} GUESS_TYPE;

typedef unsigned short USHORT; // for simplicity of declaration

struct sGUESSER_BUCKET
{
    USHORT Width;    // the actual width of the bucket
    USHORT Edge;     // the calculated edge of the bucket
    GUESS_TYPE GuessType;    // the guess type this bucket represents
};
```

Once we have defined our bucket structures, we create a vector of them:

```
typedef std::vector< sGUESSER_BUCKET > GUESS_TYPE_LIST;
GUESS_TYPE_LIST mvGuessTypeList;
```

> **NAMING CONVENTIONS**
>
> Now that the programming part of this book is starting to get more involved, perhaps it is a good time to reiterate some of the naming conventions that I use in my code.
>
> - Type and `struct` names are in all caps: `MY_TYPE`
> - `Struct` names are preceded by a lowercase "s": `sMY_STRUCT`.
> - Variables and functions are in initial caps: `MyFunction( MyVariable )`
> - Member variables of a class are generally preceded with a lowercase "m": `mMyMemberVariable`
> - List and vector names are preceded by a lowercase "l" and "v," respectively. I combine these when necessary such as in a member of a class that is also a vector. In this case the name is preceded by "mv" such as in `mvMyMemberVector`.

When we run our program, the buckets do not exist in the vector. We need to set them up with the initial data. We do this by setting the data for each bucket and pushing it onto the vector. We can isolate this process in a function such as this:

```
void CGuesser::AddBucket(GUESS_TYPE GuessType, USHORT Width)
{
    sGUESSER_BUCKET CurrentBucket;
    mMaxIndex += Width;

    CurrentBucket.GuessType = GuessType;
    CurrentBucket.Width = Width;
    CurrentBucket.Edge = mMaxIndex;
    mvGuessTypeList.push_back( CurrentBucket );
}
```

Notice that, despite the fact that our buckets have three members (`GuessType`, `Width`, and `Edge`), we only pass two variables into the `AddBucket` function. We don't need to pass in `Edge` because it is based on the running total of the bucket sizes that have been pushed before it. We track this with the member variable `mMaxIndex`, which represents the maximum array index of the vector. When we are finished pushing buckets into our vector, `mMaxIndex` will represent the combined width of all the buckets.

To add our four guesser types to this vector, we call `AddBucket()` once for each type. It doesn't matter where we get our data. For simplicity's sake, in this example, we have hard-coded the probabilities for each of the four types.

```
void CGuesser::InitBuckets()
{
    AddBucket( GUESS_33, 4 );
    AddBucket( GUESS_22, 3 );
    AddBucket( GUESS_RANDOM, 30 );
    AddBucket( GUESS_SEMI, 63 );
}
```

In the function above, we are using the same probabilities that we used in Chapter 11 and again in our initial example above. If we decide that we want to change the probability values, however, our task is much simpler now than it was when we were using the `if` statements. If we want to make the same change to the data that we did a few pages back (the "33" guessers being 5% and the semi-logical ones being only 62%), we only need to change the two relevant numbers. Our function would now read:

```
void CGuesser::InitBuckets()
{
    AddBucket( GUESS_33, 5 );
    AddBucket( GUESS_22, 3 );
    AddBucket( GUESS_RANDOM, 30 );
    AddBucket( GUESS_SEMI, 62 );
}
```

The bucket edges would now be different than they were with the original numbers. (mMaxIndex still adds up to 100).

Retrieving a Result

Once we have our buckets set up, tossing our ball in to determine a result is a fairly simple process. Originally, we generated our random number and then tested it against three if statements to find out which of our four possibilities was selected. That is not much different than what we are going to do here. Thankfully, by holding our results in vector, we can now perform this search in a loop.

```
GUESS_TYPE CGuesser::GetGuessType()
{
    // Generate a random number between 1 and mMaxIndex
    USHORT index = DieRoller.SingleDie( mMaxIndex, false );

    // Count the number of buckets
    USHORT NumBuckets = mvGuessTypeList.size();

    // Loop through all the buckets
    for ( USHORT i = 0; i < NumBuckets; i++ ) {
        // See if index fits in this bucket
        if ( index <= mvGuessTypeList[i].Edge ) {
            return mvGuessTypeList[i].GuessType;
        } // end if
```

```
        } // end for

        // Index didn't land in a bucket!
        assert( 0 && "Index out of range" );
        // As a default, however, we will return a random guesser
        return GUESS_RANDOM;
    }
```

The first thing we did in the function `GetGuessType()` is to generate our random number, `index`. There is one change to this line from the technique we used before. Instead of hard-coding the number 100, we changed our random number call to be between 1 and `mMaxIndex`. This is important. We are now set up to generate a random number between 1 and whatever the combined width of all of our buckets happens to be. For example, if we decided that our "33" guess bucket was a width of 8 wide rather than 4 *and made no other changes*, the total width of all buckets would be 104 rather than 100 (notice that we are no longer saying "percent"). If we had continued to generate a random number between 1 and 100, we would not be giving full credit to the bucket that we have now pushed to the right—ending at 104 instead of 100. We will address how dynamic bucket widths can be used to our advantage a little later on.

The next statement in the function sets `NumBuckets` to the number of buckets we have in our vector. Again, this is something that we can leverage. If we decide to add a fifth type of guesser to our experiment, this code would automatically account for it.

Once we know the number of buckets that we are going to search, we loop through them. The test is the same as we did before: We check to see if our randomly generated `index` is less than the edge of the current bucket designated by `mvGuessTypeList[i]`. If it is, we return the `GuessType` associated with that bucket. If not, we move on.

/*
Note that this code should always *return a* `GuessType` *before it exits the loop. I leave it to you, gentle reader, to insert error-trapping code of your choice (such as my* `assert()` *function), return a default* `GuessType`, *or devise any other manner of graceful exit.*
*/

There is another method of finding out in which bucket our metaphorical bouncing ball landed. It will be much more entertaining to set up a few more buckets to search before we open the lid on that method.

Converting Functions to Response Curves

As we touched on at the beginning of this chapter, response curves have another valuable role to play for us. The functions from Chapter 10 are rather inflexible in that we couldn't tweak specific areas of the curves the way we might want to. We are stuck with whatever was spit out of the equation for a given *x* value. Similarly, some of the probability distributions in Chapter 11 are function-based. While we can calculate the probability (*y*) for a given *x* value, we lack the ability to extract a random *x* value based on all of the different *y* probabilities.

While these two problems may not seem related, we can actually solve them in much the same manner using response curves. The secret to both solutions is converting the results of the function into a custom response curve. Once we have created the response curve, we have much more flexibility available to us. Before we get too far ahead of ourselves, however, we need to address the methods and code for putting the numbers into the response curve to begin with.

Simple 1-to-1 Mappings

To keep the numbers manageable at first, we will start with a simple equation:

$$y = -2x + 100$$

Because we are going to be filling a finite space with our results, it is important that we establish the range with which we are working. In this case, we will limit ourselves to the range $0 \leq x \leq 40$.

As usual, we first need to define our vector.

```
typedef std::vector< double > CURVE_VECTOR;
CURVE_VECTOR mvEquationResults;
```

The process of filling the vector is rather intuitive.

```
void CLinearFunction::FillVector( int Size )
{
    double y;

    for ( int x = 0; x <= Size; x++ ) {
        y = ( -2 * x ) + 100;
        mvEquationResults.push_back( y );
    } // end for
}
```

To fill `mvEquationResults` from 0 to 40, we simply call:

```
FillVector( 41 );
```

Below is what that data would look like:

x	y
0	100
1	98
2	96
3	94
…	…
38	24
39	22
40	20

Again, this seems ridiculously easy. In fact, it seems like a lot of wasted effort when we could have simply used the equation itself for any value of x. However, this does allow us to manipulate the results of that equation. For instance, if we want y to be the result of the equation *except* when $x = 27$, in which case we want $y = 1.0$, we can change that single entry in the vector.

```
mvEquationResults[27] = 1.0;
```

This may seem like an inconsequential benefit at the moment. However, we will soon see that this ability lies at the heart of the power behind response curves.

Just for the sake of completeness, we can recover a value by simply retrieving the contents of the vector element.

```
y = mvEquationResults[x]
```

Not a lot to it, eh?

Advanced 1-to-1 Mappings

The above example is simplified somewhat by the fact that the x range that we are working with is between 0 and 40. We have the luxury of using the vector indices that, for a group of 41 elements, start at 0 and end at 40. We are not able to do this if the range with which we want to deal starts at, for example, 125 and extends to 165.

To accommodate this, we need to abandon using the index of the vector as our x value. Instead, we create a struct that contains data for both x and y. We then can create a vector composed of that struct.

```
struct sELEMENT
{
    int x;
    double y;
};

typedef std::vector< sELEMENT > ELEMENT_VECTOR;
ELEMENT_VECTOR mvElementVector;
```

Entering Data

Filling the vector with the equation results is not much different with this new twist. Instead of simply pushing a y value onto the next element of the vector, we now store both the x and y value in an sELEMENT and push the whole thing onto the end of the vector.

```
void CLinearFunction::FillVector( int Low, int High )
{
    sELEMENT thisElement;

    for ( int x = Low; x <= High; x++ ) {
        thisElement.x = x;
        thisElement.y = ( -2 * x ) + 100;
        mvElementVector.push_back( thisElement );
    } // end for
}
```

If, as we stated above, we want to store the data for x values from 125 to 165, we call FillVector with:

```
FillVector( 125, 165 );
```

By running this new version of FillVector, we fill mvElementVector with 41 entries. The x values range from 125 to 165, with the corresponding y values being the result of our function.

For the 41 potential values of vector index *i*, the corresponding values of the elements *x* and *y* would be:

i	x	y
0	125	−150
1	126	−152
2	127	−154
3	128	−156
...	...	...
38	163	−226
39	164	−228
40	165	−230

Extracting a Value

Now that the index of the vector no longer corresponds to the *x* value, recovering the data that we need is a slightly more involved process. There are three primary ways of handling this.

Brute Force

The first option we could take is the brute force method. By iterating through the entire vector, we could check all the *x* values until we find the one we want and return the corresponding *y* value. This is a perfectly viable solution—especially for small data sets. It looks much like what we did with the guess type function earlier.

```
double CLinearFunction::GetY_BruteForce(int x)
{
    for ( int i = 0; i < mvElementVector.size(); i++ ) {
        if ( mvElementVector[i].x = x ) {
            return mvElementVector[i].y;

        } // end if
    } // end for

    // Code should never get here!
    assert( 0 && "Index not found" );
    return 0.0;
}
```

The drawback of this method is that it doesn't scale well to large data sets. The search time scales linearly with the number of members that we add to our vector. That is, if we have 41 members (as in our example above), we are going to average searching 20.5 members to find our match. If we have 1,000 members in the data set, we are going to be searching 500 of them on average… and as many as all 1,000 in the worst-case scenario.

Offset

Certainly, if we know the offset from the vector index to the lowest x value, we could leverage that to find the proper container. For example, we know that our lowest number in this exercise was 125. The lowest index in a vector is 0. Therefore, to find the container that corresponds to any given x value, we subtract 125 from the x value we actually want to look up. If we wanted to find y when $x = 130$, we could find it this way:

```
y = mvElementVector[x - 125].y;
```

If $x = 130$, the above statement would yield the equivalent of:

```
y = mvElementVector[5].y;
```

This method is problematic in that we have to keep track of the offset in a separate location—either hard-coded as a constant such as above or held separately in a variable. Either way, if we change the range of our x values, we have to remember to change this offset. We could avoid this by setting the offset to the x value of the first element in the first place:

```
Offset = mvElementVector[0].x;
y = mvElementVector[x - Offset].y;
```

The above method works in the scenario that we have set out. It also is significantly faster than the brute force method. There is a better way, however—one that allows us to do some nifty tricks down the road.

Binary Search

For those who aren't familiar with the **binary search** technique, it is, in essence, a game of "guess the number." The three possible outcomes are "higher," "lower," and "got it!" If you have every played this game, you realize that the most efficient way of guessing the number is to take a "divide and conquer" approach.

For example, if guessing a number between 1 and 100, we want to start at 50. If we are told that the number is *higher* than 50, we would guess 75. If we are then told "lower," our next guess would be 62. On each turn, we divide the remaining range in half, thereby maximizing the possibility that it is on either side of an incorrect guess. Compare this to the brute force method we listed above. That approach is analogous to guessing the lowest possible number on each iteration and being told "higher" until, one step at a time, we reach the target. Using that method, the maximum number of guesses is equal to the number of possibilities. If we are guessing a number between 1 and 100, we *could* end up guessing 100 times to determine the target (if the number was 100).

On the other hand, a binary search performs in $O(\log_2 n)$ time, where n is the number of elements. In the classic "guess the number between 1 and 100" game, we would need a maximum of seven guesses to determine the target. If we were to expand the game from 1 to *200* instead, we would only need one additional guess (eight total). Guessing a number between 1 and 400 requires only nine guesses. Between 1 and 800? Only 10 guesses. It becomes apparent very quickly that a binary search is an efficient way of finding data.

The major requirement for a binary search is that the data we are searching is stored in a sorted fashion. If it was not, then we could not determine "higher" or "lower"... only whether or not we were correct. Imagine asking someone to guess the name of an animal. When they did so, we could tell them "correct" or "incorrect." The answer of "incorrect" doesn't help them determine what direction they should take on their subsequent guess, however. If we told them that the animal they were attempting to guess was, for example, "earlier in the alphabet" or "heavier" than the one they just guessed, we would be giving them a direction in which to head. With that information, they could use a similar "divide and conquer" strategy to close in on the correct answer.

In the example we are working with, the values of x are stored in the vector in sorted order from lowest to highest. That way, when we test the value of x at a particular array index (i), we can determine if we are higher or lower (assuming we are not correct) and move in the proper direction from that point. Therefore, a binary search is a valid approach.

The code for a binary search isn't difficult to write. We need only keep track of the highest and lowest possible bounds at any given time. Then, we calculate the midpoint between them as our guess and check to see if our guess was correct, high, or low. The following searches our vector for the proper value of x to return the corresponding y.

```
double CLinearFunction::GetY_BinarySearch( int x )
{
```

```
// Get number of elements in the vector
int iCount = mvElementVector.size();

// Set the boundaries of our search range
// to the first and last elements (remember that
// the vector indices are 0-referenced... that's
// why we subtract 1 from iCount!)
int iLow = 0;
int iHigh = iCount - 1;

bool found = false;
int i = 0;   // the vector index

while ( !found ) {
    // use the mid-way point as our index guess
    i = iLow + ( ( iHigh - iLow ) / 2 );

    if ( x = mvElementVector[i].x ) {
        // the guess is correct
        return mvElementVector[i].y;
    } // end if

    if ( x < mvElementVector[i].x ) {
        // lower the high boundary to the current guess
        iHigh = i - 1;
    } else {
        // raise the low boundary to the current guess
        iLow = i + 1;
    } // end if
} // end while

return mvElementVector[i].y;
}
```

Stepping through the function from the beginning, we first determine the number of elements in the vector. We set our initial bounds for the search at 0 and one less than the number of elements. (Vectors are 0-referenced, so n elements means the last index is $n - 1$.) In the `while` loop, we set our guess index (`i`) to the halfway point between whatever the current high and low are. We then check the value of x held at the point in the vector referenced by `i`. If it matches the x we are looking for, we are finished and return the corresponding y. If not, we then determine whether our guess was too high or too low and change our upper or lower bounds accordingly. We then repeat the `while` loop to make a new guess until such time as we guess correctly.

Notice that, as written, the while loop should not end because we never change the value of `found`. If we wanted to, we could write in various error traps to avoid such things as infinite loops. I left them out here for clarity of code.

The binary search method has given us a few improvements over the prior methods. As we discussed above, the binary search method is significantly faster than the brute force method—especially when we work with larger data sets. Additionally, unlike the offset method, we no longer have to keep track of the relationship between the vector index and the data contained in the vector. This last part is significant for one last reason: by design, the vector indices necessarily have to increment by one—we may not want to hold our data to the same requirement.

CONVERTING DISTRIBUTIONS TO RESPONSE CURVES

In the previous examples, we were matching up a single x with a single y. That is, any given input generated an output. However, if we think back to the original (and delightfully simple) dentist example, we encounter a different requirement.

We can think of the "ball into bucket" metaphor as having two different types of input. First, we think of the ball in terms of dropping into one of five different segments of the range. In a way, we have recast this as being *five* buckets rather than two. In this case, buckets 1 through 4 mean that the dentist recommends sugarless gum and bucket 5 indicates that he doesn't.

If we were to create our dentist example using the 1-to-1 methods outlined above, we would be inclined to create a five-unit vector—the first four of which were mapped to one output ("sugarless") and the fifth mapped to the other ("tooth-rotting"). However, it does seem rather inefficient to have four slots in our vector all pointing to the same outcome.

On the other hand, we can also think of the ball dropping into one of only *two* buckets—the two buckets representing our two choices. It just so happens, of course, that one of those buckets is four times as large as the other one. The difference is subtle but important from an algorithmic standpoint.

It would seem that a more accurate way of modeling this idea would be to truly have *only* two buckets—that is, two items in our vector. However, we would have to also represent the reality that the first bucket was four times as large as the second one. This is where the edges come into play.

Data Structure

We don't need to change too much of our data structure to represent this method of thinking. When we use a pattern similar to what we have done already, our dentist recommendation structure would look like this.

```
typedef enum {
    SUGARLESS,
    SUGARRY
} GUM_RECOMMENDATION;

struct sRECOMMENDATION {
    USHORT Size; // The size of this bucket
    USHORT Edge; // The edge of this bucket based on its position
    GUM_RECOMMENDATION Recommendation; // The actual recommendation
};

typedef std::vector< sRECOMMENDATION > GUM_VECTOR;
```

We have replaced the *x* parameter of the `struct` with two components: `Size` and `Edge`. The first one, `Size` represents the width of the bucket. `Edge`, on the other hand, represents the position of the edge on the *x* scale. This is similar to how we were using x in the prior examples. There is not much of a functional difference between the two—the edge value is simply an *x* value after all. The difference is that we are no longer representing *every* value of *x*.

Entering Data

Entering data into the new structure works from the same premise that we used earlier. The function `AddBucket` takes a bucket size and a recommendation, places them into a temporary `struct`, and pushes that `struct` onto the back of the vector.

```
void CDentist::AddBucket( USHORT Size,
                          GUM_RECOMMENDATION Recommendation )
{
    sRECOMMENDATION CurrentRecommendation;

    mTotalSize += Size; // Calculate the new edge

    CurrentRecommendation.Size = Size;
    CurrentRecommendation.Edge = mTotalSize;
    CurrentRecommendation.Recommendation = Recommendation;
    mvRecommendations.push_back( CurrentRecommendation );
}
```

One important thing to note is how `Edge` works. As we add each bucket, we retrieve the total size of all the buckets we have added so far. That value represents the right-most edge of the whole collection. Because we are adding our new bucket on the end of the row, the edge of the new bucket is the total size plus the size of the new bucket.

We can fill our dentist recommendation list with the following function:

```
void CDentist::InitVector()
{
    mTotalSize = 0;
    AddBucket( 4, SUGARLESS );
    AddBucket( 1, SUGARRY );
}
```

This adds our two buckets to the vector. After running `InitVector()`, the data stored in the vector is:

i	Size	Edge	Recommendation
0	4	4	SUGARLESS
1	1	5	SUGARY

Converting Functions to Distributions

To convert a larger dataset such as the results of a function, we need to automate the process of adding buckets. For this example, we will use an uneven probability distribution applied to 10 items. The probabilities of the 10 items follow the formula:

$$\text{Occurrences} = -1(x - 100) + 12$$

For a visual reference, the graph of the number of occurrences looks like the one in Figure 12.3.

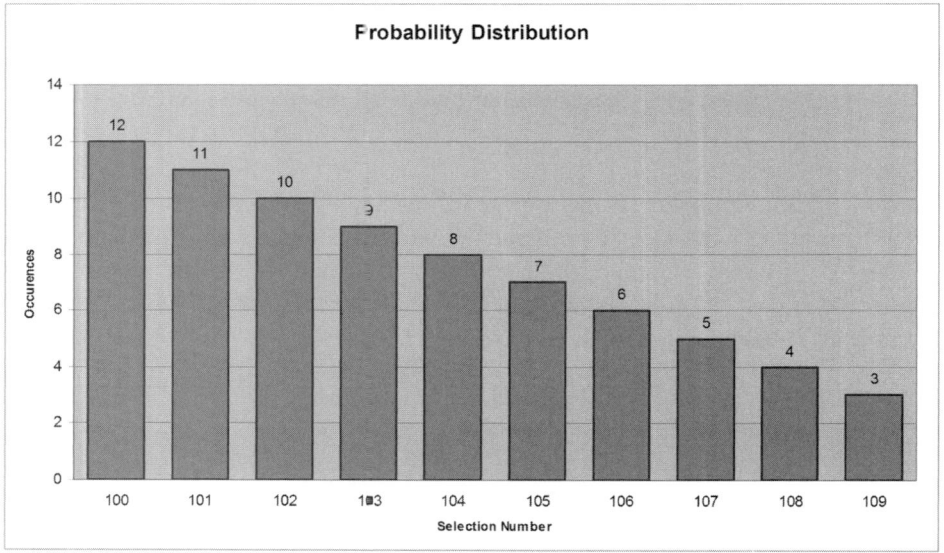

FIGURE 12.3 The histogram showing the number of occurrences of each selection is based on the formula $y = -1(x - 100) + 12$.

The first thing we do is create the `struct` that will act as our data bucket.

```
struct sBUCKET {
    USHORT Size; // The size of this bucket = probability
    USHORT Edge; // The edge of this bucket based on its position
    USHORT Result; // The result we are generating = x
};
```

As with our dentist example, each record holds the size of the bucket, its edge location, and what the result will be. We've changed the terminology slightly here.

Rather than referring to an *x* value as we have done previously, we now call this variable Result. We do this because, with a probability distribution, we are going to be selecting one of our buckets based on the probability represented by Size. We could have also named it something like "Name," "Selection," "Action," or, as in the dentist example, "Recommendation." What we call it will be case-specific. In any event, it is the name of what the bucket represents. For now, Result it is.

As usual, we create a vector to hold our distribution.

```
typedef std::vector< sBUCKET > DIST_VECTOR;
DIST_VECTOR mvDistribution;
```

We then create our function, InitVector(), that fills our vector with the 10 results that we want to track the probability of.

```
void CDistribution::InitVector()
{
    sBUCKET ThisBucket;
    USHORT ThisSize;
    USHORT MaxItems = 10;

    for ( USHORT x = 0; x < MaxItems; x++ ) {
        ThisSize = (-1 * ( x -100 ) ) + 12;

        ThisBucket[x].Size = ThisSize;
        If ( x == 0 ) {
            // this is the first entry
            ThisBucket[x].Edge = ThisSize;
        } else {
            ThisBucket[x].Edge = ThisBucket[x-1].Edge + ThisSize;
        }
        ThisBucket[x].Result = x;
        mvDistribution.push_back( ThisBucket );
    } // end for
}
```

In InitVector(), we loop through the 10 items, using the value of *x* in the equation we specified above to determine the size of the bucket that we then store.

The next step in the above function is slightly different than what we have done before. Rather than hold a separate value for the total size to determine what the edge is, we use the edge of the previous bucket. By adding the size of the current bucket to the prior edge, we determine the edge of the current bucket. (Note that for the first bucket, we don't have a *prior* bucket to use. The edge is the same as the size.) Later, when we need to know the last bucket edge—that is, the total width of the group—we can retrieve the edge value of the last bucket. As a last step, we assign the value of *x* to Result and then push the bucket onto the end of our vector.

After running InitVector(), our data will look like this (*i* is the index of the vector):

i	Size	Edge	Result
0	12	12	100
1	11	23	101
2	10	33	102
3	9	42	103
4	8	50	104
5	7	57	105
6	6	63	106
7	5	68	107
8	4	72	108
9	3	75	109

As we can see from the above table and from Figure 12.4, the edges represent the cumulative sizes of the buckets as we "lay them end to end." The total width of all 10 buckets is 75.

Selecting a Result

We can retrieve a random result out of the distribution using the binary search method outlined above. The function GetResult() is entirely self-sufficient. That is, we don't need to pass it or otherwise store the number of items in our distribution or the value of the right-most edge. When we call the function, it returns a random result from mvDistribution determined by where the generated random number lands in the distribution.

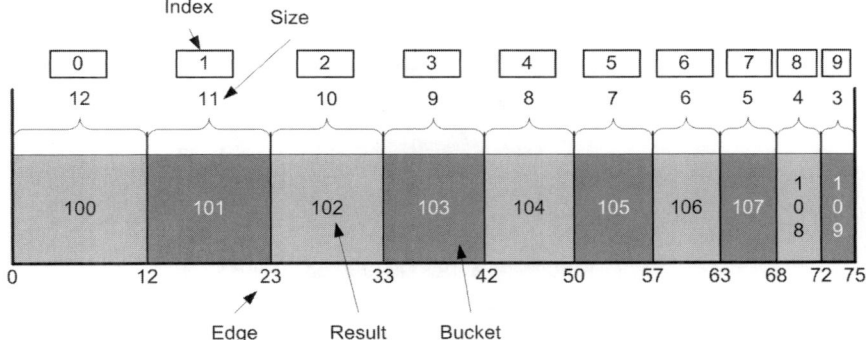

FIGURE 12.4 The histogram in Figure 12.3 rearranged to show the data generated by the InitVector() function. The terminology of the response curve data structure is labeled.

```
USHORT CDistribution::GetResult()
{
    // The number of buckets in the disribution
    USHORT NumBuckets = mvDistribution.size();

    // The maximum roll is the edge of the last bucket
    USHORT MaxRoll = mvDistribution[NumBuckets - 1].Edge;

    // The random number we are looking for
    USHORT Target = DiceRoller.SingleDie( MaxRoll, false );

    // Bucket indexes
    USHORT iHigh = mvDistribution.size() - 1;
    USHORT iLow = 0;
    USHORT iGuess;
    bool found = false;

    while ( !found ) {
        // Guess is halfway between the low and high indexes
```

```
            iGuess = iLow + ( ( iHigh - iLow ) / 2 );

            // Check for correct guess
            if ( InBucket( iGuess, Target ) ) {
                return mvDistribution[iGuess].Result;
            } // end if

            // If not correct...
            if ( Target > mvDistribution[iGuess].Edge ) {
                // guess is too low, change the bottom boundary
                iLow = iGuess;
            } else {
                // guess is too high, change the top boundary
                iHigh = iGuess;
            } // end if

        } // end while

        // Code should never get here!
        assert( 0 && "Code fell through while loop!");
        return 0;
    }
```

There is one main difference between this function and the binary search we used earlier. Because the bucket is a range rather than a discrete point on the x-axis, we must perform a slightly more involved check to see if our random number lands in it. To do this, we create a function InBucket that takes our current bucket guess and the random target as parameters.

```
    bool CDistribution::InBucket( USHORT i, USHORT Target )
    {
        if ( i == 0 && Target <= mvDistribution[i].Edge ) {
            return true;
        } // end if
```

```
        if ( Target <= mvDistribution[i].Edge &&
             Target > mvDistribution[i-1].Edge ) {
            return true;
        } else {
            return false;
        } // end if
    }
```

This Boolean function checks to see if the random number `Target` is between the edge of the specified bucket `mvDistribution[i]` and the edge of the bucket to the left of it, `mvDistribution[i-1]`. We need to take care with the operators in the two statements. Because the edge of a bucket is *inclusive*, we also need to test for equality on the current bucket but *not* equality of the previous bucket.

It is also important that we trap for the possibility that this is the lowest bucket (that is, `i` is 0). If that is the case, we cannot utilize the edge of the bucket *below* it without generating an index that is out of bounds (e.g., −1). We only check to see if `Target` is less than the edge of the bucket.

Going back to `GetResult()`, if `InBucket` returns false, then we know that our current guess, `iGuess`, is not correct. We then test to see if our random number (`Target`) is higher than the edge of our current bucket. If it is, we move the lowest bucket to search up to the current bucket. If `Target` is lower, we move the highest bucket to search down to the current bucket.

Adjusting Data

In all of the above examples, we create the response curve at the beginning and do not adjust it afterward. There are times, however, when we would want to adjust the contents of the response curve. It would be inefficient for us to erase all the contents of the existing vector and rebuild it from scratch. Depending on the change that is made, we can use a number of approaches to modify the existing data without having to start over.

One of the most common (and most useful) adjustments we can make to the data in a response curve is to adjust the weights of one or more of the buckets. When we are dealing with a 1-to-1 response curve, adjusting the *data* held in one of the buckets is inconsequential. We return the data held in the bucket that we find at the selected index.

The only difference to this approach is when we introduce the binary search. Because we are searching for our result by the edge values rather than the indices, we need to maintain the integrity of the edge values. With the distribution-based response curves, when we change the size of one bucket, we also affect the edge values of all the buckets *after* the changed one. It is a requirement that we rebuild the edge values in the vector *any* time the data changes so the change is reflected in all the edge values. For example, let's look again at the data from the above uneven distribution:

i	Size	Edge	Result
0	12	12	100
1	11	23	101
2	10	33	102
3	9	42	103
4	8	50	104
5	7	57	105
6	6	63	106
7	5	68	107
8	4	72	108
9	3	75	109

If we arbitrarily decide to change the weight ("size") of the result "104" from 8 to 10, we need to make a number of changes. Obviously, the first change is that the bucket at index 4 would now have an edge of 52 rather than 50. (It now stretches from 43 to 52.) However, looking now at the bucket at index 5, when we add its size of 7 to the new edge of 4, we arrive at 59 rather than 57. This process cascades down to the last bucket, whose edge we increase by 2 to a value of 77. The contents of the new vector are (changes from above are emphasized in bold):

i	Size	Edge	Result
0	12	12	100
1	11	23	101
2	10	33	102
3	9	42	103
4	**10**	**52**	104
5	7	**59**	105
6	6	**65**	106
7	5	**70**	107
8	4	**74**	108
9	3	**77**	109

To accomplish this properly, we need to construct a function that rebuilds the edges. Rather than rebuild *all* of the edges, however, it is more efficient (especially in larger data sets) to rebuild only from the changed bucket forward to the end of the vector. We can do this with a function such as this one:

```
void CDistribution::RebuildEdges( USHORT iStartBucket /*= 0*/ )
{
    USHORT VectorSize = mvDistribution.size();

    for ( USHORT i = iStartBucket; i < VectorSize; i++ ) {
        if ( i > 0 ) {
            mvDistribution[i].Edge =
                mvDistribution[i-1].Edge + mvDistribution[i].Size;
        } else {
            mvDistribution[i].Edge = mvDistribution[i].Size;
        } // end if
    } // end for
}
```

The function `RebuildEdges( USHORT iStartBucket )` will rebuild the edges from the array starting point identified by `iStartBucket` and continuing on to the end of the vector. If we do not specify a value for `iStartBucket`, the default of 0 is used and the entire vector is rebuilt.

As with our earlier example, we need to account for the possibility that the index is 0. In that case, attempting to access the data at `mvDistribution[i-1]` would generate an error. If the index is 0, we know that the edge is equal to the size anyway.

We can use this function every time a data element in the vector is changed. There is an exception to this approach, however. If we are going to be changing a number of elements at the same time (that is, before we try to extract data from it again), it would be redundant to keep recalculating the edges for each change. It is very likely that we will be rewriting the edge data over and over to account for each change. It is much more efficient to make all of our changes first and *then* recalculate the necessary edges. (We could either rebuild *all* the edges at that point or keep track of the lowest numbered index that was changed and start from there.)

Search Optimization

Because we are using the edge values to search for the chosen bucket, we don't necessarily have to have the buckets sorted by size. However, we can optimize searches through having our buckets sorted by size. This method works very well when there are many buckets of widely disparate sizes. We can construct an example of when this optimization is useful by using a quadratic distribution such as:

$$y = 100 - \frac{x^2}{10}$$

If we use this formula over the x range of 0 to 30, we find that the probabilities (y) of any given x range from 100 to 10. That gives us a large difference in bucket sizes. This is even more apparent when we realize that the final edge of these 31 buckets will be at 2155. The first bucket ($x = 0$) has a 4.6% chance of being picked. On the other end of the spectrum the last bucket has only a 0.5% chance.

The important factor to address, however, is the starting point of our "divide and conquer" approach. The purpose of guessing the midpoint is to reduce the amount of space left to search regardless of whether our guess was high or low. By starting with the middle bucket, we are reducing the number of buckets on each side of our guess to a joint minimum. No matter which way we missed (too high or too low), we know that we have reduced the remaining buckets to search as low as we can.

In the above examples, we started at the middle bucket found by using the formula:

```
iGuess = iLow + ( ( iHigh - iLow ) / 2 );
```

Applied to this example, our initial index would be 15 (Figure 12.5). Upon a little examination, however, we find that the edge of bucket 14 is 1399. That means that almost 65% of the data is below what we calculated as the midpoint of the vector. That also tells us that, if our initial guess of 15 is incorrect, we are going to be moving *left* more often than *right*. If that is the case, we would want to optimize for quicker searches on the side of the vector that we are going to be landing in more often.

By changing our initial guess to the bucket that is in the middle of the possible choices rather than the middle bucket, we can achieve better results. That is, rather than selecting the middle bucket, we want to select the bucket at the point where we know the ball will fall half the time on *one* side and half the time on the *other* side. We can do this by determining a theoretical bucket edge that is half the value of the farthest edge.

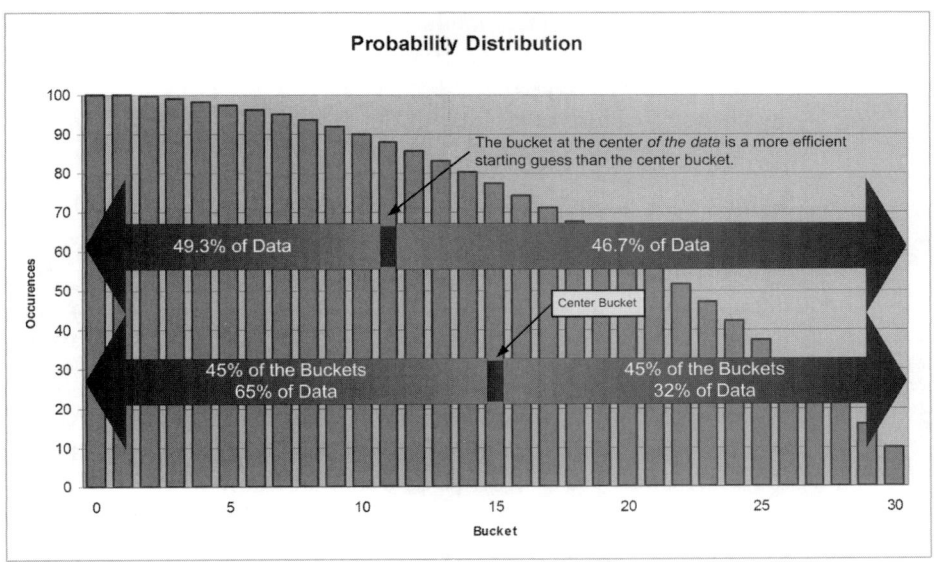

FIGURE 12.5 We can improve the performance of searching for the selected bucket by starting in the middle of the data distribution rather than the middle bucket. Most of the data occurrences are on the left side of the histogram. Therefore, we bias our search to that side by starting with bucket 11 rather than bucket 15.

In this example, the edge of bucket 30 is 2155. Half of that is 1077. The value 1077 falls into bucket 11. If we examine the bucket *below* number 11, we find that the edge of bucket 10 is 1062. That tells us that 49.3% (1062/2155) of the values are in bucket 10 or below. On the other hand, the edge of bucket 11 is 1149. There are 1005 (2155 − 1149) numbers *above* bucket 11. That represents 46.7% of the total. (Bucket 11 is the missing 4.1%.) This means, if the answer is *not* bucket 11, we have about an even chance of being either too high or too low.

To accomplish this, we need a new way to determine our starting bucket. As we explained, this is simply a matter of dividing the highest edge value in half and then searching for it via the original, slightly inefficient method. We then store that value for use in all of our regular searches.

We don't need to do this every time we search. If we did, it would be very inefficient anyway because we would be searching twice for every real search. As long as the data does not change, the suggested starting point does not change. In fact, because the binary search is so fast, as long as the data doesn't change *much*, we can still use that suggested starting point.

This point exposes the fact that these optimizations are very situation-dependant. In general, we can follow these rules:

Any change to a bucket size:	Rebuild edges
Large changes to bucket sizes:	Re-sort vector
Change in lopsided distribution:	Recalculate starting bucket

By no means is the above an exhaustive list. Depending on the number of elements in a vector, the relative sizes of the elements, the nature of the data, and even how often the data is changed or accessed, we can select our optimization and search methods to provide the best possible response.

For example, the only time that we would want to re-sort the vector and change the start bucket is if we are dealing with very large data sets (e.g., hundreds of buckets) or are doing *many* searches on a data set that changes rarely (or both). In either case, we can see some minor gains in performance. However, we need to be aware that the sort and recalculate optimizations should happen very rarely lest we give back the gained time through the time it takes to perform the actual optimization.

HAND-CRAFTED RESPONSE CURVES

Other than the occasional manual tweak, we have generated most of the response curves in this chapter through a function of some sort. This is not a necessary limitation. It is not only possible, but very useful to hand-craft a distribution to match a desired effect.

Thinking back to our five dentists, we manually created a two-bucket response curve representing the two bits of masticatory advice a dentist could offer to us: sugarless gum or sugared gum. We also manually set our two sizes of four and one, respectively to simulate the legendary "four out of five dentists surveyed" phenomenon. We also used this same approach to model the four types of guessers in the Guess Two-Thirds Game. These are very small examples of hand-crafted distribution.

Applying this process to a more extreme example, rather than go through the great pains that we went to in Chapter 11 to model the results of the Guess Two-Thirds contest run by the University of Copenhagen that we explored in Chapter 6, we could craft a 101-bucket response curve that exactly duplicated the results of the study. Rather than breaking down the four groups and then modeling the distribution of the guesses for each group, we can simply create a single response curve that holds the data for all 101 possible selections. By sizing the buckets according to how the results appeared in the actual contest, we can generate a strikingly similar distribution.

The most common method of constructing hand-crafted response curves is to save the data in a file. At run time, we read the data from the file into the response curve in almost the same looping fashion as generating it from a function. Retrieving the data uses the same process as we have discussed above.

Dynamic Response Curves

We can also generate data for a response curve at any point during run time. In fact, as we will find, response curves are at their best when storing and selecting data that is constantly changing. If we think of the buckets as decisions (e.g., "sugarless" vs. "sugary") and the sizes of the buckets as *weights*, *priorities*, or *utilities* for those decisions, we can see how being able to selected a dynamically weighted decision opens up many methods of adjusting and selecting behaviors. As the game runs, we can change the weights by any method we choose. Any time the weights change, we update the edges, re-sort the vector if necessary, and go about the business of selecting our behaviors. We will deal with this process in more detail in the next few chapters.

13 | Factor Weighting

In Chapters 7, 8, and 9 we discussed various methods of measuring utility. More importantly, we discussed that measurements of utility are a core component of the decision-making process. It behooves us to examine how we can measure, track, and adjust utility in a manner that is clean, efficient, understandable, and easy to use.

SCALING CONSIDERATIONS

When I confessed some of the intricacies of my caffeine usage earlier in the book, it would have done you, the gentle reader, very little good for me to say that I "like pop." You would have no idea what that means in the wider arena of likes and dislikes. Even if I were to say that I like pop "a lot," you have no frame of reference. Does that mean "more than average"? More than I like rutabagas? More than I like watching football? How close is "a lot" to "more than I could possibly like anything in the world"? Or is it more along the lines of "yeah… I suppose I wouldn't mind having a pop"? Without a frame of reference, many of our statements are lost in the inherent vagaries of language.

IMPOSING ARTIFICIAL LIMITS

Even when the words are very specific, we have to take them with a proverbial grain of salt. My sister, for example, has met "the funniest guy ever," seen "the funniest show ever," and eaten "the best sushi ever,"—and done all of them numerous times. In fact, she can manage to experience any one of those superlatives in startlingly rapid succession. (She once heard three "funniest joke ever" candidates within a two-hour period.) My conclusion is that she is either extraordinarily fortunate in her life's adventure, or she just misuses the word *ever*. Given the spectacularly common Internet usage of the word *ever* in the titles of videos, top 10 lists, and other such fare, I have determined that she is not alone in her overuse of the term.

To make things more complicated, our perceptions can change rapidly depending on what we are looking for, something that is the "the most" or "the best" can change from moment to moment. For instance, in a previous life, I worked at a recording studio as a composer, arranger, keyboard player, and recording engineer. (I got out of the biz when the kids wanted to eat more regularly than I was paid.) One of the phenomena that I observed there was what I termed the "climbing fader syndrome."

When I would be with a band working on the mix of their low-budget masterpiece, I was often the recipient of a nonstop barrage of requests. Most often, these took the form of "dude... I can't hear the [insert instrument here]." It doesn't take much speculation to guess that each of the members specifically focused on their own part of the project. Therefore, each person would ask to hear more of their own part. When I acquiesced to each new request by turning up their track, it caused the other members to hear less of their own respective parts. In short order, another person would complain that their part was too soft. And another... and another. I was nudging each instrument higher in the mix, one at a time until, eventually, the original complainant was, once again, tapping me on the arm and indicating I should boost him further.

The root problem that caused the climbing fader syndrome was that each person felt (consciously or subconsciously) that his part should be "the loudest"—an acoustical impossibility, to say the least. However, most of them didn't *really* think that their part should be "out front in the mix," but because it wasn't, they didn't perceive it as being there at all. I could usually prove the point fairly simply. When I received the comment "I can't hear my [instrument]," I would respond by simply turning off their track for a moment and then turning it back on. The reaction was priceless... sometimes involving the person saying, "Oh, there it is! That's a lot better!" Nothing had changed in the mix. They simply noticed their instrument again because they had missed it during the brief absence.

The lesson of the "climbing fader syndrome" is that not everything can be "the best" or "the most." And more importantly, even when something isn't at the extreme, it still is important.

So what is "the best"? What is "the most"? In a world where we reduce concepts to numbers, this is an important concept to hammer out. We could assert that "the best" selection is whatever happens to have the highest measurement at any one point. The problem with that approach is that we have no frame of reference for what "the best" *could* be. This is an important distinction.

There's Always Something More

In my recording studio example, at any one time there was a "loudest" instrument. Most of the time, however, none of them were as loud as they *could be*. That is why the climbing fader syndrome could happen. No matter what volume they were at, I could always turn them up a little bit more. Eventually, however, I would have hit the top of the range for that particular slider. I would have to then say, "It's as loud as it will go." *That point* would have been "the loudest." To make a particular track louder, the only solution would have been to turn everything *else* down.

There is a difference between the topmost value of a group and the topmost *possible* value. Making note of where this artificial edge is is essential to scaling our possible values. Sometimes there is a limit and sometimes there is not. In football, basketball, or baseball, for example, there is no upper limit to the score that a team can generate. (Sure, you eventually would run into the limitations of physics and time, but for all practical purposes, we don't consider that a problem.)

There's No Room at the Top

On the other hand, in sports like gymnastics, figure skating, and diving, there is certainly a maximum that one can obtain. Gymnasts can't get more than a 10.0, no matter how accomplished they are. (It used to be that figure skating maxed out at 6.0... I'm not sure what they do now. If you want to see multi-attribute utility theory in action, check out "ISU Judging System" on Wikipedia.) To make matters worse, there are *floors* where the gymnastics scoring starts: 8.8 or 9.2 depending on the system. You really have to work hard to merit a score below those numbers. (I was always curious to see what would happen if a skater just sat down on the ice and didn't move. Is it even *possible* to get a 0 in those sports?)

Capped systems like this can generate something of a quandary. If you, as a judge, give a contestant a 10.0 on a routine, and someone else comes along later who performs *better*, what score can you give that one? The artificial restraints of the scoring system have limited you to giving the second person a 10.0 as well. When this happens, you sound a lot like my sister saying that you have just seen "the best gymnastics routine ever"—from two different people! Certainly that is unlikely. One of them would have been better than the other—at least *marginally*.

On the other hand, if we work with a capless system, we run the risk of encountering a phenomenon similar to the climbing fader syndrome. If there is no restriction on how high a score can go, we can always justify a score by comparing it to others. Now, the second gymnast above could score a 10.1. And the next one that is better could score a 10.2. Unfettered by the practical logistics of physics and time, subjective scores can get out of hand quickly. Eventually, it is entirely possible that gymnasts of the future could be scoring 11, 20, 40, or even in the hundreds!

The solution lies in analyzing the approach that we use to generate our utility scores. To do that, we need to take into account a number of different components. We need to delve into what makes a score not only relevant, but usable. With that in mind, we can tailor our system to make it useable and meaningful without opening ourselves to pitfalls similar to the ones above.

Absolute vs. Relative Weights

We can put a lot of these issues into a better perspective by understanding the difference between types of measurements. There are three ways that we can refer to values. Each has its advantages and pitfalls. We can see each of the three illustrated in Figure 13.1. Note that the graph bars remain the same length in each of the three examples. The values that we assign to those bars change, however, depending on in what context we place them.

Absolute Weights

First, we can assign a concrete value to each bar. This approach is similar to a score in a sporting event such as baseball or basketball. The value "is what it is." This method is useful when we truly want to know what the count of something is (like the points in a game). For example, if we were calculating how many units we could kill with four different strategies, we would want to know the actual number. We could then use those values to determine **absolute weights** for each strategy.

We have already seen this idea in action. In Chapter 7, we used the actual values of the health and damage as absolute weights in our decision. We also used the actual costs of building a barracks and a tower and the estimates of how much damage they would take. Those were absolute weights as well. The numbers were exactly what they represented. If we take 10 points of damage, we represent it as "10" in our formulas.

In Figure 13.1 (left), we would determine that the rightmost bar (16) is the best of the four. However, there is nothing precluding us from selecting a different option if something better comes along. For example, a different strategy could lead us to destroy 17 units. Another could net 20. In fact, there is no real maximum for this value. Another strategy at another time may allow us to kill 100. The results of our utility function are only useful for determining which of the four strategies will give the best results.

One drawback is that we have absolutely no context in which to judge a given score. A frame of reference is required to interpret an absolute score. Unless we have other scores to compare it to, we don't know whether a score is good or bad. For instance, if I was to tell you that I achieved a score of 8,423,128 on an unnamed game, you would have no idea whether that was good or bad. Only if you have access to other people's scores, could you then compare my score directly to them and determine whether or not my braggadocio is warranted.

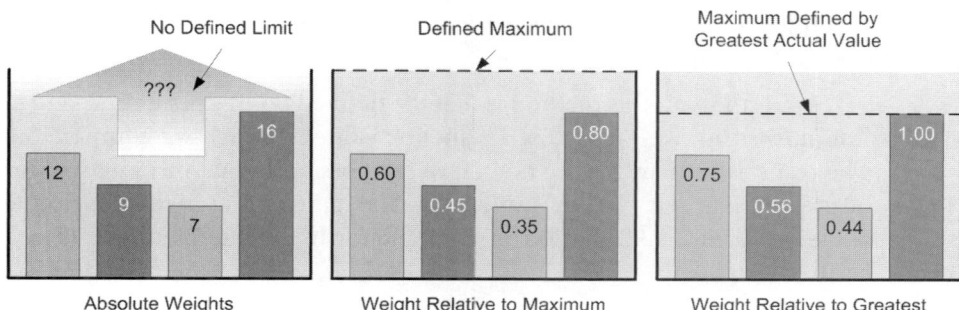

FIGURE 13.1 By changing the context, we can refer to three otherwise identical measurements in different ways. In the middle example, we have defined an arbitrary maximum at 20 units.

Weights Relative to a Maximum

The second method we can use to assign values to a score is to compare the absolute weight of what we are measuring to a different value that we predetermine as the maximum possible value. In the middle of Figure 13.1, we see the same bars as used in the left example. However, we have added the rule that the maximum value is 20. The numbers shown in the bars are the **relative weights** to what they *could be*. For example, the first bar in the graph is still an absolute size of 12, but in the context of a maximum of 20, the score is 0.60. It is 60% of what it *could be*.

Anyone who has taken a test is familiar with this sort of weighting. There is usually a maximum score that we can achieve on the test. If we compare the score that we actually receive to the maximum possible score, we arrive at a percentage. This percentage gives us two pieces of information.

First, we can still compare different scores. We know that the 0.60 for the first bar is better than the 0.45 for the second one but worse than the 0.80 of the fourth bar. However, we can also determine the fitness of the scores themselves compared to the maximum. Even if we have no other decision against which to compare, we know where it falls in relation to what it *could be*. This is similar to how, while our egos may be curious about how our test score compared to our peers, the grader only really cares about how we did relative to the maximum.

It is also similar to the gymnastics and skating scoring systems. Without knowing how the other contestants did in any given competition, we can glean information from a single score. We know that a score of 9.975 on a 10-point scale is pretty darn good. We can *not*, however, determine if the recipient of that score won that particular competition without knowing the scores of the other participants. Therefore, while a weight relative to a maximum allows us to judge the fitness of an individual score on its merit alone, we can't determine "the best" until we compare it directly to other scores.

A variation on this method is that the defined point does not need to be a maximum. Instead, we can define an **anchor value** to which we compare our values. The result is similar, but we now have the possibility that our relative weights can be greater than zero. For example, using the same bars as in our previous example, we see in Figure 13.2 that setting the anchor to a value of 10 produces different relative weights.

Weights Relative to an Anchor

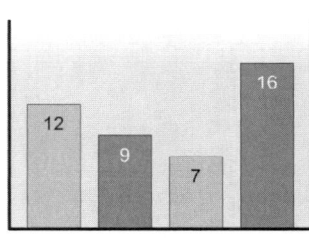
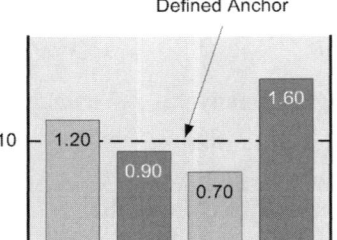

FIGURE 13.2 The value to which we are comparing our scores does not have to be a maximum. We can use other anchors. In the right-hand graph, we are comparing our absolute weights to a value of 10 to arrive at the weighted scores.

Weights Relative to Each Other

The third method, illustrated on the right of Figure 13.1, is another variation of relative weighting. In this case, the maximum is not a predetermined value. Instead, we compare all the scores to whichever score is the greatest. Therefore, the fourth bar (size of 16) is the *de facto* maximum for the moment. We score the other three bars relative to 16. For example, the first bar (size of 12) is 0.75 the size of the fourth.

One advantage to this method is that we aren't limited by an arbitrary maximum score. Because of this, the method scales itself as the scores change. For example, as a situation changes, the idea of what makes a "good score" may vary significantly.

In the example in Figure 13.1 (right), the fourth bar is the front-runner with a value of 16. Later on, the top score may be 32, for example. At that point, a score of 16 (0.50) doesn't look so hot.

Also, because of the automatic scaling of this method, the relative differences between scores yield important information. When the top score is 16, the difference between the scores of 12 and 9 are fairly significant: 0.75 − 0.56 = 0.19. However, if the top score is 32, the scores of 12 and 9 are 0.375 and 0.281, respectively. The difference between them is only 0.09 now. If the top score is 100, that difference drops to 0.03. For all intents and purposes, when compared to a value of 100, the scores of 12 and 9 are becoming identically poor.

As a variation, we don't have to use the *greatest* value as our comparison point. At times, it may be beneficial to use the *lowest* value instead (Figure 13.3). For example, if we were concerned with the least time in which an action could be performed (as opposed to the highest score), we might want to rate the other options by comparing them to the quickest one. Once again, using our original four values, we recalculate their weights relative to the smallest of the four—the third bar's size of 7. The method that we select will depend on the problem we are trying to address.

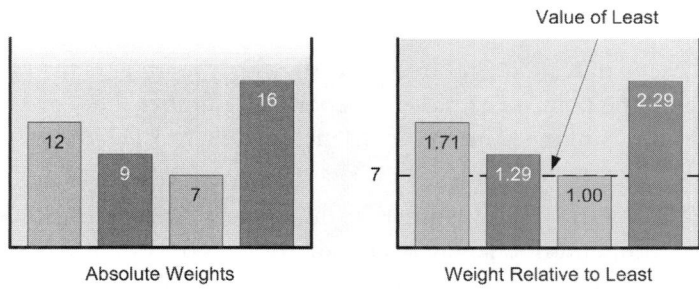

FIGURE 13.3 The value to which we compare the other scores does not have to be the maximum. At times, we may want to know how the other scores compare to the lowest selection.

Granularity

Another issue that we need to be mindful of when scaling our weight scores is **granularity**. This is comparable to the concept of *significant digits* in science and math—often with the description of *superfluous precision*. For our purposes, we can think of it in terms of the accuracy to which we need to either calculate or keep track of something.

Accuracy

One of the main considerations for establishing a correct level of granularity is **accuracy of differentiation**. This is the level at which we can discern differences between adjacent measurements. An excellent example of this is hanging in many hospital and doctor's examination rooms. Medical professionals have standardized a "pain scale" to assist in quantifying patients' otherwise (very) subjective reports of the discomfort they feel (Figure 13.4).

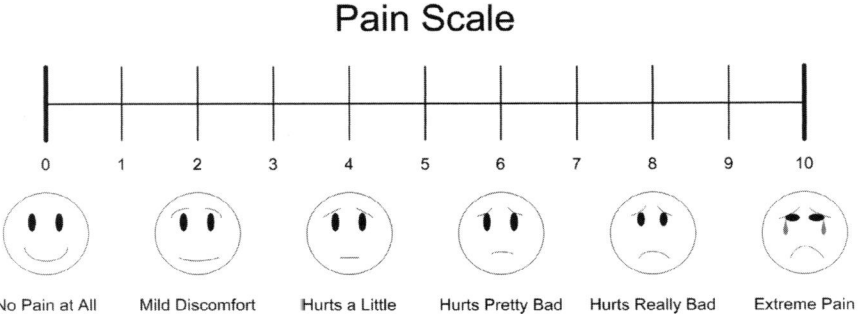

FIGURE 13.4 A typical pain chart runs from 0 (no pain) to 10 (extreme pain). The granularity of the ratings allows 11 selections. The faces allow 6 ratings.

The pain scale ranges from 0 to 10, which represents the range from "no pain" to "extreme pain." The patients report the number that corresponds to how they feel at the moment. The face icons included on most charts are helpful for children to identify how they feel.

The question that we must ask ourselves is "Why 0 to 10?" Aside from 10 being a nice round number, there is a reason the creators of the pain scale designed it with this granularity. On the 10-point scale, we can differentiate between 6 and 7. The smallest possible unit on the 10-point scale represents a gradation that we can actually discern and describe. The 11 selections are no more accurate than our own ability to sense and rate our pain level. We probably would have no reason to specify that our pain level was at a 5.5, for example.

Too Many

On the other hand, imagine that the pain scale ran from 0 to 100 instead. The smallest possible unit on a 100-point scale is one. Can we tell the difference between 60 and 61? We find that one out of 100 units is too small to be able to meaningfully differentiate the levels of pain.

A similar reason for the 0 to 10 range of the pain scale is the usability of the information. While a doctor may respond differently if you report your pain at 7 rather than 6, he is unlikely to react much differently if your pain is a 61 rather than 60. This is the portion that is similar to *significant digits* in science and math calculations. Certainly, there is a numerical difference between 61 and 60, but what does it really mean? If the granularity at which you are tracking a value is finer than the granularity at which you are able to measure the value in the first place, the extra data is *superfluous precision*.

Not Enough

On the other hand, a pain scale whose range was less than 10 may possibly not be expressive enough. For example, if we change the scale so that "extreme pain" is 3 rather than 10, it is more difficult to express exactly how we feel. ("Well, doc… I'm not a 1, and 2 seems a little high. I'm kinda somewhere between 1 and 2 but closer to 2 than to 1.") It also means that the doctor doesn't get as accurate of a picture of our condition from which to work.

Interestingly, most of the pain charts show only 6 face icons as I did in Figure 13.4. The reason for this becomes startlingly clear when we attempt to determine how we would "tweak" the faces to create ones in between the existing set. (There's only so much expression that you can present with smiley faces!) This leads to a different granularity for the "smiley face" version of the pain chart than the number line version.

However, as we will discuss later, it isn't necessarily a correct assumption that we should limit ourselves to only the outputs that we can display such as in the case of the faces. Using response curves, for example, we can always combine portions of the range into one displayed behavior. We can still benefit from tracking the underlying data without being concerned with what we can exhibit externally. This is especially important in the game development world where we are typically limited on which animations and actions we can display.

An extreme example would be a behavior that had only two outwardly visible signs such as the "fight or flee" scenario we have referenced a few times. The response curve could continue to track a more granular "degree of fear" (or some other such value) and only trigger the change to "flee" when "degree of fear" reaches a particular threshold.

The essential secret to constructing a weighting scale, therefore, is to arrange it so that there is enough granularity to express the detail you need to differentiate meaningful differences—*and no more!*

Data Considerations

Another consideration when determining granularity is the data structure we will use. Many people use a variable that can represent a plethora of decimal values from 0 to 1. That level of detail is often more than we need. Often, we only need to track a relative handful of values. For example, a single byte allows us to store 256 values. Most of the utility scales we would need to track in our games would not necessitate a finer granularity than that.

By using response curves, we can map the 256 values in a byte onto a large variety of actual figures. For example, if we wanted to represent numbers from 0 to 1,000 but didn't need to have a granularity of 1/1000, we could use a response curve that associates the indices 0 through 250 with appropriately spaced decimal values using the formula $y = 4x$. The contents of our response curve vector would look like this:

i	y
0	0
1	4
2	8
3	12
...	...
125	500
...	...
249	996
250	1,000

We are still representing numbers from 0 to 1,000, but we are not doing so with possibly unnecessary granularity. By using a `char` instead of a `short int`, we are saving one byte of data storage. While this may not seem like much at first, when multiplied many times over, the savings can add up.

Certainly, one could make the case that we could simply store the numbers 0 to 250 and multiply them by 4 when we are ready to use them. As the formulas get more complex—and especially when we hand-craft our response curves—this approach yields significant benefits.

Moreover, when dealing with arrays or vectors, by only storing token values along the way, we don't have to have an array that covers the entire range of values. In the above example, despite wanting to represent values that range from 0 to 1,000 in our array, we did so in only 251 array locations. This effect is even more noticeable when we want to store larger ranges. Just because we are storing numbers ranging from 0 to 25,000 doesn't mean we care about every individual increment. We may not need a granularity that fine.

WEIGHTING A SINGLE CRITERION

With all of the above methods, tips, and tricks in place, we are now able to approach the issue of actually scoring the value of something. To make our decisions, we need to consider information. Often, the information is not as simple as a binary "yes or no." For example, in a decision about whether or not we should get a health kit, we aren't using "alive or dead" as a factor. We are concerned with the gray areas of *how much health* we currently have. Are we fully healthy? Doing well? A little injured? Are we dragging our limbs behind us? By taking that entire spectrum of possibilities into account, we can craft deeper, more meaningful decisions.

One of the first considerations when deciding how we should weight a single criterion is whether we are tracking the actual *value* of something or the *utility*. The former case is more intuitive and certainly more common.

CONCRETE NUMBERS

We count and measure plenty of things in games: units, buildings, numbers of bullets in our guns, damage dealt over time, health, and how much money items cost. We often use these concrete numbers in our decisions. In fact, much of the heavy lifting of decision making involves concrete numbers. The game world is no exception.

For example, we may take the number of bullets remaining in our gun as a deciding factor on whether or not we should reload. Obviously, if the number drops to 0, reloading becomes relatively important. However, we can treat this in a non-binary fashion as well: the lower the number, the more we may consider taking a moment to reload.

Another decision may involve comparing our health to the damage we are expecting to receive from an opponent over time. We can compare this to the damage we are likely to deal over time and the opponent's health to determine which of us is going to survive a conflict. All of the figures in the above calculation are concrete numbers: damage (d) over time (t) vs. health (h).

ABSTRACT RATINGS

The game world is sometimes *too* enamored with concrete numbers. This is likely a by-product of the fact that computers count and perform math so well. Therefore, we programmers tend to gravitate toward using things that our computers can count and mathematically juggle. A typical thought process may sound like:

> "Ok, then we will add up the number of…, multiply it by the number of… and, if it is greater than three times the number of…, we will do [insert noble deed] as many times as it takes to construct the right number of…."

Everything there involves concrete counts and figures. "The number of…" is a very safe and comfortable place for computers (and their programmers).

As we discussed earlier in the book, concrete counts and measurements don't necessarily correspond equally to *utility*. Therefore, when dealing with these types of items, we need to determine which of the two values we are going to measure. In Chapter 8, we discussed numerous examples where we were building armies. The number of soldiers we had already built was a criterion in the decision. More importantly, however, we were measuring the marginal utility of building additional soldiers. The abstract concept of utility is different from the concrete count that we started with.

If we are using the raw number or value of an object in a calculation, there is little that we need to consider with regard to how we are weighting it as a decision criterion. However, when switching to utility, we have some subjective judgments to make. As such, the range and granularity that we select for our scale will be largely context-dependant.

In this book so far, we have covered many different examples that we would treat in a variety of manners. Even going back to my razor blades in Chapter 2, we could devise a way of scoring my relative satisfaction with the blades. We may use the number of uses as a starting point, but my satisfaction with a blade is not as linear as counting the times I have used it. For example, we could state that a blade starts with a quality of 100 when it is brand new, but, as I use it, its quality decreases rapidly at first and then gradually flattens out toward a value of 0 where I am not satisfied with it at all.

Regardless of how we arrived at the satisfaction value, our range for this value is 0 to 100. We can even think of it as a percentage of satisfaction. (Note that we don't need a lot of granularity here. Therefore, we don't need to use a decimal value. A `byte` type to store the values of 0 to 100 performs just fine in this regard.) Once we have determined our satisfaction with all five blades, we can then compare them and decide which one we are going to use.

In other examples, my daughter, Kathy, needed ways of measuring the worth of various topics that she wanted to put into her speech for her fifth grade election campaign. I needed a way of rating the quality of the food and the atmosphere at a particular restaurant when I took my family out to dinner. We could have even put a subjective value on the sense of altruism that we felt by giving more than was necessary in the Ultimatum Game.

Of course, it is certainly feasible for us to track *both* the value and the utility separately. This is often the case when the corresponding *subjective utility* for a *concrete number* of items may change based on other parameters. In our $20 bill example, the face value of $20 didn't mean the same to everyone. The 20 is a concrete value; the *utility* that people put on those $20 is an abstract rating. We will revisit this later.

COMBINING MULTIPLE CRITERIA

The important task above was to decide on the range (and, by association, the granularity) we were going to use to score our criterion. When all we are concerned about is a single criterion, we have plenty of flexibility in how we do this. However, when we plan on using one utility score in conjunction with others, it behooves us to keep the whole picture in mind.

NORMALIZING

One way of making the job of comparing, contrasting, and combining disparate numbers easier is to use the same scale for all of them. If, for example, we are tracking satisfaction ratings for various things, we want to place all satisfaction ratings on the same scale. In Chapter 9, we examined the hedonic calculus factors that could be involved in a decision on where to go out for dinner. While some of the factors were concrete (such as cost, travel time, and wait time), some of them were subjective satisfaction ratings. By making sure that we were rating all satisfaction-based values on the same scale, we can ensure that we have little difficulty later on.

Technically, the term **normalization** refers to the process of stretching or shrinking a range by a **normalizing constant** so that it fills the space from 0 to 1. This is a very common practice in probability math. While we may not be using it for exactly the same purpose, the rationale behind normalizing subjective factors is similar: put everything into one, homogenous template. For our purposes, this template doesn't have to be 0 to 1. As we have suggested above, we could use the integers 0 to 100 (pseudo-percentages), 0 to 255 (fill a `byte` variable), or something as simple as 0 to 10 such as what the pain scale uses. There is one *very* significant advantage to using 0 to 1, however: when we multiply factors that range from 0 to 1 together, the product is still in the range of 0 to 1. That is remarkably handy when producing weighted sums or weighted averages, for instance. Regardless of the range, however, the main consideration is the granularity that we require for the value.

As we mentioned above, we can normalize concrete values as well. We can do this linearly or through a function such as the ones we covered in Chapter 10.

Linear Normalization

Linear normalization is the process of converting a concrete range into a normalized range on a proportional basis. We do this by determining the normalizing constant that we need to apply to the raw value to convert it to the normalized version.

IN THE GAME   **How Much Weight?**

For example, we could convert the amount of weight a character in a role-playing game (RPG) is carrying into a normalized value. If the character can carry a maximum total weight of 75 pounds of equipment, we can use that as the endpoint of our normalized range. Therefore, 75 pounds = 1.0. In this case, the normalizing constant is 75. At any point, we can calculate the load percentage that the character is toting around by dividing the actual weight by 75.

$$W_{normalized} = \frac{W_{actual}}{75}$$

If our character is burdened with 52 pounds of items, the normalized weight would be

$$W_{normalized} = \frac{52}{75} = 0.693$$

While this may look like an unnecessary complication, one advantage we gain from normalization of factors is that we can then standardize the rules we use to apply those factors to decisions.

For example, let us assume that our game design states that different characters can carry different amounts of weight. At any time, we can calculate the character's normalized weight (burden) through

$$W_{normalized} = \frac{W_{actual}}{W_{maximum}}$$

Also, we want to determine that a character can no longer play hopscotch when he is carrying too much of a load. However, the load that prohibits playing hopscotch is based on the percentage that he is loaded (after all, stronger people can still hop around and pick up little pebbles while carrying more junk). If we state the rule that hopscotch is no longer possible once a character has more than 60% of his carrying capacity, our hapless dude in the above example is going to be left out of the game until he can rid himself of at least *some* of his burden. On the other hand (or other foot), someone who could carry a maximum of 90 pounds of equipment would still be able to play hopscotch while carrying the same 52 pounds of items.

$$\left[W_{normalized} = \frac{52}{90} = 0.578 \right] < 0.60$$

We could do the calculations for the percentage only when we need them, or we could do them ahead of time by normalizing the idea of "burden" at all times. There is a significant advantage to normalizing. The decision to play hopscotch does not need to take into account the weight the player is carrying or the maximum capacity. All we need to check is if the normalized weight (burden) is less than the threshold figure of 0.60. In fact, we can then construct *all* rules for *all* decisions that have to do with burden based on this single normalized value. We may decide that jumping rope requires a burden of less than 0.40, basketball requires less than a 0.20 burden, and that even walking requires that the character is less that 90% loaded (Figure 13.5).

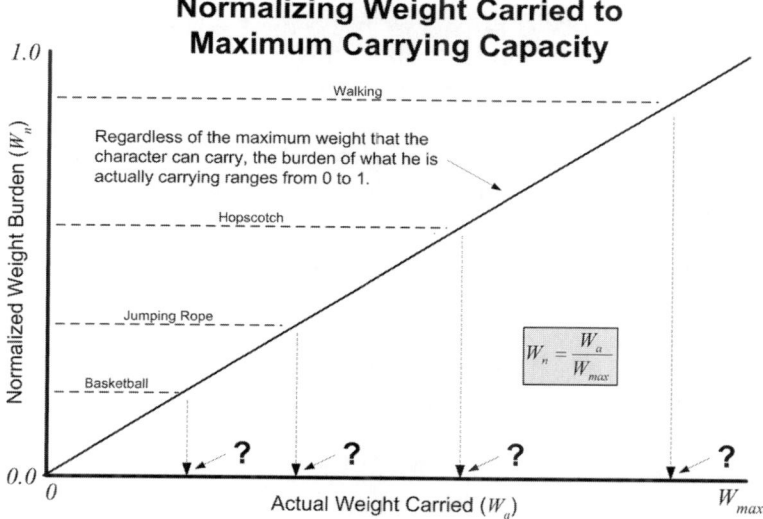

FIGURE 13.5 By dividing the actual weight carried by the maximum weight a character can carry, we can determine a normalized "burden" value that ranges from 0 to 1. We can then set thresholds for various activities all on the same scale. We don't have to know the actual weight that permits or prohibits each activity—only the normalized burden.

We can even use burden in other ways. We could state that fatigue over time is a function of relative burden rather than weight. We could represent this by the formula

$$Fatigue = W_{normalized} \times time \times FatigueConstant$$

Notice that we do not have to reference the amount of weight the character is carrying or the maximum amount that he *can* carry. We have rolled all of that information into the tidy package of the factor $W_{normalized}$. We can always expect a value of between 0 and 1 regardless of how much the character can carry or how much he has on him at the time.

Nonlinear Normalization

There are times when a direct mapping of values provided by the linear normalization method above does not suit our purposes. Thinking back to the chapters on utility (especially increasing and decreasing marginal utility), we often need a way of representing the changes in a number that reflects a particular formula. Using the same approach as we did with linear normalization, we can generate normalized values that fall within a certain range (such as between 0 and 1). Instead of using a constant to normalize the values, however, we can use a **normalizing function**. The specifics of how we would go about this vary widely depending on the type of formula we are using. The end requirement is that our values lie within a specified range.

 **IN THE GAME** Are We There Yet?

One of the examples we used earlier in Chapter 8 was building squads and armies. We used this example to show the effects of marginal utility—both increasing and decreasing. However, as with the weight example above, it could be awkward to constantly change the marginal utility formula based on a differing number of soldiers. At times, we may want to achieve a threshold of having four soldiers. At other times, for other tasks, we may want 10. For bigger, more aggressive jobs, we could say that 20 is enough. Even changes in the difficulty level of the game could warrant having slightly different numbers.

To accommodate these variable requirements, we need to normalize our marginal utility curve so that it scales to the number of units we are trying to create. We begin by deciding that our utility values for each soldier will range from 0 to 1. More accurately, they will range from 1 *down to* 0 as we add additional soldiers. We then set the utility of the *n*th soldier to the following formula, with *goal* being the number of soldiers that we will be satisfied with acquiring.

$$U_n = 1 - \frac{n^3}{goal^3}$$

As with the weight example above, the denominator of the fraction here represents the maximum value that we are using as our "endpoint." In the weight example, we divided by the constant that represented the maximum weight a character could carry. In this case, *goal* is the maximum number of soldiers we are striving for. The approach is the same—actual number divided by maximum number. The only difference is that we have an exponent in the formula. If we apply this exponent to both the numerator and the denominator, the proportion of actual to maximum remains intact.

If we graph results from a number of different values of *goal*, we find that the curve is identical for all of them (Figure 13.6). In all cases, the utility of the first soldier is 1.0. Then as we move through the range from 1 to *goal*, the utility of each soldier decreases as a rate proportional to how many total soldiers we are building. When $n = goal$, the utility is 0. (In practice, we would adjust the formula so that the utility reaches 0 *after* the last soldier by changing the denominator of the fraction to $(goal + 1)^3$. Otherwise, with a utility of 0, we would never build the last soldier. For clarity of the graphs, I did not do so here.)

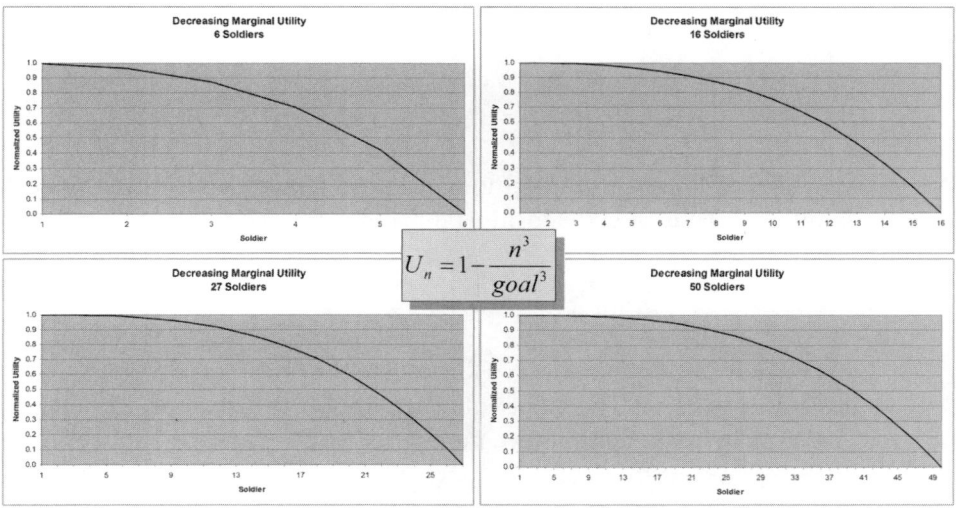

$$U_n = 1 - \frac{n^3}{goal^3}$$

FIGURE 13.6 By constructing a formula that normalizes the utility values, the results follow the same curve from 1 down to 0 regardless of how many soldiers we are building.

Comparing Normalized Values

By normalizing utility values, we can more easily use the resulting figure in a variety of comparisons and calculations that are not directly dependant on the potentially variable components that make up the utility. We have a homogenous "yardstick" that requires no additional processing to determine which is more important. As we touched on earlier, scoring systems in gymnastics and skating have a defined range in which to work. Regardless of the complicated (and sometimes controversial) processes that go into determining the final score, once we have that score, we can directly compare contestants and easily determine who performed better. We can determine the winner by the startlingly simple formula, "is $Score_A > Score_B$?"

IN THE GAME   Who's Next?

Going back to our soldier example, if we have followed a similar procedure in determining the marginal utility of building a new worker unit, we can compare that utility with the utility of building another soldier.

To illustrate this example, let us assume that the formula for workers is

$$U_W = 1 - \frac{n_W^{\,2}}{goal_W^{\,2}}$$

Also, to homogenize the nomenclature (since that's what this section is all about!), let us re-label the formula for soldiers

$$U_S = 1 - \frac{n_S^{\,3}}{goal_S^{\,3}}$$

By only raising the worker's formula to the power of two, it makes for a flatter, less cornered curve. This is the equivalent of saying that we aren't quite as driven to make sure we have a minimum number of workers as we are for soldiers.

Theoretically, the decision to build a worker instead of a soldier would then be as simple as the comparison

$$U_W > U_S$$

This direct comparison would not need to take into account how many workers or soldiers we need to build to accomplish our current civic and military agendas, respectively, as this would already be included in the normalization process for each type of unit.

To see this process in action, we will now plug in some numbers. Let's assume that our current goals and counts for workers and solders are:

Unit	Goal	Count	Utility
Worker	20	5	0.938
Soldier	20	5	0.984

By setting the goals and counts equal to each other, we show that the priority for soldiers is, indeed, higher. Let's assume that we have built a few more soldiers and see how this changes.

Unit	Goal	Count	Utility
Worker	20	5	0.938
Soldier	20	8	0.936

Once we have built our eighth soldier, the utility for the next soldier drops to the point where it is now less than the utility for the next worker. Our next build, therefore, would be our sixth worker. The utility of our *seventh* worker is 0.910, meaning we would build yet another soldier. Eventually, as we acquire more of each type, the count of workers catches up to the soldiers. (Specifically, we would build two workers in a row a couple of times. At a count of 18, the number of workers matches that of the soldiers, and they alternate again from that point.)

Different Goals for Different Folks

While this is all well and good, the power of using normalized utility is when we are working with *unequal* goals. For example, using the same utility formulas, let us assume that we would like to have 35 soldiers and 20 workers. At the beginning, our data would look like this:

Unit	Goal	Count	Utility
Worker	20	0	1.000
Soldier	35	0	1.000

After building one of each, the next *four* builds are of soldiers. Once we have five, the normalized utility of the next soldier falls to 0.997, while the normalized utility of the second worker is 0.998. Therefore, only after we have five soldiers would we build our second worker.

Unit	Goal	Count	Utility
Worker	20	1	0.998
Soldier	35	5	0.997

We build our third worker when we have eight soldiers, and so on.

Going the other way, let's assume that we only want to build eight soldiers. Remember, however, that we biased the curves to build soldiers earlier. The results are surprising. The builds alternate until we have five of each. Notice that we would then have 63% of our soldiers built but only 25% of our workers! Only then do we start building multiple workers before building another soldier. In fact, only after building our tenth worker would we build our sixth soldier.

Unit	Goal	Count	Utility
Worker	20	10	0.750
Soldier	8	5	0.756

At 13 workers, we would build our seventh soldier and at 17 workers we build our eighth soldier.

By normalizing the utility values so that they are represented on the same scale, the formulas that we used to calculate the marginal utility for each unit type are hidden from the comparison that determines what to build next. We were able to concentrate on just the single "which is greater?" expression to determine what to build next.

Soldiers, Sailors, Airmen… or Workers?

The worth of this uncomplicated method is even more apparent when we consider adding more unit types. For example, even if we have 15 or 20 different types of units, each with their own utility formulas, goal populations, and current counts, we can trust that the normalized utilities are all on the same 0 to 1 scale. Therefore, by sorting the list of units by their current utility values, we can select the highest one as the "most important" to build. This selection process would still be valid even if we changed the marginal utility formula for any of the unit types.

As we have seen, normalization is a process that helps us make sense of what would otherwise be moving targets. It is a tool that we will use often.

WEIGHTED SUMS

Most of the time, we find that a single criterion is not enough to make a decision. Many decisions are a combination of two or more criteria. Except for rare circumstances, the weights that factors have in the decision are usually not equal. One factor is typically more important than another. As we increase the number of factors to consider in a decision, the likelihood that they all have the same importance decreases.

The most common method of balancing the significance of each factor is through the process known as **weighted sums**. Through weighted sums, we construct a single value from multiple factors—each with their own value. We pair each component value with a coefficient that represents its weight in the overall decision. The resulting combined value reflects not only the component values, but the proportional "meaningfulness" for each of those components.

If we think in terms of vector math, the weights are the same as the **magnitude** of a vector. While the direction of the vector provides directional information, the magnitude tells us *how far* to move in that direction.

A generic formula for a two-component weighted sum looks like the following:

$$R_{XY} = w_X v_X + w_Y v_Y$$

In English, the weighted result of X and Y (R_{XY}) is the weight for X (w_X) times the value of X (v_X) plus the weight for Y (w_Y) times the value of Y (v_Y).

We can normalize the result by dividing by the sum of the weights.

$$R_{XY} = \frac{w_X v_X + w_Y v_Y}{w_X + w_Y}$$

This results in a **weighted mean** of the values. By doing this, we achieve the effect of putting the result on the same scale as the component values. This is especially advantageous if we have already normalized the values to the same scale. By using the weighted mean, we ensure that the result is directly comparable to the original values. For example, if the component values are normalized to a range of 0 to 1, the weighted mean is between 0 and 1 as well.

Certainly, we are not limited to two components. For the sake of completeness, the formula for *n* components is

$$\bar{v} = \frac{\sum_{i=1}^{n} w_i v_i}{\sum_{i=1}^{n} w_i}$$

Or (if you are like me and the big E sign scares you)

$$\overline{v}_{1..n} = \frac{w_1 v_1 + w_2 v_2 + \ldots + w_n v_n}{w_1 + w_2 + \ldots + w_n}$$

Deciding on Dinner

If my wife, Laurie, and I were to decide what we were going to eat for dinner (I really have to stop working on this book when I'm hungry), we may have a conversation about what we are interested in eating. Naturally, we both have preferences, and, just as naturally, those preferences may differ. We may not, however, always put equal weight on our preferences. In a typical example, Laurie may say that she really doesn't care what we have. (Whether or not I can believe that she *really* doesn't care what we eat or whether I am supposed to guess is a topic for a book on understanding women, however, and beyond the scope of this chapter.) While I don't want to entirely disregard her preferences, I can assume at this point that she wants *my* preference to have more weight than her own. To reflect this, we can weight *my* utility for varying dinner selections more than we do *her* utility for those same selections.

Let's assume that our four options for the evening are a steak dinner at a restaurant (I'm just *not* firing up my grill when it's freezing out!), Chinese take-out, nuking some burritos, and cooking a frozen pizza. First, we would establish the coefficients that we will use in the formula so that our preferences are proportional to how much consideration we put on our respective preferences. From those coefficients, we can calculate a *combined* utility that reflects our joint decision.

Because I don't want to completely disregard my wife's desires, we will establish the coefficients as:

Dave	2
Laurie	1

This means my desires are worth twice as much as hers. Put another way, instead of splitting the decision 50/50, my preferences are worth 67% and hers are worth 33%.

Put into a utility formula, this gives us:

$$U_{D+L} = 2(U_D) + 1(U_L)$$

Assuming that we have normalized the two personal utilities on a scale from 0 to 1, we can normalize the combined score by dividing by the sum of the coefficients.

$$U_{D+L} = \frac{2(U_D) + 1(U_L)}{3}$$

When we identify our personal preferences for the four potential dinner options and insert them into the above formula, we arrive at a combined utility value for each one.

Selection	Dave	Laurie	Combined
Steak dinner	1.0	1.0	1.0
Chinese take-out	0.1	0.7	0.3
Microwave burritos	0.4	0.1	0.3
Frozen pizza	0.4	0.6	0.5

Examining the data above yields a few interesting observations. First, while I look at the burritos and pizza with the same opinion, Laurie *really* doesn't like the burritos. Therefore, her preference acts a tie-breaker. We can see this reflected in the combined score where the pizza ranks higher than the burritos.

Additionally, despite the fact that she likes Chinese take-out quite a bit—more than the frozen pizza, because I'm not in the mood for Chinese, the score suffers significantly. Much to Laurie's dismay, the Chinese take-out option ends up with the *same* score as the burritos. Her difference in preference between the two is very large (0.6), whereas mine is relatively small (0.3). Because my opinion matters twice as much, however, that 0.3 difference means as much as her 0.6.

The end result is less than surprising. With both of us preferring to go out for steak, that option easily wins out. (And the agreement likely spares me the potential of annoying my wife with my choice regardless of the fact that she *said* she didn't care. *That* is a factor that carries a lot of utility value for me!)

LAYERED WEIGHTING MODELS

Even after we have calculated or combined factors to arrive at a utility function, we may not have enough information to process a decision. While weighted sums allow us to combine (and even normalize) similar information, decisions often take disparate pieces of information into account. It is usually simpler to combine similar items together first to arrive at an aggregate value. For example, we combined the two sets of dinner preferences into *one* combined dinner preference value. Once we have arrived at these combined figures, we can combine them with other figures in another step of the process. By doing this, we are creating a **layered weighting model**. In essence, we are building our decision in tiers.

We touched on this process briefly in Chapter 3 using the example of how my children's teachers calculate grades through first combining the scores for homework, tests, and quizzes together into their own scores and then combining those scores together into one aggregate score. We revisited the idea through our discussion of multi-attribute utility theory in Chapter 9. Each of these examples follows the same pattern. We start with small blocks of information that we then combine into larger blocks. Theoretically, there is no limit to how many layers we can build or how many pieces of information can go into any one aggregate.

Once again, we can use any of the above methods to do this. Typically, however, weighted sums allow us to combine the component parts together in the most flexible manner.

Constructing a Layer

The unfortunate weakness in the dinner example above is that our desire (separate or combined) is not the *only* factor in the decision. There are other thoughts that we must entertain. For example, we often have three factors that we want to take into consideration.

desire How much we desire the selection
price   The price of the selection
time   The time it takes to acquire the selection

We can address each of the three items above separately. In the previous example, we utilized weighted sums to construct a combined utility of desire. We could generate utilities for the price of the food and the time it would take to acquire it in a similar fashion. We could use weighted sums, response curves, or any other method to determine the utility of each of those factors. Regardless of *how* we calculated them, we would arrive at a single utility figure for *price* and *time*. When we have arrived at those figures, we will once again use weighted sums to combine our preferences for the four dinner options with the other factors.

You Can't Always Eat What You Want

Just as we decided how to weight my preference for dinner against Laurie's, we must do the same with the three factors that we are including in this layer of the decision. Because we have a lot of game programming (or book writing) to do, we decide that the time it takes to acquire the selection is the most important factor. Additionally, because game programming (or writing about game artificial life [AI]) doesn't make us rich, we decide that the price of our prospective forage is the second most important factor. While there is *some* consideration for how much we actually *like* the food, its impact is incidental.

Looking at the factors in order of decreasing importance, therefore, we find:

time > *price* > *desire*

The question we need to answer is, "What is the proportional relationship between these factors?" To determine this, we can assign coefficients to each of the three factors so that their respective ratios are reflective of the relative merits of the factors. Let's say, being the wise AI programmers that we have become by this point, we decide that the coefficients are as follows:

time	5
price	3
desire	2

As you can see, *price* is 1.5 times as important as *desire* but a little more than half as important as *time*. Also, *time* is 2.5 times as important as *desire*.

With the magnitude established, we can pair them with the individual utility scores for each of the factors to construct a single formula that takes all three components into account.

$$U = 5(U_t) + 3(U_p) + 2(U_d)$$

As we can see, the utility (U) is the sum of the three component utility values (t, p, d) after weighting them appropriately. By plugging in some sample data, we can test drive our formula and its weights. We are working with the assumption that we have calculated the three utility values elsewhere and come away with normalized utilities for each of them.

One important thing to note is that the time values are *inversely* proportional to the actual time that it takes to acquire the food. In this case, driving to the steakhouse and waiting for the food is the *longest* time, so it is the *lowest* utility. Microwaving a couple of burritos is the *shortest* time, giving it the *maximum* utility of 1.0. The same pattern exists for price: The steak dinner is the most expensive, thereby garnering the lowest utility score, and the frozen pizza is the least expensive.

Selection	Time	Price	Desire	Utility
Steak dinner	0.1	0.1	1.0	2.8
Chinese take-out	0.3	0.6	0.3	3.9
Microwave burritos	1.0	0.8	0.3	8.0
Frozen pizza	0.7	1.0	0.5	7.5

As we can see from the results, heating up some burritos is our selected *cena de noche*. By analyzing the chart, we can see evidence of the weighted sum in action. First, we can reflect on the somewhat depressing fact that it is the selection that we *least* desired (right along with the *kung pao* chicken). However, because we were more interested in the time factor, the quick availability of the burritos had a significant advantage. The combination of having to drive to pick up our Chinese and the fact that it is a little more expensive seriously reduced the overall utility for the take-out food.

Similarly, as we had suggested above, desire alone is not the only factor in this decision. Despite a craving to go out for steak that is *double* the utility of the second-place food (pizza), because it is the slowest and most expensive option, it dropped to last on our list. Put another way, regardless of how much we would have liked to eat steak at our neighborhood restaurant, our current priority structure (*time* > *price* > *desire*) did not allow it.

You Don't Always Have to Eat at Your Desk

For the sake of completeness, let's assume that I have finished writing this book (thereby freeing up my schedule) and that, because my publisher has anticipated that it will sell 500,000 copies, I receive a massive check from them. (OK… 500,000 is a stretch, but run with me on this, would ya?) Obviously, our priorities for a celebratory dinner would be different from a typical night of writing and programming. To reflect this, we now weigh our utilities with the following numbers:

time	1
price	1
desire	4

For the sake of example, let's assume that our utilities for desire, price, and time have not changed, nor have the relative prices of the four selections. They taste the same to us, they take the same amount of time to prepare or acquire, and they cost the same as they did before. The only change is in the *priority* of how we view those three factors.

Using the new formula,

$$U = 1(U_t) + 1(U_p) + 4(U_d)$$

our results are now:

Selection	Time	Price	Desire	Utility
Steak dinner	0.1	0.1	1.0	4.2
Chinese take-out	0.3	0.6	0.3	2.1
Microwave burritos	1.0	0.8	0.3	3.0
Frozen pizza	0.7	1.0	0.5	3.7

As we would expect, with time and price being relatively unimportant this time around, we would now elect to go out for steak. It is the *most* time-consuming and the *most* costly, yet those two factors combined cannot make up for the fact that it is also the *most* desired meal. Tonight, what we *want* to eat is twice as important as time and price combined. The frozen pizza gets some consideration by being cheap and fast, but it is not enough to overcome the very important factor of desire. Similarly, the burritos are cheap and fast, but those factors are simply not as relevant anymore.

Propagation of Change

It's worth repeating that three different dynamics are in play here—one in each of the three layers (our individual desires, the weighted combination of desires between the two of us, and the combination of desire with price and time). We can think of the multi-layered weighting model as a large filter. Changes that happen in any portion of the process will change, to some extent, the end result. The amount of change depends on the number and configuration of the filter layers through which a decision must pass. In this example, when we submit a dinner option (such as pizza), it passes through the different layers of the filter process (Figure 13.7).

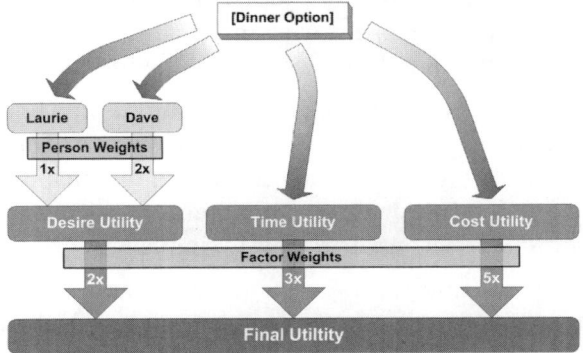

FIGURE 13.7 A multi-layered weighting model acts like a filter through which our utility information passes. Each component adjusts and weighs the data as it passes through. Changes to any part of the process will also change the end product.

First, any changes Laurie and I make to our preferences for food are going to change our personal desire utilities. (I actually do really like Chinese food most of the time!) We can change how much we desire various foods. Additionally, we could change the weights of who gets to decide. There may be times when we would weight her preference equal to—or even *greater than*—mine. However, that is only the first step in the process.

Any changes we make to process that determines the utilities of time or price for a specific meal are going to propagate from the first layer to the second just as the changes to our personal desire weights do. However, the weight of the factor where we made the change throttles the magnitude of the changes somewhat. It is entirely possible that a major change in one factor will have very little effect in the overall decision because that factor's weight is minimal. On the other hand, if a factor weighs heavily in the decision, even a minor change can cause a significant shift in the final number.

The last layer is the weights themselves. We must remember to think of the weights as their own utility function. Naturally, changes we make to those weights have a direct effect on the outcome.

After passing through all layers of the filter, we arrive at a single value that is a composite of all the processes and weights that are in place above it. We can then compare these final utility values to determine which selection has passed through "best."

COMPARTMENTALIZED CONFIDENCE

There are no limits to the depth or breadth of the multi-layered weighting process. We can have as many levels as we need. Each layer can have many different components as well. Our only limit is the information that we have available in our design. (From a design standpoint, an alternate mentality is to say, "This is the decision I want my characters to make… what information should my game track to facilitate it?") Of course, the complexity increases as we add more factors and layers.

There are methods for managing this complexity, however. Most of the methods involve making sure *we* don't confuse *ourselves* through our own process. One such method is a topic we already covered in this chapter. By ensuring the homogeneity of our data by establishing limits and practicing normalization, we keep the relationships between factors relatively simple.

As a quick example, if we were to have scored Laurie's dinner preferences on one scale and mine on another, the process of weighting them appropriately would have been more complicated. By scoring all preferences on a normalized scale of 0 to 1, we ensured that the 2:1 weight ratio between my desires and hers was, indeed,

2 to 1. If, instead, we score my ratings between 0 and 3 and hers between 0 and 5, we have to perform one extra step to say that, at the moment, *my* desires are worth twice as much as hers.

The goal is to isolate each individual component as much as possible. If we can ensure the integrity of a particular component, we do not need to know the process that generates the inputs to it, or what is going to happen to the output it generates. We have established **compartmentalized confidence** in that single portion of the decision.

If we trust that the decision model for each of our components is perfectly valid—*in its own scope*—then we can subsequently trust that they will all work together well (Figure 13.8). That is, if we believe that each step is correct, the entire decision model will be correct as well. Of course, if the outcome of the decision model doesn't seem to make sense to us, we need to go back through each layer of the model and question our premises.

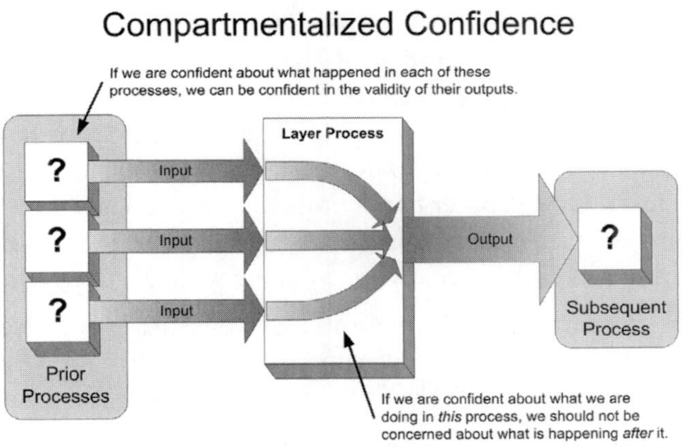

FIGURE 13.8 If we ensure the integrity of each stage of a layered weighting process, we can feel confident that the output is correct as well.

For example, if we are comfortable with the idea that time, price, and desire are the three components to our dinner decision, *and* we believe that the weights of 5, 3, and 2 (respectively) were correct for a night when time is tight and money is scarce, we should be happy with the results that these weights generate. We trust that the processes that determine the utility scores for time, price, and desire are doing their jobs. We also trust that whatever score we generate at this step will be used correctly down the road. (Theoretically, we could use the final result of the "dinner decision" example in a larger decision model—such as "plans for the evening.")

If we *do* need to make a change, we must be careful to only change components where there are problems. Of course, that necessitates finding where the problem begins in the first place. We must resist the temptation to begin tweaking one component to solve problems in another. We must locate the problem first and then change *only* that component until it generates the results we want or expect (which are not always the same thing). The process can be involved, but the end result is that our decision models can handle *many* widely disparate pieces of information in a manageable fashion.

EVERYTHING IS RELATIVE

If the prior chapters have given us the tools with which we can build our AI algorithms, this chapter gave us the rules for drawing maps and blueprints and measuring our construction materials. As with maps and blueprints, through the right application of the techniques above we can put the entire world into perspective.

I once had a social studies teacher who repeatedly proclaimed, "Everything is relative." During class discussions, he would often respond to a student's unqualified claim with "Compared to what?" For example, the word *hot* is only meaningful in context. A hot day may be 90 degrees (F). "Billy's head feels hot" may mean a 100-degree fever. On the other hand, both 90 and 100 degrees make for *comfortable*, not *hot*, bath water. I'm sure that cooking your steak over "hot coals" would suggest something hotter than what you would be willing to bathe in.

His point was that information needs to be processed together with other related information. Additionally, we can combine information with other less strongly related information if we can find some sort of common ground as an intermediary.

While this was neither his forte nor his intent, his assertion is prophetic in the realm of behavioral AI. Because we are often trying to find that *one* decision factor, we must combine many different pieces and parts. Often the information that has common ground is only meaningful when we put it in context. And for those concepts that aren't so obviously related, we define that common ground. The tools above allow us to do this. Through the iterative and layered process, we can take innumerable bits of information and construct one final expression that, in the proper context, represents to us what *should* be done.

Of course, as we shall soon revisit… just because it *should* be done doesn't mean that we *will* do it! After all, who among us is perfectly rational?

Part IV
Behavioral Algorithms

Chapter 14, "Modeling Individual Decisions," puts the tools we have assembled to use by working through a complex decision process.

Chapter 15, "Changing a Decision," addresses the caveats and complications that can arise through the process of monitoring the validity of our current plan of action—and changing decisions accordingly.

Chapter 16, "Variation in Choice," explores methods of selecting different options to ensure that our agents do not become predictable and, therefore, look less human.

14 Modeling Individual Decisions

To this point, we have pondered a lot of theory, laid out plenty of tools, and even examined ways of measuring our workspace. While all of that preparatory work was necessary, we have arrived at the point where we can put all of what we have learned to use.

Before we proceed with the glorious and rewarding process of crafting our decision models, however, we really need to determine what we are doing. Before we act, we must choose. Before we choose, we must decide what we are choosing. After all, the decision to choose (or choice to decide?) isn't one to take lightly. I've also heard it said that "if you choose not to decide, you still have made a choice." (Wow… just saying that gives me a Rush.)

With all of this choosing and deciding and acting ahead of us, perhaps a definition of terms is in order.

DEFINING *DECISION*

The most atomic structure in behavioral game artificial intelligence (AI) is the individual decision. I use the word *atomic*, not in the literal sense that it was first used—that is, "the smallest possible object"—but rather in the sense of "what bigger things are built out of." The true definition of the word *atom* is "something so small as to prohibit further division." Scientists of the past originally named atoms "atoms" because the belief was that there was nothing smaller from which an atom was made. They believed it was impossible to divide them further.

Since that point, of course, we have discovered otherwise. The etymology of the word has drifted as well. When we talk about the chemical nature of a substance, we don't make a count of the electrons, protons, and neutrons that are involved. We refer to the *atoms*. We may refer to a molecule as well, but usually that molecule is made up of atoms. We even name molecules after the atoms that are in them.

Only through changing the name slightly do we *imply* that a subatomic particle is missing or that there is an extra one along for the ride. So, despite being divisible (and putting the lie to the original meaning of their name), atoms are still the core building blocks from which everything we see, touch, and feel is made.

We can say the same for individual choices in game AI. When we look at a game character on a screen, we see many **actions**. Some are individual *choices* (e.g., "use the gun instead of my fists"), and some are actual physical events (such as "fire the gun one time").

We also witness conglomerations of multiple actions (such as "draw the gun, raise the gun, aim the gun, fire the gun"). We sometimes refer to these collections of actions as **behaviors**. Behaviors are roughly analogous to molecules (Figure 14.1). They are often composed of multiple actions (atoms). Some behaviors have many actions; some only have a few. Some actions combine well together to make a stable, understandable behavior; other actions don't bind quite as readily to each other (e.g., "draw the gun, throw the gun up in the air, pick the flower, smell the flower, aim the flower, eat the flower"). Choices and actions are the atoms we use to make up those behavior molecules.

The subatomic particles—the electrons, protons, and neutrons—in my obscure metaphor are the bits and pieces that we use to construct the individual decision.

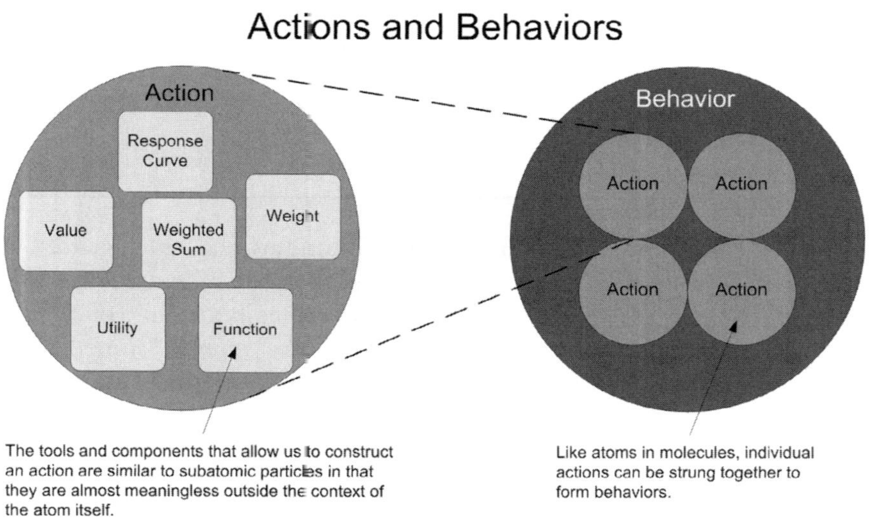

Actions and Behaviors

The tools and components that allow us to construct an action are similar to subatomic particles in that they are almost meaningless outside the context of the atom itself.

Like atoms in molecules, individual actions can be strung together to form behaviors.

FIGURE 14.1 Choices and actions are the atoms of game AI. We think of them as the smallest building blocks of character behavior.

These include the tools we have covered so far in this book: value, utility, formulas, response curves, scales, granularity, and weighted sums, just to name a few. While, like the atom, we can't construct the decision without them, we don't think about the pieces and parts *outside* the context of the decision itself. For example, a response curve doesn't have much meaning outside the context of a decision that utilizes it. Naturally, we need to understand how these tools work and how they combine. We need to understand their dynamics and how they affect the bigger picture. The entire existence of those parts, however, is given meaning by their role in forming those atoms—those decisions that our AI agents need.

Along the way through this book, we have illustrated many individual decision-making processes through our examples. Most of those were specifically constructed examples so that we could use the tool we were learning about in a context that was more familiar to us than simply an abstract theory or dry description. We will revisit some of these decisions and craft new ones throughout this chapter. Our goal is to begin to put everything we have covered into one decision-making process. Because of this, much of this chapter (and the next) falls into our familiar "In the Game" category.

Remember, while a particular example may be of a specific behavior or endemic to a stereotypical genre, it is the decision *process* that is important to learn. Strange as it may sound, deciding what weapon to use in a role-playing game (RPG) is not all that different from deciding what attraction to visit in a theme-park-style game. Deciding whom to shoot or where to hide in a first-person shooter (FPS) is similar in many respects to deciding to whom to pass the ball in a sports simulation. The genres are different, the situations are different, and the *behaviors* are different. However, the *choices* our agents are making in those examples are similar, just as the atoms that make up wildly dissimilar substances are made of the same components. And the *tools* that we use to arrive at those decisions are definitely the same. A response curve is a response curve just as an electron is an electron. The bottom line is that, while a particular example may not *seem* similar to a challenge we face in our own game, the process may certainly be what the proverbial doctor ordered. (And I give you 80% odds that the process is *sugarless*.)

DECIDING WHAT TO DECIDE

We need to go through a number of steps to construct a decision-making algorithm. Because our atom is a single decision, it is naturally the place to focus on. Once we have made some decisions, we can assemble them into behaviors. In fact, making a single decision about an action often makes a decision about a behavior as well.

For example, a decision to "attack Bad Dude with our gun" means we have made a decision about which enemy to attack, which weapon to use, that we need to draw it, aim it, fire it, and so on. All of those other actions are included in the key decision of "attack Bad Dude with our gun."

The reason we view "attack Bad Dude with our gun" as a single decision is that we are processing all of the components as a whole. We could have put it up against "attack Bad Dude with our fists," "attack Evil Dude with our gun," or even "attack Evil Dude with our fists." We were not breaking down the decision into "attack Bad Dude or Evil Dude?" or "attack with gun or fists?" While we certainly *could have* divided the quandary into two separate parts (i.e., *who* to attack and *how*), we may want to score the decision based on the *combination* of the criteria.

For example, if we compare the threats posed by Bad Dude and Evil Dude, we may find that Evil Dude is more of a threat (Figure 14.2). If we compare the relative strengths of our gun and our fists, we will likely find that our gun is a more potent weapon. Those two observations may lead us to attack Evil Dude with our gun (in the library?).

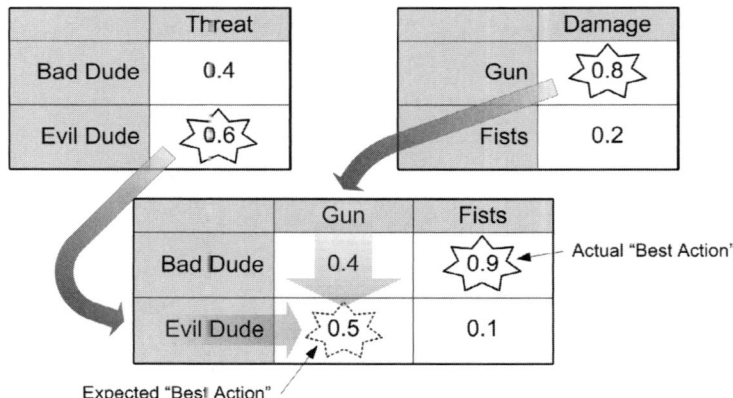

FIGURE 14.2 If Bad Dude has a particular weakness to fist attacks, separating the two decisions would not have brought us to that choice. Only by combining the factors into a single decision algorithm would we have discovered the correct action.

If we were to combine the target and weapon decisions together into one (mysterious) utility equation, however, we might find that Bad Dude has a weakness for melee attacks and that our best option (of the four combinations) would be to attack him with our fists. By making two separate decisions and gluing them together, we arrived at a suboptimal behavior. By combining them, we determined the *best* choice for the situation.

More or Less?

The way around this is for us to decide what our decision is going to entail. One action? Two? A whole cluster of them? The more actions we lump into one decision, the more complex the decision becomes. On the other hand, the fewer actions we group into one decision, the more actual decisions we need to make. We also need to be careful not to run into logical pitfalls such as the one illustrated above.

As always, the rationale for any given combination is very context-dependent. Most of the time, we want to group actions together if they are strongly related. For example, walking to an object is strongly related to the decision to pick the object up. We wouldn't separate those two actions. The statements "should I pick up the box?" and "should I walk to box?" sound odd together. If we connect the answer to the first question to the second with "therefore," however, it makes a lot more sense to us. "Should I pick up the box? Yes. Therefore, I should walk to the box." The decision (such as it is) to walk to the box is a *necessary* component of the decision to pick up the box. We can't pick it up if we don't walk to it. (You also can't pick up the box if you *can't* walk to it.) Of course, we could not have even considered picking the box up if the assumption wasn't there that we were going to walk to it. The two actions are almost inextricably linked—which means they should be considered in *one* decision.

ANALYZING A SINGLE OPTION

Once we settle on what a decision entails, we need to analyze it. By sifting all of the relevant information through the tools we've discussed, we can begin to home in on the right decision.

IN THE GAME   Which Dude to Kill?

As our example throughout this next section, we define Evil Dude and Bad Dude as types of antagonistic dudes. We will also add a boss type, Arch Dude, to the mix. (If it helps complete the picture, we can imagine all the Dudes in dark glasses and stupid hats.) There are four types of weapons that we and the Dudes can arm ourselves with: a pistol, a shotgun, a machine gun, and a rocket launcher. The decision we need to make is, when confronted by dudes of various types, armed with any of the available weapons, and at various distances from us, which of the three should we attack first (Figure 14.3)?

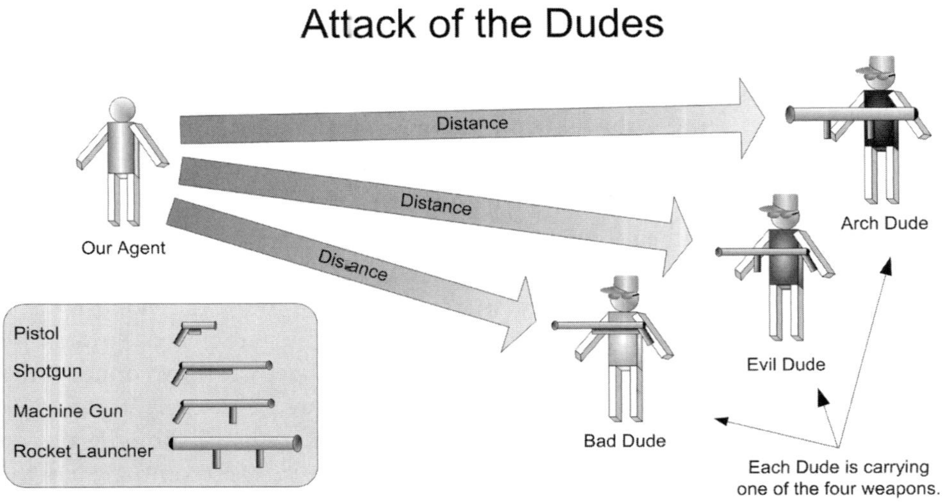

FIGURE 14.3 When our agent is confronted by Dudes of varying types, armed with any of the four weapons, and at a variety of distances, he must select which of the Dudes to attack and with which weapon.

IDENTIFYING FACTORS

Beginning as early as Chapter 2, we talked about the necessity of identifying and analyzing all the factors relevant to a decision. Throughout the examples in the book, we limited ourselves to the ones that helped illustrate the point we were trying to make at that time. We are now going to revisit this idea.

To determine which factors are relevant to our pending Dude-icide, we need to make a list of things that could help or hinder our ability to successfully attack a Dude in general. After long consideration, here is the list we will use.

- **Distance to enemy:** How far away from us is our target? This relates to the weapon range (below) as well as the threat factor to our own safety (also below).
- **Our weapon range:** How far away can we shoot with our current weapon?
- **Our weapon damage:** How much damage per second does our current weapon deal? Is the amount of damage related to the distance?
- **Our weapon accuracy:** How accurate is our current weapon? Is the accuracy related to distance?
- **Our health:** How much damage can we take?
- **Opponent's weapon range:** From how far away can they shoot us?

- **Opponent's weapon damage:** How much damage does the opponent's weapon do per second? Is it related to the distance of the shot?
- **Opponent's weapon accuracy:** How accurate is the opponent with his weapon? Is the accuracy related to distance?
- **Opponent's health:** How much damage can the target take?

While there could be other considerations, we are going to stop there for the moment. We can always add more fun stuff later on.

As we discussed in the previous chapter, we need to determine if each criterion is concrete or abstract, what range they will fall into, and at what granularity we are measuring. By doing this, we get a better idea of what we are working with. We need to know the shape of each piece before we can start fitting them together.

A quick glance through the list tells us that all of the criteria are concrete values. They are nonsubjective, measurable values. In fact, they are all values that are either listed as a property of an object (such as weapon damage) or that the game engine can calculate for us (such as distance). This simplifies our process somewhat for now.

Here a Dude, There a Dude, Everywhere a Dude, Dude...

To give us a better idea of the concrete data we are working with, we need to list the specifics for each of the three types of Dudes. Each of the three has an amount of health, with the Arch Dude being able to absorb the most damage. Additionally, they have accuracy modifiers that adjust their ability to shoot their weapons. Being the least trained, the Bad Dudes are... well... *bad*. The Arch Dudes, on the other hand, have a bonus to their weapon accuracy.

Dude Type	Health	Acc. Mod.
Bad	100	−20%
Evil	120	0%
Arch	150	+10%

Choose Your Weapon

Our agent and the Dudes can use any one of four weapons. These are a pistol, a shotgun, a machine gun, and a rocket launcher. Each of the four types has its own accuracy and damage-dealing characteristics. The weapons start with a base damage and accuracy rate. Rather than a simple concrete number, however, these values are distance-dependent.

To construct these formulas, we use some of the suggestions in Chapter 10. To exhibit the characteristic of decreasing damage, we need to have a formula that was at its maximum result at a distance of 0 (with one exception, as we shall see). From there, we want it to fall away at an increasing rate. The natural starting point was a parabolic curve that we subtract from our maximum point.

All four weapons use the same base formula. This ensures that the general, distance dependency characteristic is present. Each weapon has specific values for each variable, however, which is what separates one weapon from another. The formulas are

$$Damage = Base + Modifier - \frac{(Distance - DecayShift)^{DecayExponent}}{Divisor}$$

$$Accuracy = Base + Modifier - \frac{(Distance - DecayShift)^{DecayExponent}}{Divisor}$$

Notice that the structure of the two formulas is the same. The magic of each happens with the numbers that we plug in. There are a few things to note, however. First, it is possible that the formula can generate a number less than 0. As we shall see, this is by design. Because we can't have *negative* damage or *negative* accuracy, we need to clamp the result to a minimum of 0.

As cryptic as the formulas look in this form, they begin to make more sense as we plug in the weapon-specific values. The figures for each weapon are:

Value	Pistol	Shotgun	Mach. Gun	Rocket L.
Range	137	57	300	300
Base Damage (/sec)	10	50	30	100
Dmg. Decay Exp.	2.2	2.1	2.0	2.0
Dmg. Decay Divisor	5,000	100	5,000	1,500
Dmg. Decay Shift	0	0	0	50
Base Accuracy	0.70	0.95	0.80	0.50
Acc. Decay Exp.	1.5	2.2	1.8	2.0
Acc. Decay Divisor	3,000	15,000	50,000	30,000
Acc. Decay Shift	0	0	0	50

Unfortunately, looking at the figures in the table doesn't make them any less mysterious. To shed a little more light on how they operate together, we could use one of the weapons an example. We will leave the *Distance* and *Modifier* values blank for now, as those would be specific to the situation.

/* *A word of caution for those of us who seek to infer meaning from things: The numbers used in this example are neither specifically related to anything nor drawn from anything. Often, in the search for an* effect *for a mathematical model, we select these numbers through a trial-and-error approach. There is no "correct way" to approach this process. We end up using "whatever works."* */

Using the formula and numbers above, the damage calculation for a machine gun is:

$$Damage = 30 + Modifier - \frac{(Distance - 0)^{2.0}}{5000}$$

Assuming that the machine gun is in the hands of an Evil Dude (no modifiers) at a range of 100 feet, we can now calculate how much damage the machine gun will do per second.

$$Damage = 30 - \frac{100^{2.0}}{5000} = 28.0$$

As we can see, the travel distance of 100 reduces the damage done by the machine gun by 2 points down to 28.0. If we extend the shot further, to 200 feet, we would find that the damage is reduced further, to 22.0.

$$Damage = 30 - \frac{200^{2.0}}{5000} = 22.0$$

The formula for accuracy works the same way.

One aspect *not* shown above is the *Modifier* for the skill of user. The *Modifier* parameter directly affects the starting point of the curve. We can see this by comparing the accuracy rates for a Bad Dude and an Evil Dude. The Bad Dude has a −20% modifier to accuracy. Therefore, his accuracy with a pistol at 75 feet would be

$$Accuracy_{BadDude} = 0.70 - 0.20 + -\frac{75^{1.5}}{3000} = 0.28$$

On the other hand, the accuracy for an Evil Dude with a pistol at 75 feet would be

$$Accuracy_{EvilDude} = 0.70 - \frac{75^{1.5}}{3000} = 0.48$$

The only difference between the two is the inclusion of the *Modifier* value.

The other aspect that we haven't seen in action yet is the *Shift* parameter. If we think back to Chapter 10, we will remember that it is possible to shift the vertex of a parabola left or right. We do this by adjusting the value of x under the exponent. If we realize that *Distance* in our formula is the equivalent of x, then the placement of the *Shift* parameter along with *Distance* explains the horizontal movement of the curve.

For example, the peak accuracy of a rocket launcher is not at 0 feet. By specifying that *Shift* = 50, we ensure that the peak accuracy of the rocket launcher (i.e., the vertex of the parabola) is at 50 feet. At 20 feet, for example, the accuracy of the rocket launcher is only 47%—down from its peak of 50%.

$$Accuracy = 0.50 - \frac{(20 - 50)^{2.0}}{30000} = 0.47$$

All of this data is better visualized (and more easily constructed) by looking at graphs. Figure 14.4 shows the accuracy of the four weapons based on the data for each inserted into the accuracy formula.

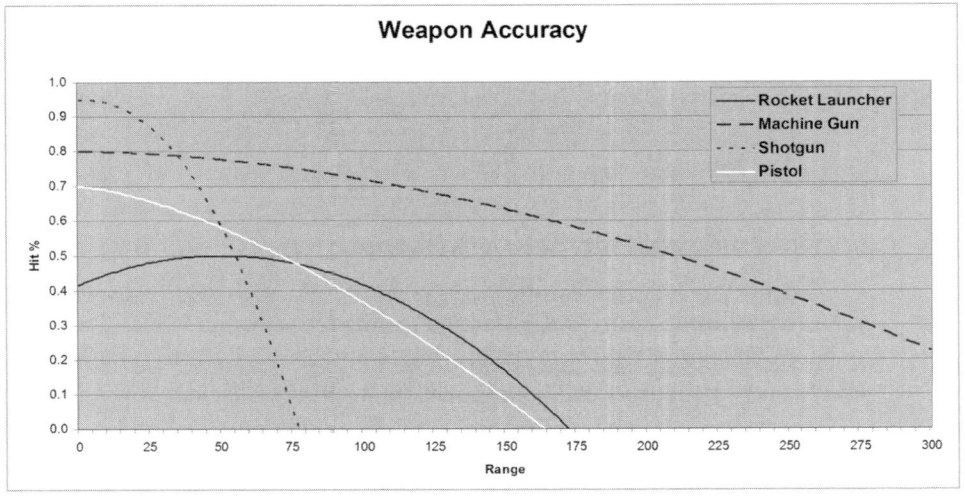

FIGURE 14.4 The accuracy curves of the four weapons are a result of the data for the respective weapons entered into the accuracy equation.

By looking at the accuracy curves on the same graph, we can see not only how each weapon performs over the given range, but also how they perform compared to each other. For example, while the shotgun is the most accurate close-range weapon (due to the scatter effect), its accuracy falls off dramatically as the distance increases. On the other hand, the accuracy of the machine gun remains relatively good over the range of the graph.

Of particular note is the graph of the rocket launcher. As we mentioned above, the *Shift* parameter moved the vertex of the parabola to the right. Rather than having a peak accuracy at a range of 0, we can see that it is at its best at a range of 50 (the *Shift* value for a rocket launcher). Both nearer and farther than 50 feet, its accuracy decreases.

We can view the results of the damage formula on a graph as well (Figure 14.5). The range of the graph is the same as in the accuracy graph (Figure 14.4). Again, we can see the telltale parabolas of the quadratic equation.

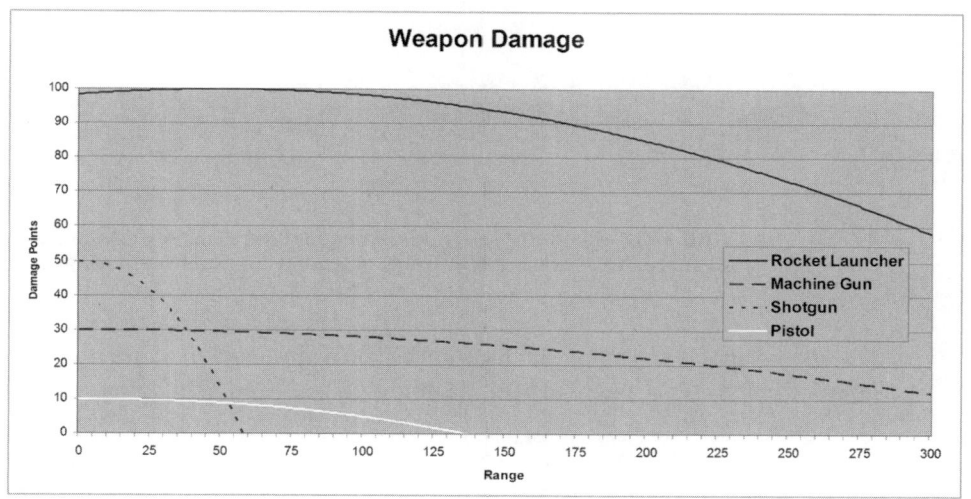

FIGURE 14.5 The damage curves of the four weapons are a result of the data for the respective weapons entered into the damage equation.

For what should be obvious reasons, the rocket launcher is the most potent of the four weapons. The lowly pistol is on the low end of the range. It is more important to note the effects of the different shapes of the damage curves as the range increases. As we would expect, a shotgun blast is fairly potent at close range. As the range increases, however, a shotgun blast loses much of its kick. In fact, at about 50 feet, it would be less powerful (per second) than being struck by a bullet from a pistol. At 60 feet, the shotgun blast does no damage whatsoever.

Whereas each of the two formulas gives us valid and important information about the four weapons, we learn a lot more about the effectiveness of the weapons when we combine the graphs. By simply multiplying the damage per second by the percent chance of scoring a hit, we arrive at a new figure: *expected damage per second.* We can then graph this combination of data in the same manner as either accuracy or damage alone (Figure 14.6).

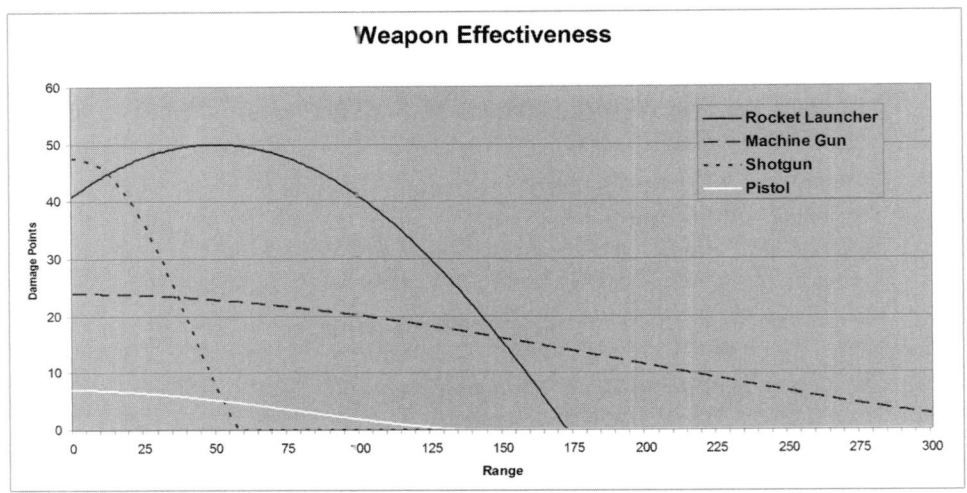

FIGURE 14.6 By multiplying the damage by the accuracy rate, we can calculate the overall effectiveness of a weapon at different ranges.

Once again, analyzing the four curves provides us with some interesting information. First, as we would expect, the high accuracy and high damage rates make the shotgun the weapon of choice at close range. While the rocket launcher certainly packs a punch close in, its accuracy rate causes it to be slightly unreliable. On the other hand, because the accuracy and damage rates of the shotgun drop so quickly, its effectiveness drops swiftly as well. That leaves the rocket launcher as a prime weapon for mid-range strikes. However, because of the poor long-range accuracy of the rockets, its formidable damage rate becomes less important as range increases. Eventually, the machine gun's reliable accuracy and moderate damage-dealing capability wins out. For longer-range strikes, it becomes the weapon of choice.

The pistol may not look impressive in the company of the other, more powerful weapons. However, we have to consider that we may not always have access to (or ammo for) the other weapons. If we only had a shotgun and a pistol, for instance, we would elect to use the pistol at ranges of over 50 feet. If we had a machine gun (and no rocket launcher), we would elect to use it instead of the shotgun for ranges of over 35 feet.

It's important for us to remember that we are not the only one with a gun. The Dudes are armed as well. Other than the accuracy modifiers that we identified above, the Dudes' weapons perform identically to ours.

Did I Mention the Detonator?

The above information helps us determine what the optimum weapon is for each range. That goes a long way toward helping us make our decision. If we know the range to each Dude, his health, and what weapon he is carrying, we can determine which Dude to attack first and what the optimum weapon is for us to attack him with. The solution is to determine which Dude is some combination of the biggest threat and the easiest kill. However, before we go further, we are going to add one last wrinkle to our example.

We will now assume that there is an important point in the area. In true epic James Bond style, we will say that it is a detonator for a large explosive device. (On second thought, this could be in Austin Powers style, too. Or Jack Bauer style. Or Jedi Knight sty–... never mind.) We now have two goals to address.

First, as before, we need to avoid allowing ourselves to be killed by a Dude. That is what we were addressing above when we were going to dispatch the biggest threat–easiest kill combination. However, our second goal is to prevent someone from triggering the detonator. By adding a parameter to each Dude "range to goal," we can determine who is the most dangerous target in *that* respect. The two priority systems may not yield the same answer. For example, a Dude who we may have judged as the *lowest*-priority target before may suddenly become extremely *important* to attack if he moves close to the detonator (Figure 14.7).

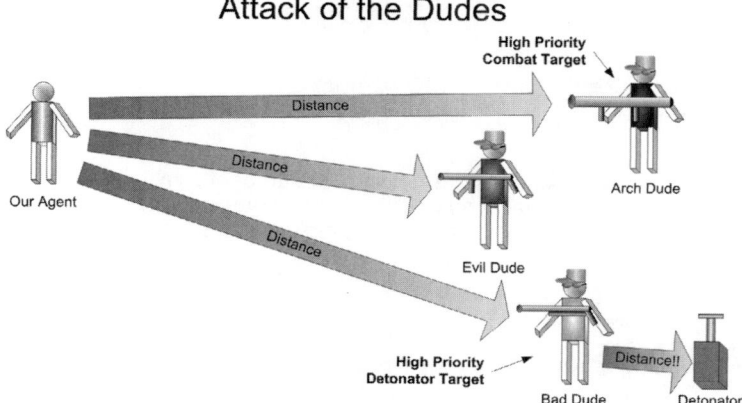

FIGURE 14.7 The poor fighter (Bad Dude) with a poor weapon (shotgun) at long range would normally be the lowest-priority target. If he is standing next to the dreaded detonator, however, his priority as a target increases significantly.

We need to include a way of adding that priority into our target selection algorithm. Before we do that, however, we need to define what "close to" and "increased priority" mean. To do that, we construct another formula. Once again, we tap into a type of formula from Chapter 10. We will define *Urgency* as the result of a formula with an exponent that is less than 1 (a *root*). By subtracting from the high value, 1.0, we arrange it so that as distance from the detonator increases, the urgency of the target drops away from 1.0. The formula we will use is

$$Urgency = 1 - \frac{Distance^{0.4}}{10}$$

Once again, the effect of this formula is easier to visualize as a graph (Figure 14.8). In this case, we are using a parabola to simulate the rise in *Urgency* as the range decreases. The nature of an exponent-based curve is such that the range of change is very significant near the vertex (*Range* = 0, *Urgency* = 1.0). While there is an increase in *Urgency* as the distance diminishes throughout the entire range of the graph, the rate of change increases markedly as the distance approaches 0.

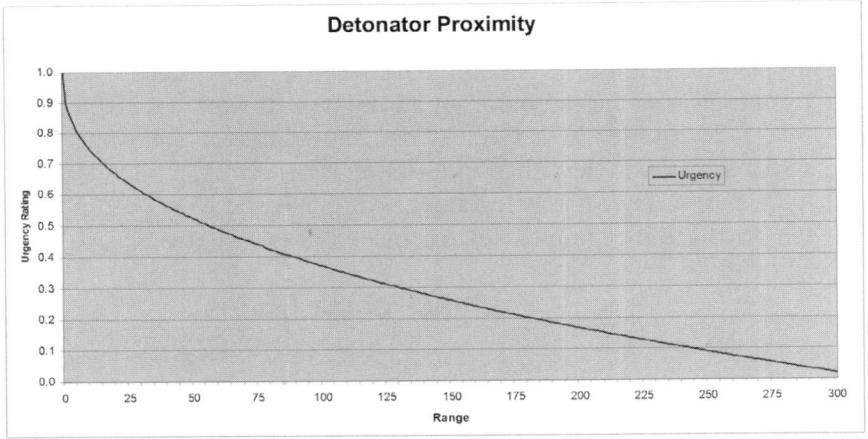

FIGURE 14.8 As the range to the detonator increases, the urgency level for the target drops. As the target's range to the detonator decreases, especially as it closes within 25 feet, the urgency rises rapidly.

A Jumble of Blocks

We have now defined all of the pieces and parts that we will use in our decision. We have not only set values for the various Dudes that we will encounter, but we have established formulas for calculating more complex (yet still concrete) values such as the range-based damage and accuracy figures. However, none of these parts work *together*. We have lots of facts and formulas, but no cohesion.

Before we start putting these blocks together, we need to ensure that we have them built correctly. To establish the compartmentalized confidence we talked about in Chapter 13, we need to ensure that we are comfortable with each component. Only then can we trust that what we *build* with the blocks will be valid.

PUTTING IT IN CODE

There are three major components in this example: the agent (us), Dudes, and weapons. Accordingly, we create classes for the three types of entities (`CAgent`, `CDude`, and `CWeapon`). Additionally, for Dudes and weapons, we create collection classes to hold the individual objects (Figure 14.9). We will look at the basics of each of the classes for clarity.

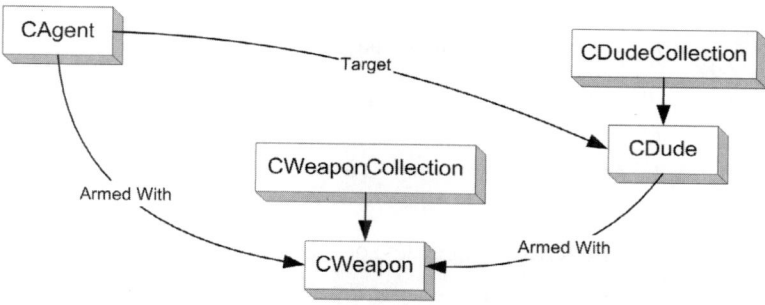

FIGURE 14.9 The class structure for the "Shoot Dudes" example. `CDudeCollection` contains a vector of `CDude` objects. `CWeaponCollection` contains an array of four `CWeapon` objects.

/*
This logical arrangement is optional, of course. This book is not meant to be an educational tome on design patterns or memory management. I have stripped the example down to a simple, easy-to-understand model. Feel free to insert the AI logic into a design of your own choosing.
*/

Weapons

Because we utilize `CWeapon` in both `CDude` and `CAgent`, we will begin by defining it. First, we should note that we have enumerated a type to make referencing the weapons easier throughout the entire program.

```
typedef enum {
    WEAPON_PISTOL,
    WEAPON_SHOTGUN,
    WEAPON_MACHINEGUN,
    WEAPON_ROCKETS
} WEAPON_TYPE;
```

The header of CWeapon is self-explanatory. (For space purposes, I have cut out the constructor, destructor, and the usual "get and set" accessor functions.)

```
class CWeapon
{
public:
    //[Ctor/Dtor snipped for space…]

    //[Accessors snipped for space…]

    //////////////////
    // Accuracy and Damage Calculations
    //////////////////
    double GetAccuracy( USHORT Dist = 0, double Modifier = 0.0 );
    double GetDamage( USHORT Dist = 0, double Modifier = 0.0 );

private:
    //////////////////
    // Member Variables
    //////////////////

    char* mName;              // Name
    USHORT mMaxRange;         // Max range

    USHORT mBaseDamage;       // Base (max) damage
    double mDmgDecayExp;      // Decay formula exponent
    USHORT mDmgDecayDiv;      // Decay formula divisor
    USHORT mDmgDecayShift;    // Decay formula shift (horiz.)
```

```
    double mBaseAccuracy;      // Base (max) accuracy
    double mAccDecayExp;       // Decay formula exponent
    USHORT mAccDecayDiv;       // Decay formula divisor
    USHORT mAccDecayShift;     // Decay formula shift (horiz.)
};
```

The member variables for the weapons hold the numbers that we used for the damage and accuracy calculations. For both damage and accuracy, we have a base, a decay exponent, a decay divisor, and a decay shift. Based on the formulas we laid out above, those are the only figures that we need to define the appropriate curves.

By calling GetDamage() and GetAccuracy() with the distance and any modifiers (e.g., the accuracy modifiers for the different types of Dudes), we receive the appropriate damage value or accuracy percentage. These two functions operate very simply.

```
double CWeapon::GetAccuracy( USHORT Dist /*= 0*/,
                             double Modifier /*= 0.0 */ )
{
    double Accuracy = mBaseAccuracy + Modifier -
        (pow(( Dist - mAccDecayShift ), mAccDecayExp )) / mAccDecayDiv;

    if ( Accuracy < 0 ) { Accuracy = 0; }

    return Accuracy;
}


double CWeapon::GetDamage( USHORT Dist /*= 0*/,
                           double Modifier /*= 0.0 */ )
{
    double Damage = mBaseDamage + Modifier -
        (pow(( Dist - mDmgDecayShift ), mDmgDecayExp )) / mDmgDecayDiv;

    if ( Damage < 0 ) { Damage = 0; }

    return Damage;
}
```

Notice that, because our formulas can generate values that are less than 0, we must clamp the minimum on both values to 0. We can't do *negative* damage, and we can't have *less than* a 0% chance of hitting our target. Other than that, the formulas for calculating the values are familiar as code-ese translations of their mathematical versions we expressed above.

We define an array of `CWeapon` objects in the `CWeaponCollection` as follows:

```
#define MAX_WEAPONS 4
CWeapon mWeapons[MAX_WEAPONS];   // Array of all weapons
```

`CWeaponCollection` also has accessors for looking up information about any of the members of its array by index. These accessors simply pass the request on to the matching accessor of the referenced object.

The important function that `CWeaponCollection` performs, however, is to initialize the array with the four weapons we have defined in our game. We do this through the function `InitOneWeapon()`.

```
void CWeaponCollection::InitOneWeapon( WEAPON_TYPE Type,
                                       char* Name,
                                       USHORT MaxRange,
                                       USHORT BaseDamage,
                                       double DmgDecayExp,
                                       USHORT DmgDecayDiv,
                                       USHORT DmgDecayShift,
                                       double BaseAccuracy,
                                       double AccDecayExp,
                                       USHORT AccDecayDiv,
                                       USHORT AccDecayShift )
{
    mWeapons[Type].SetMaxRange( MaxRange );
    mWeapons[Type].SetBaseDamage( BaseDamage );
    mWeapons[Type].SetDmgDecayExp( DmgDecayExp );
    mWeapons[Type].SetDamageDecayDiv( DmgDecayDiv );
    mWeapons[Type].SetDamageDecayShift( DmgDecayShift );
    mWeapons[Type].SetBaseAccuracy( BaseAccuracy );
    mWeapons[Type].SetAccDecayExp( AccDecayExp );
```

```
    mWeapons[Type].SetAccDecayDiv( AccDecayDiv );
    mWeapons[Type].SetAccDecayShift( AccDecayShift );
    mWeapons[Type].SetName( Name );
}
```

In the function `InitWeapons()`, we call `InitOneWeapon()` once for each of our four weapons.

```
void CWeaponCollection::InitWeapons()
{
    InitOneWeapon( WEAPON_PISTOL, "Pistol", 137,
                   10, 2.2, 5000, 0,       // Damage
                   0.7, 1.5, 3000, 0 );    // Accuracy



    InitOneWeapon( WEAPON_SHOTGUN, "Shotgun", 57,
                   50, 2.1, 100, 0,        // Damage
                   0.95, 2.2, 15000, 0 );  // Accuracy

    InitOneWeapon( WEAPON_MACHINEGUN, "M/G", 300,
                   30, 2.0, 5000, 0,       // Damage
                   0.8, 1.8, 50000, 0 );   // Accuracy

    InitOneWeapon( WEAPON_ROCKETS, "R/L", 300,
                   100, 2.0, 1500, 50,     // Damage
                   0.5, 2.0, 30000, 50 );  // Accuracy
}
```

In each call to `InitOneWeapon()`, we are passing in the numbers from the characteristics table that we laid out earlier. Once we have defined the weapon parameters, the damage and accuracy functions have all the information that they need to do their magic. If we want to change the characteristics of one weapon, we simply change the initialization parameters that we pass in when we create the `CWeapon` object. The formula does the rest. (In a production environment, we would store these values in a configuration file so that we can tweak them without touching the code.)

What Makes a Dude a Dude?

We now turn our attention to `CDude` and `CDudeCollection`. There really isn't a lot to `CDude` in our implementation. As we did with the weapons, we define an enumerated type for the three different types of Dudes.

```
typedef enum {
    BAD_DUDE,
    EVIL_DUDE,
    ARCH_DUDE
} DUDE_TYPE;
```

The header file contains the usual suspects. The constructor takes the arguments that set all the member variables. (Again, I have snipped the accessor functions.)

```
class CDude
{
public:
    //////////////////
    // Ctor/Dtor
    //////////////////
    CDude( DUDE_TYPE Type,
           char* Name,
           USHORT Health,
           USHORT Location,
           USHORT DistToGoal,
           CWeapon* pWeapon );
    virtual ~CDude();

    //[Accessors snipped for space...]


    void SetAccAdjust()

private:
    //////////////////
    // Member Variables
    //////////////////
```

```
    char* mName;           // Name of Dude
    DUDE_TYPE mType;       // Dude Type
    USHORT mHealth;        // Health of this Dude
    USHORT mLocation;      // Location (1D) of this Dude
    USHORT mDistToGoal;    // Distance to the goal
    double mAccAdjust;     // Accuracy adjustment
    CWeapon* mpWeapon;     // Pointer to weapon armed
};
```

Please note that, for purposes of our example, we are tracking the positions of the Dudes and our agent in *one* dimension only. Therefore, the distance between them is simply a linear measurement on a single axis.

The only function in `CDude` that is not *precisely* an accessor is `SetAccAdjust()`. When a Dude is created, the constructer calls `SetAccAdjust()` to set the accuracy adjustment based on the type of Dude.

```
void CDude::SetAccAdjust()
{
    switch( mType ) {
    case BAD_DUDE:
        mAccAdjust = -0.2;
        break;

    case EVIL_DUDE:
        mAccAdjust = 0.0;
        break;

    case ARCH_DUDE:
        mAccAdjust = 0.1;
        break;

    default:
        mAccAdjust = 0.0;
        break;
    } // end switch
}
```

The `CDudeCollection` is just as bland. It contains, as its member variable, a vector containing `CDude` objects.

```
typedef std::vector < CDude > DUDE_LIST;
DUDE_LIST mlDudes; // List of Dudes in the game
```

We fill this vector with our Dudes when the constructor for `CDudeCollection` calls `InitDudes()` which, in turn, calls `InitOneDude()`.

```
void CDudeCollection::InitDudes()
{
    InitOneDude( BAD_DUDE, "Baddie",
                 100, 180, 50, WEAPON_SHOTGUN );

    InitOneDude( EVIL_DUDE, "Evilmeister",
                 120, 200, 150, WEAPON_MACHINEGUN );

    InitOneDude( ARCH_DUDE, "Boss Man",
                 150, 150, 110, WEAPON_ROCKETS );
}


void CDudeCollection::IritOneDude( DUDE_TYPE Type,
                                   char* Name,
                                   USHORT Health,
                                   USHORT Location,
                                   USHORT DistToGoal,
                                   WEAPON_TYPE Weapon )
{
    CWeapon* pWeapon = mpWeaponCollection->GetWeaponPointer( Weapon );

    CDude NewDude ( Type, Name, Health, Location, DistToGoal, pWeapon );
    mlDudes.push_back( NewDude );
}
```

The Mind of an Agent

The last class we need to establish is `CAgent`. This is where our AI decision-making process will be taking place, of course. Before that, however, we need to establish what our class looks like.

The `CAgent` class uses a pair of `structs` to help track its information. The first one is for keeping track of the weapons that we have on our person.

```
struct sWEAPON_INFO
{
    CWeapon* pWeapon;
    USHORT Ammo;
};


typedef std::vector < sWEAPON_INFO > WEAPON_VECTOR;
```

Each item in a vector of type `WEAPON_LIST` contains a pointer to a weapon and a record of the amount of ammunition that we carry for this weapon.

We also have a similar structure for our list of targets.

```
struct sTARGET_INFO
{
    CDude* pDude;
    CWeapon* pWeapon;
    double Score;

    bool operator<( const sTARGET_INFO& j ) {return Score > j.Score;}
};
typedef std::vector < sTARGET_INFO > TARGET_VECTOR;
```

The information contained in `sTARGET_INFO` may be confusing at first until we discuss what our decision process will entail. We will be making a choice that is actually two in one. We must decide the best *combination* of which enemy we are going to kill and with what weapon. As we touched on earlier in this chapter, deciding on our target separately from the weapon we want to use may lead us to a false "best solution." Therefore, we have to address them as part of the same decision process. Each entry that we place into a `TARGET_LIST` will be a combination of an enemy and a weapon. We will then score that *combination* individually and select the best entry.

We overload the < operator for the `std::sort` algorithm because we have to explain to the compiler that we are sorting by a particular member of the `sTARGET_INFO` (specifically, `Score`).

Rather than list the entire header file here and spoil the surprise, we will look only at a few key items of `CAgent`. First, there are no surprises in the member variables.

```
USHORT mHealth;       // Current Health
USHORT mLocation;     // Current Location in 1D

TARGET_LIST mvTargets;     // List of available targets
WEAPON_LIST mvWeapons;     // List of available weapons

CDude* mpCurrentTarget;        // Current target to attack
WEAPON_TYPE mCurrentWeapon;    // Current weapon to use
```

We have defined two member list variables—one for our current targets and one for our current weapons.

When the agent needs the distance to a selected enemy, we call the function

```
GetDistToTarget( CDude* pTarget )
```

The implementation is simply

```
USHORT CAgent::GetDistToTarget(CDude *pTarget)
{
    USHORT Dist = abs( mLocation - pTarget->GetLocation() );
    return Dist;
}
```

The constructor for `CAgent` sets `mLocation` = 0 and `mHealth` = 100. Its other function is to initialize our weapons. We do this through the functions `InitWeapons()` and `AddWeapon()`.

```
void CAgent::InitWeapons()
{
    AddWeapon( WEAPON_PISTOL, 20 );
    AddWeapon( WEAPON_MACHINEGUN, 100 );
    AddWeapon( WEAPON_SHOTGUN, 10 );
```

```
        AddWeapon( WEAPON_ROCKETS, 6 );
    }

    void CAgent::AddWeapon( WEAPON_TYPE WeaponType, USHORT Ammo )
    {
        sWEAPON_INFO ThisWeapon;

        ThisWeapon.Ammo = Ammo;
        ThisWeapon.pWeapon =
            mpWeaponCollection->GetWeaponPointer( WeaponType );

        mvWeapons.push_back( ThisWeapon );
    }
```

All Dressed Up and No One to Kill

By this point, we have created our objects and filled our lists. Our weapons have stats and functions describing their abilities, our enemies have stats and weapons, and our agent has stats, weapons, and enemies. None of that veritable cornucopia of information, however, yields a decision on its own. All we have is *information*. Even the nifty formulas that calculate the accuracy and damage that the weapons cause are only different forms of information.

We have assembled the factors that we believe will be important to our decision just as a glance at the ingredient list for a cake tells us what we need to have handy. It does *not* tell us how we should combine those ingredients or what we need to do with them once they are in the same bowl. For that, we need to begin to identify how these components will work together.

IDENTIFYING RELATIONSHIPS

The first step we must take in combining our data into something meaningful is to identify the items that are directly related. We already touched on a few simple relationships. For example, our formulas for weapon damage and accuracy use distance as one of their components. Therefore, if we know the distance to a target, we can enter that into the formula for a particular weapon and generate a result. We have established a relationship between our location, that of our target, and the weapon.

Another relationship we identified earlier also involved the weapons. The strength of a weapon is neither based *only* on the damage that it can do nor *only* on the accuracy with which it can be used. We combine these two factors into a single measurement. We measure it as the amount of damage that a weapon can do per second when we factor in the probability of a hit. In the graph in Figure 14.6, we labeled this "effectiveness." By combining these two pieces of data into one concept, we establish a relationship.

We can add another component to this relationship. This one makes it far more useful and relevant to the decision we are trying to make. By taking into account the health of the target that we are considering, we can determine how long it would take for us to kill that target with a given weapon at a given distance.

$$TimeToKill = \frac{TargetHealth}{Accuracy \times Damage}$$

Of course, what is missing in the above equation is that *Accuracy* and *Damage* are the results of the distance-based formulas for the weapons. Figure 14.10 shows the entire cascade of relationships that leads us to the *TimeToKill* value.

FIGURE 14.10 As we add more relationships between our individual components of data, we create data that is more useful to our overall decision process.

 PUTTING IT IN CODE

The code for this relationship is as simple as it seems. We create a function that takes the accuracy rate, the damage rate, and the target's health and combines them into one figure based on the formula above.

```
double CAgent::TimeToKill( USHORT Health,
                           USHORT Damage,
                           double Accuracy )
{
    USHORT TimeToKill;

    double DamagePerSec = ( Accuracy * Damage );

    // avoid divide by zero
    if ( DamagePerSec != 0 ) {
        TimeToKill = Health / DamagePerSec;
    } else {
        // if damage/sec is 0, clamp time to 1000
        TimeToKill = 1000;
    } // end if

    return TimeToKill;
}
```

Notice that the process in this function is broken into two steps so that we can avoid "division by zero" errors. We are serving another purpose here. If the amount of damage per second that we can inflict is 0, there is no way that we can injure, much less *kill* the target with the selected weapon. We want to exclude this target-weapon combination from *reasonable* consideration. By setting `TimeToKill` to an absurd value such as 1,000, we are ensuring that it will significantly reduce any further calculations that we perform with it. However, we are *not* removing it from consideration entirely. If we find ourselves in a situation where *none* of the weapons are effective against *any* of the targets, we would still want to use the best combination to at least do *some* damage.

Processing this relationship is as simple as sending the appropriate data into the function. The data comes from a few simple functions as well. First, we have to retrieve the accuracy and damage rates based on the weapon and distance. The following functions provide that information for us.

```
USHORT CAgent::GetDamage( CWeapon* pWeapon, USHORT Dist )
{
    USHORT Damage = pWeapon->GetDamage( Dist );
```

```
        return Damage;
}

double CAgent::GetAccuracy( CWeapon* pWeapon, USHORT Dist )
{
    double Accuracy = pWeapon->GetAccuracy( Dist );
    return Accuracy;
}
```

Therefore, the entire process for determining the time it takes to dispatch a particular enemy is:

```
USHORT Dist = GetDistToTarget( pTarget );
USHORT TargetHealth = pTarget->GetHealth();
USHORT DamageIDeal = GetDamage( pWeapon, Dist );
double MyAccuracy = GetAccuracy( pWeapon, Dist );
double TimeToKillEnemy = TimeToKill( TargetHealth,
                                     DamageIDeal,
                                     MyAccuracy );
```

What Goes 'Round Comes 'Round

Because we know what weapon our enemy is carrying, his accuracy rate (adjusted for the type of Dude if necessary), and our own health, we can reverse the above process and determine how long it would take for a particular enemy to dispatch *us*. The only difference in the functions is that GetAccuracy() must account for the Dude adjustment. By passing a pointer to the selected enemy into an overloaded version of GetAccuracy(), we can add that bit of additional information.

```
double CAgent::GetAccuracy( CWeapon* pWeapon,
                            USHORT Dist,
                            CDude* pDude )
{
    // Get Dude's accuracy adjustment
    double AccAdjust = pDude->GetAccAdjust();

    // Get weapon accuracy adjusted for Dude's skill
```

```
        double Accuracy = pWeapon->GetAccuracy( Dist, AccAdjust );

        return Accuracy;
}
```

Assembling the data requires a similar set of function calls.

```
double DamageITake = GetDamage( pTarget->GetWeapon(), Dist );
double EnemyAccuracy =
        GetAccuracy( pTarget->GetWeapon(),
                     Dist,
                     pTarget->GetPointer() );
double TimeToKillMe = TimeToKill( mHealth,
                                  DamageITake,
                                  EnemyAccuracy );
```

Through the processes above, we know how long it will take for us to kill a selected enemy and how long it will take for him to kill us… but now what? What do we do with this information?

As we discussed in the first half of the book, the utility of an action is not always as obvious as we would like it to be. Sometimes we have to add a little bit of subjectivity as well.

BUILDING CONNECTIONS

Certainly, each of the two values, `TimeToKillEnemy` and `TimeToKillMe`, is important. It is helpful to know how long it would take us to mow down a Dude with a particular weapon. It is also helpful to know how long we can expect to survive an onslaught from a particular Dude. However, there is not an inherent "cause and effect" relationship between `TimeToKillEnemy` and `TimeToKillMe`. We have to define a meaningful connection between the two.

As with our simple example earlier, we cannot base our decision solely on one or the other of these two factors. Anecdotally, if we select the Dude we can kill the quickest, we may be exposing ourselves to a Dude who can kill us the quickest. Alternatively, if we elect to assault the one who is the greatest threat, we may be overlooking the fact that we could have quickly dismissed his weaker pals. What we must do is build a connection between these two independent values that expresses a *combined* utility to us.

In Chapter 9, we explored the idea of relative utility. The decision that we often had to make at each step of the process was to decide if two items or actions were equally important or if one was more desirable than the other. We also had to decide *how much more* important one selection was than the other. This leads to a decision on how to weigh the utility of each action (Chapter 13). This is what we must do now to build a connection between the independent values of `TimeToKillEnemy` and `TimeToKillMe`.

Certainly, we would prefer a situation where it takes us less time to vanquish our foe than it does for him to annihilate us. On the other hand, we also want to pick off the targets that are quick for us to kill. If we get them out of our hair, we have less to worry about. We will call the figure we are calculating *ThreatRatio*.

After experimenting with various combinations, we can arrive at something that "feels" reasonable. We will define *ThreatRatio* with the following formula:

$$ThreatRatio = \frac{TimeToKillMe + (3 \times TimeToKillEnemy)}{4}$$

By multiplying `TimeToKillEnemy` by 3, we are making it three times as important as `TimeToKillMe`. By dividing the weighted sum by 4, we are converting it to a weighted average.

It's worth noting that we are, once again, relying on the principle of compartmentalized confidence. We trust that the processes that led us to the two "time to kill" values are valid. With that trust, we can turn all of our exploration and experimentation to the components we are adding—the numbers involved in the weighted sum.

By selecting a few examples, we can visualize the effect of our formula. For now, we will ignore *how* we arrived at these numbers (because we are confident, remember?) and instead focus only on the effect of the weighted average.

TimeToKillMe	TimeToKillEnemy	ThreatRatio
5.1	3.3	3.76
5.1	427.1	321.56
12.6	4.7	6.69
12.6	1,000.0	753.15
39.9	1.0	10.72
39.9	10.7	18.02

In the examples above, we can see a few extremes. The "best" score is the lowest, so we see that the first line is the best option for us to select. In that example, we are facing an enemy who can kill us more quickly than the other examples (5.1 seconds).

On the other hand, by using whatever weapon is represented in the first line, we will dispatch him in a fairly rapid 3.3 seconds.

Further examination of the data shows how it is working. For example, the second line is the same dangerous enemy. However, our selection of weapon is less than stellar. It would take us a tragic 427 seconds to finish him off. The threat ratio score reflects this with a very poor result.

On the other hand, if we had based our decision solely on how quickly we can kill an enemy, we would have elected to go with the fifth line. In that combination, we can kill the enemy in a single second. However, looking at the first column shows that dispatching that enemy is a pressing problem. We have almost a full 40 seconds in which to deal with him.

One other item to note is the appearance of the 1,000-second time in the fourth line. This is due to a weapon choice where the damage per second *would have been* zero and we manually overrode the value. We still calculate a threat ratio for that selection in case we find ourselves in a hopeless situation where we must choose the "lesser of two evils." The threat ratio of 753 effectively puts that selection out of the running, however.

Remember that Detonator?

While the formula above successfully connects the two expected kill times into a single threat value, we still have the messy problem of the detonator to worry about. The connection between the time to kill values was relatively obvious. We could sum it up with the trite phrase "kill him before he kills you!" However, the Dude's proximity to the detonator is less directly related.

We could calculate the amount of time that it would take a Dude to reach the detonator based on the Dude's speed and distance, but that assumes that the Dude is moving directly for it without anything else on his mind. Instead, because we constructed a utility curve that yielded the value, *Urgency*, we will use that as our sole measurement.

As with the two "kill times" above, we need to construct an abstract connection between *ThreatRatio* and *Urgency* that meaningfully describes their relative merit in our overall decision. We begin by making an assertion that we believe is important: "If a Dude is close to the detonator, he becomes the most dangerous enemy."

While this assertion is indisputably relevant, it still doesn't tell us *how important* the factor is. For example, when we say "if a Dude is close to the detonator," what do we mean by "close?" The *Urgency* function already accounts for the phenomenon that "closer means more urgent," but until we relate it to the threat ratio, the notion of "more urgent" is rather vague. As a result, we have no idea when the enemy would become the "most dangerous" one out there. That depends on a lot of factors.

If the Dudes arrayed before us all have the same threat ratio, a small tweak in the distance to the detonator could make the difference. On the other hand, if there is a large difference between the threats that the various Dudes present, it may not matter much how close any one of them is to the detonator. As with many occurrences of subjective ratings, we are left to the obscure and very nonscientific method known as "pulling numbers out of the air to see what works."

Thankfully, by performing a simple division, we can significantly affect our result as both of our two factors change. Consider the formula

$$Score = \frac{ThreatRatio}{Urgency}$$

Because we had already established that a lower *ThreatRatio* is more important, it helps for us to keep that arrangement. We also constructed *Urgency* so that the *maximum* value is 1. We want *Score* to be at its extreme (lowest) when *Urgency* = 1. By placing it in the denominator, we achieve this effect. As *Urgency* goes down, the value of the fraction would go up—that is, the target would become *less* of a priority. Likewise, if *Urgency* stayed the same and *ThreatRatio* increased (became less important), *Score* would increase as well—again, making the target *less* of a priority. Therefore, the arrangement of dividing *ThreatRatio* by *Urgency* achieves the desired effect.

SCORING THE OPTION

We can run some numbers through the formula to ensure that this is working properly. Consider the following values:

ThreatRatio	Urgency	Score
3.8	0.26	14.64
3.8	0.32	11.85
4.1	0.26	15.77
4.1	0.32	12.81
10.9	0.51	21.37
10.9	0.80	13.62

Again, as we peruse these examples, some things jump out at us. First, consider the first two lines. The threat ratio stays the same, but the urgency increases from the first to the second line. As we would expect, the value for the score decreases (or becomes more important). Using the same two urgency values but increasing the threat ratio slightly shows that the resulting scores increase as well. However, we can see that a *ThreatRatio* of 4.1 and an *Urgency* of 0.32 yields a lower *Score* than the lower threat ratio (3.8) and lower *Urgency* (0.26). This exhibits the subtlety in the combination of the two values.

In the last two lines, the threat of 10.9 isn't terribly dangerous in and of itself. When combined with a significantly higher *Urgency* value (the last line), however, the final score falls into the same range as the more threatening situations. This would be comparable to a nonthreatening foe approaching the detonator. Whether he can kill us or not, he becomes a priority target. In fact, if we increase the *Urgency* of that last line to 0.95, the final score for that enemy becomes 11.47. That would make it the lowest score (i.e., highest priority) of the ones shown.

PUTTING IT IN CODE

Assuming we are now comfortable with the relationships and connections we have established, we can now go about coding the scoring process. We looked at a portion of this process already when we laid out the function calls that generated the time-to-kill values. We will now put it into the whole function.

```cpp
void CAgent::ScoreTarget( CDude* pTarget, sWEAPON_INFO Weapon )
{
    CWeapon* pWeapon = Weapon.pWeapon;

    USHORT Dist = GetDistToTarget( pTarget );

    // Calculate time to kill enemy
    USHORT TargetHealth = pTarget->GetHealth();
    USHORT DamageIDeal = GetDamage( pWeapon, Dist );
    double MyAccuracy = GetAccuracy( pWeapon, Dist );
    double TimeToKillEnemy = TimeToKill( TargetHealth,
                                         DamageIDeal,
                                         MyAccuracy );

    // Calculate time for enemy to kill me
    double DamageITake = GetDamage( pTarget->GetWeapon(), Dist );
    double EnemyAccuracy =
```

```
                GetAccuracy( pTarget->GetWeapon(),
                             Dist,
                             pTarget->GetPointer() );
    double TimeToKillMe = TimeToKill( mHealth,
                                      DamageITake,
                                      EnemyAccuracy );

    // Calculate threat ratio
    double ThreatRatio = ( TimeToKillMe + ( 3 * TimeToKillEnemy ) ) / 4;

    // Calculate target urgency based on proximity to the goal
    double Urgency = CalcTargetUrgency( pTarget->GetDistToGoal() );

    // Create and store the target information
    sTARGET_INFO ThisTarget;

    ThisTarget.pDude = pTarget;
    ThisTarget.pWeapon = Weapon.pWeapon;
    ThisTarget.Score = ThreatRatio / Urgency;

    mvTargets.push_back( ThisTarget );
}
```

The function `ScoreTarget()` takes a pointer to a `CDude` and a weapon type as its parameters. We will see where these come from in a moment.

The beginning of the function is familiar. First, we calculate the time it takes us to kill the selected enemy. Second, we calculate the same information in the other direction—the time it would take for the selected enemy to kill us. This is the portion we addressed above. Immediately after that, however, we calculate `ThreatRatio` according to the weighted average formula we defined earlier.

We then calculate the urgency of the target based on his distance from the detonator. The function we call to do this is simple.

```
double CAgent::CalcTargetUrgency( USHORT Dist )
{
    double Urgency = 1 - ( pow( Dist, 0.4) / 10);
```

```
    // Clamp negative urgency to 0
    if ( Urgency < 0.0 ) {
        Urgency = 0.0;
    } // end if

    return Urgency;
}
```

Once we have `ThreatRatio` and `Urgency`, we proceed with building the information about this target. Remember that `sTARGET_INFO` represents a combination of a Dude and a weapon that we are scoring for comparison purposes. We create a new instance of `sTARGET_INFO`, set the appropriate Dude and weapon information, and then save the score using the simple equation we decided on above.

```
ThisTarget.Score = ThreatRatio / Urgency;
```

We then push it onto the list of targets and exit the function. That is the entire process for scoring the utility of attacking one of our enemies with one of our weapons.

COMPARING OPTIONS

Of course, we need to repeat `ScoreTarget()` for each of the enemies we face and for each of the weapons we carry. If we are facing three Dudes and have four weapons available to us, we have 12 options to score. By looping through the two lists, we can call `ScoreTarget()` for each of the 12 combinations.

```
void CAgent::ScoreAllTargets()
{
    sWEAPON_INFO ThisWeapon;
    CDude* pThisEnemy;

    USHORT ei, wi; // loop indexes

    mvTargets.empty(); // start with a fresh list of targets
```

```
        for ( ei = 0; ei < mpDudeCollection->GetSize(); ei++ ) {
            pThisEnemy = mpDudeCollection->GetPointer( DUDE_TYPE(ei) );

            for ( wi = 0; wi < mvWeapons.size(); wi++ ) {
                ThisWeapon = mvWeapons[wi];

                // Only consider loaded weapons
                if ( ThisWeapon.Ammo > 0 ) {
                    ScoreTarget( pThisEnemy, ThisWeapon );
                } // end if

            } // end for
        } // end for
    }
```

We have also placed our call to `ScoreTarget()` inside an `if` statement that checks to see if we have ammo for the selected weapon. If not, there is no need to check it and add it to the list.

SELECTING AN OPTION

At the end of `ScoreAllTargets()`, we have a list of all the possible attack combinations. Selecting an option is a simple exercise at this point. Because we built our scoring algorithm so that the *lower* the value, the better the option, we can logically deduce that the target with the *lowest* score is the best option for us to select. We can sort `mvTargets` of targets by the `Score` value so that the lowest value is at the beginning of the vector. (Naturally, we could simply walk the list and make a note of the lowest-scored item. I sort it here because doing so will come in handy in Chapter 16.) We then set our target and weapon to the values held in that location. The entire function for selecting a target is:

```
    CDude* CAgent::SelectTarget()
    {
        ScoreAllTargets();
        std::sort( mvTargets.begin(), mvTargets.end() );
```

```
            mpCurrentTarget = mvTargets[0].pDude;
            mpCurrentWeapon = mvTargets[0].pWeapon;
    }
```

Reading it in order, we score all the targets, sort the vector by the score, set our target, and change our weapon. That's it. Easy enough. We did all the heavy lifting in the layers of formulas that we built piece by piece (Figure 14.11).

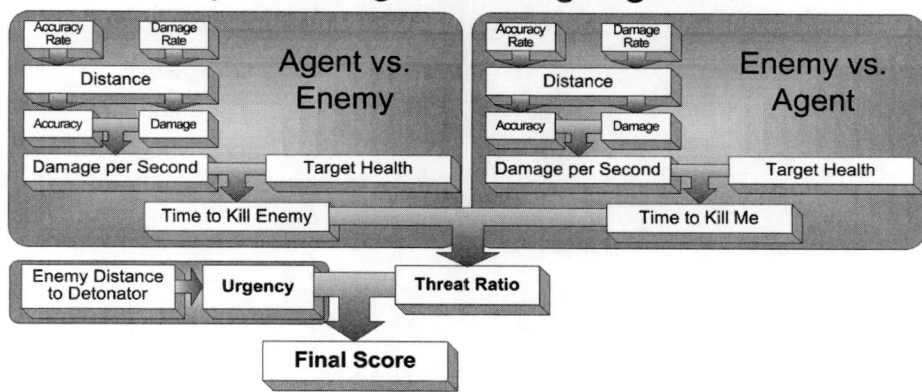

FIGURE 14.11 The scoring algorithm for selecting a target and a weapon combination cascades through many levels. We combine Time to Kill Enemy with Time to Kill Me, to arrive at Threat Ratio, which we then combine with Urgency to yield our final score for the target.

/* *In Chapter 16, we will show some alternatives for selecting options that will allow us to create less predictable, deeper-looking behaviors in our agents.* */

TESTING THE ALGORITHM

We will now take our new algorithm for a complete test drive to test some combinations of factors. When conducting this process, it is best to start with something simple and predictable. For example, if we place our three Dudes the same distance away from us and the same distance away from the detonator, and arm them all with the same weapon, we eliminate many of the possible variables.

Parameters:

Dude	Distance	Dist. to Det.	Weapon
Baddie	150	100	Machine Gun
Evilmeister	150	100	Machine Gun
Boss Man	150	100	Machine Gun

Results:

Name	Weapon	Threat	Urgency	Score
Baddie	Pistol	754.6	0.369	2,044.7
Baddie	M/G	6.9	0.369	18.8
Baddie	Shotgun	754.6	0.369	2,044.7
Baddie	R/L	7.0	0.369	19.0
Evilmeister	Pistol	753.1	0.369	2,040.8
Evilmeister	M/G	6.6	0.369	18.1
Evilmeister	Shotgun	753.1	0.369	2,040.8
Evilmeister	R/L	6.7	0.369	18.3
Boss Man	Pistol	752.7	0.369	2,039.6
Boss Man	M/G	7.4	0.369	20.1
Boss Man	Shotgun	752.7	0.369	2,039.6
Boss Man	R/L	7.5	0.369	20.4

As we can see, because all the Dudes are at the same distance and using the same weapon, their threat ratios are very similar. The difference comes from two factors. First, the differences in their accuracy rates adjusts how much damage they can do to us. Boss Man will be a little more dangerous to us, and Baddie will be slightly less so.

Second, the different types of Dudes have different amounts of health (50, 75, and 100). This makes a significant difference in how long it takes us to kill them. This yields an interesting result. Notice that killing the lowly Baddie is the second-most-preferable option. Despite the fact that Baddie is a less dangerous attacker, because of his lower health, we can kill him quickly. The difference is small, but in such a similar situation as this, we might as well get him out of the picture. In this situation, though, our algorithm suggests that killing an Evil Dude (in this case, Mr. Evilmeister) is our best bet. Also, given the distance, our trusty algorithm informs us that our best choice is the machine gun.

Because the distance to the detonator is the same for all three Dudes, the urgency ratings are all the same. Therefore, there is no change in the best choice as reflected by the final score. We should whip out our trusty machine gun and let Evilmeister have it!

Here... Use This Instead

If we make one change to the above scenario and give Evilmeister a shotgun, his threat ratio drops significantly. At 150 feet away, he can't hurt us. Replacing only his lines from the above table, we can see how his threat ratio (and his final score) changes.

Name	Weapon	Threat	Urgency	Score
Evilmeister	Pistol	1,000.0	0.369	2,709.7
Evilmeister	M/G	253.5	0.369	687.0
Evilmeister	Shotgun	1,000.0	0.369	2,709.7
Evilmeister	R/L	253.6	0.369	687.3

Evilmeister's threat scores are high enough that he is taken completely out of the running as our prime target. (Lucky him!) Notice that the threat ratio for using a pistol or a shotgun is pinned at 1,000. This is as we designed. Because a pistol and shotgun can't reach him at 150 feet, the damage we could due with those two weapons is 0. They are not even considered.

Because Evilmeister is no longer a threat, we turn our attention to Baddie the Bad Dude, who still comes in with a score slightly under (more important than) Boss Man.

Back Off, Son!

We will grudgingly give Evilmeister back his machine gun for the moment. There is something else we need to test. What would happen, for example, if Baddie were to begin to approach us? If we change the distance to Baddie to 100 feet rather than 150, his accuracy and damage rate go up. That makes him more dangerous. Of course, our rates go up as well, making it easier for us to kill him. As we would expect, Baddie becomes a higher priority as he gets closer to us. Again, showing only Baddie's new data:

Name	Weapon	Threat	Urgency	Score
Baddie	Pistol	29.0	0.369	78.6
Baddie	M/G	5.3	0.369	14.3
Baddie	Shotgun	753.4	0.369	2,041.6
Baddie	R/L	4.3	0.369	11.8

When we recall that the prior best score before Baddie made his move was Evilmeister's 18.1, we can see how much those 50 feet meant. Not only should we now attack Baddie, but we should do it with our rocket launcher. The reason for the weapon switch is because of the accuracy and damage curves that we designed very early on. A quick glance at Figure 14.6 reminds us that the rocket launcher is our most effective weapon at a range of 100 feet. (We should notice as well that while the shotgun is still not a good choice, the pistol is now something to at least consider.)

Don't Touch That!

So far, all we have changed is the Dudes' distance to us. Because we have not changed their respective distances to the detonator, the urgency scores have not changed. To test the effect this has on our scenario, let's assume that Boss Man has made a break for the dastardly device. His path takes him no nearer to us, however. The only distance that is changing is the range to the detonator—to which he is coming alarmingly close. To complete the picture, we will leave Baddie at his closer range of 100 feet. The updated parameters, therefore, are:

Dude	Distance	Dist. to Det.	Weapon
Baddie	100	100	Machine Gun
Evilmeister	150	100	Machine Gun
Boss Man	150	20	Machine Gun

As we would expect, as Boss Man gets closer to his goal, our urgency to drop him increases. To help us make the various comparisons, we will list all 12 options again.

Name	Weapon	Threat	Urgency	Score
Baddie	Pistol	29.0	0.369	78.6
Baddie	M/G	5.3	0.369	14.3
Baddie	Shotgun	753.4	0.369	2,041.6
Baddie	R/L	4.3	0.369	11.8
Evilmeister	Pistol	753.1	0.369	2,040.8
Evilmeister	M/G	6.6	0.369	18.1
Evilmeister	Shotgun	753.1	0.369	2,040.8
Evilmeister	R/L	6.7	0.369	18.3
Boss Man	Pistol	752.7	0.669	1,125.9
Boss Man	M/G	7.4	0.669	11.1
Boss Man	Shotgun	752.7	0.669	1,125.9
Boss Man	R/L	7.5	0.669	11.3

Checking back against our original results shows us that the threat scores for Boss Man have not changed. This makes sense because his weapon, our weapon, and the distance between us have not changed. On the other hand, because he is now only 20 feet away from the detonator, our urgency level for him has climbed to 0.669. Despite the fact that Baddie and Evilmeister have a more important (lower) threat ratio than does Boss Man, the Arch Dude's proximity to the awful annihilatory apparatus drops his final score under that of the other options. Our decision would now be to attack Boss Man with our machine gun.

Dude, There Were Dudes Everywhere!

In one last test, our original three Dudes are joined by reinforcements. There are now eight Dudes total: four Bad Dudes, three Evil Dudes, and their infamous Arch Dude leader, Boss Man. They are armed with different weapons, and arrayed at different distances away from us and from the detonator.

Dude	Distance	Dist. to Det.	Weapon
Baddie 1	40	50	Pistol
Baddie 2	80	125	Machine Gun
Baddie 3	30	130	Shotgun
Baddie 4	60	90	Shotgun
Evil Genius	120	80	Rocket Launcher
Evil Knievel	180	40	Machine Gun
Evilmeister	60	110	Machine Gun
Boss Man	90	125	Rocket Launcher

At first glance, it is difficult to sort through the list and determine who might be the highest-priority target. Consider the following observations:

- Baddie 3 is closest to us and has a powerful shotgun.
- Evil Knievel is closest to the detonator.
- Baddie 1 is close to us *and* to the detonator.
- Baddies 1 through 4 have only 50 points of health and are, therefore, the easiest to kill.
- Boss Man is the most accurate shot and has a rocket launcher.

Unfortunately, none of those observations bring us to the correct conclusion. Only when we run the information through our algorithm do we take *all* of that information into account, rate it according to the formulas we have devised, combine it in the ways we have defined, and arrive at a single score do we come to the most logical answer:

Use our rocket launcher to kill Evil Genius.

Because there are eight enemies and four weapon choices for each, there are 32 entries in our target list. Rather than clutter things up, we will only list the best weapon for each of the eight targets. (It's not much of a surprise that it's usually the rocket launcher, is it?)

Name	Weapon	Threat	Urgency	Score
Baddie 1	R/L	14.1	0.5218	27.0
Baddie 2	R/L	4.0	0.3101	13.1
Baddie 3	R/L	2.9	0.2992	9.7
Baddie 4	R/L	250.7	0.3950	634.7
Evil Genius	R/L	3.2	0.4229	7.7
Evil Knievel	M/G	8.0	0.5626	14.3
Evilmeister	R/L	3.3	0.3445	9.8
Boss Man	R/L	2.6	0.3101	8.5

As we ponder the stats, we begin to see why Evil Genius didn't immediately attract our attention. He ranks third on threat ratio (remember, lowest is most threatening) and third on urgency (higher is more urgent). If we had looked only at the disconnected data such as distance to us, distance to the detonator, weapon strength, and so on, we would not have detected the combination of information that makes Evil Genius the highest-priority target. (Rather ingenious of him, in an evil sort of way... don't you think?)

SUMMARIZING THE DECISION PROCESS

While it seems like it was a long road to accomplish the decision of which Dude to assault with which weapon, by breaking it down into individual steps, we were able to simplify the *entire* process.

One of the important decisions *we* made about constructing our *agent's* decision is what the decision was going to entail. As we theorized early in the chapter and subsequently confirmed in our last example, we could not have separated the two individual choices of who to attack and what weapon to use. Doing so may have led us to less-than-optimum results. This is reminiscent of the Prisoner's

Dilemma, where thinking *only* about our own choice rather than taking into consideration our partner's mindset led us to an acceptable yet not optimal solution. Only when we considered *both* of the inputs and results did we arrive at the best possible outcome.

Once we decided what it was we were going to decide, we identified the individual components of the whole decision and dealt with each portion individually. Establishing compartmentalized confidence in each of those steps as we went along freed us up to concentrate *only* on the next step. For example, we were confident that the formulas for the accuracy of the weapons were accurate. We were also confident that the formulas for the damage from the weapons were accurate. Feeling good about both of those *as individual functions*, we felt comfortable combining the two into *damage per second*. Feeling that damage per second was an accurate measurement of strength, we felt quite secure in the validity of comparing *our* damage-dealing power with that of the enemy. We continued the process of adding more layers—each layer *only* concerned with the one immediately before it. In the end, we arrived at our final decision of who to attack and with what.

One of the payoffs of the time we spent in developing this model is that our agent is now highly dynamic. It responds well to changes in its environment. As Dudes move, it adapts. Adaptation and change in AI agents is one of the major steps in making AI seem more "alive" than mechanical and scripted.

There's Always Something Bigger

That doesn't have to be the end, however. We could have continued to combine this result with something else. For example, we could introduce the idea of other actions that are *not* related to attacking: fleeing, hiding, surrendering, grabbing a health pack or a new weapon, running to a detonator of our own, or even pausing to take a photo to memorialize the occasion.

To incorporate these other possibilities, we would build a process similar to the one for attacking and, as we have done a few times already, define a connection algorithm between them. Our process above then becomes part of a bigger picture. Rather than simply asking, "Who do we kill and with what?" a higher-level component would be asking, "*If we decide to attack*, who would we kill and with what?" There is a subtle difference between those two statements. The former is a final decision; the latter is a suggestion.

The difference becomes clearer if we imagine processing the decision from the top down, instead. Imagine that our first decision was between the nebulous concepts of *attack*, *flee*, *hide*, *get health*, *get weapon*, and *take memorial photo*. How can we decide between them without knowing more about their relative merits? Sure, we can decide that *get health* is a high priority if we are low on health, but if there is no health pack nearby, the arbitrary decision to "go get some health" could send us off on a wild goose chase (because everyone knows that geese provide health). We can't decide to hide unless we know there are decent hiding places nearby. What constitutes "nearby" anyway? And what are we hiding *from*? What if we could easily win the battle because the *attack* decision tells us the Dudes that are arrayed against us have no hope at all? We would have no reason to hide even if there *was* "the very bestest hiding place in the history of ever" right next to us! In fact, because we completely overpower them, we *can* take a moment to fulfill that burning desire to pause and take a photo of the poor Dudes for our MySpace page prior to blowing them up.

The point is, all of those decisions are related through information that is specifically tied to them. Based on criteria that each would process on its own—*hide* needing a convenient hiding spot, for example—the possible decisions would generate their own utility values. We can then compare and contrast these utility values to decide which action best suits our needs at the moment.

The moral of the story of the Dudes is:

- We can't make decisions without information.
- Information is often ambiguous until we relate it to something.
- We can combine lots of little decisions into bigger decisions.
- We can roll bigger decisions into huge decisions.
- Beware the Evil Genius with the rocket launcher!

There is one problem with all of the above, however: Information rarely stays the same—and especially not for very long.

So *then* what do we do?

15 Changing a Decision

In the last chapter, we illustrated many aspects of what goes into a making a decision. Indeed, throughout much of this book, we have thought about a decision as a static, isolated event—a puzzle to be solved. We have even examined some of the examples from various starting states.

In the example in Chapter 13, we looked at how the weighted decision model for "what to do for dinner" yielded a different output *if* we offered it different inputs. We didn't address the situation in terms of *when* the inputs change. The scenario for a given evening (i.e., the time and price restrictions and our desire for types of food) was presented as inputs to the algorithm. The algorithm crunched the numbers and gave us an output. We were done. There was no further consideration given to what to have for dinner. One situation led to a single choice.

Similarly, in Chapter 14, we laid out numerous starting conditions for our Dude assault. What types of Dudes are we facing? What weapons are they carrying? Where are they? Where is the detonator? We can represent all of those conditions in a single slice of time—the world as it is *now*. That slice is as thin as the simulation rate—a single frame of information… literally, a fraction of a second. We proceed with the decision process based only on that snapshot and yield a decision just as static. This is what we are doing *now*.

But then what?

The problem with a static, thin-sliced mentality is that time and circumstances are usually fluid. Situations change. Information varies. Inputs fluctuate. Accordingly, our decisions must adapt as well. On the other hand, changing our decision can be a weakness as well as a strength, as we shall examine in a little bit. Before we get too involved with the caveats, however, we need to address whether we need to change our minds in the first place.

Monitoring a Decision

Just because a decision is valid at one point in time doesn't mean it will always be so. When we base a decision entirely on information that we input into it from the world, we tie the decision itself directly to that information. That is not to say that *any* change in input would automatically yield a different decision. The problem we have is that we don't necessarily know *what* changes will cascade into a different output.

For instance, looking back at our Dude example from the previous chapter, it is unlikely that if any one of the Dudes took one step in any direction there would be a significant enough effect in the output to warrant a change in the decision. But how many steps *would* constitute enough of an adjustment? And what if *all* the Dudes were moving? And what if *all* of the Dudes' health levels were fluctuating? And what if our ammo was changing? If all the inputs are changing, even in small amounts, the combination of all the changes makes for a dizzying array of possibilities.

To account for the possibility that our results *will* change, we need to establish a method of monitoring those inputs so that our agent can respond accordingly. Unfortunately, there is no single solution to this problem. The approaches to monitoring a scenario are as widely varied as the procedures for generating the decision in the first place. As we have seen throughout this book, there is no single, all-encompassing answer. However, we do have some general considerations that we can take into account. By matching these tools to the task at hand, we can build our routines in a way that solves the problem we are attempting to address.

Time Frames

One of the first concerns that we must address is *how often* we are going to check ourselves. We can think of this in the same manner as the concept of granularity that we discussed in Chapter 13. We want to establish a "Goldilocks" rule on how often to reprocess our decisions that is a balance between too often and not often enough.

Sometimes the time frame of the decision is obvious. For example, it would be overkill to process the "what to do for dinner" decision very often. In fact, one could make the case that once a night is enough (although we will throw a wrench into that in a minute). Other times, the notion of how often to reanalyze our decision may be a little more obscure.

If we were driving down the street in traffic, how often should we consider changing lanes? Is it something that we, as *human* drivers think about multiple times per second? Every second? Every five seconds? (On second thought, I know some people who seem to follow that rule.) What if we were on a highway in western

Nebraska with no other traffic in sight? Would you need to *ever* think of changing lanes? (For my gentle readers who have not been to western Nebraska, think of a highway on the moon instead.)

It could be just as awkward to think about changing lanes over a longer period such as five minutes, however. What if a situation arose where a lane change was not only available, but desirable? Or even necessary? We would look a little silly sitting there waiting patiently for our "lane-change timer" to expire. (On second thought, I know people like this, too.) The problem is that there is no "natural" interval at which we should consider changing lanes.

While the correct approach to any given problem may be a little obscure at times, we can generally narrow it down to one of four approaches:

- Every frame (continuous recalculation)
- Defined time periods
- Polling for changes
- In response to an external event

Let's examine the strengths and weakness of each approach.

Continuous Recalculation

The term *continuous recalculation* doesn't evoke a lot of mystery about how often we are reprocessing the world. In a nutshell, this method recalculates a decision every frame. The only variation is how many frames per second we are running. Suffice to say, for all intents and purposes, this method is equivalent to "as fast as we possibly can."

There are uses for this approach throughout much of artificial intelligence (AI). Simulation of flight, racing, aiming, and other continuous forms of movement, for example, depends heavily on continuously updating speed and directional control to match the information of the exact moment. Animation AI needs to know the position of body, the states various limbs are in, what objects are in the way, and what forces are present. One could make the case, however, that these items are *reactions* and not *decisions* or *behaviors*. While reactions certainly do need to be updated quickly, continuous updates aren't as appropriate for behavioral AI.

Above, we suggested that our decision on what to do for dinner should be calculated once per evening. Barring certain contingencies (such as receiving a phone call from friends inviting us over), imagine our dinner decision being constantly monitored with the question, "Are we still having microwave burritos? Are we still having microwave burritos? Are we still having…" (I'll quit there. You probably get the point.) The continual analysis of a decision that we have already made and that is unlikely to change quickly is horribly inefficient (and sounds amazingly like a four-year-old).

Defined Time Periods

Going back to the reactions vs. behaviors question, from a pragmatic standpoint, one argument to *not* use continuous processing is a matter of reaction time. Human reaction time to a stimulus generally runs in the range of 150–300 milliseconds. A game running at 50 frames per second averages 20 ms per frame. Therefore, a human reaction time would be about 7 to 15 frames.

For purposes of calculation, let us use 12 frames (240 ms) as our typical benchmark. If our agent reprocesses the world every frame, and *reacts* to changes in the world *in that same frame*, it is acting in *1/12* the time that a human would. What's more, if the stimulus continues to change every frame, our agent could theoretically make 12 different decisions in the time it *should* take for a real human to even react to the *first* stimulus.

/*

You can test yourself (and see the results of other people's tests) at http://www.humanbenchmark.com/tests/reactiontime/. All they ask is that you click the mouse when the image changes from red to green. (This is similar to the test that cab drivers in major urban areas put the rest of us through at stoplights—their horns being the punishment for failure.)

It's actually startling to realize how long it takes humans to react to things. I refuse to divulge what my average was... but I'm old. Let's just say that my teenagers fared significantly better. Even my teenagers' relatively rapid times and those of the people on the "high score" board make the idea of a single frame reaction look a little absurd.

*/

As we can see, continuous recalculation makes for serious overkill. We can mitigate this effect somewhat by ensuring that we don't process more than one reaction in a set amount of time. By waiting for an animation to finish before we check for another stimulus, for example, we can slow down our agent's hypersensitivity. If a "fire weapon" animation takes a full second, we can only decide to check for a new target at the end of each fire animation. We have limited the processing to once every 50 frames.

We can also set an arbitrary limit on how often an agent will process decisions. If, for example, we use the 240 ms reaction time as our guide, we can elect to have an agent only process a decision every 12 frames. By setting this pace for the reactions of one agent, we open up those frames to allow *other* agents to make their decisions.

Theoretically, 1/12 of our agents will be making a decision in any given frame. (We can actually specifically enforce this balance if we like.) This allows us to process *more* agents and still have a short enough reaction time to make our agents look and feel like they are reacting in human-like time spans. We aren't really modeling reaction time with this method, only taking advantage of the time that it gives us. The possibility still exists, for example, that the decision would be processed in a single frame.

We can make use of this time savings in other ways. If we use those extra frames to process *more information* about the world in *more depth*, we can possibly construct better behaviors. Using 12 frames rather than 1 to make a decision can be rather freeing. Exactly how we would do this depends largely on the type of decision we are making and the architecture we are using. Although an extended discussion on these techniques is beyond the scope of this book, some suggestions are multithreading and the well-documented techniques for spreading search algorithms (such as A*) over multiple frames.

Polling for Changes

While we mentioned above that one of the inefficiencies of constant recalculation is when the data hasn't changed much, there is the possibility that the data has not changed *at all* from frame to frame. If the data that we are incorporating in the decision has not changed, we are processing the same inputs only to repeatedly arrive at the same decision. To avoid this problem, we first check to see if any of our inputs have changed. If they have, we can then proceed with recalculating the decision. We refer to this method of asking the world for information as **polling**.

Polling has serious drawbacks, however. To check if something has changed, we have to remember what it was before. This means that an agent would have to remember the state of *all* of the inputs that it uses in *all* of its decisions. Multiply this by multiple agents and the data demands can increase rapidly.

Continuously polling the world to see if an event has happened that would require a change in decisions is taxing to the processor. Imagine the simple act of an agent determining if anyone in the local area has thrown a grenade that he would need to react to. That seemingly simple test involves the following steps:

1. Determine enemies in range of agent.
2. Determine if agent has line of sight to enemies.
3. Check each visible enemy to see if they have thrown a grenade since the last time we checked.
4. Determine if grenade will land close to us.
5. *If necessary*, process the reaction.

Simply recalculating the enemies in range and determining if we have a line of sight to them (items 1 and 2) is an expensive proposition. Asking each enemy if he has thrown a grenade every frame (or even every few frames) when it is statistically likely that they have *not* done so, is wasting precious clock cycles. For example, if an agent only throws a grenade on average every 30 seconds, that is 1,500 times we must ask (at 50 frames per second, or fps) to receive *one* "yes" answer. If we also decide to check to see if they have aimed a weapon, fired a weapon, taken a step in any direction, surrendered, died, or stopped to take a memorial photo of the moment, we are asking a lot of repetitive questions for very little gain.

Event-Driven Recalculations

The usual solution to "polling paralysis" is an event-driven model. Rather than having each agent poll the environment to see if anything has changed in the 20 ms since he last checked, we can instruct agents to tell each other if *they* have done anything. We call this an **event-based** system.

In our dinner example, receiving a phone call from friends inviting us over is an event that we can specifically associate with the dinner decision. Naturally, despite having made our decision earlier, we can use this excuse to recalculate our plans (with the addition of a new option).

Using an event-based system, we broadcast actions performed by *one* agent to *other* agents. For example, if our agent throws a grenade, he performs steps one and two above and sends a message to the other nearby agents informing them that he has done something that is worth of their attention. Only *then* do the other agents know to include the new grenade in their decision process. The new action list is now:

1. Determine enemies in range of agent.
2. Determine if enemies have line of sight to agent (notice we reversed this).
3. *If necessary*, inform each affected agent of the event.

More importantly, rather than performing the above tasks every frame, we only execute them when there is something to say. In our grenade example, if we only lob a grenade every 30 seconds, we only send a "grenade!" message out every 30 seconds. We have achieved a 1:1 efficiency rate.

Unfortunately, this is not a completely fail-safe solution either. We may not *want* our decision-making agent to wait until the state of the world changes. We have all played games where an enemy sat and waited, doing *nothing* until some trigger event happened. This is most noticeable in games where an enemy gets "aggroed" (angered into attacking) by the proximity or line of sight to a player. In older games, the agent would idle in either a state of suspended animation or an idle loop.

Some recent games have incorporated more realistic-looking combinations of idle behaviors that don't rely on player-triggered events. Despite the *appearance* of added complexity, however, the enemy is still "waiting for something."

A completely event-triggered method can also be extremely brittle. Depending on when and in what order the messages arrive, our agents may react in different and unexpected ways. Even messages that arrive in the *same frame* may be processed in an order that leads to problems simply because of the order they were placed in the message queue. Also, considering that some of the actions that we may trigger as a result of a message can take a significant amount of time to perform (especially when measured in 20 ms frames), we may effectively preclude a response to something that needs to be considered.

For example, if we receive a message that causes our agent to decide to do something relatively mundane (such as answering the phone), we initiate that task, and *then* receive information of a high priority (the grenade), we may not process that information until much later. Our agent can get stuck doing the mundane task when he needed to consider something else.

The mechanics of event-driven architectures, the messaging systems that support them, and the difficulties involved in interrupting animations are well documented in other books. However, it is important to be aware that they exist from a conceptual standpoint.

A Hybrid Approach

As we have seen with the various tools and techniques throughout this book, a combination approach is often called for. We can draw from the strengths of the different methods to build an appropriate self-monitoring scheme. As we discussed at length in Chapter 2, observation of our own behaviors holds many clues to what the proper approach is. Just as we broke down a decision process into smaller values, formulas, and algorithms, we can subdivide the decision-monitoring process into component parts.

For example, think about what we do when we drive a car—an example we touched on briefly above. The decisions we make require a reevaluation of our environment to determine that our current course of action is the correct one. For simplicity's sake, let's list only the factors we consider to determine if we should change our speed. While we monitor many items on a regular basis, we monitor none of them on a *continual* basis—that is, taking up *all* of our attention. We tend to alternate our attention between the following:

- Our current perceived speed
- Our current reported speed

- The current posted speed limit
- The proximity of the next traffic light
- The state of the next traffic light
- The proximity of the nearest traffic ahead of us
- The speed of the nearest traffic ahead of us
- The speed of traffic *ahead of* the traffic ahead of us
- The speed of traffic near us that may help or interfere with our plans (for a lane change, for example)
- Unexpected events to which we may have to react

While all of those components are factors that we would want to build into a decision on whether to speed up, slow down, apply the brakes, or maintain our current velocity, we certainly don't think about them all at the same time. How often do we make a mental note of our speed, for example? Every few seconds? Most of us likely check our speedometer even less than we make a mental note of our speed—perhaps every 10 seconds. How often do we consciously look for the posted speed limit? More likely in the process of "scanning the world" we happen to notice the sign and compare it to our mental record of what we thought it was.

While we may make a note of how far away the next traffic light is, we don't continually monitor its state until it is close enough that we would need to react to a change. (My father gleefully tells the story of how, when I was three years old, upon seeing a traffic light at the next corner turn red, I would stop walking… even if I was in the middle of the block. Obviously my AI was still being debugged at age three.)

Determining Minimum Granularity

Most of the examples in the above list are addressable by setting different timers for checking information. One problem with this analogy, however, is that we have a hard time differentiating between the *collection* of information and the *reprocessing* of a decision. In a computer situation, the information is already there. We aren't necessarily modeling the sensory system of "checking the speed." Our driver agent already "knows" the speed. We aren't modeling the process of looking out the window at the scenery and occasionally glancing at the car ahead of us or the distant traffic light. All of that information is immediately accessible. By only processing the decision calculations occasionally rather than continuously, we are leveraging the fact that people *don't* process stimuli that quickly.

If we were to list the time periods between updates of the different actions in the list, we would find a range of times. We, as drivers, may perform some of the actions every second, some every few seconds, and some every minute or so. It would not make sense for us to wait until we have updated *everything*, however. In fact, the opposite is true. If we have updated *any* of our information, we need to reprocess the *entire* decision using the information that we already have. What we are establishing is a **minimum granularity**. If the shortest update interval is one second, for instance, it is possible that our information would change in as little as one second. Therefore, we need to reprocess our decision at that interval.

Interrupting with an Event

The one glaring exception that doesn't work on a timed-update-based system is the final item: unexpected events. Almost by definition, continually checking for an unexpected event is counter-productive. This is where the event-based system is helpful. Putting our driving example into computer terms, if the driver ahead slams on his brakes, that car sends an "I'm braking!" message to other nearby cars. The effect is much like the grenade message earlier. This event would immediately trigger a recalculation—not necessarily to stop (what if the driver "ahead of us" is a full block ahead?), but to recalculate our current situation and construct an appropriate decision. In essence, the message is telling us, "You *really* need to recalculate everything *right now*!"

Timers as Interrupts

By constructing the timers we discussed above so that they send messages as well, we effectively combine the two methods. The difference is minor and mostly logistical. The agent's message receiver (again, beyond the scope of this book) would not need to differentiate whether the message instructing him to recalculate the decision arrived from an internal timer or an external event. The result is the same: "Recalculate now."

| IN THE GAME | **Dudes Revisited** |

In the previous chapter, we constructed an elaborate method of determining who the "best" target is for us to shoot. Let us now examine the possible solutions for how and when to reexamine our decision and, possibly, reevaluate our target.

First, we *do* have a natural division that we can work from—one shot. The rationale for using a single shot as the minimum granularity is simple; we can't change targets in the middle of a shot. Of course, the time period that each shot may take is different. Shooting our machine gun is a fairly rapid event. Similarly, a pistol is quick but requires more effort to aim. The shotgun doesn't require as much time to aim, but the reload time is going to be more involved. Lastly, the rocket launcher is slower to wield, slower to aim, *and* slower to reload. The result of this is that, while we have a defined *action* that constitutes a single decision, we don't have a single amount of *time*.

The solution, therefore, is to recalculate the decision of whom to shoot next after the conclusion of each shot. As we prepare to shoot the next target, we proceed with all the nifty stuff that goes into facing the target and aiming. Upon completion of that shot (regardless of how long that takes), the decision about whom to pummel next is reevaluated and the process starts anew.

This seems simple and foolproof at the moment, but there are plenty of wrenches that we could find haphazardly lobbed into our tidy little process. For example, consider the following sequence:

1. We complete a shot at Bad Dude.
2. We reload our weapon.
3. We process the decision of whom to shoot next.
4. We turn toward the target.
5. We raise our weapon.
6. We aim our weapon.
7. We get ready to fire… and…
8. We find that Bad Dude is *already dead!*

Somewhere between step 3 and step 8, the decision of whom to dispatch was rendered irrelevant. While this might not look too out of the ordinary for a fast-firing weapon such as a machine gun or a pistol, our agent would look startlingly ridiculous going through the protracted action of aiming a rocket launcher at the space *formerly* occupied by a Bad Dude. If we only build our model to recalculate *after* a shot, we have to go through with the shooting process to select a new target. What's more, if the game code insists that the actual act of shooting requires a valid, live target to complete, we may now be stuck.

To avoid all of this, we can add a verification process throughout steps 3 through 7. In essence, we are asking the simple question, "Can I still do this?" If not, we can trigger our decision evaluation process immediately (through an event message, for example).

To make this process more involved, let us return to the idea that the decision about "who to shoot" is only a part of the whole. At the end of Chapter 14, we listed other actions that we could consider: fleeing, hiding, surrendering, grabbing a health pack or a new weapon, running to a detonator of our own, or (as we so glibly joked) pausing to take a photo to memorialize the occasion. When we consider those actions as well, the line that demarks when we should process a new decision is a little more blurry.

If we are hiding, for example, when do we peek out? How often do we think about peeking out? If we have decided to head off in pursuit of the health pack in the distance, what happens if someone else takes it first? Or shoots a rocket at it? Or simultaneously makes a break for the world-ending detonator? All of those are situations that *may* cause us to change our mind about what we should be doing. Continuing on with our current course of action could make us look… well… *less than intelligent*.

The answers to some of those events are triggers. A Dude shooting a rocket at us is certainly a trigger that would get our attention and spur us into careful reconsideration of our priorities. On the other hand, some of the criteria are polling-based. "Is the health kit still there?" is very similar to checking to see if our target is still alive, for example.

Other answers are a little harder to nail down. For instance, we don't want to trigger an event *every* time a Dude moves. We would never stop triggering events! We can stick to polling the relevant information about the location of the Dudes to determine if any one of them is either an urgent threat or an opportunistic easy kill. However, if our polling interval is too long, the Dude may get a jump on his dash for the doomsday switch before we can react.

Again, there isn't a "right" answer that covers every contingency. We must keep in mind, however, is that we must find that elusive balance between useless reprocessing and the accuracy of the current decision.

PERSEVERANCE AND DECISION MOMENTUM

While changing our mind at appropriate times and for appropriate reasons is a necessity to building agents that react adequately to their surroundings, problems can result. Even a *seemingly* logical decision change—in both the timing and content—can be perceived as odd, unproductive, or incorrect. What's worse, by making our agents reactive to their environment, we can be opening them up to manipulation and exploits.

Rather than doing theory first and then an example, let's reverse the process.

IN THE GAME — Flotilla of Futility

Consider the following example (Figure 15.1):

In a tile-based strategy game, we have assembled our naval fleet for a bombardment and invasion. We analyze the coastal cities of our enemy to determine which one is the most vulnerable. After using our complicated utility algorithm, we decide to attack Dudetown (I just had to use the Dudes again!), an ill-defended city on the western side of the continent. Our fleet sets out in the direction of the soon-to-be-ravaged city (1).

When the fleet has traveled a significant portion of the distance (2), we reevaluate the situation by once again analyzing the coastal cities. Much to our surprise, we find that another city, Suckerville, is completely unprotected! Our trusty attack algorithm determines that you can't get much better than an undefended city. We issue new orders to our fleet to head in the direction of Suckerville. Unfortunately, our new target happens to be on the *eastern* side of the continent. Oh well, for the easy spoils, it is worth the trip.

All the way around the continent (3), we continue to check our status. Every time, the still-undefended Suckerville comes up on top of our priority list. Upon closing to attack range of Suckerville (4), we are astounded to discover that, at the last moment, our enemy has moved large numbers of defensive units into the city. Strangely (and almost simultaneously, it seems), the heretofore well-fortified Dudetown is now devoid of military occupation!

Well aware that an attack on Suckerville would be met with fierce resistance, we see Dudetown once again as a *far* more attractive target. Our ships turn around (5) and begin the long trip back around the continent toward what *must be* inevitable victory on the western rim of this vast land (6).

As we once again spot the doomed city of Dudetown on the horizon (7), we check our intelligence reports one last time and find… wait a minute… *are you kidding me?!?*

Anyone who has played strategy games probably uttered a knowing chuckle about two paragraphs in. It turns out that Suckerville was appropriately named. Our decision model, and by association, our fleet, was exploited by the enemy.

This is a common technique to confuse the AI. It is most effective in tile-based games where there is a distinct grid space that defines "in the city." Moving all the military units one space outside of a city causes the AI that is analyzing the potential targets to see the city as being completely undefended.

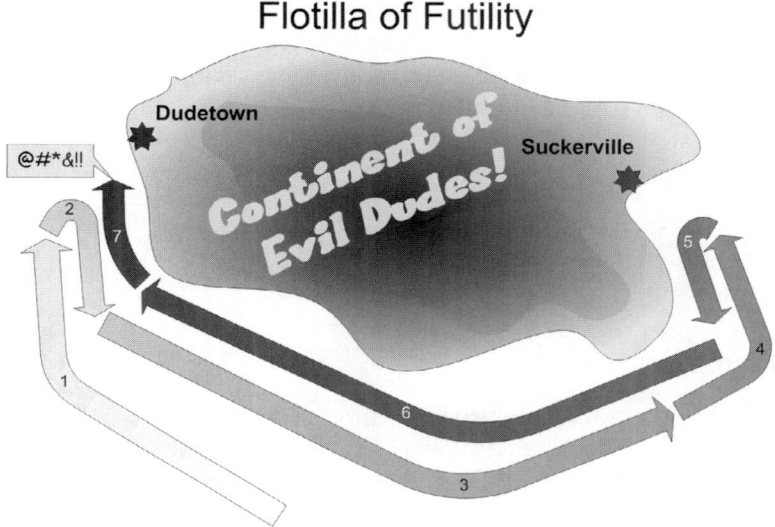

FIGURE 15.1 By not taking the travel time into account, the AI fleet does not realize that it is wasting significant time alternating between two distant goals.

When the fleet approaches the city, the player moves the units back into the city. Simultaneously, the player removes units from a distant and otherwise safe city somewhere else. The AI, upon recalculating the situation, views the *second* city as a prime target—especially when compared to the original target that is now mysteriously bristling with defenders. Using the same, simple utility model, the AI picks the "best target" and sets off.

The player can repeat this process with a minimum of attention and effort. It also effectively takes the AI player's navy completely out of the game. None of the player's cities get attacked because the AI can't ever settle on a decision—at least not long enough to act on it. If the naval forces are an *invasion* force to the continent, the benefits are even more significant. The player can live quite comfortably as long as he needs to in relative peace. He has not built defenses of stone and steel; he has built a defense of flawed logic and confusion.

Oh yeah… and the AI looks bad. We may as well put him in dark glasses and a stupid hat.

There are a number of ways that our AI can stumble in the manner exemplified above. The AI in the above scenario fell prey to one of the classic blunders (the most famous of which is, never get involved in a land war in Asia): It didn't take into account all of the possible inputs. We will explore the exact mechanics of what went wrong in a moment. By not taking key factors into account, it allowed itself to be led into alternating between decisions. This is a phenomenon known as **strobing**, **flip-flopping**, or even just **flipping**.

While strobing can manifest in many ways, the common thread is the effect that strobing has—*nothing*. In mild cases, strobing AI can look inefficient or muddled. At its worst, strobing leads to the behavior seen in our example above where the fleet alternated between sailing toward one city and the other, never attacking either one.

IGNORING FUTILITY

While that example implied a nefarious player intentionally exploiting the decision algorithm of the fleet, AI agents can strobe between behaviors based on less direct and less obvious changes in their decision factors. In fact, a worse problem is when our game model generates strobing behaviors entirely on its own.

Agents that depend on each other for decision criteria can enter into a joint concert of strobing. To illustrate with a simple example (with yet another nod to Brother Occam), imagine two agents facing off in a Rock-Paper-Scissors contest. There is a twist to the game, however: each agent can see the other player's intention *before* they make their play and elect to change what they are going to do.

At first, each player selects randomly. Then, upon examination of the pending match, they can elect either to proceed or to change their selection. Because this is a zero-sum game, the only two outcomes are a win-loss combination or a draw. Unless there is a draw, *one* player is going to be on the losing side of the match. (Even a draw is less than preferable.) Naturally, one would expect the soon-to-lose player to be dissatisfied with this outlook and decide to change his play. Additionally, because he can see the other player's choice, he changes his selection such that it will put him in the position to win.

This act, of course, causes his *opponent* to be in the potential losing role. The logical reaction is for the second player to switch *his* play as well. You can see where this is headed, I'm sure. None of them will ever be satisfied with the pending outcome to actually *commit* to playing. Between the two of them, they will spend all of their time switching "weapons" in the battle and never fire a shot.

While this example might seem absurd, consider a scenario such as the Dude assault from Chapter 14. As part of the decision process, our agent took into account both the weapon that he was using and the one the *other* player was using. If the scenario was drawn up so that there were distinct strength vs. weakness correlations (as there are in Rock-Paper-Scissors), two agents with the same decision algorithm may engage in much the same dance.

The reason that we, as intelligent people, find this behavior absurd is that we recognize the futility of the situation. In fact, the popular (and generally very accurate) layman's definition of *insanity* is "doing the same thing over and over and expecting a different result." Given that one of the early structural flaws about which beginning programmers are cautioned is the "infinite loop," most of us are very cognizant of the fact that computers are blissfully unaware of the existence of, much less the absurdity of, futility. Unless instructed otherwise or until a different complication (such as your processor chip melting) brings it to a halt, a computer will contentedly repeat mundane tasks *ad infinitum*.

One of our tasks, then, is to make sure our AI agents *understand* the concept of futility. We can do this through pattern recognition or a variety of other esoteric techniques. However, it is usually better to avoid the situation altogether by providing the agent with more information and a better decision model.

BUILDING DECISION MOMENTUM

We often refer to the antithesis of strobing as **decision momentum**. The use of the word *momentum* is not entirely figurative. It actually is appropriate in a metaphorical sense. We use the word in the same sense as we use it in physics. In the world of Sir Isaac Newton, when something is barreling along in one direction, it is going to take something pretty big to get it to change direction, much less reverse its direction entirely.

Remember that in Newtonian physics, mass is only part of the equation. The momentum of an object is a product of its mass *and* its velocity. When two objects of equal mass meet in a collision, the one that is moving will "win" against the one that it is at rest. For example, imagine a moving billiard ball colliding with a stationary one. Despite their equal mass, the velocity of the system continues in the direction that the original, moving ball was going prior to the collision. However, if the moving billiard ball were to collide with something more massive such as a bowling ball (to extend things to easily illustrative lengths), the larger (albeit stationary) mass is going to be rather convincing that the hapless billiard ball needs to head back in the other direction. To sum up, the bowling ball had enough weight to reverse the direction of the entire system.

We can apply this to our choices as well. Once we have set about doing something, we have added velocity to our decision. (This is not a stretch, really. Don't we say that we have "put a plan in motion?") We can elect to continue performing that action—*unless and until* something "big enough" comes along to change our direction. Because information is the impetus that puts our decisions into motion in the first place, it is reasonable to assume that information is the force that would act upon our decisions to get them to change their course.

To do this, we judge the weight (now being used figuratively) of new information not only against the weight of the previous information, but against that weight times the velocity that the action is already traveling. If we already have committed heavily (see how these weight words work so well?) to a decision, the momentum of the system will be fairly significant. If information of equal weight to what we already used is placed in front of our decision, the idea of decision momentum tells us that we would continue on in the same direction. However, if we encounter new information that has *greater* weight than what we originally had considered, the pace of our overall decision system will slow down somewhat. The greater the difference in the weight of the information, the greater the effect it has on our decision. Eventually, if the new information becomes massive enough, it will act as the bowling ball above did, and our decision will reverse in the face of this imposing new mass of data.

Keeping this in mind, rather than focusing on stopping our decisions from strobing *after the fact*, we can ensure that enough of the relevant information is available for the agent to take into account so that the problem doesn't occur in the first place. Often, by making the agent a little more aware of information and a little more mindful of ramifications, we are giving it more "mass" and, therefore, more decision momentum. Rather than changing a decision on the fluctuations of the moment, our agents can persevere with their chosen course of action.

Time Commitment

In the Flotilla of Futility example above, there was one more piece of information that, if the AI had considered it, may have made the difference in its decision: *time*.

In Chapter 7, we spent some time pondering the utility of time as a component to consider in decisions. We discussed time *spent*, time *saved*, time *wasted*, and other such ways that we can view chronological matters. In one example, we set out a scenario in which we were deciding whether we wanted to accomplish goal A before goal B or vice versa. We illustrated how the decision depended on factors such as the relative value of the goals and the time it would take to travel to them. We complicated the situation a little more by introducing decay in the value of the goals over time. By doing so, we caused the time we spent traveling to the goals to be even more influential in the final decision calculation. All of those factors are transferable to the example of the aimless armada.

In the example above, the AI calculated the relative utility of attacking the two cities (and presumably others as well). The AI would have to weigh various pros and cons about his own fleet, the defenders, and so on. This is, of course, similar to the Dude Assault example from Chapter 14. This is where the calculation stopped, however. Unlike our decision regarding which Dude to fire a single shot at, there is a significant time commitment involved in execution of the naval attack. While a portion of the solution was the continual monitoring of the prospective targets for a change in their status, the weakness in the process was not monitoring what the resultant decision would entail.

The "attack" that we were deciding to launch only took into account the expected odds of success or failure and the relative worth of the target. All of those factors take place between the time the first shot is fired and the time the last defender (or attacker) gives up and throws down his weapons. There is no accounting for the *entirety* of the action. Put another way, rather than a decision about "what city to attack," the decision needed to be "what city to *travel to* and *then* attack." By considering the *whole* process as one decision, time is automatically included in the calculation.

Information Expiry

In addition to the utility of the time we would spend traveling to someplace or doing something, there is another reason that we need to consider time heavily in the decision-making process. An *intentional* exploit by a player is not the only reason we should treat the decision to attack a particular city with caution. In the highly dynamic environment that games tend to be, information has a "shelf life." Units are created and moved, defenses are constructed, values change… in short, *things happen*. Even if the decision to attack a city is a legitimate one based on the information we have, we have to question the likelihood that the information will still be valid by the time we get there.

This is similar, but not identical, to the "fog of war." The legendary "fog" encompasses how information may change while we are not able to view it. **Information expiry** deals with the prospect that information probably *will* change over time whether we are watching it or not.

We touched on this above when we discussed the value of updating information. However, by factoring in the possibility that the situation will be different as part of the initial decision process, we are taking a more proactive approach. Rather than the "we can always change our mind" method that continual updates provide, we are saying, "let's not even start."

While we could conduct complicated analyses of fluctuation frequencies and ranges, it is usually simpler to build the *idea* that the state of the world *could* change into the weight given to the time that we will need to spend. We can do this through biasing the marginal utility in a nonlinear way. Using a simple exponential model, we could say that our confidence in the validity of information drops away from 100% at an accelerating rate as time passes.

The graph in Figure 15.2, for example, follows one of our trusty formulas from Chapter 10.

$$Confidence = 1 - \frac{Turns^2}{1000}$$

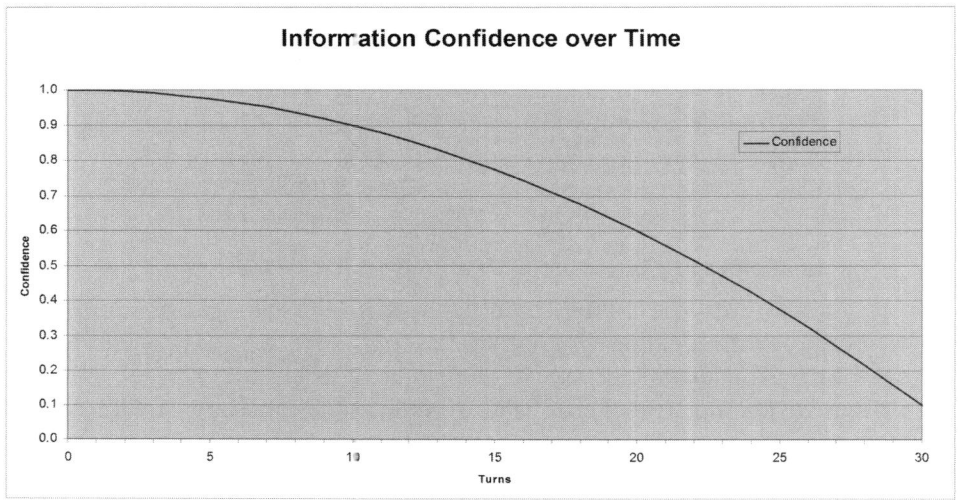

FIGURE 15.2 By constructing a decreasing marginal utility curve such as this one, we can simulate our gradual loss of confidence that what we know now will be relevant later.

If we can act on our decision in the next turn, we can remain fairly confident that the information we are acting on is going to still be valid when we get there. On the other hand, if it will take us 10 turns to arrive, we may only ascribe 90% confidence to the data. As the time frame lengthens, we grow *less* confident *more* quickly. Doubling the distance (and therefore the time) to a target would yield a 60% confidence rate per the formula above. At 25 turns, our confidence is 38%, and if it will take us 30 turns to arrive, we may only believe there is a 10% chance that our estimate will be correct.

We would only apply this confidence rating to information about items that are *not* in our control. In the example above, we would only apply it to the makeup of the city's defenses. The value of the city as a strategic target likely wouldn't change, and we know that the makeup of *our* forces won't change. (If it does, we would need to recalculate our plans anyway.)

Exactly *how* we apply this factor would depend largely on how we constructed the decision algorithm in the first place. However, it is usually a good idea to bias a distant objective pessimistically. For example, we would not serve ourselves well if we assumed that, by the time we arrived, the enemy will have graciously removed all their defenders.

In that respect, another method of biasing our decision is to *add* a pessimistic, time-based value to the strength of the opponents in the city. Imagine flipping the curve in Figure 15.2 upside down. Instead of a confidence factor moving *downward* from 1.0 toward 0, we could create a multiplier that moves *up* from 1.0. By using this value as a coefficient for the defenses, we are artificially inflating our estimate of the defense capabilities of the enemy. This could represent the possibility that they will see us coming and have time to move units into the city, for example. The result is that we will be *less* likely to consider that option as viable.

On the other hand, we must also take care to not paint such a bleak picture of *all* distant targets that our fleet despondently remains at anchor and doesn't do *anything*. Remember, much of the time we are using the information to bias an otherwise equal decision one way or another… not negate the whole process of action entirely.

The Value of Thoroughness

Not all of the considerations on whether or not to switch from one task to another are based on time, of course. Another significant factor reoccurs in many different types of decision processes—completing the task at hand. Unfortunately, one of the side effects of the task monitoring that we discussed at the beginning of the chapter is that our agent may be tempted to abandon what it was doing to perform what it believes is a higher priority task. While that is certainly laudable, and is a necessary part of a proper decision framework, we don't want our agents simply abandoning what they were doing because something else comes up. We would often end up with many partially finished projects and nothing that ever gets *completed*.

One simple illustration of this effect is a slight modification of our fleet example. Imagine that our little armada actually began to *attack* Dudetown rather than changing its goal before the assault. However, just as the last battered and bleeding defenders were about to fall, we received word that the distant Suckerville was undefended. If we leave at that moment and *don't* finish the sacking of Dudetown, we give the residents time to rebuild, the military time to regroup and heal, and perhaps even allow time for reinforcements to arrive. Even if we are only gone for a few turns, we may be right back where we started in our quest to eradicate Dudetown of all Dudes. What did we accomplish by our initial attack?

Finish Him!

In a similar way, we can extend our Dude assault example from Chapter 14. If we have selected our target, fired on him enough to *almost* kill him, and yet changed to target someone else who has become even *slightly* more preferable, we are still exposed to the threat of the original target. However, if we incorporate the utility of finishing the job, we would decide to continue attacking the wounded warrior until we have eliminated him. This is analogous to the mindset, "I have noticed that the Dude over *there* is now important. I will need to attack him next… *after* I finish killing this Dude."

This is especially important in games where the offensive capabilities of a unit are not reduced by the damage that it has sustained. For example, if we face four dudes who can do 10 points of damage each second, it doesn't matter if they each have 50% health remaining. We will still face all four of them and, as a result, continue to take 40 points of damage per second. On the other hand, if we had used the same firepower over time to completely kill two of the four dudes, we would have done the same amount of damage and yet reduced the damage to ourselves to 20 points per second instead of 40. The difference was, we *finished the job*. Taken to an extreme, if we were to continue alternating between different Dudes, we could theoretically face four Dudes who each have 1% health remaining—and are still dishing out 10 points of damage per second each. Obviously, this is not an efficient way to handle business.

We can return to the principles of increasing marginal utility (Chapter 8) to help us bias our decisions and imbue our current course of action with some extra momentum. We incorporated some of this already in our Dude assault algorithm by using the amount of remaining health that a Dude had left (instead of his maximum health) in our calculations. To recall two equations from Chapter 14, we first constructed *TimeToKill* out of some relevant information.

$$TimeToKill = \frac{TargetHealth}{Accuracy \times Damage}$$

We then used two different *TimeToKill* values to calculate *ThreatRatio*.

$$ThreatRatio = \frac{TimeToKillMe + (3 \times TimeToKillEnemy)}{4}$$

The effect that the *TimeToKill* results had on *ThreatRatio* was linear, however. If we replace the raw *TimeToKillEnemy* with a value that represents the *marginal utility* of the time it would take to kill an enemy, we could increase the meaningfulness of that factor in the formula as the time decreased. To do this, we could pass *TimeToKill* through a function that converts it from linear to exponential, for example.

Notice that this is different from simply changing the *weight* of the factor compared to *other* factors. This is utilizing a response curve to change the weight of the factor compared to *itself* over other ranges. For instance, we may not care so much if the target has 100% health or 90% health. That 10% difference doesn't mean much to us. We may be slightly more interested as the health drops to 80%. If the target's health is only 20%, however, we become *very* interested in trying to finish this Dude off—and need to increase the utility of this factor accordingly. Inflicting that last 20% of damage to the Dude is far more important to us than doing the first 20%.

Just Gimme a Minute, Boss!

Changing genres to something more constructive, we can use the concepts of marginal utility once again with regard to completion of buildings in a strategy game. If our game involves the allocation of time, labor, and resources to construct a building, we may want to continually check to see if there is something more important that the units should be building or doing. There would definitely be circumstances that would warrant a worker putting down his hammer for a moment to take up another task. (Being *attacked* comes to mind as something that Mr. Carpenter would find mildly distracting.) We may even decide that, despite our partially finished building, our labor or money needs to be diverted to a more important building. However, it would be tragic (and our players would view it as ridiculous) if our workers were to abandon a 99% completed building to start a new one elsewhere. Even if the new building is important, is it so urgent that our laborers couldn't simply finish the one they were working on first?

The incorporation of *increasing* marginal utility as we near completion artificially biases the importance of each successive hammer swing. As the building nears completion, we generate sufficient decision momentum to cause the workers to be more interested in completing their current task than shuffling off to a new one.

OUR FINAL DECISION ON CHANGING DECISIONS

As has been something of a mantra throughout this vast tome, there is no "right answer." What we have discussed above is a handful of considerations, caveats, and strategies. "Ways to think" is probably more accurate. There are a few things to remember.

First, we need to be willing to change decisions. We need to not be afraid to allow our agents to do so. After all, we *real* people do it all the time—and usually for good reason. On the other hand, the ability to change a decision is like a powerful weapon that can be deadly if it falls into the wrong hands.

Second, decisions do not exist in a vacuum. We can't simply process the world *as it is at that moment* and expect consistently realistic-looking results. Somehow we need to step out of the present and look at the whole picture—whether it is the repetitive strobing behaviors of the past or the possibility that the decision we make now will not be valid in the future.

Third, we must find that balance between making more decisions or fewer. More active processing adds to the responsiveness of our agent—but can make him *too* responsive and flighty. Less processing is more efficient and even somewhat more realistic but can lead to an appearance of indifference, bewilderment, or outright stupidity.

We can throw one final twist into our decision-making engine, however, and *this* is where the human-ness really sinks in! Rather than changing our mind about a decision we already made and replacing it with a newer, *better* decision, how about changing our mind about a decision that we are making and, before we act on it, decide to replace it with a *worse* one?

Confused? You could always decide to turn the page… unless you have changed your mind.

16 Variation in Choice

In the past few chapters, all of our examples have been solved by finding "the best" answer to the problem. We built all of our utility functions to rate and score the aspects of the decision, sorted the options by the score, and selected the one with "the best" score (be that highest or lowest). Naturally, this sounds strikingly like normative (or prescriptive) decision theory. In fact, if we recast it in the vernacular we used in Chapter 4, we were determining what we *should* do. Remember that normative decision theory assumes that our agent:

- Has *all* of the relevant information available
- Is able to *perceive* the information with the accuracy needed
- Is able to perfectly *perform* all the calculations necessary to apply those facts
- Is perfectly *rational*

We spent a good deal of time in Part II of this book showing examples of how humans just don't do what is *perfectly rational*. On the other side of the spectrum, descriptive decision theory tells us what people *elect* to do. More specifically, it reports what they have *already* done. Because our data for how demons from the underworld will counter the assault of a single space marine is somewhat lacking, we have to construct our own models—which defies the survey-based definition of descriptive decision theory.

Our goal, however, is to create behaviors that only *look* like they are born out of the wide palette of descriptive decision theory's data. The first step in this direction is *away* from the single "best answer" that normative decision theory gives. That is, we are looking for *variation* in our decisions. How do we create this variation without data from which to work? To find the answer, let's first examine why we want variation in the first place.

REASONS FOR VARIATION

There are a number of reasons why we would want to create variation in the decisions our agents make. We can illustrate some of them best by using examples of what it looks like when variation is *not* present. Imagine the following:

We enter a bank containing 20 customers, and 5 employees. We approach the middle of the lobby and begin yelling loudly that we are robbing the bank. As we look around to assess the impact that our display is having on the people, we are stunned to realize that all 25 people are reacting in exactly the same way. They are all standing there in stunned silence, too afraid to move. Not a single one has screamed or spoken. Not a single one has taken a step away from us—or toward us, for that matter. All 25 people have reacted in *exactly* the same way!

Curious about this odd display of solidarity, we reach into our jacket for our gun. The moment our hand disappears into our pocket, *every single customer* in the bank shrinks into a crouch, ready to either duck or run. *All of them*. A glance at the tellers behind the counter shows that *all five of them* have raised their hands.

As we pull out our gun and wave it wildly in the air, every player in this peculiar show drops to the floor and screams. None of them only duck. None of them try to run for the door. None of them are still paralyzed with fear. None of them even fall to the floor faster or slower than the others.

The tellers, in the mean time, have *all* raised their right hands toward us in a placating gesture. Exactly two seconds later, their left hands reach into their bank tills. Simultaneously, all five say, "Here, take the money!"

Dying to find out what this impromptu synchronized exhibit will do next, we turn the gun to point it at our own head. The customers all stop screaming, even the small girl in the corner. The employees all put down their hands in such rigid precision it seems like they are about to bust into a group version of the Macarena.

We pull the trigger on the gun and the water inside squirts against the side of our head. All 25 people gasp in surprise in what sounds like a single, magnified intake of breath.

As the water trickles to the floor, we yell "Hey folks! I was just kidding! It was a joke!" As if cued by the producer of a bad TV sit-com, all 25 people begin laughing.

We put our now empty squirt gun back into our pocket, whereupon all 25 people turn back to what they were doing prior to our entrance. To a man, they all seem completely unfazed by the trauma we just inflicted on them.

On the other hand, *we* are a little disturbed by what we just witnessed. We turn to the door, muttering under our breath, "Wow... it was like a bad video game or something."

Variation between Actors

As ludicrous as the above scenario seems, many of us have probably experienced something like this in games. The underlying technical problem with the above scenario (if you didn't get it already) is that all the agents were using the same algorithm to determine their reaction to a stimulus. Every time we changed the world state through our actions, we fed the 25 people the same information with which to calculate their decisions. As a result, they all arrived at the same conclusion about what the "best" reaction should be.

The only difference in the actions of the various people was that the employees and the customers had different reactions at one point. The reason for that is that they had different programmed reactions to the stimulus of us waving our gun around. The customers dropped to the floor and began screaming; the employees tried to placate us. The only reason for this occurring is that, at some point, either a designer or a programmer differentiated between the two: "When the player does [insert action], I want the customers to [insert reaction] and the employees to [insert reaction]."

While the separation of customer vs. employee is admirable and was certainly a logical division, there is a subtle implication in that statement. Imagine the above statement rephrased this way: "When the player does [insert action], I want *every single* customer to [insert reaction] and *every single* employee to [insert reaction]." By inserting the specifier "every single..." we draw attention to the inherent weakness in this line of thinking.

The differentiation between customer and employee was based on the reasonable premise that customers and employees would likely react to the situation in different ways. This is a logical assumption given the fact that their roles in a bank robbery would be different. They enter the scenario of a bank robbery with different goals. The customers' primary goal is "don't get killed." The employees have two goals: "don't get killed" and "defuse the situation by giving the really scary man what he wants." The problem with the artificial intelligence (AI) as theoretically designed in our example is that every person's solution for how to reach those goals was exactly the same as every *other* person's.

If we were to imagine how a scenario such as this one would go in real life (or even in a movie, for those of you who can't envision yourself in the position of the bank robber), we likely would have a different picture than the one painted above. Simply making a list of possible customer reactions is enlightening.

- Stand paralyzed with fear
- Scream
- Scream and run
- Scream and duck
- Scream and grab your child/parent/husband/wife/random stranger
- Just run (no screaming)
- Just duck (no screaming)
- Just grab your child/parent/husband/wife/random stranger (no screaming)
- Move slowly away from the robber
- Move *toward* the robber
- Try to get behind a desk
- Try to jump *over* a desk
- Reach for the robber's gun
- Reach for our own concealed weapon
- Try to call 911 on our phone
- Laugh because the robber is wearing dark glasses and a stupid hat

As we can see, there are a lot of options that the customers and the employees *could have* chosen from. There are probably many more. Add to this list that most of these actions could be done with various delays and speeds. For example, not *everyone* is going to scream at exactly the same time.

If we can anecdotally list so many actions that our agents *could* select, the fact that they all selected the same action becomes even more startling. Variation in behavior is what makes humans look… well… *human*. Because, as we are fond of saying, "no two people are exactly alike," it is unlikely that their reactions to a given set of stimuli will be the same

VARIATION BY A SINGLE ACTOR

While it is important to consider the behaviors of a group of actors, we also need to consider the actions of a single actor. Imagine, if you will, the following scenario:

We enter a bank containing 20 customers and 5 employees. We approach the middle of the lobby and begin yelling loudly that we are robbing the bank. The woman to our left shrieks in terror. The man to our right drops to the ground and assumes the fetal position. The teenager in back looks up from her phone where she is text-messaging, shrugs, and looks back down.

The security guard by the wall turns toward us and stares slack-jawed in disbelief and, after two seconds, reaches for the gun at his belt. The girl in the pink dress says, "Look at the man with the dark glasses, Mommy! His hat is stupid!"

After displaying our nifty squirt gun trick to the bank patrons and employees (and shooting an annoyed look at the little girl with the big mouth), we leave the bank.

Later in the day, we return to the bank, which (surprisingly) still contains 20 customers and 5 employees. We approach the middle of the lobby and begin yelling loudly that we are robbing the bank. The woman to our left shrieks in terror. The man to our right drops to the ground and assumes the fetal position. The teenager in back looks up from her phone where she is text-messaging, shrugs, and looks back down. The security guard by the wall turns toward us and stares slack-jawed in disbelief and, after two seconds, reaches for the gun at his belt. The girl in the pink dress says, "Look at the man with the dark glasses, Mommy! His hat is stupid!"

Wow. That's odd. Did I just step into my own version of the movie *Groundhog Day*? What's *with* these people? That's exactly what they did earlier today! Wait a minute... let's try this again.

We step outside onto the sidewalk and count to ten before we reenter the bank lobby. We approach the middle of the lobby and begin yelling loudly that we are robbing the bank. The woman to our left shrieks in terror. The man to our right drops to the ground and assumes the fetal position. The teenager in back looks up from her phone where she is text-messaging, shrugs, and looks back down. The security guard by the wall turns toward us and stares slack-jawed in disbelief and, after two seconds, reaches for the gun at his belt. The girl in the pink dress says, "Look at the man with the dark glasses, Mommy! His hat is stupid!"

My guess is that you, my ever-gentle reader, skipped the last paragraph of our little story above. Why? Because it was stale the third time around. You knew what was going to happen. You had already seen how each person was going to react to our declaration of impending robbery. If I asked you what the woman on the left would do if we reentered the bank and once again made our threat, you would be able to tell me with unflagging certainty that she was going to shriek in terror. After all, we have been presented with the impression that she *always* shrieks in terror. Every time. Without fail. Why would we think anything else?

Not only is rigid predictability *boring* to us, the observer, but it is not even remotely human. If we think of a situation in our own lives that occurs regularly, it is likely that we can also make a list of our actions or reactions to that situation at different times. For the sake of continuity, let's look again at the list of bank robbery reactions above. How many of them could we see ourselves *possibly* exhibiting? Some of them might be more likely than others, of course, but we would have at least a *small* chance of doing a great number of them. There also may be a few that we may never consider. (I can no longer see myself jumping *over* a desk, for example.)

More importantly, if we found ourselves in a bank robbery situation again later (hopefully not the same day!), would we pick the exact same reaction? We still would have the same list of things we *might* do, but could we guarantee that any one of them is the one we would do *every time*? It is far more likely that we would react different ways each time we were faced with a bank robbery situation. If we experienced ten different robberies that were all similar in nature, how many different reactions would we exhibit? Two or three? Five? Would we have *ten* different reactions? (At this point in our saga, I am thinking that banking exclusively online would also start to look more attractive.)

The quandary becomes apparent when we juxtapose having all those choices that we *might* select from against a formula or algorithm that tells us that this is "the best" reaction to have *every time*. Just as it was a false assumption to think that *every person* in the bank would react the same as every other person *one time*, it is likewise a tenuous assertion to say that *one person* would react the same way *every time*.

EMBRACING RANDOMNESS

Individual people make decisions based on a massive collection of information—only some of which is the current environment. The adage goes that "we are the sum of our life experiences." Those experiences were, themselves, information at one time. Now, however, they have taken on a different role in our lives. What were events at the time have become memories. Experiences have shaped beliefs. Traumas have begotten fears. Pleasures have nurtured cravings and desires. Put into mathematical terms, those life experiences of the past are now the formulas, equations, and algorithms through which we pass the inputs of the current environment.

The problem is, even if we were to analyze our own life in great detail, we would be hard-pressed to codify our own psychology accurately enough to construct the algorithms that would yield the "right way" for us to respond to those inputs. Even if we could do so, the construction of such a system would be prohibitively labor-intensive. (Yes, this is a massive understatement.) Additionally, the computations involved would be processor-intensive. Oh yeah... don't forget that we would have to model the game world in such excruciatingly fine detail that we may as well be creating the *holodeck* from *Star Trek*. To sum up, *it ain't gonna happen*.

Of course, constructing one algorithm to tell us what we "would do" is a lot like the normative decision theory approach of one algorithm to tell us what we "should do." That's what got us into this problem in the first place. To return to our bank example, we would have to construct algorithms to replicate the life experiences of 20 typical bank customers and 5 typical bank employees. And when the cops show up at the bank to arrest us, we would have to create three or four individual "life experience models" of typical police officers. If constructing and using *one* such model was prohibitive, we probably don't have a word for what the prospect of creating *dozens* of them would be like. (I nominate "insane.")

Never Mind All That...

Remember, however, that we really don't care about how a bank customer got to the point in his life that would cause him to react in a particular way; we care about the *result* of all of that information and experience-building. This is the same rationale that we used with the dentists dispensing their helpful advice. We don't know or care *why* four of the five dentists recommended sugarless gum or *why* the fifth did not. We just know that they did. If we were going to create our Dental Advice Simulator, we would not have to worry about the fact that one of the dentists' spouses recently died of complications due to diabetes and another is taking kickbacks from the Sugar Growers of the World Association. To *simulate* the dentists we would simply codify that 80% of dentists we encounter recommend sugarless gum and the remaining 20% do not. We can leave it up to the players to overlay such creative interpretations if they *really* feel the driving need to do so.

As we dealt with in Chapters 11 and 12, probability distribution and random selection is something we can model rather well. How hard is it, after all, to recommend sugarless gum 80% of the time? Using that simple procedure, our Dental Advice Simulator could simulate a whole *convention hall* full of dentists! We have substituted simple probability distributions for the complex (and largely unnecessary) process of generating the minutia of what goes into individualized human decisions. The results are strikingly compelling, however. When we query our faux dentists about their thoughts on sugarless gum, rather than acting in rigid unison, 80% of them (give or take a few, I'm sure) would raise their hands. A player of our Dental Advice Simulator would see that, nod to himself, and say, "Wow… looks like about four out of five to me. That's a reasonably accurate simulation of dentists!"

A Framework for Randomness

It's important to note that we did not make the decision completely random. We did not flip a coin to decide. Doing so would have generated a 50/50 split on the

Great Sugarless Debate. We used a random number process in conjunction with a carefully constructed probability distribution (i.e., four out of five).

Yes, the dentist example was simple, but we can do far more if necessary. In fact, we explored some of this in Chapter 11 when we randomly created a population of guesses in the Guess Two-Thirds the Average Game that was similar to the results of the Danish study. Our approach in that exercise was to use random generation of guesses based on a combination of specifically tailored probability curves.

Thinking further back to Chapter 6, recall the real lesson of the Guess Two-Thirds the Average Game. We were trying to find the sweet spot between the purely rational (yet very unlikely) answer of 0 and a completely random (and also unlikely) guess. That is, we were trying to get away from the rigid rationality of normative decision theory and move toward the more human-like descriptive decision theory. Our solution at the time was the carefully crafted and controlled application of structured randomness.

The question that we still must answer, however, is how do we build that structure around our randomness? In the Guess Two-Thirds the Average Game, we had an example from which to work. It was much like how I was able to paint my somewhat realistic-looking pig because I was looking at a photo of a pig. From an artistic standpoint, I couldn't draw a pig from scratch. However, by looking at one, I could copy the bits and pieces and replicate what was already there. We did this in Chapter 11 by reconstructing the guesser distribution one part at a time. We weren't modeling *why* they were guessing the way they did, only that they did so because a survey told us, "This is how 19,000 Danes guessed."

Unfortunately, we don't always have a handy survey to tell us how people divided themselves among the choices that range between "the best" and "the most ridiculous ever." We need to have a more procedural way of outlining the framework that will support our otherwise stochastic process. Surprisingly, we are already closer to the solution than we might think.

SELECTING FROM MULTIPLE CHOICES

Let's break our problem down into the features we need in our decision model and the features we don't want.

- We want more variety than "the best" answer.
- We *don't* want to include "the worst" answer.
- We *do* want to include "reasonable" answers.
- We don't want to include "unreasonable" answers.

In the above criteria for what we do and don't want, we were coming at the problem from both ends. We want more than just the best choice. We acknowledged that there are other choices that might be acceptable. On the other hand, we certainly don't want the *worst* choice, and there are likely a lot of choices that aren't the *worst* but are pretty darn bad as well. We want to avoid those. But how do we separate the good from the bad?

RANDOM FROM TOP *n* CHOICES

If we list our choices ranked from optimum down to downright silly, someplace in the middle is a meeting point between the good ones and the bad ones. The problem is that we don't know where that point happens to be. This causes us to get a little arbitrary at first.

In our Dudes example, we scored each combination of Dude and weapon. By selecting the best score (in this case, the lowest number), we chose which weapon to use and which Dude to target. However, that means that *every time* we encounter that exact arrangement of Dudes, we will do exactly the same thing. While this may not be startling in and of itself, what if there are two of us… or five… or a whole *bank full* of us all running the same algorithm. We would all respond exactly the same way. We would all pull out the same weapon and fire at the same Dude.

Never mind that this collective response is a tactical nightmare; it just looks silly. It looks even more ludicrous when we translate it back *out* of our Dude scenario and into something like our bank example. Even if everyone was processing the same inputs, would *everyone* react exactly the same way? Not likely. Therefore, despite the fact that there may be a single *best* Dude to attack with a single *best* weapon, it probably does not behoove us to insist that we follow that model rigidly.

Opening the Playbook

Thankfully, one of the advantages of ranking the scores was that we learned more than simply which one was *best*. We also are aware that there were others that were decent choices as well… just not the *best*. To confirm this, let's examine the results of our final Dude example from Chapter 14. (Note that in Chapter 14, we had limited our list to only the best weapon for each Dude. Here, we include them all. We'll see why in a moment.)

Name	Weapon	Score
Evil Genius	R/L	7.7
Boss Man	R/L	8.5
Baddie 3	R/L	9.7
Evilmeister	R/L	9.8

Evil Genius	M/G	10.8
Baddie 3	Shotgun	11.2
Baddie 3	M/G	12.6
Baddie 2	R/L	13.1
Evilmeister	M/G	13.8
Evil Knievel	M/G	14.3
Boss Man	M/G	14.8
Baddie 2	M/G	16.3
Baddie 1	R/L	27.0
Baddie 3	Pistol	28.7
Baddie 1	M/G	28.8
Baddie 1	Shotgun	29.4
Baddie 1	Pistol	38.6
Evilmeister	Pistol	44.0
Baddie 2	Pistol	54.2
Boss Man	Pistol	100.0
Evil Genius	Pistol	257.7
Baddie 4	R/L	634.7
Baddie 4	M/G	637.0
Baddie 4	Pistol	654.5
Evil Knievel	Pistol	1,339.7
Evil Knievel	Shotgun	1,339.7
Evil Knievel	R/L	1,339.7
Evil Genius	Shotgun	1,777.0
Evilmeister	Shotgun	2,183.4
Boss Man	Shotgun	2,421.3
Baddie 2	Shotgun	2,428.8
Baddie 4	Shotgun	2,531.1

Remember that we had 8 enemies and 4 weapon choices for each, giving us 32 possible combinations. We have ranked them here in order from the best choice to the worst. Recall that our eventual selection in this scenario was to kill Evil Genius with our rocket launcher. After all, our delightfully thorough algorithm told us that was the best answer.

Wheat and Chaff

Now that we have looked at all the possibilities, however, we can see that, while "shoot Evil Genius with the rocket launcher" is, indeed, the lowest score, there were plenty of other options that were very close. How much worse would it have been for us to attack Boss Man with the rocket launcher instead? In the heat of battle, would it have looked completely illogical for us to attack Boss Man instead of Evil Genius? (After all, he's *Boss Man!* And *he's* got a rocket launcher too!) What about Baddie 3 (who was 30 feet away with his potent shotgun) or Evilmeister (only 60 feet away with his machine gun)? Those would certainly have been understandable and legitimate targets for us—and we see this reflected in the scores.

On the other end of the spectrum, we can see that there were plenty of options that would have looked just plain odd. With all these Dudes running around near and far, why would we elect to attack the ones that are far away with a shotgun that is all but useless at those distances? That explains the bottom five options in the list. They are simply out of the question.

Drawing a Line

As we theorized, someplace in the middle of this list, the good meets the bad (by blending into the mediocre). While we would have been comfortable selecting one of the "reasonable" answers, we want to avoid the "unreasonable" ones. The trick is deciding where that line is. Everything under 10? Under 50? Under 500?

Pragmatically, we realize that we can't even use the scores in this list as a guide. In a different situation, we may not have *any* options that score under 10… or even 50. The scores will change all the time relative to whatever arbitrary line in the sand we draw. However, one thing is certain: No matter what the scores are, we can always arrange them relative to *each other*. After all, that's how we determined the best option before. "Attack Evil Genius with our rocket launcher" was the best *relative to the other scores*. The solution, therefore, lies not in basing the threshold on an absolute score but on the score relative to other scores.

Instead of limiting ourselves to *only* the single best item, we can select from a handful of the best scores. How many options we elect to choose from will be very problem-specific. (Certainly, you are getting tired of hearing that by now.) We could, for example, choose to select from the top 10 options. However, what if there are fewer Dudes and fewer weapons available to us? We may not *have* 10 options from which to select.

Usually, it is a better idea to use the top n% of the choices rather than the top n choices. In the case of the Dudes, for example, we could decide that our cut-off is 25% of the total possible choices. In this case, we would consider the top eight items. If we had more options, that number would increase. As we removed Dudes from the battlefield and perhaps ran out of ammo for some of our weapons, the total number of options available to us would decrease, and the number that we would consider would contract with it.

Now that we have decided that we will consider the top eight choices, we have truncated our list to:

Name	Weapon	Score
Evil Genius	R/L	7.7
Boss Man	R/L	8.5
Baddie 3	R/L	9.7
Evilmeister	R/L	9.8
Evil Genius	M/G	10.8
Baddie 3	Shotgun	11.2
Baddie 3	M/G	12.6
Baddie 2	R/L	13.1

Those all look like fairly reasonable actions for us to take. Their scores are so similar, it almost doesn't matter which one we choose. Therefore, a simple solution would be to pick one of them randomly.

PUTTING IT IN CODE

We can do this very simply by changing the selection code in `CAgent`. The original `SelectTarget()` function sorted the vector and selected the target in the 0 index—the lowest-scored combination.

```
void CAgent::SelectTarget()
{
    ScoreAllTargets();

    std::sort( mvTargets.begin(), mvTargets.end() );

    mpCurrentTarget = mvTargets[0].pDude;
    mpCurrentWeapon = mvTargets[0].pWeapon;
}
```

By adding two lines, we can determine how many records we should consider (25% of the total number) and generate a random vector index in that range. Rather than returning the record at index 0, we are returning a random one between index 0 and (NumberToConsider − 1).

```
void CAgent::SelectTarget()
{
    ScoreAllTargets();

    std::sort( mvTargets.begin(), mvTargets.end() );
    USHORT NumberToConsider = mvTargets.size() * 0.25;
    USHORT i = rand() % ( NumberToConsider - 1 );

    mpCurrentTarget = mvTargets[i].pDude;
    mpCurrentWeapon = mvTargets[i].pWeapon;
}
```

Selecting randomly may seem counterintuitive and even mildly alarming. Why, after all the work we went through in Chapter 14 to arrive at these scores, would we seemingly cast it all aside and go back to random selection?

The answer to this is in the lessons we learned all the way back in Chapter 5. In the Ultimatum Game, we determined through similarly mathematical methods that the best option for the Giver to bestow upon the Receiver was $1. That was the most logical answer. Likewise, it was in the best interests of the Receiver to accept that amount. (After all $1 > $0, right?) And yet, people placed in those two roles rarely do either of those "best" actions.

We explored this further in Chapter 6 with examples such as the Pirate Game, the Guess Two-Thirds the Average Game, and even the Monty Hall Problem. We humans like to talk about how rational we are, but, for a variety of reasons, we usually aren't *completely* so. We may occasionally select the "best" answer but usually only get close by selecting a *reasonable* answer.

The Payoff

That is what we accomplish by using a hybrid of our scoring system (pure rationality) and random selection (inexplicable irrationality). By allowing our agent to select from a number of reasonable-*looking* choices, we are effectively modeling all the little vagaries of humanness that we don't care to model. Perhaps when our agent asked for his first rocket launcher at the age of eight, someone told him "You'll put your eye out, kid," and he's been a little wary of them ever since. Perhaps he is particularly offended by the dark glasses and stupid hat that Baddie 3 has donned for this encounter. It doesn't really matter *why* they act differently; humans simply *do*. Therefore, we don't need to model the *whys* of the different decisions. We simply provide a mechanism that simulates those different (but still somewhat reasonable) decisions.

Think back to Chapter 1 and the definition of a game provided by Sid Meier: "A game is a series of interesting choices." We examined that notion by using examples such as Rock-Paper-Scissors, Tic-Tac-Toe, Blackjack, and Poker. Rock-Paper-Scissors is predominantly random. The choices in Tic-Tac-Toe are almost entirely predictable. Blackjack has random components, but the dealer's choices are entirely rule-bound; we don't know what either of us will get next, but we know exactly what the dealer will do with it when he gets it. Only when we get to Poker do we see a challenge provided by the other player (i.e., the agent). The reason this is so compelling is that while we have an idea of what he *might* do, we can't predict exactly what he *will* do. Responding to *his* interesting choices is what makes *our* choices that much more interesting.

We will find that the result of changing our agent's model to include more options is that he will display broader behavior than when he was restricted to only the one choice. In fact, if the agent were to encounter the same circumstances again, he may or may not select the same approach. If we are playing as one of the Dudes, this is actually a boon. Just as with the Poker player, the agent's interesting (yet reasonable) variation of choices makes our choices that much more interesting as well.

From a player's standpoint, it also helps avoid situations like that uncomfortable moment in the bank when everyone reacted in exactly the same way. In this case, if we were a Dude facing multiple AI agents, they would look just as peculiar all doing exactly the same thing It seems that not only is variety the spice of life, but it keeps AI from looking like the Stepford Wives—completely identical in thought and deed... and *horribly boring*.

WEIGHTED RANDOM FROM TOP *n* CHOICES

We still have one problem with the approach we are using. We arbitrarily chose to randomly select from the top 25% of options. In the case of our primary example, that meant there were eight possibilities in play. Once we had split those eight options off, for all intents and purposes, we treated them equally. We didn't bias the random selection whatsoever. Because the top eight options were similar, there was little difference between them anyway. We can see this in the black bars of Figure 16.1.

While that approach worked for our sample data, imagine that our scores had turned out more like what we see with the gray bars in Figure 16.1. In that example, there is a large jump between the score of the first two and the rest of the options. We can no longer consider these eight options as being equal. That hamstrings our idea of selecting randomly from that list of eight.

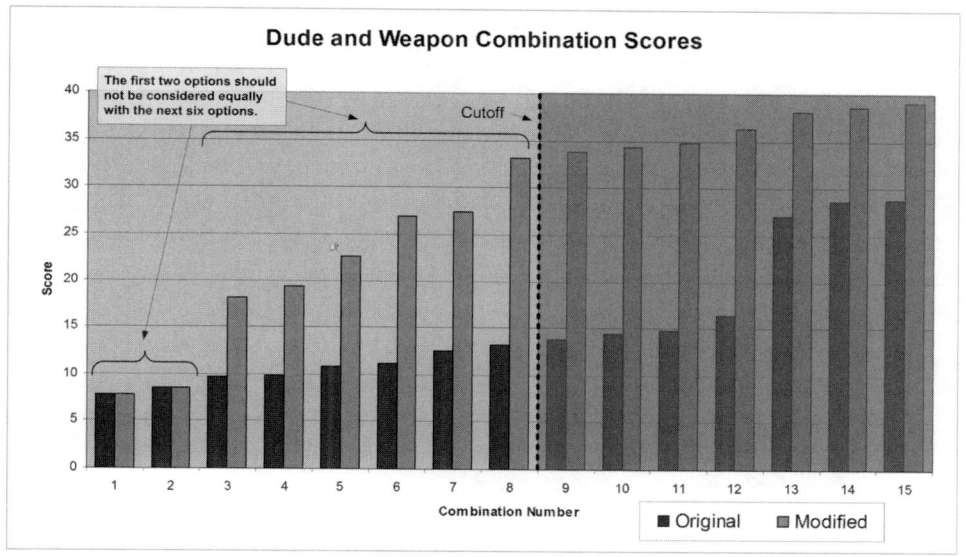

FIGURE 16.1 If there is a significant difference between the scores of our top *n* selections, we should not treat them equally.

One possible solution to this problem is to reduce our cutoff to two possibilities instead of eight. However, that almost negates the purpose of expanding it in the first place. Also, we have no way to predict where that cusp will be on any iteration of this process. Looking at our original data (black bars), we could have included the first *12* records before we saw a significant jump in the scores.

To continue to provide some variety in our choices, we would like to continue drawing from the top eight selections (or, more generally, the top 25% of the possible selections). What we do *not* want to do, however, is to treat all eight possibilities as equal.

Thankfully, our scoring system provided us with something other than an ordinal ranking of the possibilities. The very fact that the scores vary from one option to the next reminds us that these differences are proportional. In layman's speak, some options are "more better" than the options that come after them. We need a way to leverage these proportional differences.

We already know that we would like for the "better options" to occur more often than the "not quite as good" options. We discussed in Chapter 12 that response curves are excellent at helping us tailor customized distributions. We can then select randomly from the weighted options, knowing that the more weight we give to an option, the more often that option will occur. The first thing we need to address is how to weight our options. We want to convert our somewhat abstract "score" into a proportional weight.

As a general rule, the larger the weight we want to set an option at, the larger the number we will need to use to set the size of the bucket for that option. When we look at our score values for the options, we might have a moment of concern—our better options have *smaller* scores. Our scores are an abstract rather than concrete value, however; they do not represent something we are measuring. All we are concerned with is their relationship to each other. We don't have to preserve any sanctity of the actual numbers.

Assigning Weights

In Chapter 13, we discussed a method of weighing scores *relative* to other scores. If we put all the other scores in terms of the best score, we preserve the relationship between them. To set our benchmark, we set the best option's score to 1.0. For each of our options, i, we score them as

$$Weight_i = \frac{Score_1}{Score_i}$$

Naturally, $Weight_1 = 1.0$ because we are dividing it by itself. The next item in our original list, Boss Man with the rocket launcher, scored an 8.5, compared to 7.7 for the best option (Evil Genius with the rocket launcher).

$$Weight_2 = \frac{7.7}{8.5} = 0.91$$

Therefore, the second option would have a smaller weight and be slightly less likely than the first. Continuing through our eight options, we find:

Name	Weapon	Score	Weight	Edge	%
Evil Genius	R/L	7.7	1.00	1.00	16.5
Boss Man	R/L	8.5	0.90	1.90	14.8
Baddie 3	R/L	9.7	0.79	2.69	13.0
Evilmeister	R/L	9.8	0.78	3.47	12.9

Name	Weapon	Score	Weight	Edge	%
Evil Genius	M/G	10.8	0.71	4.18	11.7
Baddie 3	Shotgun	11.2	0.69	4.87	11.4
Baddie 3	M/G	12.6	0.61	5.48	10.0
Baddie 2	R/L	13.1	0.59	6.07	9.7

Examining the weights of the options, we can see how the weights are proportional to how often we would like them to occur. For example, the last option (Baddie 2 with the rocket launcher) would occur about 60% as often as our top choice.

The last two columns give us another look at our results. The fifth column, Edge, shows us what the edges of the buckets would be if we put all our weighted options end to end. The final column shows the percentage chance of each option occurring based on the weights. If we had picked randomly, each option would have had a 12.5% chance of being selected. Because of the application of our weights, those percentages now range from 16.5% for our most preferable selection to 9.7% for our eighth-place option.

The Haves and Have Nots

While it is noticeable, there is not much of a spread between the percentages of those eight options. We can see a more distinct difference when we use data that is more disparate—such as the modified data (gray bars) in Figure 16.1.

Name	Weapon	Score	Weight	Edge	%
Evil Genius	R/L	7.7	1.00	1.00	25.8
Boss Man	R/L	8.5	0.91	1.91	23.5
Baddie 3	R/L	18.1	0.43	2.34	11.1
Evilmeister	R/L	19.3	0.40	2.74	10.3
Evil Genius	M/G	22.6	0.34	3.08	8.8
Baddie 3	Shotgun	26.9	0.29	3.37	7.5
Baddie 3	M/G	27.4	0.28	3.65	7.2
Baddie 2	R/L	33.1	0.23	3.88	5.9

Because the scores for this batch of data are more widely spread, the resulting occurrence percentages are significantly different as well. We can see that the two options with the relatively low scores of 7.7 and 8.5 will occur 25.8% and 23.5% of the time, respectively. That is almost 50% of the time between the two of them. We are not precluding the other six options from selection, however. They will occur, but at a reduced frequency that is on par with their proportional score.

A Different Edge

We will notice one problem with the numbers that we have generated above when we try to use a response curve to select an option, however. Remember that to use a response curve, we need to generate a number between 0 and whatever the outermost edge is—that is, the edge of the last bucket. In the case of the example above, that edge is 3.88. Because some random number generators tend to yield integers, however, we would have to do a conversion from the integer result to generate a number between 0 and 3.88. While we certainly could do that conversion, there is another approach we could take.

Remember, the actual values of the weights themselves do not matter—only the proportion between them. Therefore, to avoid this problem, we could multiply the weight formula by a coefficient. The result is the same but has the benefit of converting our bucket edges to integers instead of decimal values.

The actual coefficient that we should select is a little difficult to ascertain, however. Again (say it along with me, folks), *it is a very problem-specific issue.* The main consideration is that we want to achieve enough granularity to express subtleties in the sizes of the buckets. Because we are going to have to round to the nearest whole number, if the coefficient is too small, we risk rounding similar numbers off to the same size when we would rather they remain distinctly different. For example, if we were to multiply the weight scores above by a coefficient of 2, we would get the following numbers:

Name	Weapon	Score	Weight	Edge	%
Evil Genius	R/L	7.7	2.00	2.00	25.8
Boss Man	R/L	8.5	1.82	3.82	23.5
Baddie 3	R/L	18.1	0.86	4.68	11.1
Evilmeister	R/L	19.3	0.80	5.48	10.3
Evil Genius	M/G	22.6	0.68	6.16	8.8
Baddie 3	Shotgun	26.9	0.58	6.74	7.5
Baddie 3	M/G	27.4	0.56	7.30	7.2
Baddie 2	R/L	33.1	0.46	7.76	5.9

Note that only the weights and the edges changed. The percentage scores and the percentages are still the same. This process is not changing the distribution of choices; we are only attempting to make selecting a choice a more accurate process.

The problem we would still have with the above data is that the granularity is still too coarse. If we rounded the data off, we would have two 2s, five 1s, and even a 0. Ignoring the problem of having a bucket size of 0, we still have to deal with the fact that five of our buckets are the same size again. We have lost all the subtlety of the scores between 18.1 and 27.4 by compressing them into a bucket width of 1 each.

If we increase the coefficient to 10, our numbers now are a little more workable:

Name	Weapon	Score	Weight	Edge	%
Evil Genius	R/L	7.7	10.00	10.00	25.8
Boss Man	R/L	8.5	9.06	19.06	23.4
Baddie 3	R/L	18.1	4.25	23.31	11.0
Evilmeister	R/L	19.3	3.99	27.30	10.3
Evil Genius	M/G	22.6	3.41	30.71	8.8
Baddie 3	Shotgun	26.9	2.86	33.57	7.4
Baddie 3	M/G	27.4	2.81	36.38	7.3
Baddie 2	R/L	33.1	2.32	38.70	6.0

As we look at the weights for each option, we see that our buckets are a variety of different sizes. The third and fourth end up with a rounded size of 4, and the fifth, sixth, and seventh round to a size of 3, however; we still are losing some of our fine shades of difference. In the original example where the eight scores were closer together, the loss of detail would be even more pronounced.

Automatic Scaling

Thankfully, we don't have to guess what size would be an appropriate coefficient. We can rewrite our weight equation to help us automatically scale our weights to a reasonable granularity. It *does* involve one extra step, however.

To generate the weights above, we scaled everything relative to the lowest score. That is, the lowest score was the anchor point of 1.0 (before the application of a coefficient). The other, higher scores generated smaller weights as a result. We had no way of accounting for what the other scores were because we were using the single score as our only frame of reference.

Because we are generating proportions of the whole that each option represents, we need to begin with what the *whole* looks like. If we sum the scores in our list of options, we can then further calculate the proportion of the whole that each individual score represents using the following formula:

$$Weight_i = \frac{Score_1 + ... + Score_n}{Score_i}$$

Looking back at our data table, the sum of the eight scores is 163.6. Therefore, the weight of our first option would be

$$Weight_1 = \frac{163.6}{7.7} = 21.25$$

Rounded off to an edge-friendly integer, the *Weight* of our first bucket is 21. Checking our accuracy, we find that 21 is 25.9% of 163.6. This is reasonably close to the 25.8% that this option represented before. Applying this method to the other options, we arrive at the following new data:

Name	Weapon	Score	Weight	Edge	%
Evil Genius	R/L	7.7	21	21	25.9
Boss Man	R/L	8.5	19	40	23.5
Baddie 3	R/L	18.1	9	49	11.1
Evilmeister	R/L	19.3	8	57	9.9
Evil Genius	M/G	22.6	7	64	8.6
Baddie 3	Shotgun	26.9	6	70	7.4
Baddie 3	M/G	27.4	6	76	7.4
Baddie 2	R/L	33.1	5	81	6.2

For those of us who are curious, if we had still been using the previous method of generating weights to arrive at this set, we would have needed to use a coefficient of 21. Of course, we had no way of knowing that ahead of time, nor did we have any reasonable method of guessing it. (Any guess we had used may not have worked for some arrangements of data, anyway.)

A glance down the list shows that our granularity is such that we still show the subtlety of variation between the options. The only two items that have the same weight are the sixth and seventh options. Looking at their scores, however, we have to concede that they were almost identical anyway. For our purposes, the 0.1% difference is loose change.

More importantly, our weights are now integers; therefore, our edges are now integers as well. By generating a random number between 0 and 81, we can select a random option whose rate of occurrence reflects the percentages shown. Our agent is now still *reasonable,* but neither rigidly predictable nor boring. Out of the 32 original possibilities, we will observe our agent selecting from among the eight best options proportionally distributed by their relative merit.

Putting It in Code

To accommodate the above discussion, the changes that we make to our code are relatively minor. First, we must change the `struct` that we use for the target information to hold an edge value.

```
struct sTARGET_INFO
{
    CDude* pDude;
    CWeapon* pWeapon;
    double Score;
    USHORT Edge;

    bool operator<( const sTARGET_INFO& j ) {return Score < j.Score;}
};
```

Next, we need to add a function that calculates the edges. Because we need to have the scores completely filled out to determine weights and edges, the process of calculating this information cannot begin until we have finished scoring all the targets. `BuildEdges()` also uses the functions `SumScores()` and `ScoreToWeight()`.

```
void CAgent::BuildEdges(USHORT NumBuckets)
{
    double TotalScore = SumScores( NumBuckets );

    mvTargets[0].Edge = ScoreToWeight( mvTargets[0].Score, TotalScore );

    for ( USHORT i = 1; i < NumBuckets; i++ ) {
        mvTargets[i].Edge = mvTargets[i-1].Edge +
            ScoreToWeight( mvTargets[i].Score, TotalScore );
    } // end for
}

double CAgent::SumScores(USHORT NumBuckets)
{
    double TotalScore = 0;
```

```
        for ( USHORT i = 1; i < NumBuckets; i++ ) {
            TotalScore += mvTargets[i].Score;
        } // end for

        return TotalScore;
    }

    USHORT CAgent::ScoreToWeight(double ThisScore, double TotalScore)
    {
        // note the 0.5 addition to round rather than simply truncate
        USHORT Weight = USHOFT( ( TotalScore / ThisScore ) + 0.5 );
        return Weight;
    }
```

As we can see, `SumScores()` simply loops through a number of items in `mvTargets` set by the value `NumBuckets` and totals their scores. We can then pass `TotalScore` into `ScoreToWeight` with each of the records' scores to calculate the new weight value. Despite its simplicity, we have split `ScoreToWeight()` out as a separate function. We never know when we may want to modify (and likely complicate) the algorithm later.

In this example, notice that we don't store the actual weight of each bucket but rather use it immediately to calculate the new edge of that bucket. If we ever needed to, we could calculate the weight of any bucket by comparing its edge to that of the bucket preceding it. On the other hand, depending on how often our data changed and how much of the data we expected to change at any one time, there are times when storing the weights would be advantageous. This is the approach we used in Chapter 12.

Because we need to sort our target vector to determine the top *n* targets (in this case, eight), we put the call to `BuildEdges()` into `SelectTarget()` after we have already scored and sorted the target information.

```
    void CAgent::SelectTarget()
    {
        ScoreAllTargets();

        std::sort( mvTargets.begin(), mvTargets.end() );
```

```
    USHORT NumberToConsider = mvTargets.size() * 0.25;
    BuildEdges( NumberToConsider );

//  USHORT i = rand() % ( NumberToConsider - 1 ); // <- The old way

    USHORT Guess = rand() % ( mvTargets[NumberToConsider - 1].Edge );
    USHORT i = GetResult( Guess, NumberToConsider );

    mpCurrentTarget = mvTargets[i].pDude;
    mpCurrentWeapon = mvTargets[i].pWeapon;
}
```

Notice that, for comparison purposes, we have left in the original method for determining the index of the target to select (commented out). In that method, we selected a random index between 0 and the last record we were considering (`NumberToConsider` − 1). Instead, rather than generating a random index, we generate a random *guess* between 0 and the edge of the last bucket (in our example, 81). We then need to find out into which bucket the random guess falls. We do this by passing it into `GetResult()`.

Our implementation of `GetResult()` here is similar to the one that we originally used in Chapter 12. The implementation is the same "divide and conquer" binary search. The only difference is that we have included a parameter, `NumBuckets`, to state how many of the buckets we are searching.

```
USHORT CAgent::GetResult( USHORT Target, USHORT NumBuckets )
{
    // Bucket indexes
    USHORT iHigh = NumBuckets;
    USHORT iLow = 0;
    USHORT iGuess;

    bool found = false;

    while ( !found ) {
        // Guess is halfway between the low and high indexes
        iGuess = iLow + ( ( iHigh - iLow ) / 2 );
```

```
        // Check for correct guess
        if ( InBucket( iGuess, Target ) ) {
            return iGuess;
        } // end if

        // If not correct...
        if ( Target > mvTargets[iGuess].Edge ) {
            // guess is too low, change the bottom boundary
            iLow = iGuess;
        } else {
            // guess is too high, change the top boundary
            iHigh = iGuess;
        } // end if

    } // end while

    // Code should never get here!
    assert( 0 && "Code fell through while loop!" );
    return 0;
}
```

`GetResult()` returns the index of the target record that we are randomly selecting. We have now replaced the evenly distributed random target selection with a selection process that proportionally weighs the relative scores of those targets.

We are now relieved of the problem of not knowing how those top eight selections are distributed ahead of time. They can be similar or widely disparate, and our algorithm would account for it. We could also change the number of buckets we are searching. If the number of possible target selections was larger or smaller, the 25% of them that we are allowing for consideration would grow or shrink, respectively. Even if we changed our minds and decided that we wanted to consider more or less than 25%, our algorithm would score, weigh, and select from among the choices.

WEIGHTED RANDOM FROM ALL CHOICES

Let's recap a few points. Our algorithm adapts to changing numbers of options. It automatically puts those options into the proper distribution to account for how well (or poorly) the option scored when we analyzed our situation. The question is, if our algorithm takes all of that into account, why are we limiting our choices anyway?

We have already noted not only the *difficulty* in determining an abstract cutoff point, but we have noted that by having a cutoff point at all, we risk disqualifying potentially viable options. Looking back at our original data for the Dude example, while we cut off the options at eight, the difference in score between the first *12* options is minimal. Why wouldn't we consider those extra four?

Thankfully, the weighted random approach biases our results toward the options we want and biases *away* from the options we don't. We have reduced the options that are *very* bad to having almost *no* chance whatsoever of being picked. To see this effect, we can run the weighting algorithm on all 32 of our possible options.

Name	Weapon	Score	Weight	Edge	%
Evil Genius	R/L	7.7	2,343	2,343	10.07
Boss Man	R/L	8.5	2,114	4,457	9.08
Baddie 3	R/L	9.7	1,860	6,317	7.99
Evilmeister	R/L	9.8	1,834	8,151	7.88
Evil Genius	M/G	10.8	1,670	9,821	7.18
Baddie 3	Shotgun	11.2	1,607	11,428	6.90
Baddie 3	M/G	12.6	1,430	12,858	6.14
Baddie 2	R/L	13.1	1,374	14,232	5.90
Evilmeister	M/G	13.8	1,303	15,535	5.60
Evil Knievel	M/G	14.4	1,254	16,789	5.39
Boss Man	M/G	14.8	1,221	18,010	5.25
Baddie 2	M/G	16.3	1,106	19,116	4.75
Baddie 1	R/L	27.1	666	19,782	2.86
Baddie 3	Pistol	28.7	628	20,410	2.70
Baddie 1	M/G	28.8	627	21,037	2.69
Baddie 1	Shotgun	29.4	613	21,650	2.63
Baddie 1	Pistol	38.6	468	22,118	2.01
Evilmeister	Pistol	44.0	410	22,528	1.76

Baddie 2	Pistol	54.2	333	22,861	1.43
Boss Man	Pistol	100.0	180	23,041	0.77
Evil Genius	Pistol	257.7	70	23,111	0.30
Baddie 4	R/L	634.7	28	23,139	0.12
Baddie 4	M/G	637.0	28	23,167	0.12
Baddie 4	Pistol	654.5	28	23,195	0.12
Evil Knievel	Pistol	1,339.7	13	23,208	0.06
Evil Knievel	Shotgun	1,339.7	13	23,221	0.06
Evil Knievel	R/L	1,339.7	13	23,234	0.06
Evil Genius	Shotgun	1,777.0	10	23,244	0.04
Evilmeister	Shotgun	2,183.4	8	23,252	0.03
Boss Man	Shotgun	2,421.3	7	23,259	0.03
Baddie 2	Shotgun	2,428.8	7	23,266	0.03
Baddie 4	Shotgun	2,531.1	7	23,273	0.03

There are a few things to notice about this data. First, a quick glance shows that our selections at the bottom are all but disqualified from consideration. We only have a 1% chance of selecting one of the 12 worst options *combined*. But the percentages for the good choices are not that much different from what they were when we were only considering eight options. Our best option, Evil Genius with the rocket launcher, represented 16.5% of the choices originally. In this variation, it will occur slightly more than 10% of the time.

However, we have now included more potential options from which our agent can select. In particular, the 9th through 12th options are in play with reasonable frequency. Our original arbitrary choice of selecting from only eight options had excluded these choices despite having similar scores to the top eight. Only after the 12th item (Baddie 2 with the machine gun), when the score jumps from 16.3 to 27.1, does the percentage chance of occurrence drop from around 5% to below 3%.

We only have to make two changes to our code. One is to pass the *total* number of buckets into `GetResult()` rather than the 25% (or whatever) that we had calculated and passed before.

The other, more beneficial change is that we can now remove the call to `std::sort()` that we had made prior to calling `BuildEdges()` and `GetResult()`. Because we're now selecting from all of our options, we no longer have to be concerned with the order in which they appear in our vector. The sizes of the buckets determine the probability of selection, not the order in which they appear. If we're processing a decision many times—especially if it is for many agents—sorting the list to provide either the single best option or the top *n* candidates can be a major performance hit. Now, by considering all options, we only need to pass through the vector once to weight them and build the edges, and then select.

Remind Me Why We Did This?

Spreading the behavior possibilities around over more options may not seem important when considering *one* agent acting *one* time. When we think back to our bank example, however, we remember that when we use one algorithm to simultaneously drive many agents, we run the risk of having those agents exhibit identical behaviors. If the Dudes faced 100 agents whose weaponry and distances from the Dudes were equal, they would see a large variety of reactions from those agents.

Most of them (approximately 82) would select from those top 12 "reasonable" behaviors—between 5 and 10 agents selecting each of the 12. About 17 of them would select from the 8 "not quite as good" behaviors—making about 2 agents for each behavior. And *one* of our 100 agents is going to look...*ahem*... like he's only burning about 15 watts, if you know what I mean.

This may be alarming to some people. "Why would we want any of our agents to do something that looks dumb?!" The simple answer is... *because real people sometimes do things that look dumb*. The more involved answer is based more on the idea that we are facing many, many agents. In the previous example, having 1 of the 100 agents doing something odd provides a function of variety rather than one of accuracy. He is the person who guessed the impossible solution of greater than 66 in the Guess Two-Thirds the Average Game. Our focus is on the people who guessed reasonably despite the fact that there are unreasonable guessers in the mix.

By making some of the 100 agents more dangerous, it provides us with an "interesting choice." As a player, we would have to determine which of the enemies is more of a threat to us rather than simply take the "kill 'em all!" approach. This aspect can make the encounter more engaging, interesting, and fun.

Similarly, one agent running the algorithm with the same inputs many times in succession can produce repetitive behaviors. By stepping away from the narrow view that we should only consider the best-scoring action, we open up far more varied behaviors. More importantly, because we've already done all the work to score each of the potential actions anyway, the extra few steps above are only a small addition.

Expanding Our Horizons

One last aspect of this approach is worth mentioning again. In the previous example, we had 32 possible choices. By approaching this problem in such an open-ended fashion and by utilizing the very scalable binary search method, we do not have to be daunted by including scores—or even *hundreds*—of possible choices.

Imagine for a moment a character in a role-playing game (RPG). The character may have 4 different weapons to select from just as our agent above did. In addition to that, however, our character may have 3 offensive magic items, 2 defensive magic items, 8 different types of potions, 20 spells (some offensive, some defensive), and a number of non-combat options. If he was also facing multiple opponents whom he could attack (in any of those methods) and had multiple allies whom he could assist, the number of possible actions would increase geometrically.

Using the methods we have discussed, we can score each of the possibilities in the same manner, weight them appropriately, and easily select a weighted random result from among them—*even if there are hundreds of possible actions*. We do not need to be horrified by the prospect of our agents having that flexibility. We can give them the freedom to choose and feel comfortable that they will exhibit that precious balance of rationality and variety.

SCORES AND WEIGHTS

We made one very significant assumption in the examples in this chapter: Scores can be easily converted to weights. In both methods of converting the Dude assault score to a weight, we proceeded on the premise that the distribution of scores would provide proper weights for us with a minimum of manipulation. In this case, the outcome seemed reasonable. However, that may not always be the case. (For that matter, we don't even know that this *is* the case in what we did above.)

If we think back to the gymnastics and skating examples, the scoring systems that they use have all of the contestants compressed into a very small range. There is little difference between them. Furthermore, the 0.05 difference between 9.85 and 9.90 may not mean the same as the 0.05 difference between 9.45 and 9.50. We just don't know what those scores *mean*. Because of the lack of differentiation between the scores, it might be difficult to convert this scoring system into a weighted selection system that represents the range from excellent to horrible.

We can say the same for our abstract score for the dudes. As we processed that score, we went from very concrete numbers like "damage per second" and "distance to detonator" to more abstract "threat ratios." Unlike the concrete values, our final score is not something that we can look at and mentally decipher. Thankfully, it seems that this system worked properly. Testing and observation may lead us to adjust the formula that we use to convert the scores to weights, but for the most part we are in the right neighborhood.

Measure Twice, Cut Once

It is generally a good idea, however, to build our process with this eventuality in mind. If we are planning on using weighted randoms to select from among our scored behaviors, we need to ensure that our scoring system will enable the process of weighting. That is not to say that the scores themselves need to be weights, but we need to design them in such a fashion that they are convertible.

To an extent, we helped ourselves in this fashion when we decided to set the undesirable "we can't kill him with this weapon" selections to 1,000. This effectively took those options off the table. If we had elected to use a smaller number such as 100, those options would have been scored much more favorably *relative to the other scores* and would, therefore, have been weighted more highly. By changing that value to 2,000, we would have achieved the opposite effect—minimizing the probability of those options occurring even more than they already are.

Use the Right Tool for the Job

Additionally, remember that we discussed a number of techniques in Chapter 10 that helped us convert one set of numbers to another. These tools are very powerful when they are wielded by the hands of creativity. If we wanted to bias the Dude's scores more toward the best possible selection, we could have used a coefficient—or even an *exponent*—to decrease the weights of the less-preferable selections and increase the weights of our preferred options.

Using the more advanced functions such as the logistic curve can provide interesting results as well. In a situation where the "right answer" is in the middle of the group, for example, we can use the logistic curve to weigh the other answers above and below that midpoint in a more expressive fashion than the data may otherwise exhibit.

In other cases, which we didn't touch on here, we could have applied a random value generated by a normal distribution to account for errors in observation, measurement, or just plain differences in personality. Think of what the effect would be if we had applied a small *plus-or-minus x%* value to any or all of the steps along the way. This has the effect of "fuzzying up" variables from one iteration to the next so that we don't arrive at the same outcome every time.

Most importantly, remember the principle of compartmentalized confidence. If we know that we are eventually going to use the scores as weights, we can apply these functions along the way to minimize the manipulation in that final step of converting a score to a weight.

The possibilities are dizzying. And because the depth and breadth of human behavior is just as immense, there are no final answers. To say it one final time in this chapter, *every solution is problem-specific*.

The power is in *your* hands.

Epilogue

If you have turned the page from the last chapter, I have to assume that you are looking for more answers. You won't find any more in this book. That doesn't mean that there are no more answers out there *somewhere*. In fact, when I set out on this adventure, I had the noble (if overly optimistic) intention to provide them all. That is simply not feasible; there are too many problems and too many approaches to ever cover them all. For example, I could write another entire book on the deterministic mechanics of chaos theory in stable and unstable multi-agent environments. Maybe someday I will. (The very inclusion of this sentence means I will be getting an inquisitive email from my darling editor.)

The point is that there *are* no answers—only tools. No one book, instructional course, or Web site can tell you exactly how to design and program game artificial intelligence (AI), just as there are no "ultimate designs" for how to build a house—only ideas, observations, methods, materials, and tools. However, there is one aspect of designing and building game AI (or houses) that many people in our industry often overlook or minimize. There *are* ways to think. There *are* ways to approach a problem long before we ever write code, a formula, or even a number. We have to get inside our own heads and the heads of those around us.

Even though we didn't cover *everything* that could ever be discussed about game AI, let's walk through what we have presented (and hopefully learned):

- In Chapter 1, we invoked the words of Sid Meier: "A game is a series of interesting choices." We discussed how a game can be more interesting when it involves not only the choices that *we* make, but the choices that our opponent might make as well. If our opponent is either entirely random or entirely predictable, we run the risk of limiting our own choices as well. We also discussed (with the help of my pig) the difficulty involved in determining what proper behavior "should be"— a step we must take before we can begin to model behavior.

- In Chapter 2, we walked through the observations we must consider when attempting to replicate decisions and behaviors. First, we must identify the important components—both apparent and obscured—that could possibly affect our decision. We then must determine a way to quantify that information into a language our programs can understand.

- Chapter 3 briefly explored how numbers can be placed into formulas and algorithms to become decisions.

- We then explored how neither the purely logic-based normative decision theory nor the survey-based descriptive decision theory are entirely adequate for our needs. We suggested that there might be a way to combine the logic of what people *should do* with the relative illogic of what people *tend to do* that would yield our solution.

- We visited the world of John von Neumann and Oskar Morgenstern and their tribute to Sir Occam. Their examples of game theory, such as the Prisoner's Dilemma, showed us how the solutions to even seemingly simple decisions can be elusive. More importantly, through games such as the Ultimatum Game, we discovered how humans don't necessarily act logically even when the "right answer" is well within their reach.

- This led us to our exploration of what goes into rational and irrational behavior. The Pirate Game, the Guess Two-Thirds the Average Game, and a visit to Monty Hall were very clear in their exhibition of the gulf between perfect rationality and what we humans actually decide. On the other hand, we also discovered how sometimes it is perfectly acceptable to *not* be *perfectly* rational. In the end, human behavior lies somewhere in that chasm between perfect rationality and complete randomness. But where in that chasm?

- Chapter 7 is where we started applying the language of mathematics to our problems. We discussed how *utility* differs from *value*. Blaise Pascal reminded us that we always need to know what's at stake in making a decision. We also examined how we can measure utility in other ways, such as *time*.

- Our examination of *marginal utility* further complicated things by suggesting that not all utility is alike. The same $20 means different things to different people. In fact, it may mean different things to the *same* person at a different *time*. We also learned that there may be more than one threshold of utility as our goals change. What we thought was "good enough" before might no longer be so once we reach it.

- In Chapter 9, we were introduced to Jeremy Bentham. His hedonic calculus was an attempt to codify the sins and pleasures of the world into a version of multi-attribute utility theory (MAUT). While his rules may not directly apply to all of our game situations, his approach was important. Through MAUT, we can combine different pieces and parts into one final measurement of overall utility. However, we also learned how difficult comparing some inputs can be. Not only are there no direct translations from some aspects of life to others, but our inherent flaws of perception, categorization, and understanding color our views of what we are measuring. We also learned that rats do a pretty good job of budgeting root beer.

- Part III, Chapters 10 through 13, laid out our mathematical tool box. After learning about the use of specialized functions, probability distributions, techniques such as response curves, and various methods of combining criteria, we came away equipped to begin constructing those "interesting choices" that we spoke of early on.

- We then set about modeling decisions for our agents. We took all the theory we had learned about *how* to build and began assembling those ideas with the tools we had laid out. We showed how we could start with the smallest, seemingly unrelated pieces such as strengths and distances, hone them with formulas and curves, and gradually assemble them into one final number.

- Once we had made a decision, it didn't take us long to consider changing it. We discussed the strategies for not only *how* but *when* to change our minds. More importantly, we addressed the potential pitfalls (such as decision strobing) that changing our minds can lead to. Our primary solution was to include decision momentum in whatever we were doing at the time lest we look a little flighty.

- Finally, we admitted that *always* doing the *best* thing resembled the very unrealistic, un-human-like normative decision theory. (And looked a little startling when we were faced with a bank full of people!) We built a number of methods of selecting actions *other* than the best one. Thankfully, by being careful, the decisions that our agents could select from still looked reasonable (and therefore intelligent) if not perfect.

Again, despite all the material we have covered, there is one underlying theme throughout this entire book.

Designing AI is not about code… it's about decisions.

Our approach to those decisions determines how we eventually need to design our code. Break down the problem into smaller and smaller pieces. Question everything. Don't simply ponder *what* is happening… ponder *why* it happens. This last piece is probably the most important consideration for designing truly reactive, dynamic AI. I can illustrate with one last family anecdote.

When my kids were younger, I made a point of not simply telling them *what* to do but discussing *why* with them. I made a point of making sure that *they* were engaged in that process of searching for the "why" of any situation. The result was interesting.

One example I remember well is the classic "don't run into the street" lecture. Upon engaging them in the discussion of "what do you think might happen if you do that?" we walked through, "there might be a car," "he might hit me," "I might get hurt," "I might have to go to the hospital," "Mom and Dad might be sad," and the entire gamut of potential ramifications.

The result of this approach was that, *on their own*, my kids applied this method to any similar situation that might result in this sequence of events. Their mother and I would listen in amazement as they would admonish each other, "Don't run there! It has cars so it's kinda like a *street* and we might get hit by a car!" They applied it to anywhere that might involve a vehicle of some sort: parking lots, driveways, and even the local bike path near our house. If we had only told them "Don't run in the street," they may not have made that connection to other, similar situations for some time. Instead of giving them a rule, we gave them a "way of deciding."

There are other examples of this form of teaching. We didn't simply tell them "Be quiet" in public places. We explained why (primarily so as not to disturb other people). If we had only told them *what* to do rather than explain the cause-and-effect rule base, they may have only been quiet when we told them to be. Instead, we could stand back and watch as they applied that lesson *on their own* to other venues: restaurants, movie theaters, stores, school events, you name it. Again, because of their similar ages, we could listen to them say things to each other along the lines of, "Remember, if we are loud, we might bother those other people over there… it's just like a *restaurant*." They were able to apply the *whys* of the situation on their own regardless of the environment they were in.

This is what we are trying to do with our AI. We can script an AI agent to react to a single case (the "what"), or we can teach the AI to pay attention to its world and apply the rules we have taught it to whatever situation it finds itself in. By doing so, our AI can react much more fluidly regardless of the specific minutia surrounding it.

The challenge, then, is to determine how we explain those rules to our little electronic progeny so they can go forth full of "whys" rather than "whats." I hope this book has illustrated some methods of how we can communicate those instructions and admonitions.

Now, where did I put my sunglasses and that stupid hat?

—Dave Mark

Index

68-95-99.7 rule, 253

A
accuracy formulas, 358–361
accuracy of differentiation, 326
actions, 352
ad hoc functions, 240
AddBucket function, 293, 304–305
AddWeapon( ) function, 374–375
algorithms
    converting behaviors to
        overview, 29
        using algorithms to construct numbers, 37–41
        using numbers to define, 33–36
        using numbers to select, 30–33
    decisions testing, 387–392
    scoring, 387
    statistical handicapping, 99
anchor values, 324
asymmetric games
    Cutting Cake, 70–72
    defined, 56
    Dictator Game, 75–76
    overview, 69–70
    Trust Game, 76–77
    Ultimatum Game
        failure to act rationally, 74–75
        looking from other side, 73–74
        overview, 72–73
attack formula, 36
automatic scaling, 435–436

B
Battalio, Raymond, 210
behavioral mathematics, 3–13
    challenges
        actions, 11–12
        looks, 10–11
        perfect actions, 12–13
    choices, 4–9
    overview, 3
behaviors
    converting to algorithms
        overview, 29
        using algorithms to construct numbers, 37–41
        using numbers to define, 33–36
        using numbers to select, 30–33
    defined, 352
bell curves, 250. *See also* normal (Gaussian) distributions
Bentham, Jeremy, 448
Bernoulli, Daniel, 171
Bertrand's Box Paradox, 101
Blackjack
    asymmetry, 70
    basic strategy card, 6
    choices in, 5, 8–9
    predictability, 46–47
bounded rationality
    calculations, 97
    defined, 110
    ignoring relevant information, 100–105
    misusing irrelevant information
        football statistics, 99–100
        inventorying backyard, 97–99
    overview, 96
BuildEdges( ) function, 437–438
BuildTower( ) function, 136, 138

C

CAgent class, 365, 373–374
capped scoring systems, 321
categorization, problems with, 207
CDF (cumulative distribution function), 249
CDude class, 365, 370–371
certainty dimension, 196
choices
    See also variation in choice
    overview, 4–9
    Prisoner's Dilemma Game, 66–68
class structure, Shoot Dudes example, 365
climbing fader syndrome, 320–321
combinatorial explosion, 9
comparative values, 112
confidence formula, 412
constructing response curves, 286–295
continuous random variables, 249
continuous recalculation, 397–398
continuous triangular distribution, 270
cooperative game, 56
cost
    of calculation, 107–109
    of information, 105–107
creativity, 17
cumulative distribution function (CDF), 249
curves
    bell, 250. See also normal (Gaussian) distributions
    defined, 244
    exponential, 275–276
    generating, 256–259
    response
        and granularity, 327–328
        selecting options, 434
    shifting, 266–267
    skewing, 261–266
    utility, 171, 181
Cutting Cake Game, 70–72, 105
CWeapon class, 365–366

D

D&D (Dungeons & Dragons), 255
damage formulas, 358–359, 361
damage rate, 157–159
data, response curves, 311–313
decay rate, value, 150–154

decision matrix
    Capture the Flag, 119–120
    Marci's Monopoly strategy, 118
    Matching Pennies, 58
    Pascal's Wager, 114
    Prisoner's Dilemma, 62
    rocket launcher example, 66
    Rock-Paper-Scissors, 4
    Ultimatum Game, 74
decision theory, 45–54
    descriptive
        faulty data, 50–51
        overview, 48–49
        past performance, 49–50
    hybrid, 51–53
    normative
        overview, 45–46
        predictable "shoulds", 46–47
decisions
    changing, 395–416
    combining actions into, 353–355
    defining, 351–353
    intelligent, 27–28
    momentum
        building, 409–415
        ignoring futility, 408–409
        overview, 405–408
    options
        analyzing, 355–382
        comparing, 385–386
        scoring, 382–385
        selecting, 386–387
    testing algorithm, 387–392
decisions under risk
    Monopoly example, 116–117
    overview, 112–113, 115–116
    Pascal's Wager
        overview, 113–114
        strictly dominant strategy, 115
Dental Advice Simulator, 423
dentist example, 242–244, 286
Department of Economics, University of Copenhagen, 91–92
descriptive decision theory
    faulty data, 50–51
    overview, 48–49
    past performance, 49–50
Dictator Game, 75–76

die-roll combinations, 255–269
  changing curve shape, 259–260
  code for, 257–259, 263–266
  distribution checklist, 267–269
  generating curves from, 256–257
  overview, 255–256
  shifting curve, 266–267
  skewing curve, 261–263
  triangular distribution, 269–270
differentiation, accuracy of, 326
discrete random variables, 249
dispersion, 253
distance over time, 145–150
distribution checklist, 267–269
distribution terms, 249
Dungeons & Dragons (D&D), 255
duration dimension, 196
dynamic bucket widths, 295
dynamic response curves, 317

E

edges, 287
engagement decision, 33–36, 201
event-driven recalculation, 400–401
expected utility, 124–127
exponential curves, 275–276
exponential functions, 231
extent dimension, 196

F

factors
  finding hidden
    supply and demand, 22–23
    turning human decisions into AI decisions, 23–24
  identifying
    class elections example, 17–20
    observations without order, 20–21
    overview, 16–17
    Shoot Dudes example, 356–375
fecundity dimension, 196
felicific calculus, 196, 215–216, 220
finite state machine (FSM), 30–33
first standard deviation, 253
flip-flopping, 407–408
Foundation **trilogy, 48**
FSM (finite state machine), 30–33

functions, 292
futility, ignoring, 408–409

G

game theory
  asymmetric games
    Cutting Cake Game, 70–72
    Dictator Game, 75–76
    overview, 69–70
    Trust Game, 76–77
    Ultimatum Game, 72–75
  Matching Pennies Game, 57–60
  overview, 55–57
  Prisoner's Dilemma Game
    best interests, 63–64
    making choices, 66–68
    Pareto improvement, 64–69
    strictly dominant strategies, 61–63, 68–69
games
  See also Guess Two-Thirds Game
  defined, 4, 430
  role playing games (RPGs)
    finite state machine (FSM), 30–33
    linear normalization, 332–334
    relative utility, 216–219
  strategy games
    income vs. expense comparison in, 216–219
    marginal utility in, 172–176
    morals in, 224
    multiple thresholds in, 191–194
    tile-based, 406–407
Gaussian distributions. *See* **normal (Gaussian) distributions**
Gaussian function, 254
GetAccuracy( ) function, 367, 378
GetBestAction( ) function, 160–162
GetDamage( ) function, 367
GetGuess( ) function, 280–282
GetGuessType( ) function, 280, 294–295
GetResult( ) function, 308–309, 311, 439–440
Giffen goods concept, 210–219
GoalUtility( ) function, 154, 156
granularity, minimum, 402–403
Guess Two-Thirds of Average Game
  adding buckets, 287–289
  code for, 289–294
  distribution in, 279–283
  guessing, 90–92

Guess Two-Thirds of Average Game *(continued)*
  iteratively eliminating irrational answers, 88–89
  logical irrationality, 94–95
  measuring depth of rationality, 92–94
  overview, 87–88
  randomness, 424
  retrieving results in, 294–295
  segmenting population in, 244–247
guessing, 90–92

H
hand-crafted response curves, 316–317
Harmony, 49
hedonic calculus, 196–198, 215–216, 220
histograms
  dentist data, 242, 286
  Guess Two-Thirds Game, 245–247
  InitVector() function, 309
  probability distribution, 315
human behavior, 11

I–J
idle behaviors, 400–401
if statements, 290–291
imperfect knowledge, 56
InBucket function, 310–311
income versus expense comparison, 216–219
increasing marginal utility, 171, 414–415
infinity, 184
information expiry, 411–413
information momentum, 18–20
InitDudes() function, 372
InitOneWeapon() function, 368–369
InitVector() function, 305, 307–309
InitWeapons() function, 374–375
intelligent decisions, 27–28
intensity dimension, 196
International Society on Multiple Criteria Decision Making, 199
interrupting
  with events, 403
  with timers, 403–405
irrationality, logical, 94–95
irrelevant information, misusing
  football statistics, 99–100
  inventorying backyard, 97–99

iterative rationality
  eliminating irrational answers, 88–89
  overview, 81–83
  questioning, 84–85

K–L
Kagel, John, 210
Kahneman, Daniel, 208

latent inhibition, 17, 97–99
law of large numbers, 242
Let's Make a Deal game, 100–101
linear difference, 148
linear distribution, 272–273
linear functions, 229–230
list names, 292
logical irrationality, 94–95
logical notation, 124
logistic curve, 445
logistic function, 236–238
logit function, 239–240

M
magnitude, vector, 339
marginal utility, 414–415, 448
  changes in
    decreasing, 170–176
    increasing, 177–181
    overview, 169
  defining thresholds, 187–188
  multiple utility thresholds, 188–194
  overview, 167–168
  St. Petersburg paradox
    marginal utility of reward, 184–185
    marginal utility of risk, 186
    maximizing difference, 186–187
    overview, 181–184
  versus utility, 168–169
  utility of, 194
  versus value, 168–169
Marshall, Alfred, 212
Matching Pennies Game, 57–60
mathematical functions
  ad hoc functions, 240
  linear functions, 229–230

quadratic functions
  reshaping parabola, 234–236
  shifting quadratic, 231–232
  tilting parabola, 233
sigmoid functions
  logistic function, 236–238
  logit function, 239–240
MAUT. *See* **multi-attribute utility theory**
mean, 251–252
median, 251–252
Meier, Sid, 4, 430, 447
member variables, 292
minimum granularity, 403–404
mixed strategy, 59
mMaxIndex member variable, 293
mode, 251–252
momentum, decision
  building, 409–415
  ignoring futility, 408–409
  overview, 405–408
money
  utility versus risk, 123–140
  value versus utility, 121–123
Monty Hall Problem, 100–105
moral dilemmas, 219–225
Morgenstern, Oskar, 448
multi-attribute utility theory (MAUT)
  analyzing attributes, 201–202
  assembling blocks, 202–203
  defined, 448–449
  final connection, 204–205
  overview, 198–200
  subjectivity, 203–204
multi-layered weighting model, 345
MultipleDie( ) function, 259

N

naming conventions, 292
negative skew, 252
[!non-zero-sum game, 56
normal (Gaussian) distributions
  generating
    changing shape, 259–260
    distribution checklist, 267–269
    generating curve, 256–259
    overview, 254–256
    shifting curve, 266–267
    skewing curve, 261–266
  properties of
    mean, 251–252
    median, 251–252
    mode, 251–252
    range, 250–251
    skew, 252–253
    standard deviation, 253–254
normalizing constant, 331
normalizing function, 334
normative decision theory
  combining with positive decision theory, 52
  criteria for, 85
  descriptive decision theory and, 49
  overview, 45–46
  predictable "shoulds", 46–47
numbers
  making decisions based on, 27–28
  turning observations into, 26–27
  using algorithms to construct
    compartmentalization, 38–41
    grading, 37–38
  using to define behaviors, 33–36
  using to select behaviors, 30–33
NumBuckets parameter, 439

O

observation log, 15
observations
  factors
    finding hidden, 22–24
    identifying, 16–21
  needing more than, 28
  overview, 15–16
  quantifying
    making decisions based on numbers, 27–28
    razor example, 24–26
    turning observations into numbers, 26–27
Occam's razor, 56
Official Rock-Paper-Scissors Decision Die (ORPSDD), 7
opinion propagation, 4, 19–20
options
  analyzing
    connections, 379–382
    identifying factors, 356–375
    identifying relationships, 375–379
    overview, 355–356
  comparing, 385–386

options *(continued)*
  scoring, 382–385
  selecting, 386–387
ORPSDD (Official Rock-Paper-Scissors Decision Die), 7
outbreak problem, 208–210

P

pain scale, 326–327
parabola
  reshaping, 234–236
  tilting, 233
parabolic distributions, 274–276
parametric building, 270–272
Pareto improvement, 64
Pareto optimum, 64
Pascal, Blaise, 112–113, 448
Pascal's Wager
  overview, 113–114
  strictly dominant strategy, 115
PDF (probability density function), 249
Perceived Morale, 204–205
perception problems, 206
perfect knowledge, 56
perfect rationality
  flawed, 109
  Guess Two-Thirds of Average
    guessing, 90–92
    iteratively eliminating irrational answers, 88–89
    logical irrationality, 94–95
    measuring depth of rationality, 92–94
    overview, 87–88
  Pirate Game
    iterating perfectly rational decisions, 81–83
    overview, 80–81
    questioning iterative rationality, 84–85
    superrationality, 85–87
Pirate Game
  iterating perfectly rational decisions, 81–83
  overview, 80–81
  questioning iterative rationality, 84–85
  superrationality, 85–87
Piston, Walter, 49
PMF (probability mass function), 249
Poisson distribution, 276–279
Poker, 5, 9

Politiken, 91–92
polling, 50, 399–400
population, 241
position, distribution checklist, 267
positive decision theory, 48–49, 52
positive skew, 252
predictability, 419–421
prescriptive decision theory, 45–47, 52
Prisoner's Dilemma Game
  best interests, 63–64
  Guess Two-Thirds of the Average Game, 88
  making choices, 66–68
  Pareto improvement, 64–69
  strictly dominant strategies
    versus optimal strategies, 68–69
    overview, 61–63
  utility, 111
probability density function (PDF), 249
probability distributions
  converting functions to distributions, 306
  distributing, 279–283
  identifying population features
    analyzing single segment, 247–248
    overview, 242–243
    segmenting population, 244–247
    turning tables, 243–244
  normal (Gaussian) distributions
    generating, 254–269
    properties of, 250–254
  overview, 241
  parabolic distributions, 274–276
  Poisson distribution, 276–279
  search optimization, 315
  triangular distributions
    parametric building, 270–272
    simplified normal distributions, 269–270
    substituting for Poisson, 279
  uneven distributions, 272–273
  uniform distributions, 248–250
probability mass function (PMF), 249
production over time, 141–145
propinquity dimension, 196
psychohistory, 48
psychophysics, 206
PurchaseWarranty( ) function, 130
pure strategy, 57–58, 90
purity dimension, 196

Q

quadratic distribution, 314
quadratic functions
    reshaping parabola, 234–236
    shifting quadratic, 231–232
    tilting parabola, 233
quantifying observations
    making decisions based on numbers, 27–28
    razor example, 24–26
    turning observations into numbers, 26–27

R

random from top *n* choices, 425–430
    drawing line, 427–429
    opening playbook, 425–426
    payoff, 429–430
    Wheat and Chaff, 427
randomness, 422–424
range, 250–251, 267
rat experiment, 210–216
rate of decay of value, 150–154
rational behavior
    bounded rationality
        calculations to use, 97
        ignoring relevant information, 100–105
        misusing irrelevant information, 97–100
        overview, 96
    combining approaches, 109–110
    overview, 79–80
    perfect rationality
        Guess Two-Thirds of Average, 87–95
        Pirate Game, 80–87
    rational ignorance
        cost of calculation, 107–109
        cost of information, 105–107
rational ignorance
    cost of calculation, 107–109
    cost of information, 105–107
reaction time, 398
RebuildEdges (USHORT iStartBucket) function, 313
recursion, 83
relationships, identifying, 375–379
relative difference, 148
relative utility
    apparent contradictions
        Giffen goods concept, 210–219
        moral dilemmas, 219–225
    computer plus warranty example, 130–136
    hedonic calculus, 196–198
    inconsistencies
        categorization, 207
        overview, 205
        perception, 206
        understanding, 207–210
    multi-attribute utility theory
        analyzing attributes, 201–202
        assembling blocks, 202–203
        final connection, 204–205
        overview, 198–200
        subjectivity, 203–204
    overview, 195
    relative benefit of, 225
relevant information, ignoring, 100–105
remoteness dimension, 196
response curves
    constructing, 286–295
    converting distributions, 303–313
    data adjustments, 311–313
    dynamic, 317
    and granularity, 327–328
    hand-crafted, 316–317
    selecting options, 434
reward, marginal utility of, 184–185
risk
    marginal utility of, 186
    versus utility
        effect of changes, 136–140
        generalizing formulas, 127–130
        inputs and outputs, 125–127
        relative utility, 130–136
        warranties, 123–125
Rock-Paper-Scissors Game, 4, 6
role playing games (RPGs)
    finite state machine (FSM), 30–33
    linear normalization, 332–334
    relative utility, 216–219

S

scaling, automatic, 435–436
score formula, 382–383
ScoreAllTargets( ) function, 386
scores, 444–445
ScoreTarget( ) function, 384–386
ScoreToWeight( ) function, 437–438

scoring algorithm, 387
scoring systems, 321
search, optimizing, 314–316
second standard deviation, 253
SelectGoal( ) function, 155–156
SelectTarget( ) function, 428
semi-logical guessers, 247–248
SetAccAdjust( ) function, 371
sGUESSER_BUCKET struct, 291–292
Shoot Dudes example
    identifying factors, 356–375
    random choices, 425–428
sigmoid functions
    logistic function, 236–238
    logit function, 239–240
SingleDie( ) function, 258, 265–266
Situational Morale, 204
68-95-99.7 rule, 253
skew, 252–253, 261–267
slope-intercept form, 229
slopes, 229
solution concept, 63
St. Petersburg paradox
    marginal utility of reward, 184–185
    marginal utility of risk, 186
    maximizing difference, 186–187
    overview, 181–184
standard deviation, 253–254, 267
standard normal distribution, 253
statistical handicapping algorithm, 99
statistical notation, 124
strategy games
    income vs. expense comparison in, 216–219
    marginal utility in, 172–176
    morals in, 224
    multiple thresholds in, 191–194
    tile-based, 406–407
strictly dominant strategy, 63, 71, 88, 115
strobing, 407–408
structs
    entering data, 304–305
    naming conventions, 292
    vectors and, 298
SumScores( ) function, 437–438
superrationality, 85–87
supply and demand, 22–23
symmetric game, 56

T

target priority, 363–364
TBS (turn-based strategy), 143–145
Theory of Games and Economic Behavior, 57
thoroughness, 413–415
threat ratio, 380–383, 414
Three Prisoners, The, 101
three standard deviations of mean, 253
thresholds
    defining, 187–188
    multiple utility, 188–194
Tic-Tac-Toe Game
    choices in, 5, 7–8
    perfect rationality, 80
    predictability, 46
tile-based strategy game, 406–407
time
    changes in utility over time, 150–165
    distance over time, 145–150
    overview, 140–141, 410–411
    production over time, 141–145
time distance dimension, 196
Time to Kill relationships, 376–378, 414–415
tools, 29
Total Threat, 203–204
transition percentages formulas, 35
travel distance, 145–146
triangular distributions
    parametric building, 270–272
    simplified normal distributions, 269–270
    substituting for Poisson, 279
triggers, 405
Trolly Moral Dilemma, 220–224
Trust Game, 76–77
Turing, Al, 7
Turing Test, 7
turn-based strategy (TBS), 143–145
turtling, 119–120
Tversky, Amos, 208
two-person game, 56

U

Ultimatum Game, 72–75, 84
uncertainty dimension, 196
understanding, 207–210
uneven distributions, 272–273
unexpected events, 403

uniform distributions, 248–250
urgency, 364, 381–383
usage patterns, razor blade, 24–28
utility
    decisions under risk
        no pain, no gain, 115–121
        overview, 112–113
        Pascal's Wager, 113–115
    versus marginal utility, 168–169
    of marginal utility, 194
    of money
        utility versus risk, 123–140
        value versus utility, 121–123
    overview, 111–112
    summary, 165–166
    of time
        changes in utility over time, 150–165
        distance over time, 145–150
        overview, 140–141
        production over time, 141–145
utility curves, 171, 181

V

value
    versus marginal utility, 168–169
    versus utility, 121–123
variables, 249, 292
variation in choice, 417–445
    random from top n choices, 425–430
        drawing line, 427–429
        opening playbook, 425–426
        payoff, 429–430
        Wheat and Chaff, 427
    randomness, 422–424
    reasons for
        overview, 418
        variation between actors, 419–420
        variation by single actor, 420–422

    scores and weights, 444–445
    weighted random from all choices, 441–444
    weighted random from top n choices, 430–440
        assigning weights, 432–433
        automatic scaling, 435–440
        different edge, 434–435
        haves and have nots, 433
vectors
    advanced 1-to-1 mappings
        entering data, 298–299
        extracting values, 299–303
    names of, 292
    simple 1-to-1 mappings, 296–297
vectors, magnitude of, 339
vertices, 231
von Neumann, John, 55, 448

W–Z

warranties, 123–125
weapon accuracy formulas, 358–361
weapon effectiveness, 362
weighted mean, 339
weighted random
    from all choices, 441–444
    from top n choices
        assigning weights, 432–433
        automatic scaling, 435–440
        different edge, 434–435
        haves and have nots, 433
        overview, 430–432
weighted sums, 339
weighted values, 37–38
weights, 444–445
while loops, 303
widget production, 141–142
WorksOdds( ) function, 128

zero-sum game, 56

Challenges for Game Designers
1-58450-580-X ■ $24.99

Game Graphics Programming
1-58450-516-8 ■ $64.99

Game Character Development
1-59863-465-8 ■ $44.99

Video Game Design Revealed
1-58450-562-1 ■ $39.99

See our complete list of beginner through advanced game development titles
online at **www.courseptr.com** or call **1.800.354.9706**

THE BEGINNING SERIES FROM COURSE TECHNOLOGY PTR

Essential introductory programming, game design, and character creation skills for the game developers of tomorrow.

 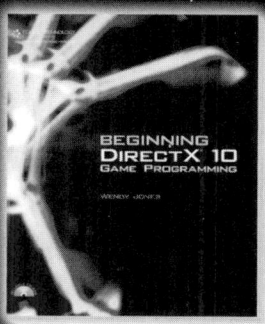  

Beginning Game Programming, Second Edition
1-59863-288-4 ■ $29.99

Beginning DirectX 10 Game Programming
1-59863-361-9 ■ $29.99

Beginning Java Game Programming, Second Edition
1-59863-476-3 ■ $29.99

Beginning Game Programming with Flash
1-59863-398-8 ■ $29.99

See our complete list of beginner through advanced game development titles online at **www.courseptr.com** or call **1.800.354.9706**